D1245833

Crisis of Conscience

CRISIS *of* CONSCIENCE

RAYMOND FRANZ

Former member of the
Governing Body of Jehovah's Witnesses

COMMENTARY PRESS · ATLANTA · 1983

Unless otherwise indicated, Scripture quotations are from the *New World Translation of the Holy Scriptures,* published by the Watchtower Bible and Tract Society of New York, Inc. Abbreviations of Bible translations referred to in the footnotes:

JB   *The Jerusalem Bible*
NEB *The New English Bible*
NIV *The New International Version*
RSV *The Revised Standard Version*

Wherever possible, and for the sake of authenticity, an effort has been made within this book to present quotations from other publications by direct photocopies. Since certain of these publications are as much as fifty years old, the quality of the type may not always be of the highest standard.

PAPERBACK EDITION, First printing, August 1984
Second printing, May 1985
All rights reserved.
Copyright © 1983 by Raymond Franz
Published by Commentary Press
P.O. Box 43532, Atlanta, Georgia 30336
Manufactured in the United States of America
ISBN: 0-914675-03-6
Library of Congress Catalog Card No.: 83-62637

When persons are in great danger from a source that they do not suspect or are being misled by those they consider their friends, is it an unkindness to warn them? They may prefer not to believe the warning. They may even resent it. But does that free one from the moral responsibility to give that warning?

—The *Watchtower* magazine,
January 15, 1974.

Life is uncertain and when a man dies what he knows dies along with him—unless he passes it on while still in life.

What this book contains is written out of a sense of obligation to people whom I sincerely love. In all good conscience I can say that its aim is to help and not to hurt. If some of what is presented is painful to read, it was also painful to write. It is hoped that the reader will recognize that the search for truth need never be destructive of faith, that every effort to know and uphold truth will, instead, strengthen the basis for true faith. What those reading this information will do with it is, of course, their own decision. At least it will have been said, and a moral responsibility will have been met.

Contents

1

PRICE OF CONSCIENCE

WHETHER we like it or not, moral challenge affects each of us. It is one of life's bittersweet ingredients from which there is no successful escape. It has the power to enrich us or impoverish us, to determine the true quality of our relationships with those who know us. It all depends on our response to that challenge. The choice is ours—it is seldom an easy one.

We have the option, of course, of surrounding our conscience with a sort of cocoon of complacency, passively "going along," shielding our inner feelings from whatever might disturb them. When issues arise, rather than take a stand we can in effect say, "I'll just sit this one out; others may be affected—even hurt—but I am not." Some spend their whole life in a morally 'sitting' posture. But, when all is said and done, and when life finally draws near its close, it would seem that the one who can say, "At least I stood for something," must feel greater satisfaction than the one who rarely stood for anything.

Sometimes we may wonder if people of deep conviction have become a vanishing race, something we read about in the past but see little of in the present. Most of us find it fairly easy to act in good conscience so long as the things at stake are minor. The more that is involved, the higher the cost, the harder it becomes to resolve questions of conscience, to make a moral judgment and accept its consequences. When the cost is very great we find ourselves at a moral crossroads situation, facing a genuine crisis in our lives.

This book is about that kind of crisis, the way people are facing up to it and the effect on their lives.

Admittedly, the story of the persons involved may have little of the high drama found in the heresy trial of a John Wycliffe, the intrigue of the international hunt for an elusive William Tyndale, or the horror of the burning at the stake of a Michael Servetus. But their struggle and suffering are, in their own way, no less intense. Few of them could say it as eloquently as Luther, yet they take very much the same stand he took when he said to the seventy men judging him:

> "Unless I am convinced by the testimonies of the Scriptures or by evident reason (for I believe neither pope nor councils alone, since it is manifest they have often erred and contradicted themselves), I am bound by the Scriptures I have quoted, and my conscience is held captive by the word of God; and as it is neither safe nor right to act against conscience, I cannot and will not retract anything. Here I stand; I cannot otherwise; God help me. Amen."[1]

Long before any of these men, the apostles Peter and John of nineteen centuries ago confronted essentially the same issue when they stood before a judicial council of the most respected members of their life-long religion and frankly told them:

> "Whether it is right in the sight of God to listen to you rather than to God, you must judge; for we cannot but speak of what we have seen and heard."[2]

The people I write of are from among those I know most intimately, persons who have been members of the religious group known as Jehovah's Witnesses. I am sure, and there is evidence to show, that their experience is by no means unique, that there is a similar stirring of conscience among people of various faiths. They face the same issue that Peter and John and men and women of later centuries confronted: *the struggle to hold true to personal conscience in the face of pressure from religious authority.*

For many it is an emotional tug-of-war. On the one hand, they feel impelled to reject the interposing of human authority between themselves and their Creator; to reject religious dogmatism, legalism and authoritarianism, to hold true to the teaching that Christ Jesus, not any human religious body, is "the head of every man."[3] On the other hand, they face the risk of losing life-long friends, seeing family relationships traumatically affected, sacrificing a religious heritage that may reach back for generations. At that kind of crossroads, decisions do not come easy.

What is here described, then, is not merely a "tempest in a teapot," a major quarrel in a minor religion. I believe there is much of vital benefit that any person can gain from considering this account. For if the numbers presently involved are small, the issues are not. They are

---

1 These were Luther's concluding words in making his defense at the Diet of Worms, Germany, in April of 1521.
2 Acts 4:19, 20, RSV.
3 1 Corinthians 11:3.

far-reaching questions that have brought men and women into similar crises of conscience again and again throughout history. At stake is the freedom to pursue spiritual truth untrammeled by arbitrary restrictions and the right to enjoy a personal relationship with God and his Son free from the subtle interposition of a priestly nature on the part of some human agency. While much of what is written may on the surface appear to be distinctive of the organization of Jehovah's Witnesses, in reality the underlying, fundamental issues affect the life of persons of any faith that takes the name Christian.

The price of firmly believing that it is "neither safe nor right to act against conscience" has not been small for the men and women I know. Some find themselves suddenly severed from family relationships as a result of official religious action—cut off from parents, sons and daughters, brothers and sisters, even from grandparents or grandchildren. They can no longer enjoy free association with long-time friends for whom they feel deep affection; such association would place those friends in jeopardy of the same official action. They witness the blackening of their own good name—one that it has taken them a lifetime to earn—and all that such name has stood for in the minds and hearts of those who knew them. They are thereby deprived of whatever good and rightful influence they might exercise on behalf of the very people they knew best in their community, in their country, in all the world. Material losses, even physical mistreatment and abuse, can be easier to face than this.

What could move a person to risk such a loss? How many persons today would? There are, of course (as there have always been), people who would risk any or all of these things because of stubborn pride, to satisfy the desire for material gain, for power, prestige, prominence, or simply for fleshly pleasure. But when the evidence reveals nothing indicating such aims, when in fact it shows that the men and women involved recognized that just the opposite of those goals was what they could expect—what then?

What has happened among Jehovah's Witnesses provides an unusual and thought-provoking study in human nature. Besides those who were willing to face excommunication for the sake of conscience, what of the larger number, those who felt obliged to share in or support such excommunications, to allow the family circle to be broken, to terminate long-standing friendships? There is no question about the sincerity of many of these persons, or that they felt and still feel distress from carrying out what they deemed a necessary religious duty. What convictions and reasonings motivated them?

Notably, as regards the cases here dealt with, many if not most of those involved are persons who have been associated with Jehovah's Witnesses for twenty, thirty, forty or more years. Rather than a "fringe element," they have usually been among the more active, productive members of the organization. They include persons who were prominent members of the Witnesses' international headquarters staff at Brooklyn, New York; men who were traveling superintendents and elders; women who spent long years in missionary and evangelistic work. To become Witnesses, they had often cut off all previous friendships with persons of other faiths, since such associations are discouraged among Jehovah's Witnesses. For the rest of their life their only friends have been among those of their faith. Some had built their whole life plans around the goals set before them by the organization, letting these control the amount of education they sought, the type of work they did. Their "investment" was a large one, involving some of life's most precious assets. And now they have seen all this disappear, wiped out in a matter of a few hours.

This is, I believe, one of the strange features of our time, that some of the most stringent measures to restrain expressions of personal conscience have come from religious groups once noted for the defense of freedom of conscience.

The examples of three men—each a religious instructor of note in his particular religion, with each situation described occurring in the same year—illustrate this:

One, over the past decade, wrote books and regularly gave lectures presenting views that struck at the very heart of the authority structure of his religion.

Another gave a talk before an audience of more than a thousand persons in which he took issue with his religious organization's teachings about a key date and its significance in fulfillment of Bible prophecy.

The third made no such public pronouncements. His only expressions of difference of viewpoint were confined to personal conversations with close friends.

Yet the strictness of the official action taken toward each of these men by their respective religious organizations was in inverse proportion to the seriousness of their actions. And the source of the greatest severity was the opposite of what one might expect.

The first person described is Roman Catholic priest Hans Küng, professor at Tubingen University in West Germany. After ten years, his outspoken criticism, including his rejection of the doctrinal infallibility of the Pope and the bishops, was finally dealt with by the Vatican itself and, as of 1980, the Vatican removed his official status as a Catholic theologian. Yet he remains a priest and a leading figure in the Catholic university's ecumenical research institute; even students for the priesthood attending his lectures are not subject to church discipline.[4]

The second is Australian-born Seventh Day Adventist professor Desmond Ford. His speech to a layman's group of a thousand persons at a California college, in which he took issue with the Adventist teaching about the date 1844, led to a church hearing. Ford was granted six months leave of absence to prepare his defense and, in 1980, was then met with by a hundred church representatives who spent some fifty hours hearing his testimony. Church officials then decided to remove him from his teaching post and strip him of his ministerial status. But he was not disfellowshiped (excommunicated) though he has published his views and continues to speak about them in Adventist circles.[5]

The third man is Edward Dunlap, who was for many years the Registrar of the sole missionary school of Jehovah's Witnesses, the Watchtower Bible School of Gilead, also a major contributor to the organization's Bible dictionary (*Aid to Bible Understanding*) and the writer of its only Bible commentary (*Commentary on the Letter of James*). He expressed his difference of viewpoint on certain teachings only in private conversation with friends of long standing. In the spring of 1980, a committee of five men, none of them members of the organization's Governing Body, met with him in secret session for a few hours, interrogating him on his views. After over forty years of association, Dunlap was dismissed from his work and home at the international headquarters and disfellowshiped from the organization.

Thus, the religious organization that, for many, has been a symbol of extreme authoritarianism showed the greatest degree of tolerance toward its dissident instructor; the organization that has taken particular pride in its fight for freedom of conscience showed the least.

Herein lies a paradox. Despite their intense activity in door-to-door witnessing, most people actually know little about Jehovah's Wit-

---

4 They simply receive no academic credit for such attendance.
5 In conversation with Desmond Ford at Chattanooga, Tennessee, in 1982, he mentioned that by then more than 120 ministers of the Seventh Day Adventist church had either resigned or been "defrocked" by the church because they could not support certain teachings or recent actions of the organization.

nesses aside from their position on certain issues of conscience. They have heard of their uncompromising stand in refusing to accept blood transfusions, their refusal to salute any flag or similar emblem, their firm objection to performance of military service, their opposition to participation in any political activity or function. Those familiar with legal cases know that they have taken some fifty cases to the Supreme Court of the United States in defense of their freedom of conscience, including their right to carry their message to people of other beliefs even in the face of considerable opposition and objections. In lands where constitutional liberties protect them, they are free to exercise such rights without hindrance. In other countries they have experienced severe persecution, arrests, jailing, mobbings, beatings, and official bans prohibiting their literature and preaching.

How, then, is it the case that today any person among their members who voices a personal difference of viewpoint as to the teachings of the organization is almost certain to face judicial proceedings and, unless willing to retract, is liable for disfellowshipment? How do those carrying out those proceedings rationalize the apparent contradiction in position? Paralleling this is the question of whether endurance of severe persecution and physical mistreatment at the hand of opposers is, *of itself*, necessarily evidence of belief in the vital importance of staying true to conscience, or whether it can simply be the result of concern to adhere to an organization's teachings and standards, violation of which is known to bring severe disciplinary action.

Some may say that the issue is really not as simple as it is here presented, that there are other crucial matters involved. What of the need for religious unity and order? What of the need for protection against those who spread false, divisive and pernicious teachings? What of the need for proper respect for authority?

To ignore those factors would admittedly show an extreme, blindly unbalanced, attitude.

Who can challenge the fact that freedom, misused, can lead to irresponsibility, disorder, and can end in confusion, even anarchy? Patience and tolerance likewise can become nothing more than an excuse for indecision, nonaction, a lowering of all standards. Even love can become mere sentimentality, misguided emotion that neglects to do what is really needed, with cruel consequences. All this is true and is what those focus on who would impose restraints on personal conscience through religious authority.

What, however, is the effect when spiritual "guidance" becomes mental domination, even spiritual tyranny? What happens when the desirable qualities of unity and order are substituted for by demands for institutionalized conformity and by legalistic regimentation? What results when proper respect for authority is converted into servility, unquestioning submission, an abandonment of personal responsibility before God to make decisions based on individual conscience?

Those questions must be considered if the issue is not to be distorted and misrepresented. What follows in this book illustrates in a very graphic way the effect these things have on human relationships, the unusual positions and actions persons will take who see only one side of the issue, the extremes to which they will go to uphold that side.

Perhaps the greatest value in seeing this is, I feel, that it can help us understand more clearly what the real issues were in the days of Jesus Christ and his apostles, and why and how a tragic deviation from their teachings and example came, so subtly, with such relative ease, in so brief a span of time. Those who are of other religious affiliations and who may be quick to judge Jehovah's Witnesses would do well to ask first about themselves and about their own religious affiliation in the light of the issues involved, the basic attitudes that underly the positions described and the actions taken.

To search out the answers to the questions raised requires going beyond the individuals affected into the inner structure of a distinctive religious organization, into its system of teaching and control, discovering how the men who direct it arrive at their decisions and policies, and to some extent investigating its past history and origins. Hopefully the lessons learned can aid in uncovering the root causes of religious turmoil and point to what is needed if persons trying to be genuine followers of God's Son are to enjoy peace and brotherly unity.

2

CREDENTIALS AND CAUSE

"I am speaking the truth as a Christian, and my own conscience, enlightened by the Holy Spirit, assures me it is no lie. . . . For I could even pray to be outcast from Christ myself for the sake of my brothers, my natural kinsfolk."
—Romans 9:1, 3, *New English Bible*.

WHAT has thus far been said gives, I believe, good reason for the writing of this book. The question may remain as to why I am the one writing it.

One reason is my background and the perspective it gives. From babyhood up into my sixtieth year, my life was spent in association with Jehovah's Witnesses. While others, many others, could say the same, it is unlikely that very many of them had the range of experience that happened to be my lot during those years.

A reason of greater weight is that circumstances brought to my knowledge information to which the vast majority of Jehovah's Witnesses have absolutely no access. The circumstances were seldom of my own making. The information was often totally unexpected, even disturbing.

A final reason, resulting from the previous two, is that of conscience. What do you do when you see mounting evidence that people are being hurt, hurt deeply, with no real justification? What obligation does any of us have—before God and toward fellow humans—when he sees that information is withheld from people to whom it could be of the most serious consequence? These were questions with which I struggled.

What follows expands on these reasons.

In many ways I would much prefer passing over the first of these since it necessarily deals with my own "record." The present situation seems to require its presentation, however, somewhat in the way circumstances obliged the apostle Paul to set out his record of personal experiences for Christians in Corinth and afterward to say to them:

> "I am being very foolish, but it was you who drove me to it; my credentials should have come from you. In no respect did I fall short of these superlative apostles, even if I am a nobody [even though I am nothing, *New International Version*]."[1]

I make no pretence of being a Paul, but I believe that my reason and motive at least run parallel with his.

My father and mother (and three of my four grandparents) were Witnesses, my father having been baptized in 1913 when the Witnesses were known simply as Bible Students. I did not become an *active* Witness until I was sixteen. Though still in school, I was before long spending from twenty to thirty hours a month in "witnessing" from door to door, standing on street corners with magazines, putting out handbills while wearing placards saying "Religion is a snare, the Bible tells why. Serve God and Christ the King."

That year, 1938, I had attended an assembly in Cincinnati (across the Ohio River from our home) and listened to Judge Joseph F. Rutherford, the president of the Watch Tower Society, speak from London, England, by radio-telephone communication. In a major talk entitled "Face the Facts," Rutherford's opening words included this:

> "Because the full statement of facts tends to shock the susceptibilities of some persons [this] furnishes no excuse or justification to withhold from the public any part thereof, particularly when the public welfare is involved. . . . Previous belief or opinion should never be permitted to hinder one in receiving and considering a statement of facts."[2]

That appealed to me as a worthwhile principle to follow in life. I felt receptive to the facts he would present.

Among major points emphasized were these:

> "God has made it clearly to be seen by those who diligently seek the truth that religion is a form of worship but which denies the power of God and turns men away from God. . . . *Religion and Christianity are therefore exactly opposite to each other*."[3]

---

1 2 Corinthians 12:11, NEB; compare 3:1, 2; 5:12, 13; 6:4–10; 11:21–29.
2 *Face the Facts*, p. 3.
3 Ibid., pp. 7, 8. (Jehovah's Witnesses now view "religion" as an acceptable term for true worship.)

"According to the prophecy of Jesus, what are the things to be expected when the world comes to an end? The answer is world war, famine, pestilence, distress of nations, and amongst other things mentioned the appearance of a monstrosity on the earth. . . . *These are the indisputable physical facts* which have come to pass *proving that Satan's world has come to an end*, and which facts cannot be ignored."[4]

"Now Germany is in an alliance with the Papacy, and Great Britain is rapidly moving in that direction. The United States of America, once the bulwark of democracy, is all set to become part of the totalitarian rule. . . . Thus the indisputable facts are, that there is now in the earth Satan's dictatorial monstrosity, which defies and opposes Jehovah's kingdom. . . . *The totalitarian combine is going to get control of England and America. You cannot prevent it. Do not try.* Your safety is on the Lord's side. . . ."[5]

I have italicized statements that particularly engraved themselves in my mind at that time. They created in me an intensity of feeling, of near agitation, that I had not experienced before.

His other major talk, "Fill the Earth," developed the view that as of 1935 God's message, till then directed to persons who would reign with Christ in heaven, a "little flock," was now being directed to an earthly class, the "other sheep," and that after the approaching war of Armageddon these would procreate and fill the earth with a righteous offspring. Of these he said:

"They must find protection in God's organization, which shows that they must be immersed, baptized or hidden in that organization. The ark, which Noah built at God's command, pictured God's organization. . . ."[6]

Pointing out that Noah's three sons evidently did not begin to produce offspring until two years after the Flood, the Watch Tower president then made an application to those with earthly hopes in modern times, saying:

"Would it be Scripturally proper for them to now marry and to begin to rear children? No, is the answer, which is supported by the Scriptures. . . . It will be far better to be unhampered and without burdens, that they may do the Lord's will now, as the Lord commands, and also be without hindrance during Armageddon."[7]

---

4 Ibid., p. 9. (The teaching then was that, since Satan's lease of power ended in 1914, the "world ended" in that sense. The Society's publications no longer teach this.)

5 Ibid., pp. 16, 17, 27. (The Society now gives a different application to the "abomination of desolation" [Matthew 24:15] here referred to as the "monstrosity.")

6 Ibid., pp. 40, 41. (This view of the ark's symbolic significance has changed, though the role of the organization as essential to salvation as presented is basically the same.)

7 Ibid., pp. 46, 47.

Joseph Rutherford spoke forcefully and with a distinctive cadence of great finality. These were *facts*, solid truths on which to build life's most serious plans. I was deeply impressed with the importance of the organization as essential to salvation, also that the work of witnessing must take precedence over, or at least mitigate against, such personal interests as marriage and childbearing.[8]

In 1939 I was baptized and in June, 1940, on graduating from high school I immediately entered full-time service in witnessing activity. That year was a turbulent one for the world and for Jehovah's Witnesses. World War II was under way, the work of Jehovah's Witnesses came under ban in several countries and hundreds of Witnesses were imprisoned; in the United States children of Jehovah's Witnesses were being expelled from school for refusal to salute the flag (viewed as a form of image worship); the Witnesses' stand of neutrality toward war often inspired violent antagonism on the part of those priding themselves on their loyalty and patriotism; vicious mob attacks were starting to spread.

That summer our family went to Detroit, Michigan, to attend a major Witness convention. A spirit of tense anticipation prevailed, a sense of being under siege. At the close of the assembly Judge Rutherford indicated that 'this might be the last assembly we would have before the great tribulation struck.' When the autumn of 1940 came and I put my summer clothes away, I remember thinking that I would likely never take them out again—that either Armageddon would have come or we would by then all be in concentration camps, like many Witnesses in Nazi Germany.

Mob violence reached a crescendo during the early 1940's. In Connersville, Indiana, I attended a trial of two women Witnesses charged with seditious activity ("riotous conspiracy"), simply because they studied Watch Tower publications as part of a home study group. The trial ran five days and on the last day, after night had fallen, the jury brought in its verdict of guilty. On leaving the courthouse, the defense attorney (a Witness named Victor Schmidt) and his wife were violently assaulted by a mob and were forced to walk, in a driving rain, the entire distance to the city limits. On the way the horror of the situation caused Schmidt's wife suddenly to begin to menstruate. I had in my car group a Witness representative (Jack Rainbow) who had

---

8 It was not until 1959, when I was 36, that I finally married; my wife and I are childless, having been vigilant in birth control until recent years.

earlier been threatened with death by some of these men if he returned to "their city." On arriving at the city limits and seeing Schmidt and his wife, followed by a remnant of the mob, I felt obliged to take the risk of picking them up and was able to do so. Another Witness had attempted this but only got a broken car window for his efforts. Schmidt's wife broke out into hysterical screaming when we got her into the car; her husband's face was bruised and covered with blood from deep cuts where he had evidently been hit with brass knuckles.[9]

To experience firsthand such raw and callous intolerance left a vivid impression on my young mind. I felt all the more convinced of the rightness of my course with those who were quite evidently the true servants of God.

Later, as a tactic recommended by the Watch Tower Society's legal counsel, Hayden Covington, a large group of seventy-five Witnesses from the Cincinnati, Ohio area, including my parents, my two sisters and myself, traveled to Connersville in a "blitzkrieg" witnessing effort. With one exception, we all, men, women and children, were arrested and wound up in various jails, being locked up for one week until bail could be worked out. Still in my teens, it was my first time at experiencing the feeling that comes with seeing a massive metal door swing shut, hearing the bolt shoved in place and realizing that your freedom of movement is now taken from you.

Some months later I was in Indianapolis, Indiana, for a superior court hearing involving the Connersville events. My uncle, Fred Franz, a member of the Watch Tower headquarters staff since 1920 and a close associate of Judge Rutherford, was also there from Brooklyn as sort of an expert witness on the Society's behalf. The local congregation asked him to speak to them one evening. During the course of his talk he began discussing the attitude of so many that the work of witnessing was nearing its end, just about finished. To put it mildly, I was stunned to hear my uncle speak to the contrary, saying that at Brooklyn they were not expecting to close down, that 'anyone who wanted to send in a subscription for the *Watchtower* magazine needn't send it in for just six months—he could send it in for a full year or for two years if he wanted!'

The thrust of his remarks was so contrary to the comments of the Society's president at the Detroit assembly that it seemed clear to me

---

9 See the *1975 Yearbook of Jehovah's Witnesses*, pp. 186–188; also the booklet *Theocracy*, published in 1941, pp. 44, 45.

that my uncle was speaking on his own, not presenting some duly authorized message from the Society. I actually felt like going to him and urging caution lest his remarks get back to Brooklyn and be viewed as disloyal, as having a dissipating, undermining effect on the sense of extreme urgency that had developed. Although then in his late forties, my uncle was a relatively young man compared to Judge Rutherford and I found myself uncertain as to whether to accept his remarks as proper or discount them as the product of an independent, somewhat brash attitude.

Leaving home that year to become the partner of a young fellow Witness in the coal mining region of West Virginia and eastern Kentucky, I found myself in an area where the threat of violence was faced almost on a daily basis. Some mining camps consisted of long wooden "row houses" strung along the highway. At times, upon reaching the last of such a section of houses, we could look back to the point where we had begun our calls and see men and boys excitedly running about, gathering a mob.

At the "Octavia J" mining camp in Kentucky, our old "Model A" Ford car was surrounded by a group of angry miners and we were told to 'get out of there and out of the State of Kentucky and not come back if we valued our lives.' Attempts to reason only provoked greater anger. We did return a couple of months later and before we got out were shot at and pursued, escaping only by a ruse that led us over back roads and across a mountain until we could finally make our way home. More so than patriotic fervor, religious bigotry seemed to have been the force motivating the miners. Our disbelief of the teaching of a literal hell fire torment (causing young boys to yell out "no-hellers" as we drove by) weighed almost as heavily as our stand toward war.

I found that close-minded bigotry appalling then. I was happy to be part of an organization free from such intolerance.

The summer of 1941 came and, contrary to my expectation, I found myself attending another assembly, held in St. Louis, Missouri. I still remember seeing crowds gather around as Judge Rutherford was driven up to the assembly site in a large car with Hayden Covington and Vice-President Nathan Knorr, both men of large build, standing on the running boards as bodyguards. On the final day of the assembly, Rutherford had all the children from five to eighteen years of age seated before the platform. After his prepared speech, he talked to them extemporaneously. A tall man of usually stern appearance and stern tone, Rutherford now spoke with almost fatherly persuasion and recommended to these children that they put marriage out of their minds until the return of Abraham, Isaac, Jacob and other faithful men and women of old who would soon be resurrected and would guide them in their selection of mates. A free copy of a new book entitled *Children* was given each one. As a vehicle for developing the material, it presented a fictional young Witness couple, John and Eunice, who were engaged but who had decided to postpone their marriage until the arrival of the New Order so near at hand. In the book, John said to Eunice:

> "Our hope is that within a few years our marriage may be consummated and, by the Lord's grace, we shall have sweet children that will be an honor to the Lord. We can well defer our marriage until lasting peace comes to the earth. Now we must add nothing to our burdens, but be free and equipped to serve the Lord. When THE THEOCRACY is in full sway it will not be burdensome to have a family."[10]

I was then nineteen, and today at sixty-one I can still remember the inner emotional stirrings, a strange mixture of agitation and depression, those expressions generated in me. At my age, to be confronted with statements of that kind that, in essence, called upon me to make a decision and set aside interest in marriage for an indefinite time, had an unsettling effect. I could perhaps appreciate better what young men contemplating entering the priesthood of Catholicism experience. Of course, the force of the Watch Tower president's urgings lay in the shortness of time till Armageddon. As the September 15, 1941, *Watchtower* magazine in describing the occasion later said:

> "Receiving the gift [the book *Children*], the marching children clasped it to them, not a toy or plaything for idle pleasure, but the Lord's provided instrument for most effective work in the remaining months before Armageddon."[11]

Years later I learned that Judge Rutherford was at that point dying of cancer. He had been separated for many years from his wife, who was also a Witness and who lived as an invalid in California; his one son on reaching adulthood had shown no interest in the religion of his father. My uncle, Fred Franz, said that the Judge's failing condition, coupled with his strong desire that the "end" come while he was still alive to see it, motivated many such expressions as those made in 1940 and 1941. I have thought since that, had the couple in the book

---

10 *Children*, published in 1941, p. 366.
11 See the *Watchtower* of September 15, 1941, p. 288.

been real instead of fictional, their engagement period would have been rather long, in fact, would still be in effect. All the young girls present at that assembly would be well past the childbearing age now, being at least in their late forties. Some of those who were then present as children, however, did loyally follow through on the counsel heard and remained single through what might be called their normal marriageable years on into bachelorhood and spinsterhood.

In 1942, a "special pioneer" assignment in Wellston, Ohio, brought other experiences.[12] Another young Witness and I lived in a small trailer house, a homemade "box on wheels" six feet wide and fourteen feet long. It had no insulation whatsoever in the walls and our small coal stove held a fire for at most a few hours. Many wintry nights saw the water in the pail *inside* the trailer freeze over and it was not uncommon to awaken and then be unable to get back to sleep because of feet throbbing with pain from the cold. We could afford nothing better since, aside from our share of the contributions people gave for literature, we each received as a monthly allowance from the Society a maximum of fifteen dollars.[13] During the better part of a year, our main meal of the day usually consisted of boiled potatoes, oleomargarine and day-old bread (half the cost of fresh bread). My partner had an old car but we rarely had the money to put fuel in it.

In this town, too, animosity flared. At one time or another young boys broke every window in the trailer. One night I returned home to find it thrown completely over on its side. I again experienced arrest and spent a night in the local jail. The place literally crawled with bed bugs and, unable to bring myself to lie on the jail bunk, I spent the entire night sitting on an empty tin can someone had left in the cell.

In 1944, an invitation came to attend a missionary school, the Watchtower Bible School of Gilead, for a five-months course. Upon graduation and while awaiting a missionary assignment, I spent a year and a half in traveling work, visiting congregations in a "Circuit" that

---

12 "Special pioneers" are full-time representatives ("pioneers") given special assignments by the Society, with a higher quota of hours and a monthly allowance to aid in expenses.

13 The request form for this allowance had spaces to indicate what had been received from contributions for literature, what had been spent, and the difference. Since at times the difference did not come quite to fifteen dollars, I felt the right thing to do was to ask for less. But this resulted in my consistently winding up short of funds and then requesting smaller and smaller amounts. As I realized later, most "special pioneers" just asked for the straight fifteen dollars.

took in the state of Arizona and a large section of California. When visiting congregations in the San Diego, California, area I spent five nights at "Beth Sarim" (meaning "House of Princes"). This was a large home built by the Society and said to be 'held in trust' for the faithful men of old, from Abel onward, to be used by them upon their resurrection.[14] Judge Rutherford, who had had some lung problems, spent the winters there during his life. I recall that the place gave me somewhat of a sense of unreality. San Diego was a nice city, the home was a fine, upper-class residence. But I could not see why the men I had read about in the Bible would have any interest in being placed there; something did not seem to fit.[15]

Assigned first to France as a missionary, I was unable to go due to the refusal of my draft board to grant me permission to leave the country. Then I was assigned to the island of Puerto Rico. Before leaving, in 1946, Nathan Knorr, now president of the Society (Rutherford having died in early 1942), talked to a group of us, all young men being sent out to do supervisory work in different countries as "Branch Overseers." Among other things he strongly stressed that if we wished to remain in our missionary assignments we should avoid anything that might lead to courtship and marriage. The policy was: Loss of singleness means loss of assignment.[16]

In Puerto Rico it was not long before our "missionary home" group in San Juan consisted of one married couple, seven young girls in their twenties and me, all living in a two-story, six bedroom house. Though I followed Knorr's counsel and kept very busy (sometimes conducting more than fifteen home Bible studies a week), the announced policy on marriage and the circumstances in the close quarters of the home created pressure that wore ever more heavily on me. Bouts with dysentery, then a paratyphoid infection with its griping pain and passage of stools of blood, and later a case of infectious hepatitis did nothing to help. (I worked in the office right through the cases of dysentery and paratyphoid infection and was off only one week as a result of the hepatitis, though I felt so weak I could hardly climb the stairs to the office.) After eight years the combined strain brought me near to a nervous breakdown. Upon writing the president, I was relieved of my Branch responsibilities (I had not requested this) and was given the

---

14 See the book *Salvation*, published in 1939, pp. 311, 312.
15 Not many years later Beth Sarim was sold. The belief in the return of the "faithful men of old" before Armageddon was also set aside.
16 Basically the same rule applied at the international headquarters and all Branch Offices; in the mid-1950's this rule was changed; Knorr himself married.

option of returning to the States to do traveling work there. I asked to be allowed instead to remain in my assignment in Puerto Rico and was transferred to another town. Though the town, Aguadilla, was one I did not care for personally, I had requested it since it seemed the need was greater there.

Within a year or so I was assigned to do traveling work, visiting congregations in the island and in the neighboring Virgin Islands (lying to the east of Puerto Rico). An added feature was that periodically the Society asked me to make trips to the Dominican Republic where the work of Jehovah's Witnesses had been banned by the government of dictator Rafael Trujillo. The purpose was primarily to smuggle in copies of Watch Tower literature.[17] I did so a number of times and then, in 1955, was asked to try to deliver a petition personally to the dictator. Knowing that people who incurred his disfavor had a way of simply disappearing, I accepted the assignment with a measure of apprehension. Arriving in Ciudad Trujillo (now Santo Domingo), I sent a telegram to the Generalissimo presenting myself solely as a "North American educator with information of great importance to you and your country." The interview was granted at the National Palace and I was able to deliver the petition into his hands.[18] To my surprise I was not expelled and continued to make my periodic "smuggling" trips without being apprehended.

Then in 1957 all the American missionaries of the Witnesses were expelled from the Dominican Republic in the wake of a wave of violent persecution, many local Witnesses being brutally beaten and imprisoned. A major issue had been the refusal of male Witnesses to do "marching" as required by military training laws, but there was also considerable religious opposition expressed, priests and others making inflammatory statements in the newspapers. The Society asked me to go in and check on the conditions of the Dominican Witnesses. I had been in just shortly before to deliver instructions to the missionaries and had brought out detailed accounts of the persecution and these

---

17 Though of medium height, my average weight while in the Caribbean was only 117 pounds. I could place several magazines around my body beneath a double set of undershirts and slip an opened, 384-page book inside my shorts and still look normal. The only problem was that while seated on the plane the corners of the opened book cut into my thighs causing some discomfort.

18 The Generalissimo received me in full uniform with all his medals on (many, if not most, of these being self-bestowed). When he found out what my mission actually was, the interview ended fairly soon. It apparently created a favorable impression, nonetheless, since some time later the ban was lifted for a period of about a year and then was reimposed.

were prominently featured in Puerto Rican newspapers. As we learned from a source close to him, this adverse publicity enraged Trujillo. Feeling like a marked man, I recall that my first night at a hotel in Ciudad Trujillo I was given a room on the ground floor with French windows right next to the bed. My sense of real danger was strong enough to move me to rig up the appearance of a form on the bed while I slept on the floor behind it. Again, however, I was able to make it in and out without incident and made other trips in the following years.

Later the Society changed its policy on marriage, and thirteen years after arriving in Puerto Rico I married. Cynthia, my wife, joined me in traveling work. Economic conditions in the islands were poor, considerably beneath today's level. We lived with the people we served, sharing their little homes, sometimes with running water and electricity, sometimes not; sometimes with a measure of privacy, often with very little. Relatively young, we adjusted, though my wife's health was due to be seriously affected.

Only a few months after our marriage, while serving in a small island, my wife fell ill with a severe case of gastroenteritis, evidently from bad water or tainted food. The home we were staying in belonged to a fine West Indian couple with lovable children. Unfortunately the house they were renting was overrun with roaches, a creature that inspires near panic in my wife. At night we regularly checked our bed for any roaches before letting the mosquito netting down. Suspecting that a large box in a corner containing clothes was the creatures' headquarters, one day I took some insect spray and went to the box and lifted the top garment. I quickly let it down, for the box was alive with what looked to be hundreds of small roaches and I feared the spray could send them everywhere. For added measure a large rat each night entered the kitchen (next to our room and next to the only bathroom), its size being enough to make the tins of food on the shelves move.

In these circumstances my wife now began to experience the gastroenteritis, developing extreme diarrhea and regular vomiting. I was able to get her to the island's one doctor and an injection temporarily stopped the vomiting. Late that night it began again and this, coupled with the constant diarrhea, brought Cynthia to the point of dehydration. I ran about a mile to rouse the doctor from sleep and we carried her in his jeep to a little clinic. Her veins had nearly collapsed and the nurses tried again and again before they could finally get a needle in to administer saline solution. She was able to leave a few days afterward but her health was never quite the same. A later parasite infection (whipworm) added to the problem.

We continued in traveling work until 1961 and then were transferred to the Dominican Republic. Trujillo was assassinated shortly before our arrival.

During our nearly five years there, we saw the fall of four separate governments and in April of 1965 experienced a war that centered around the capital where we were located. Most Americans and other foreign residents fled the country. Our missionary group felt no inclination to abandon the Dominican Jehovah's Witnesses and our assignment, and so we learned what wartime life is like. Nights were filled with the crack of hundreds of rifles, the rattle of machine guns, the boom of bazookas and other heavier weapons. Lulls came in the fighting during the day and we were able to get outside and carry on some activity, though sometimes almost pinned down by the eruption of gunfire. To this day I have wondered just how close bullets must come for the distinct buzzing sound like that of angry bees to be heard as they fly past your head. One soldier comfortingly told me, "There's no need to worry about those. You won't hear the one that hits you."

The remaining fifteen years of full-time service were quite different, as they were spent at the international headquarters in Brooklyn, New York. My reason for describing in some detail the earlier years up to 1965 is that their content seems to be more of the fabric (though greatly inferior in quality) of the experiences the apostle focuses on in setting forth the evidence of the genuineness of his service to God and Christ, saying:

> "We prove we are servants of God by great fortitude in times of suffering: in times of hardship and distress."

In the words that follow, he makes no mention of his speeches, gives no figures of great audiences he addressed, cites no examples of organizational feats in building up large numbers of believers.[19]

I make no claim that what I went through was any more than what many others have experienced, either as missionaries of Jehovah's Witnesses or of other religions. The record is simply set out for the reader to decide upon its relative worth, particularly as regards assessing the validity and integrity of the information supplied in the rest of this publication.

19 2 Corinthians 6:4–20, JB.

CIRCUMSTANCES AND CONSEQUENCES

*"We cannot but speak of what we have seen and heard." —Acts 4:20,
Revised Standard Version.*

What I saw, heard and experienced during the next fifteen years had a
great impact on me. Whether the reaction of the reader will coincide
with mine, I have no way of knowing, but one thing is certain and
that is that no one could understand what brought me to a crisis situation without knowing these developments. The proverb is apt: "When
anyone is replying to a matter before he hears it, that is foolishness on
his part and a humiliation."[20]

The year before the war in the Dominican Republic, and following
an attack of dengue fever which left my nerve endings hypersensitive,
I had attended a ten-month course at Gilead School.[21] At the close,
the Society's president, N. H. Knorr, asked me to leave my missionary service in the Caribbean and come with my wife to the international headquarters (called "Bethel") in Brooklyn, where I would serve
in the Writing Department. Though doubtless this would have been
viewed as an honor by others, I frankly had no interest in leaving the
place where I was. Speaking to Brother Knorr in his office I explained
how much I enjoyed my current assignment, enjoyed the people, enjoyed the work. This apparently was viewed as a lack of appreciation
for the opportunity offered; he seemed somewhat offended. I then told
him I simply had wanted him to know my feelings, my love for missionary activity, and that I would accept the change of assignment.

A few months after our arrival and after I had done some work in
writing, President Knorr showed me into an office containing a table
piled high with stacks of typed papers and asked me to undertake the
development of a Bible dictionary. The papers were the result of assignments that had been parceled out to 250 men around the world.
Those assignments, however, were generally made on the basis of
their organizational position (as Branch Office personnel, Factory
Overseers, and so forth). Few of the men had writing experience and
fewer still had either the experience, the time or the library facilities
for doing research. I believe it can be conservatively said that at least
ninety percent of the submitted material was not used.

I began with "Aaron," and continued with "Aaronites," "Ab,"

---

20 Proverbs 18:13.
21 Dengue fever is like malaria in being transmitted by mosquitoes but is self-limiting. Its
permanent effect on me may have been due to an earlier, childhood case of scarlet fever.

"Abaddon," and so on but the impracticality of one writer undertaking the task soon became obvious. First, a Director of the Watch Tower Society, Lyman Swingle, was assigned; shortly thereafter Edward Dunlap, the Registrar of Gilead School was also assigned. Eventually Reinhard Lengtat and John Wischuk, of the Service and Writing Departments respectively, joined the project group. Others shared intermittently for varying periods but the five persons mentioned carried the project through until the 1,696-page reference work, called *Aid to Bible Understanding*, was completed five years later.[22]

Near the start, President Knorr made a statement that proved a key factor in our approach to the project. It was not intended the way we understood it but that undoubtedly was fortuitous. Talking to those of us then assigned, he said, "We just want to present what the Bible says; there is no need to look up everything in the Society's publications."

His intent in saying this, as we realized later, was so that the project could get done quickly and so it would produce something relatively small, a "handbook" as he later expressed it. By just restating what was in the particular Bible verses relating to a subject, with very little additional clarification, there would be only a minimal amount of time needed for research. We misunderstood him to mean that we should strive always to present what the Bible *actually* said rather than feel obliged to present things the way the Watch Tower publications presented them. A considerably different kind of publication resulted than would otherwise have been the case. The material sent in by the 250 men almost without exception presented information according to the 'accepted viewpoint' of the Society's publications. Our research often revealed differences.

The Society's vice president, Fred Franz, was acknowledged as the organization's principal Bible scholar. On a number of occasions I went to his office to inquire about points. To my surprise he frequently directed me to Bible commentaries, saying, "Why don't you see what Adam Clarke says, or what Cooke says," or, if the subject primarily related to the Hebrew Scriptures, "what the Soncino commentaries say." Our Bethel library contained shelf after shelf after shelf filled with such commentaries. Since they were the product of scholars of other religions, however, I had not given much importance to them and, along with others in the department, felt some hesitancy, even

---

22 The five of us received our assignments of subjects through Karl Adams, then the head of the Writing Department.

distrust, as to using them. As Karl Klein, a senior member of the Writing Department, sometimes very bluntly expressed it, using these commentaries was "sucking at the tits of Babylon the Great," the empire of false religion according to the Society's interpretation of the great harlot of Revelation.[23]

The more I looked up information in these commentaries, however, the more deeply impressed I was by the firm belief in the divine inspiration of the Scriptures the vast majority expressed. I was impressed even more so by the fact that, though some were written as early as the eighteenth century, the information was generally very worthwhile and accurate. I could not help but compare this with our own publications which, often within a few years, became "out of date" and ceased to be published. It was not that I felt these commentaries to be without error by any means; but the good certainly seemed to outweigh the occasional points I felt to be mistaken.

When the subjects of "Older Man [Elder]" and "Overseer" were assigned to me, research into the Scriptures themselves soon made evident that the congregational form of supervision employed by us did not conform to the first-century arrangements. (We had no bodies of elders in our congregations; one man in each congregation was the sole "overseer.") Somewhat disturbed, I approached my uncle with the evidence. Again his response took me by surprise. "Don't try to understand the Scriptures on the basis of what you see today in the organization," he said, and added, "Keep the *Aid* book pure." I had always looked upon the organization as God's one channel for dispensing truth and so this counsel sounded unusual to say the least. When I pointed out that the Society's *New World Translation* rendering of Acts, chapter fourteen, verse 23, evidently inserted the words "to office" in connection with the appointment of elders and that this somewhat altered the sense, he said, "Why don't you check it in some other translations that may not be as biased."[24] I walked out of his office wondering if I had actually heard what I had heard. In future days I was to remind him of these statements on more than one occasion during Governing Body sessions.

---

23 I find it hard to believe he meant this as seriously as it sounded, since he made use of the commentaries himself and knew that Fred Franz used them quite frequently.

24 Later editions of the *New World Translation* dropped the added phrase. The first editions had read: "Moreover, they appointed older men to office for them in the congregation and, offering prayer with fastings, they committed them to Jehovah in whom they had become believers."

That conversation strongly affected my approach to Scripture. I deeply appreciated the integrity toward Scriptural truth his remarks indicated. I began to appreciate more than ever before how vitally important *context* was in discerning the meaning of any part of Scripture, and that realization seemed to be true of others of the group who were working regularly on the *Aid* project. We also came to realize the need to let the Bible define its own terms rather than simply taking some previously held view or letting an English dictionary definition control. We began to make greater use of the Hebrew and Greek lexicons in the Bethel library, and concordances that were based on the original language words rather than on English translations.

It was an education and it was also very humbling, for we came to appreciate that our understanding of Scripture was far less than we had thought, that we were not the advanced Bible scholars we thought we were. I personally had been on such a "treadmill" of activity over the previous twenty-five years that, although reading through the Bible several times, I had never been able to do such serious, detailed research into the Scriptures, in fact never felt great need to do so since it was assumed that others were doing it for me. The two courses at Gilead School I had attended were so tightly programmed that they gave little time for meditation, for unhurried investigation and analysis.

Now having both time and access to the extra Bible helps, the lexicons, commentaries, Hebrew and Greek concordances, and so forth, was an aid. But above all it was seeing the need always to let the context guide, always to let the Scriptures themselves control, that made the major difference. There was no overnight change of viewpoint but, over a period of years, a gradual deepening of appreciation of the crucial need to let God's Word speak for itself to the fullest extent possible. I could see why those one-hundred and two-hundred-year-old commentaries in our Bethel library were comparatively timeless in their value. The very fact of their verse-by-verse approach more or less obliged them to stay within the contextual meaning and thereby considerably restricted them from taking excursions into sectarian views or interpretative flights of fancy.

Thus the material in the *Aid* book relating to elders and the congregational direction in Bible times was very different from the position then held by Jehovah's Witnesses, where a more or less "monarchical" arrangement had prevailed. The Scriptural arrangement of bodies of elders had been summarily ended in 1932 by Judge Rutherford due to a lack of cooperation on the part of some elders with the Society's programs and policies.²⁵ His position as President gave Rutherford the necessary authority to take such a stand and all congregations were invited to vote for the disbanding of bodies of elders and their replacement by a Society-appointed "Service Director." For the next forty years there were no bodies of elders in the congregations. That is why the *New World Translation* of the Bible published by the Society in the 1950's regularly used the rendering "older men" rather than "elders," a then officially discredited term.²⁶

After completing the subjects "Older Man" and "Overseer" I submitted these. Normally, President Nathan Knorr and Vice President Fred Franz were not attempting to read the large volume of copy for the *Aid* project. However, Karl Adams, as head of the Writing Department, told me that upon reading the information he went to Brother Knorr and said, "I think you should read this. It changes a lot of things." After reading the material, Knorr went into Fred Franz's office and, with considerable vehemence, said, "What does this mean? Does this mean we have to change everything at this late date?" Fred Franz replied, No, that he did not think that would be necessary. That the existing arrangement could be continued without problem.

When Karl Adams later passed this information on to me, I found it hard to believe and went to my uncle's room one evening to inquire about it. He confirmed that he felt no need to make adjustments. Knowing that the *Aid* book was to be released to the brothers in completed form that summer at the District Assemblies, I asked what effect he thought it would have on them to read the evidence that there were bodies of elders in the first-century congregation, that all elders served as overseers, and then to find out that we had no intention of following this Scriptural example? He said calmly that he did not think it would cause any problem, that the existing arrangement could be "accommodated" to the information in *Aid*. I expressed deep concern that this setting aside of the Scriptural precedent could be very unsettling to the brothers. Holding to his position, he related how brothers of earlier decades had reasoned that, since Christ had taken Kingdom

25 Generally, in justifying this action, focus is placed on the lack of cooperation by some elders in sharing in the door-to-door witnessing which was now being strongly promoted. They are represented as men who were only interested in conducting meetings and giving talks. It is never mentioned that the Watch Tower president, Judge Rutherford, followed exactly that same course. The explanation given was that his responsibilities did not allow for him to share in the door-to-door activity.
26 Later editions of the *New World Translation* use "elders" but only in Revelation in texts referring to the 24 elders by God's throne.

power in 1914, there could rightly be changes in the way things were administered on earth. He added that he had believed and still believed that Christ Jesus would direct and administer the affairs of his servants earthwide by the use of, or through the office of, just a single individual, and that this would be the case until the New Order came. The tenor of these expressions seemed so different from those he had made on earlier occasions that I found it difficult to reconcile them.

Sometime later, however, the vice president prepared some convention material that indicated that a change in the congregational direction *would* take place. When the copy of this material reached Karl Adams he saw the implications and immediately contacted President Knorr, saying to him, "I think you had better talk with Brother Franz again. I believe he has changed his mind." Brother Knorr did and Brother Franz had. And the forty-year-old arrangement changed as a consequence.

When the subject "Chronology" was assigned to me this similarly led to serious questions.[27] A major teaching of Jehovah's Witnesses is that Bible prophecy had pointed to the year 1914 as the end of the "Gentile Times" of Luke chapter twenty-one, verse 24, and that in that year Christ Jesus actively took up his Kingdom power and began to rule invisibly to human eyes. In Daniel chapter four, references to a period of "seven times" were the foundation for the calculations leading to that date and, by use of other texts, these "seven times" were translated into a period of 2,520 years beginning in 607 B.C.E. and ending in 1914 C.E. The starting date, 607 B.C.E., was held to be the time of the destruction of Jerusalem by Babylonian conqueror Nebuchadnezzar. I knew that the 607 B.C.E. date seemed to be peculiar to our publications but did not really know why.

Months of research were spent on this one subject of "Chronology" and it resulted in the longest article in the *Aid* publication.[28] Much of the time was spent endeavoring to find some proof, some backing in history, for the 607 B.C.E. date so crucial to our calculations for 1914. Charles Ploeger, a member of the headquarters staff, was at that time serving as a secretary for me and he searched through the libraries of the New York city area for anything that might substantiate that date historically.

We found absolutely nothing in support of 607 B.C.E. All histori-

---

27 I was also assigned most of the historical subjects, dealing with the rulers and history of Egypt, Assyria, Babylon (rulers only), Medo-Persia and others.
28 It runs from page 322 to page 348, a total of twenty-seven pages.

ans pointed to a date twenty years later. Before preparing the *Aid* material on "Archaeology" I had not realized that the number of baked-clay cuneiform tablets found in the Mesopotamian area and dating back to the time of ancient Babylon numbered into the tens of thousands. In all of these there was nothing to indicate that the period of the Neo-Babylonian Empire (in which period Nebuchadnezzar's reign figured) was of the necessary length to fit our 607 B.C.E. date for the destruction of Jerusalem. Everything pointed to a period twenty years shorter than our published chronology claimed. Though I found this disquieting, I wanted to believe that our chronology was right in spite of all the contrary evidence. Thus, in preparing the material for the *Aid* book, much of the time and space was spent in trying to weaken the credibility of the archeological and historical evidence that would make erroneous our 607 B.C.E. date and give a different starting point for our calculations and therefore an ending date different from 1914.

Charles Ploeger and I made a trip to Brown University in Providence, Rhode Island, to interview Professor Abraham Sachs, a specialist in ancient cuneiform texts. We wanted to see if we could obtain any information that would indicate any flaw or weakness whatsoever in the astronomical data presented in many of the texts, data that indicated our 607 B.C.E. date was incorrect. In the end, it became evident that it would have taken a virtual conspiracy on the part of the ancient scribes—with no conceivable motive for doing so—to misrepresent the facts if, indeed, our figure was to be the right one. Again, like an attorney faced with evidence he cannot overcome, my effort was to discredit or weaken confidence in the witnesses from ancient times who presented such evidence, the evidence of historical texts relating to the Neo-Babylonian Empire.[29] The arguments I presented were honest ones, but I know that their intent was to uphold a date for which there was no historical support.

So, despite our heightened appreciation of certain principles, the *Aid* book nonetheless contained many examples of our efforts to be loyal to the Society's teachings. In many respects, what we learned through our experience did more for us than it did for the publication. Still, the *Aid to Bible Understanding* book did serve to quicken interest in the Scriptures among many Witnesses. Perhaps its tone, its approach, the effort put forth by most of the writers to avoid dogmatism, to acknowledge that there might be more than one way of seeing certain matters, not to make more of something than the evidence hon-

---

29 *Aid to Bible Understanding*, pp. 326–328, 330, 331.

estly allowed—these things may have been of principal benefit, though in these too we certainly fell short at times, allowing preconceived ideas to control, failing to hold as firmly as we should have to the Scriptures themselves. I know this was true in my own case in preparing such subjects as the "Appointed Times of the Nations," "Faithful and Discreet Slave," and "Great Crowd," all of which contain arguments designed to uphold current teachings of the Watch Tower publications. Simply because in my mind those teachings were then equivalent to "fact," I found myself doing what the "Foreword" I later wrote said was not intended. On page 6 under the heading "Its Aim," the words appear, *"Aid to Bible Understanding* is not intended to be a doctrinal commentary or an interpretative work." Also, that whatever application was made of figurative and symbolic expressions, this was not done "arbitrarily or to conform to a creed." In the main, that was true. But ingrained beliefs sometimes overrode our efforts to hold to that standard.

The year the completed *Aid* book was released, I was invited to become a member of the Governing Body of Jehovah's Witnesses, the Body that now directs the activity of Jehovah's Witnesses in some 205 countries of the world. Up to that point it had been composed of seven members who were identical with the seven members of the Board of Directors of the corporation called the Watch Tower Bible and Tract Society, a corporation founded originally in Pennsylvania by Charles Taze Russell, the first president. On October 20, 1971, along with three others, I was appointed as a member of the now expanded Governing Body. This circumstance, perhaps more than any other, brought me face to face with some realities that I had never expected to encounter.

Many of Jehovah's Witnesses took exception to a statement that appeared in a *Time* magazine article (February 22, 1982) in which my name figured prominently. The writers of the article referred to the organization of Jehovah's Witnesses as "secretive." It may seem odd to use a term like that about an organization that encourages vigorously a work of the most public kind—house-to-house activity in cities, towns and countryside around the world. The *Time* reporters evidently wrote what they did because they found it extremely difficult to obtain any comment from the international headquarters about the situation described in the first chapter of this book.

But the fact is that even among Jehovah's Witnesses very few have any clear idea as to how the central part of the organization functions.

They do not know how decisions as to doctrinal teachings are reached, how the Governing Body that directs all their activities worldwide conducts its discussions, whether decisions are consistently unanimous or what is done if there is disagreement. All this is cloaked in secrecy as the Governing Body meets in closed sessions. I can only recall two or three occasions in the nine years that I was a part of the Body when persons other than appointed Members were allowed to be present at a regular session of the Body. And on those occasions their presence was simply to give a report requested by the Governing Body, after which they were dismissed and the Governing Body then carried on its deliberations in private—the importance of their reports did not qualify those persons to share in the discussion. Also, no specific information is ever given to Witnesses as a whole as to the Society's income, expenditures, assets or investments (although they have received a brief expense report in the annual *Yearbook*).[30]

Thus numerous factors that are relatively common knowledge in many religious organizations are known only vaguely, if at all, by the vast majority of Jehovah's Witnesses. Yet the decisions made by the small group of men forming that Body can, and often do, affect their lives in a most intimate way and are supposed to be applied globally.

Which brings me to the final reason for writing, the most important since without it the previous ones are of little consequence.

OBLIGATION

"Whatever you wish that men would do to you, do so to them; for this is the law and the prophets." —Matthew 7:12, *Revised Standard Version.*

That principle stated by Jesus Christ binds any of us claiming to be Christian, in whatever we do. No honest person can claim to carry out those words perfectly and I make no such claim. But I believe I can say that what is here written owes to a sincere desire to follow that principle.

The apostle Paul spoke of himself as a "debtor" to persons of all kinds.[31] He felt an obligation toward them, and I feel a similar sense of obligation. If someone else had knowledge of facts that could be of

---

30 In 1978 a financial report to the Governing Body listed $332 million in assets (properties, deposits and so forth). Even on the Governing Body, few members know much about the nature of the financial holdings of the Society.

31 Romans 1:14.

value to me in making vital decisions, I would want him to make these available to me—not to make my decision for me, but to supply the information, leaving it to me to weigh its value or significance. If he were a friend, a genuine friend, I believe he would do that.

The nine years spent on the Governing Body had great impact on me and particularly on my conscience. I found myself facing a major crisis in my life, a crossroads situation I had never expected to encounter. The decision I made was my own and the resulting cost was considerable. But I do not regret it nor do I regret having gained the information that contributed toward it. Others might decide differently; some have. That is their privilege, something between them and God.

After I resigned as a member of the Governing Body in May, 1980, I received numerous calls from newspapers and magazines wanting information about the situation existent within the organization. I consistently directed the inquirers to the headquarters in Brooklyn. The inquirers, in turn, consistently said that they had tried that avenue with no success: "No comment." My reply was simply that I could not be their source of information. I maintained that position for nearly two years. What has happened in those two years, not merely as regards myself but as regards others, has caused me to reassess that position.

During those two years, the motives, character and conduct of persons who conscientiously disagreed with the organization have been portrayed in the worst of terms. Their concern to put God's Word first has been represented as the product of ambition, rebellion, pride, as sin against God and Christ. No allowance is made for the possibility that any of them acted out of sincerity, love of truth or integrity to God. No effort to distinguish is made, but all are 'lumped' together. Any misconduct or wrong attitude on the part of some who have left the organization is attributed to all who have left. For those who do display a wrong attitude, no effort is made to appreciate that the wrong attitude may be a result of frustration, disappointment and hurt. An enormous amount of rumor and even gutter-level gossip has circulated among Witnesses, internationally. Faithful Christians with high standards of morality are accused of being wife swappers, homosexuals, hypocrites, egoists interested in establishing their own personal cult. Older ones are often dismissed as being "mentally disturbed" or "senile."

The only ones who could restrain such talk, simply by pointing out the possibility that such persons *could* be genuinely sincere, *could* have true concern for conscience—as well as by reminding the sowers of rumor how repugnant false testimony is to God—these persons have in reality contributed to the spread of rumor by what they have published.[32]

Consider, for example, this material found in the August 15, 1981, *Watchtower* (pages 28, 29), circulated in the millions of copies in many languages around the earth:

> [14]From time to time, there have arisen from among the ranks of Jehovah's people those who, like the original Satan, have adopted an independent, fault-finding attitude. They do not want to serve "shoulder to shoulder" with the worldwide brotherhood. (Compare Ephesians 2:19–22.) Rather, they present a "stubborn shoulder" to Jehovah's words. (Zech. 7:11, 12) Reviling the pattern of the "pure language" that Jehovah has so graciously taught his people over the past century, these haughty ones try to draw the "sheep" away from the one international "flock" that Jesus has gathered in the earth. (John 10:7–10, 16) They try to sow doubts and to separate unsuspecting ones from the bounteous "table" of spiritual food spread at the Kingdom Halls of Jehovah's Witnesses, where truly there is 'nothing lacking.' (Ps. 23:1–6) They say that it is sufficient to read the Bible exclusively, either alone or in small groups at home. But, strangely, through such 'Bible reading,' they have reverted right back to the apostate doctrines that commentaries by Christendom's clergy were teaching 100 years ago, and some have even returned to celebrating Christendom's festivals again, such as the Roman Saturnalia of December 25! Jesus and his apostles warned against such lawless ones.—Matt. 24:11–13; Acts 20:28–30; 2 Pet. 2:1, 22.

Thus, in one paragraph, persons are described as *like Satan, independent, faultfinding, stubborn, reviling, haughty, apostate* and *lawless*. What had they actually done to earn this array of charges? Among the "wrongs" mentioned is that of disagreeing in some unspecified way with some unspecified part of the organization's teachings; also, holding that God's inspired Word alone is sufficient and that large meetings in a building are a nonessential.

Could these things *of themselves* place a person in the Satan-like category described? Nothing is said to indicate otherwise and, incredible as it may seem, in the minds of many Witnesses, including elders and traveling representatives, this has been considered enough to so categorize them and to deal with them accordingly.

Below is a chart made from the Governing Body records of the worldwide activity of Jehovah's Witnesses, showing year by year the number of persons baptized and the total number actively associated for the years from 1970 to 1979, inclusive:

32   Exodus 20:16; Leviticus 19:16; Psalm 15:3; 1 Peter 2:21–23.

Year	Baptized that year	Total number reporting activity that year
1970	164,193	1,384,782
1971	149,808	1,510,245
1972	163,123	1,596,442
1973	193,990	1,656,673
1974	297,872	1,880,713
1975	295,073	2,062,449
1976	196,656	2,138,537
1977	124,459	2,117,194
1978	95,052	2,086,698
1979	113,672	2,097,070
Total baptized in 10 years:	1,793,898	

This reveals that during a ten-year period ending in 1979 a total of 1,793,898 persons were baptized. The organization customarily estimates that 1% of those associated die each year. Figuring this out year by year, it would mean an estimated 185,308 were lost in that way. If we reduce the baptismal figure by that amount it leaves 1,608,590 as the increase gained in that ten-year period if all persons remained in the organization.

What do we find? Adding 1,608,590 to the number active in the year previous to this ten-year period, 1,256,784 (in 1969), gives a total of 2,865,374 that should be associated in 1979. But the report for that year shows only 2,097,070 associated. That means that during the ten-year period some 768,304 persons left the organization or ceased activity. This is equal to *four out of every ten persons* baptized in that same period. Or, put another way, for every three persons still in the organization, one had left.

The reasons producing this "revolving door" situation are multiple. I have no illusions that all of these more than a half million persons who left the organization in those ten years did so for reasons of conscience or that every one of them is necessarily a humble, rightly motivated person, more concerned about truth than about self. Many quite evidently are not; some have pursued a course of immorality either before or after leaving; some who left because of disagreement have become guilty of the same wrongs they objected to, expressing vindictiveness, using ridicule, half-truths and exaggerations. Some have even created disturbances at meetings or assemblies of Jehovah's Witnesses, conduct that I find deplorable. But I know personally many,

many persons who are not like that, who give every indication of being decent, God-fearing, compassionate persons. If viewed from a selfish standpoint, they had everything to lose and nothing to gain from the stand they took and the course they have followed thereafter.

In many cases it was not some unkind treatment they themselves experienced that disturbed them; it was seeing such treatment meted out to others, seeing people suffer because of the rigidity, narrow-mindedness, even arrogance of men in charge, elders and others, or recognizing the hurtful effects of certain edicts of the organization that did not rest on a solid Scriptural foundation. Rather than disgruntled, vindictive complainers, they have simply pleaded for greater compassion, a closer adherence to the example of God's own Son, the Master of the Christian household of faith.

This *feeling for others* is, I believe, a decisive factor as to the genuineness of motive. Similarly, a concern for truth, a concern not to be guilty of misrepresenting God's own Word, a concern not to be hypocritical in appearing to believe what they do not believe, support what they cannot conscientiously support, condemn what they cannot see that Scripture itself condemns—such concern is, I think, also determinative as to genuineness of motive of any taking such a stand. I know many persons who clearly evidence such concern, yet who are labeled as "apostates," "antichrists," "instruments of Satan." In case after case after case, the sole basis for such condemnation is that they could not honestly agree with all the organization's teachings or policies.

I feel an obligation toward such persons. In virtually every instance, a small group of three to five men (a "judicial committee") met with them in secret meetings, where those who came as witnesses could only give their testimony but not stay to witness the discussion. Later a brief disfellowshiping announcement was read to the congregation that presented none of the testimony and none of the evidence in support of the disfellowshiping action. After the reading of that announcement no Witness was supposed to talk with the persons disfellowshiped, thereby shutting down any possibility of their expressing themselves by way of an explanation to friends and associates. For them to have done so *before* the disfellowshiping would have been counted as 'proselytizing,' 'undermining the unity of the congregation,' 'sowing dissension,' 'forming a sect.' For anyone to talk to them *afterward* would jeopardize that person's own standing, make him liable for similar disfellowshipment.

An effective "quarantining" is thus accomplished; a "lid" is placed on any discussion of the matter. The record of the disfellowshiping and any claimed evidence now resides in one of the many voluminous files at the Brooklyn Service Department (or the files of a Branch Office), stamped "Do Not Destroy." This file containing the charges made against them, like their hearing, is also secret, not subject to review.

The Scriptures tell us that, "A true companion is loving all the time, and is a brother that is born for when there is distress."[33] I once thought I had many, many such friends. But when the crisis reached a decisive point I found I had only a few. Still, I count those few precious, whether they said little or much on my behalf. Because of past prominence, people inquire about me. However, almost no one ever inquires about the others who lack such prominence, although they have suffered through the same experience with essentially the same costs and agonies.

What must it mean to a mother, who has seen a baby daughter come forth from her own body, has nursed that baby, cared for it through illness, has trained the young girl through the formative years of life, living her problems with her, feeling her disappointments and sadnesses as if they were her own, shedding tears along with her tears— what must it mean to that mother to have her daughter, now an adult, suddenly reject her, and do so simply because her mother sought to be true to her conscience and to God?

What must it do to a father or mother to see a son or daughter marry and be told, for the same reason, that 'it would be best if they did not appear at the wedding,' or know that a daughter has given birth to a child and be told that they should not come to see their grandchild?

This is not imagination. Exactly those things are happening to many parents who have been associated with Jehovah's Witnesses.

Consider here just one example, from a mother in Pennsylvania who writes:

"I have children in the organization, married, who at the time of my disassociation even offered for me to come to their home, for a rest, and their opinion of me as a person was not altered. When the information came through later [in the September 15, 1981, *Watchtower* which set forth detailed instructions as to association with any who thus disassociated themselves] I've been

33 Proverbs 17:17.

shunned by them ever since and they will not talk to me on the phone or have contact with me. I've got to do something about it but I don't know what. I make no move lest it be a wrong move and alienate them further. I don't phone them for fear they'll get an unlisted number, and I don't write, as I said, for fear of saying anything they might construe as offensive. I've been hospitalized during this time for emotional exhaustion and I suffered an additional crisis all within a short time of each event which proved, unfortunately, overwhelming.

"Perhaps you share this experience. I do not know how I am going to handle the loss of my children (and future grandchildren). The loss is monumental."

If my past prominence could now contribute in some way to the situation of such persons being considered with a more open mind and could aid others to revise their attitude toward persons of this kind, I feel that such prominence would thereby have served perhaps the only useful purpose it ever had.

I think here of Paul's words when he says:

"What we are is plain to God, and I hope it is also plain in your conscience. We are not trying to commend ourselves to you again, but are giving you an opportunity to take pride in us, so that you can answer those who take pride in what is seen rather than in what is in the heart."

"Make room for us in your hearts. We have wronged no one, we have corrupted no one, we have exploited no one. I do not say this to condemn you; I have said before that you have such a place in our hearts that we would live or die with you."[34]

If the information presented in this book could help toward one such mother being viewed by her children, not with shame, but with pride for staying by her conscience, all the effort involved would be worth it.

That is basically why this book will present things that I saw, heard and experienced during my nine years on the Governing Body of Jehovah's Witnesses. It is evidently necessary in order to get at the root of what is a heart-breaking problem for many, on both sides of the issue.

What is presented is not intended as some kind of "exposé." While it is true that some things were shocking to me, they are not presented for their shock value. Their presentation is because they illustrate and exemplify very fundamental problems, very serious issues. They demonstrate the extremes to which "loyalty to an organization" can

---

34 2 Corinthians 5:11, 12; 7:2, 3, NIV.

lead, how it is that basically kind, well-intentioned, persons can be led to make decisions and take actions that are both unkind and unjust, even cruel. Names along with times and places will generally be cited because that seems necessary for a credible, factual presentation. I am quite sure that without these many would doubt or deny the factualness of what is said. Where these features seem unnecessary and where they could, by their use, cause needless difficulty for individuals involved, names or other identifying factors will not be stated. Personalities are dealt with only as they figure into the overall picture. If some persons, such as Nathan Knorr and Fred Franz, are quoted with great frequency it is because they had much to say and said it with greater influence and effect than others. Others, such as Lyman Swingle and Karl Adams, may at times be quoted more often because my work brought me into closer contact with them than with some others.

I have sought to be fair in such quotations, not taking them out of context, not seeking to give them a meaning that is not there. I believe the quotations made are typical of the persons quoted, not something out of character with their usual outlook, approach and personality. Nonetheless, I have kept a few quotations anonymous, including certain quotations by members of the Governing Body, because of wishing to avoid unnecessary difficulty for the individual or those closely related to him, or because of considering particular circumstances, at times tragic, relating to the person. It is, obviously, impossible to do this in all cases or the account would become meaningless. I believe, too, that none of us can expect to receive total exemption from the responsibility indicated by Jesus' statement: "I tell you that men will have to give account on the day of judgment for every careless word they have spoken. For by your words you will be acquitted, and by your words you will be condemned."[35] We may seek, and gain, forgiveness for wrong or hurtful things said. But we are still responsible for them.

Some will likely condemn certain information as an 'airing of our dirty linen before the public.' Strangely, these same ones generally do not object to the airing of the 'dirty linen' of other religions and may, in fact, take great interest in it, even publicize it widely. But they feel that what happens within their own religious organization should not be discussed outside its confines.

The hard fact is, however, that among Jehovah's Witnesses today

35 Matthew 12:36, 37, NIV.

there is simply no possibility for such discussion to take place. Anyone's attempting to do so would be viewed as showing a rebellious spirit and would only result in further disfellowshiping. Since the information cannot be discussed within, and if it is not to be discussed outside the structure, that means that it must be left undiscussed, ignored. Some, of course, would like it to remain that way, but is it right that it should?

It is true that the Christian rightly relies on God to see all things and to be the true and final Judge of all matters. Undeniably, He alone can fully and finally right all wrongs committed. There is never any justification for angry retaliation, spiteful recrimination. There is no room for 'smear tactics.' The Scriptures leave no doubt in that regard.[36] Does this, however, call for maintaining total silence about injustice? Does it require keeping silent when error is propagated in the name of God? Is, perhaps, the discussion thereof evidence of 'disrespect for divinely constituted authority'?[37]

The position of the organization is that no injustice exists. That what has been, and is being, done is in full harmony with the Scriptures, in fact that the Scriptures *require* such action to be taken. If that is so, then there should be no objection to a frank discussion of things. Such discussion should actually result in the rightness of the organization's position becoming more evident, should vindicate it of any charge of injustice. Only persons truly responsible for injustice prefer silence and seek to impose it, as has long been the case with dictatorial governments and authoritarian religions in past as well as recent times.

Do Scriptural examples themselves urge against disclosure of wrongs where these involve those in high places of authority? It does not seem so, since the work of the Hebrew prophets frequently focused on such ones, those prophets making known the ways in which those leaders and men in authority had strayed from God's standards with resulting problems. Jehovah's Witnesses have often pointed to such candor and openness as one of the evidences that the Bible is truthful, genuinely God's Book.[38]

What, too, of Jesus' apostles and disciples? It was the very authority structure of God's covenant people—its Sanhedrin, its elders, and

---

36 Psalm 37:5–9, 32, 33; Romans 12:17–21; 1 Peter 2:21–23.
37 The August 15, 1982, *Watchtower* in discussing Jude's remarks regarding those "speaking abusively about glorious ones" (verse 8) states that those glorious ones include "appointed Christian overseers" and warns against the "tendency to disregard God-given authority." See also the boxed information on page 29 of that issue.
38 See the book *"All Scripture Is Inspired of God and Beneficial,"* published in 1963, p. 341.

the divinely constituted priestly authority—that objected strenuously to the publicizing done by the apostles of the unjust handling of Jesus' case.[39] In both cases, that of the Hebrew prophets and that of the Christian disciples, those publicizing the wrongs did so out of respect for, and in obedience to, a *higher* authority, and in the interests of the people who needed to know.

Obviously, no one today has a divine commission as a prophet or an apostle. But one does not have to be a prophet to take a course that follows the *example* of God's prophets. Otherwise Jesus' words would lose their meaning when, speaking to those who were reproached and about whom every sort of wicked thing was being said, he encouraged them to rejoice, saying, "for in that way they persecuted the prophets before you."[40] It was because they were following a parallel course that those Christians were receiving parallel treatment. One does not have to be an apostle to follow the example of the apostles, nor does he have to be, or pretend to be, a Messiah in order to walk in the footsteps of Jesus Christ.[41]

There is, of course, an enormous difference between the treatment accorded God's Son—as to importance, significance and consequence—and that accorded to the persons involved in this modern-day situation. But it would seem that the principle of open disclosure that God approved in the above examples has force in this present-day situation, gives some indication at least that He is by no means averse to having injustice and misrepresentation uncovered, provided that the motivation is that of helping, of alerting people to realities that can aid them in arriving at right conclusions. The saying that "evil prevails when good men remain silent" seems to have some validity here.

Regardless of the seriousness of the matters here made known, they alone did not lead me to a decision. But they did cause me to ponder more seriously than ever before the meaning of major portions and teachings of the Bible—why the apostle Paul could stress salvation by faith, "not owing to works, in order that no man should have grounds for boasting," what the real difference is between the righteousness produced by lawkeeping and the righteousness resulting from God's grace or undeserved kindness, the importance of the role of God's Son as Head of the Christian congregation, what the true purpose of the congregation is, the reason for God's granting authority therein and

---

39 Acts 4:5–23; 5:17–40.
40 Matthew 5:11, 12, compare James 5:10, 11.
41 1 Corinthians 11:1; Ephesians 5:1; 1 Peter 2:21.

how that authority can be misused. The things that I saw, heard and experienced as a member of the Governing Body of Jehovah's Witnesses, part of the inner executive circle, brought home to me more than ever before the crucial importance of those teachings.

Many others of Jehovah's Witnesses, not having the information I here supply, arrived at the same crossroads and made their own decision, doing so simply on the basis of what they had read in the Bible. Others, however, face a serious crisis of conscience and do so with uncertainty, with a sense of confused anguish, even of guilt. My hope is that what is presented in this book may be of help and I feel it is owed to them. It is offered to be used in whatever way their conscience may lead, as they submit to the guidance of God's spirit and word.

3

GOVERNING BODY

"Not that we are the masters over your faith,
but we are fellow workers for your joy, for it is
by your faith that you are standing."
—2 Corinthians 1:24.

THE above-quoted statement of Paul repeatedly came into my mind during the nine years of my participation in the Governing Body of Jehovah's Witnesses. I could wish that all Witnesses might have the experience of participation. Perhaps then they could understand what words alone cannot convey.

To clarify what the Governing Body is:

Jehovah's Witnesses understand that Christ Jesus, as Head of the congregation, feeds and governs his congregation by means of a "faithful and discreet slave" class. This class is now composed of a remnant of the 144,000 persons anointed as heirs of Christ's heavenly kingdom.[1] But from among such class there is a small number of men who act as a Governing Body and perform all administrative functions for the global congregation, not only for the present number of 9,500 "anointed ones" out of whom these men are drawn, but also for the more than two million other persons associated who are not considered to be among the heavenly heirs.[2]

It seemed an awesome responsibility for me when I became one of eleven members of the worldwide Governing Body in 1971 (the number later grew to as many as eighteen in 1977 and today stands at

---

1 The term "faithful and discreet slave" is drawn from Jesus' parable at Matthew 24:45–47, the number 144,000 is taken from Revelation 7:4 and 14:3.
2 See the *1983 Yearbook of Jehovah's Witnesses*, p. 31.

fifteen).[3] The first sessions of the weekly meetings attended, however, proved quite different from what I expected.[4]

A rotational chairmanship had recently been put into effect and Vice President Fred Franz was that year's chairman. But the matters to be discussed were determined by the corporation president, Nathan Knorr. Whatever he considered advisable for the Body to discuss he brought to the meeting and generally that was the first time we had any knowledge of the matter under discussion. During some weeks the meetings consisted simply of a consideration of lists of recommendations for traveling representatives in different countries—the name, age, date of baptism, whether of the "anointed" or not, the years of full-time service being read out. In the vast majority of cases these were just names to us; we seldom knew any of the individuals involved. So after listening to such readings of lists from Suriname or Zambia or Sri Lanka, we would vote on the appointment of these men. I recall that Thomas Sullivan (usually called "Bud") was then in his eighties, nearly blind and in poor health. He repeatedly would give in to sleep during these sessions and it seemed a shame to wake him to vote on things he knew little about. At times the entire meeting lasted but a few minutes; one that I recall lasted only seven minutes (including the opening prayer).

Then from time to time President Knorr would bring some "problem correspondence" involving questions as to certain conduct by individual Witnesses, and the Body was to decide what policy should be adopted regarding these, whether the particular conduct called for disfellowshiping, some lesser discipline, or no action at all. During that period (and on up until 1975) all decisions were expected to be unanimous. After discussion, a motion would be made, seconded, and then the Chairman called for a show of hands. If a unanimous vote was not obtained, as occasionally different ones would not vote for a motion, generally some compromise solution was developed that could gain unanimity. As is but natural in those circumstances, there was a certain sense of pressure to go along with the majority rather than take a lone stance on matters and thus appear as independent or out of harmony. There were votes where I did not raise my hand, but as a

---

3 At that time the eleven members were: Nathan Knorr, Fred Franz, Grant Suiter, Thomas Sullivan, Milton Henschel, Lyman Swingle, John Groh (these seven also being the Directors of the Watch Tower Society), then, William Jackson, Leo Greenlees, George Gangas, Raymond Franz. Sullivan, Groh, Knorr, Jackson' and Suiter are now deceased.
4 The Governing Body as a whole meets every Wednesday.

rule I conformed. In the few instances where my not having voted resulted in someone's proposing a compromise motion, even though the compromise motion still did not seem fully right to me I would concede and vote with the majority. It appeared necessary to conform if matters were to be decided and expedited rather than stalemated. However, issues began arising that made this more and more difficult for me.

As weeks went along discussions were held on such subjects as whether a father qualifies as an elder if he allows a son or daughter to marry when only eighteen years of age; whether one qualifies as an elder if he approves of his son or daughter taking higher education;[5] whether one qualifies as an elder if he does shift work and sometimes (while on night shift) misses congregational meetings; whether elders can accept circumstantial evidence of adultery, or the testimony of a wife that her husband confessed adultery to her, and whether this is sufficient to allow for Scriptural divorce and remarriage; whether a divorce is Scripturally acceptable if, even where adultery has been committed, the one obtaining the divorce is the guilty mate rather than the innocent mate;[6] what validity a divorce has when obtained on grounds other than adultery if, after the divorce is granted, evidence of *pre*-divorce adultery comes to light; what the situation is if such a divorce is obtained and there is *post*-divorce adultery; whether an innocent mate's having sex relations with an adulterous mate (subsequent to learning of the adultery) cancels out the right to divorce that mate and be free to remarry; whether it is proper for a Witness to pay a fine if that fine is imposed because of an infraction of law resulting from his witnessing activity or because of some stand he had taken in order to adhere to Witness beliefs;[7] whether it is proper to send food or other assistance to persons by means of the Red Cross (the main issue here being that the cross is a religious symbol and so the Red Cross organization might be quasi-religious; this discussion was quite lengthy and was carried over to a subsequent meeting); issues about the Society's existing practice of using irregular channels to funnel money into certain countries (Indonesia as one example) in a way that would gain greater value for the American dollars involved, doing this

---

5 Higher education is generally frowned upon as conducive to loss of faith and as providing an atmosphere likely to contribute to immorality.

6 At that time the ruling was that only if the *innocent* mate got the divorce was it Scripturally valid.

7 The policy had been that the fine should not be paid, that in these circumstances it would be an admission of guilt and hence a compromise of one's integrity. This policy has changed.

even though the particular country had laws ruling this illegal; also as to getting certain equipment into some countries without having to pay the heavy import tax imposed by law; whether Witnesses belonging to labor unions can accept strike duty assignments or can accept a union order to do cleaning work on the union premises in lieu of accepting such assignments as picketing; whether Witnesses could respond to military conscription simply to do work in cotton fields (this from Bolivia).

These are only a partial sampling of things discussed during the first two years or so of my being on the Body. The effect of our decisions was considerable in its impact on the lives of others. In matters of divorce, for example, the congregation elders serve as a sort of religious court and if they are not satisfied as to the validity of a divorce action, the individual who goes through with such a divorce and then later remarries becomes subject to disfellowshiping.

A matter, not among those just mentioned, but which brought considerable discussion involved a Witness couple in California. Someone had seen in their bedroom certain literature and photographs dealing with unusual sex practices. (I do not recall that we learned just how the person reporting this happened to have access to the couple's bedroom.) Investigation and interrogation by the local elders confirmed that the couple did engage in sexual relations other than by simple genital copulation.[8] Correspondence from the elders came in to Brooklyn and the Governing Body was called upon to rule as to what action if any should be taken toward the couple.

Until the correspondence was read to us that morning, none of us aside from the president had had any opportunity to think about the subject. Yet within a couple of hours the decision was reached that the couple was subject to disfellowshiping. This was thereafter set out as a formal published policy, applicable to any persons engaging willfully in similar practices.[9]

The published material was understood and applied in such a way that marriage mates generally felt obliged to report to the elders if any such practice existed or developed in their marriage, whether mutually agreed upon or done solely at the initiation of one of the mates. (In

8 An article in the December 15, 1969, *Watchtower* (pp. 765, 766) had first focused attention on such sexual relations, discussing them at considerable length, and this doubtless served to sensitize the elders to reports of such conduct, in fact, was likely responsible for this report about people's private bedroom matters being made in the first place.

9 See the *Watchtower*, December 1, 1972, pp. 734–736; also November 15, 1972, pp. 703, 704.

the latter case the noninitiating mate was expected to come forward and convey this information to the elders if the initiating mate was unwilling to do so.) To fail to come forward generally is viewed as indicative of an unrepentant attitude and as weighing in favor of disfellowshiping. The belief that disfellowshiping cuts one off from the one organization where salvation can be found, as well as from friends and relatives, exercises heavy pressure on the person to conform, no matter how difficult confession (or reporting) to the elders may be.

The Governing Body's decision in 1972 resulted in a sizeable number of "judicial hearings" as elders followed up on reports or confessions of the sexual practices involved. Women experienced painful embarrassment in such hearings as they responded to the elders' questions about the intimacies of their marital relations. Many marriages where one of the mates was not a Witness underwent a turbulent period, with the non-Witness mate objecting strenuously to what he or she considered an unwarranted invasion of bedroom privacy. Some marriages broke up with resulting divorce.[10]

An unprecedented volume of mail came in over a period of five years, most of it questioning the Scriptural basis for the Governing Body members inserting themselves into the private lives of others in such a way, and expressing inability to see the validity of the arguments advanced in print to support the stand taken. (The principal portion of Scripture relied upon was Romans, chapter one, verses 24–27, dealing with homosexuality, and those writing to the Society pointed out that they could not see how it could rightly be applied to heterosexual relations between man and wife.) Other letters, often from wives, simply expressed confusion and anguish over their uncertainty as to the properness of their "sexual foreplay."

One woman said she had talked to an elder and he had told her to write to the Governing Body "for a sure answer." So she wrote, saying that she and her husband loved each other deeply and then she described the "certain type of foreplay" they were accustomed to, stating "I believe it's a matter of conscience, but I am writing you to be sure." Her closing words were:

> "I am scared, I am hurt, and I am more worried at this time about [my husband's] feeling for the truth. . . . I know you will tell me what to do."

10 In a memorandum to the Governing Body, dated August 9, 1976, a headquarters staff member handling correspondence states: "Many, many problems have resulted from the position taken, often where there is an unbelieving [meaning a non-Witness] husband. Wives have refused to allow such husbands to stimulate them in this way or to stimulate the husbands in this way. As a result marriages have broken up."

In another typical letter an elder wrote, saying that he had a problem he wanted to get straightened out in his mind and heart and that
to do this he felt "it's best to contact the 'mother' for advice."[11] The
problem dealt with his marital sex life and he said that he and his wife
were confused as to "where to draw the line in the act of foreplay
before the actual act of sex." He assured the Society that he and his
wife would "follow any advice you give us to the letter."

These letters illustrate the implicit trust these persons had come to
place in the Governing Body, the belief that the men forming that
Body could tell them where to "draw the line" in even such intimate
aspects of their personal lives, and that they should rightly hew to that
line "to the letter."

Many letters went out from the Society in response. Often they
endeavored to provide some limited clarification (saying without *exactly* saying) as to what sexual foreplay fell within the bounds of condemned actions, other foreplay thereby being exempt.

A memo from a member of the Society's Service Department, in
June of 1976, discusses a telephone conversation with an Instructor of
seminars (held with elders). The memo relates that the Instructor had
phoned about an elder attending the seminar who confessed to certain
disapproved sexual practices within his marriage. The memo states:

> "Brother [here giving the name of the Instructor] closely discussed the mat-
> ter with him to determine whether it was really oral copulation that was in-
> volved. . . . [The Instructor] had told him in view of the circumstances that
> he ought to go to the other members of the committee and it happened that the
> other two members of the committee were in the class and so he went and
> talked with them. Now [the Instructor] was wondering what else should be
> done. . . . It was suggested to [him] that he write a full report on this to the
> Society so that in the future when he has any such case come up he will have
> direction on how to handle the matter and he will not have to call."

This illustrates the extent to which interrogation went in intimacy
and the extent to which the headquarters organization supervised the
whole situation.

Letter after letter reveals that the persons involved felt positively
responsible before God to report to the elders any deviance from the
norm established by the Governing Body. A man in a midwestern state
who confessed to an infringement of the Governing Body's decision

---

11 Many Witnesses refer to the organization as "our mother," and this is because the *Watchtower* magazine has used this term in such way, as in the February 1, 1952, issue, p. 80,
and the May 1, 1957, issue, pp. 274, 284.

as regards his marital relations with his wife was told by the elders that they were writing about this to the Society; he also wrote an accompanying letter. Eight weeks passed and finally he wrote again to Brooklyn, saying that "the waiting, anxiety and anticipation is almost more than I can bear." He said that he had been removed from all congregational assignments, including offering prayer at the meetings, and that "almost weekly I am losing something that I have worked and prayed for for thirty years." He pleaded for an early answer, saying:

> "I do need some mental relief as to how I stand with Jehovah's organization."

Some elders endeavored to take a moderate approach to the matter. Doing so, however, could make them liable for reprimand from the headquarters' offices in Brooklyn. Consider this letter:

```
            SCE:SSE              August 4, 1976

Body of Elders of the
W███████ Congregation
of Jehovah's Witnesses, M███████
c/o ██████████████████████
███████████████████████
W██████ M█████████████

Dear Brothers:

        We have a copy of the letter dated July 21 from the committee
of the S█████████ Congregation in California in which they write
about matters involving J███████.

        Please let us know if any of the elders in the congregation
have been giving incorrect advice with regard to matters involving
oral sex.  If any of the elders in the congregation have advised
married persons that it would not be improper for them to engage
in oral sex, then on what basis was such counsel given?  If wrong
counsel was given, then let us know if appropriate steps have been
taken to correct any misunderstanding on the part of individuals
who were given wrong counsel and let us know if the elders con-
cerned now are in agreement with what has been stated in the
Society's publications with regard to oral sex.

        If any of you brothers as elders have been advising in-
dividuals that oral sex would be permissible as foreplay prior
to having actual sex relations, then such advice was not correct.

        Thank you for your attention to the above matter.  May
Jehovah's rich blessing go with you as you endeavor always to
care for your responsibilities as elders in an exemplary manner.

                        Your brothers,




cc:  Judicial Committee of the
     S█████████ Congregation
     of Jehovah's Witnesses, Ca
```

The preceding letter is a photo copy of that sent by the Society's Service Department to one Body of Elders (names and specific places have been blocked out).[12]

Interestingly, some elders actually felt that the Governing Body's position was, if anything, somewhat lenient or limited. A letter sent by an elder in the United States says:

"Some of the older brothers felt that the Governing Body could have gone even further in condemning unnatural practices among married couples to include assuming certain positions when performing the sexual act. . . ."

Later the elder expressed his own feelings saying:

"Since Jehovah went into great detail in this chapter [18] of Leviticus as well as other chapters on sexual behavior, why is there no statement made to married couples as to acceptable or unacceptable forms of copulation? Would it not be likely that Jehovah would have done so if he wanted this personal and private area of the marriage union open to the scrutiny or opinions of the 'Judges' or 'Older men' of Israel so that appropriate action could be taken against offending individuals?"

Some of those affected by the organization's ruling were persons whose normal sexual functions had been seriously impaired by an operation or by an accident. Some of these expressed dismay at the position the Governing Body's decision placed them in.

One such person who had become impotent in this way, had, during the years that followed, been able to perform a sexual role through one of the means now condemned by the organization. Before the Governing Body's ruling he said he had been able to stop feeling like half a man, because he could still please his wife. Now, he wrote saying that he could not see the Scriptural proof for the stand taken in the *Watchtower* magazine but that his wife felt duty bound to obey, and because he loved her he acceded. He said he knew that he was the same as before, yet emotionally he was crumbling since he feared their marriage would be seriously affected. He pleaded to be told if there was not some "loophole" in God's will that would allow him the satisfaction of pleasing his wife.

All of these situations put considerable strain on the conscience of elders called upon to deal with offenders against the Governing Body's

---

12 This copy is of the carbon copy and hence bears no stamped signature. The symbol "SCE" identifies the writer of the letter as Merton Campbell of the Service Department.

decision. At the conclusion of the earlier mentioned letter from an elder, he says:

> "I find I can only use what Bible laws and principles I understand with any degree of sincerity and conviction in representing Jehovah and Christ Jesus, and if I have to administer these laws and principles in exercising my responsibility as an elder in the congregation I want to do it not because I have come to take for granted that this is Jehovah's organization and I'm going to follow it no matter what it says, but do it because I truly believe it to be scripturally proven and correct. I truly want to continue believing as Paul admonished the Thessalonians in the second chapter, verse 13, to accept the word of God, not as of men, but as it truthfully is, as the word of God."

Though I find the sexual practices involved to be definitely contrary to my personal standards, I can honestly say that I did not favor the disfellowshiping decision made by the Body. *But that is all that I can say.* For when the vote came I conformed to the majority decision. I felt dismayed when the Body assigned me to prepare material in support of the decision, yet I accepted the assignment and wrote it as was desired by the Body, in conformity with its decision. Thus I cannot say that I acted according to the same fine outlook expressed by the elder just quoted. My belief in the organization as God's only agency on earth caused me to do what I did at that time without particularly great qualms of conscience.

The bulk of the correspondence on this subject never reached the Governing Body, being handled by the staff members assigned to "Correspondence Desks" or by the members of the Service Department. I am sure, however, that the various Governing Body members must have been made aware, likely through personal contacts and conversations, that many felt they had improperly invaded people's private lives. When finally, after some five years, the matter came up again on the agenda, the disfellowshiping policy was reversed and the Governing Body in effect now withdrew itself from that intimate area of others' lives. Again the Body assigned me to prepare material for publication, this time advising of the change. I found it personally satisfying to be able to acknowledge, even though rather obliquely, that the organization had been in error.

The February 15, 1978, *Watchtower*, pages 30 and 32, carried the material and included these points:

> ". . . in view of the absence of clear Scriptural instruction, these are matters for which the married couple themselves must bear the responsibility be-

fore God and . . . these marital intimacies do not come within the province of the congregational elders to control nor to take disfellowshiping action with such matters as the sole basis. . . . [This] expresses a keen sense of responsibility to let the Scriptures rule and to refrain from taking a dogmatic stand when the evidence does not seem to provide sufficient basis."

Actually, I felt that way about a whole host of matters that came before us, that there was really no basis in Scripture for taking dogmatic stands on the vast majority of things we were ruling on. I expressed that view here and it was accepted by the Body on this point. I expressed it again and again in the future but it was rarely accepted.

Looking over the letters at hand, some of which have been presented, whatever satisfaction it brought to write that corrective material seems rather hollow. For I know that no matter what was said, it could never in any way compensate for or repair all the damage in embarrassment, mental confusion, emotional distress, guilt pangs, and broken marriages that resulted from the earlier decision—a decision made in a few hours by men almost all of whom were approaching the matter 'cold,' with no previous knowledge, thought, meditation, specific prayer on the matter or searching of Scriptures, but whose decision was put in force globally for five years and affected many people for a lifetime. None of it needed to have occurred.

Another issue that arose, somewhat linked to the above, involved a Witness in South America whose husband had confessed to having sexual relations with another woman. The problem was that he said that the relations were of the kind involved in the issue earlier described, in this particular case anal and not genital copulation.

The decision of the Governing Body was that this did not qualify as adultery; that adultery required strictly genital copulation 'capable of producing children.' Therefore the man had not become "one flesh" with the other woman and hence the decision was that the wife had no grounds for Scriptural divorce and future remarriage.

The existing rule of voting required unanimity of decision and I conformed. I felt genuinely disturbed, however, at thinking about this woman and her being told that she could not Scripturally choose to become free from a man guilty of such an act. The decision also meant that a husband who engaged in homosexual acts with other men or who even had relations with a beast was not subject to Scriptural divorce, since a man could not, with any procreative possibilities, become "one flesh" with another man or with an animal. A *Watchtower* magazine earlier that year had, in fact, specifically ruled this way.[13]

The emotional upset I felt moved me to make a study of the original language terms (in Greek) used in Matthew, chapter nineteen, verse 9. The Society's *New World Translation* there presents Jesus as saying:

> "I say to you that whoever divorces his wife, except on the ground of fornication, and marries another commits adultery."

Two different words are used, "fornication" and "adultery," yet the *Watchtower* publications for many decades had taken the position that they both referred essentially to the same thing, that the "fornication" meant a man's having adulterous relations with a woman other than his wife (or a wife's having such relations with a man not her husband). Why then, I asked myself, did Matthew, in recording Jesus' statement, use two different words (*porneia* and *moikheia*) if the same thing, adultery, was actually meant in both cases?

Searching through the many translations, Bible dictionaries, commentaries and lexicons in the Bethel library, the reason became obvious. Practically every book I opened showed that the Greek term *porneia* (rendered as "fornication" in the *New World Translation*) was a very broad term and applied to ALL types of sexual immorality and for this reason many Bible translations simply render it as "immorality," "sexual immorality," "unchastity," "unfaithfulness."[14] Lexicons clearly showed that the term was also applied to homosexual relations. The conclusive point to me, however, was realizing that in the Bible itself *porneia* is used at Jude, verse 7, to denote the notorious homosexual conduct of people in Sodom and Gomorrah.

I prepared fourteen pages of material containing the results of the research and made copies for each member of the Body. But I felt very uncertain as to how this would be received and so I went to Fred Franz's office and explained what I had done, expressing my doubt that the material would be favorably accepted. He said, "I don't believe there will be any difficulty."

Though very brief, the words were spoken with a tone of confidence. When I inquired if he would like to see what had been found, he declined and again said he thought there would be "no problem."

---

13 See the *Watchtower* of January 1, 1972, pp. 31, 32.

14 The word "adultery" appearing in the original Greek of Matthew 19:9 is *moikheia* and, unlike *porneia*, is not broad but very limited in meaning, being restricted to adultery in the ordinary sense of the term.

My impression was that he was already aware of some of the points my research had revealed, though for how long I had no way of knowing. Since he had been the principal translator of the Society's *New World Translation* I felt he must surely have at least been apprised of the true sense of the word *porneia* ("fornication").[15]

When the matter came up in the Governing Body session, the material I submitted was accepted, Fred Franz having expressed his support, and I was assigned to prepare articles for publication in the *Watchtower* presenting the changed stand this would bring about.[16]

I still remember, some time after the articles appeared, a letter that came in from a Witness who some years before had discovered her husband having sexual relations with an animal. As she said, "I couldn't live with a man like that," and she divorced him. Later she remarried. The congregation then disfellowshiped her for so doing as she was not "Scripturally free." After the *Watchtower* articles appeared, she now wrote and asked that, in view of the changed position, something be done to clear her name of the reproach she had suffered as a result of the disfellowshiping action. I could only write her that the articles published were themselves a vindication of her course.

Though again it had been satisfying to prepare the material acknowledging the organization's erroneous view and rectifying it, the sobering thought remained that this could never undo whatever harm the previous position had caused over decades of time and—only God knows—to how many people.

The Governing Body at that time was, in reality, both a judicial court and also—because its decisions and definitions had force of law for all Jehovah's Witnesses—a legislative body. It was a "Governing Body" in the sense that the Sanhedrin of Bible times might be called such, its functions being similar. Just as all major questions involving Jehovah's name people of that period were brought to the Sanhedrin in Jerusalem for settlement, so with the Governing Body of Jehovah's Witnesses in Brooklyn.

15 The *New World Translation* bears no translator's name and is presented as the anonymous work of the "New World Translation Committee." Other members of that Committee were Nathan Knorr, Albert Schroeder and George Gangas; Fred Franz, however, was the only one with sufficient knowledge of the Bible languages to attempt translation of this kind. He had studied Greek for two years in the University of Cincinnati but was only self-taught in Hebrew.

16 See the *Watchtower* of December 15, 1972, pp. 766–768.

But it was not an administrative body in any sense of the word. The administrative authority and responsibility rested exclusively with the corporation president, Nathan H. Knorr. I had not expected this because the same year of my appointment Vice President Franz had given a speech, later carried in the December 15, 1971, *Watchtower*, in which he described the role of the Governing Body, contrasting this with that of the corporation, the Watch Tower Bible and Tract Society. Spoken of by some as the "tail wagging the dog talk," its language was unusually bold and frank, stating again and again that the corporation was simply an "agency," a "temporary instrument" used by the Governing Body (pages 754, 760):

> [29]This worldwide evangelizing organization is not tailored according to any present-day legal corporation that may be required under the laws of man-made political governments that now face destruction in the "war of the great day of God the Almighty" at Har-Magedon. (Rev. 16:14–16) No legal corporation of earth shapes the evangelizing organization or governs it. Rather, it governs such corporations as mere temporary instruments useful in the work of the great Theocrat. Hence it is patterned according to His design for it. It is a theocratic organization, ruled from the divine Top down, and not from the rank and file up. The dedicated, baptized members of it are under Theocracy! Earthly legal corporations will cease when the man-made governments that chartered them perish shortly.

> ———————

> So the Society's voting members see that this governing body could most directly use that "administrative agency" as an instrument in behalf of the work of the "faithful and discreet slave" class by having members of the governing body on the Board of Directors of the Society. They recognize that the Society is not the administrative body, but is merely an agency for administering matters.

> Hence the Society's voting members do not desire that there be any basis for conflict and division. They do not want to cause anything like a situation where the "administrative agency" controls and directs the user of that agency, which user is the governing body as representing the "faithful and discreet slave" class. No more so than to have the tail wag a dog instead of the dog's wagging its tail. A legal religious instrument according to Caesar's law should not attempt to direct and control its creator; rather, the creator of the legal religious instrument should control and direct it.

These were powerful expressions. The problem was that they presented a picture that was completely contrary to fact.

The Governing Body did not control the corporation, not at the time that the aforementioned talk was given by the vice president, nor at the time the material was published, nor for some four years thereafter.

The picture presented eventually *did* come to be true, but only as the result of a very drastic adjustment, one unpleasantly fraught with heated emotions and considerable division. Strange as it may seem to most Jehovah's Witnesses today, the kind of Governing Body described in that talk *had never existed in the whole history of the organization.* It took over ninety years for it to come into being and its present existence covers only a brief span of eight years. I will explain why I make such a statement and why it is factual.

THREE MONARCHS

"You know that in the world, rulers lord it over their subjects, and their great men make them feel the weight of authority; but it shall not be so with you." —Matthew 20:25, 26, *New English Bible.*

The history of Jehovah's Witnesses becomes one of record particularly with the publication of the first issue of the *Watch Tower* magazine on July 1, 1879. The corporation called the Watch Tower Bible and Tract Society was formed in 1881 and incorporated in 1884. It is certainly true that back there the corporation did not 'shape, govern, control or direct' (to use the words of the vice president) the governing body of those associated with the Watch Tower. It did not, and in fact could not do so, for the simple reason that no "governing body" existed.

Charles Taze Russell personally started the *Watch Tower* as his own magazine and was its sole editor; during his lifetime all those associated with the Watch Tower Society accepted him as their one and only Pastor. It is true, of course, that the Society, once formed, had a Board of Directors (Russell's wife, Maria, originally being one of these). But that Board was not viewed as a governing body nor did it serve as such. Yet the *Watchtower* of December 15, 1971, pages 760 and 761, makes this statement:

"According to the facts available, the governing body became associated with the Watch Tower Bible and Tract Society of Pennsylvania. C. T. Russell was patently of that governing body back there in the last quarter of the nineteenth century."

What do the "facts available" actually show?

Concerning the Board of Directors, Russell himself states in the *Watch Tower* of January, 1891, page 16:

> Having up to December 1, 1893, thirty-seven hundred and
> five (3,705) voting shares, out of a total of sixty-three hun-
> dred and eighty-three (6,383) voting shares, Sister Russell
> and myself, of course, elect the officers, and thus <u>control the
> Society</u>; and this was fully understood by the Directors from
> the first. *Their usefulness, it was understood, would come
> to the front in the event of our death."* [17]

That Russell clearly did not view the Directors (or any others) as a
governing body along with himself is obvious from the course he consistently followed. The *Watch Tower* of March 1, 1923, page 68, says:

> Often when asked by others, Who is
> that faithful and wise servant?—Brother Russell would
> reply: "Some say I am; while others say the Society
> is."

The article then goes on to say:

> Both statements were true; for Brother Russell
> was in fact the Society in a most absolute sense, in this,
> that he directed the policy and course of the Society
> without regard to any other person on earth. He some-
> times sought advice of others connected with the Society,
> listened to their suggestions; and then did according to
> his own judgment, believing that the Lord would have
> him thus do.

In answer to a question from some *Watch Tower* readers, C. T. Russell wrote in 1906:

> No, the truths I present, as God's mouthpiece, were not
> revealed in visions or dreams, nor by God's audible voice,
> nor all at once, but gradually, especially since 1870, and
> particularly since 1880. Neither is this clear unfolding of
> truth due to any human ingenuity or acuteness of per-
> ception, but to the simple fact that God's due time has

---

17 Mrs. Russell resigned as associate editor of the *Watch Tower* in October, 1886, due to
disagreement with her husband and on November 9, 1897, she separated from her husband. She remained a Director of the Society, however, until February 12, 1900. In 1906
she obtained a divorce.

come; and if I did not speak, and no other agent could be
found, the very stones would cry out. [18]

Believing himself to be "God's mouthpiece" and his agent for revelation of truth, it is understandable why he would see no need for a
governing body. The year after this statement, Russell prepared a "Last
Will and Testament" which was published in the December 1, 1916
Watch Tower magazine following his death in that year. Since nothing
illustrates more clearly the total control Charles Russell exercised over
the *Watch Tower* magazine, the full text of this will is presented in the
Appendix. We may here note what is said in the second paragraph of
this published Will:

> However, in view of the fact that in donating the journal,
> ZION'S WATCH TOWER, the OLD THEOLOGY QUARTERLY and the
> copyrights of the MILLENNIAL DAWN SCRIPTURE STUDIES
> Books and various other booklets, hymn-books, etc., to the
> WATCH TOWER BIBLE AND TRACT SOCIETY, I did so with the
> explicit understanding that I should have full control of all
> the interests of these publications during my life time, and
> that after my decease they should be conducted according to
> my wishes. I now herewith set forth the said wishes—my
> will respecting the same—as follows:

Although he donated the *Watch Tower* magazine to the corporation
(at its incorporation in 1884), he clearly considered it *his* magazine,
to be published according to his will even after his death. He directed
that, upon his death, an Editorial Committee of five men, personally
selected and named by him, should have entire editorial charge of the
Watch Tower magazine.[19] He also willed all his corporation voting
shares to five women named by him as Trustees, and provided that if
any member of the Editorial Committee should be impeached, these
women would serve along with the other corporation trustees (evidently the Directors) and the remaining Editorial Committee members
in acting as a Board of Judgment to decide the case of the Editorial
Committee member accused.[20]

Since one person cannot form a collective body, the facts show that
during C. T. Russell's lifetime, that is up until 1916, there was not
even a semblance of a governing body. That continued to be the case

---

18 The *Watch Tower*, July 15, 1906, p. 229.
19 Russell did not list Rutherford among these five but placed him in a second group of five
    who might serve as replacements if occasion required.
20 The book *Jehovah's Witnesses in the Divine Purpose*, published in 1959, p. 64, says that
    by law Russell's votes died with him.

during the presidency of his successor, Joseph F. Rutherford. One might assume that the members of the Editorial Committee, along with the Board of Directors, would compose such a governing body. But the facts show that that assumption would be wrong.

At the annual corporation meeting in January, 1917, Rutherford was elected to replace Russell as president. Early in his presidency, four of the seven Directors (a majority) took issue with what they viewed as arbitrary action on the part of the president. He was not recognizing the Board of Directors and working with it as a body but was acting unilaterally, taking actions and informing them later of what he had decided to do. They did not feel that this was at all in harmony with what Pastor Russell, the "faithful and wise servant," had outlined as the course to follow. Their expressing objection led to their swift elimination.[21]

Rutherford found that, though they were personal appointees of C. T. Russell as Directors for life, the directorship of these four had never been confirmed at an annual corporation meeting. According to A. H. MacMillan, then a prominent member of the headquarters staff, Rutherford conferred with an outside lawyer who agreed that this allowed for dismissing the men—on a legal basis, that is.[22]

Rutherford thus had an option. He could acknowledge the objections of the majority of the Board and seek to make amends. (If he had viewed these men as the majority of a "Governing Body" of the kind described in the 1971 *Watchtower* he would have been morally bound to do so.) Or, he could avail himself of the legal point mentioned and use his presidential authority to dismiss the Directors who disagreed with him.

He chose the latter course, appointing Directors of his own choice to replace them.

21 Typical of this course was Rutherford's decision to publish a book titled *The Finished Mystery*, presented as the 'posthumous work of Russell,' but actually written by Clayton J. Woodworth and George H. Fisher. Rutherford not only had not consulted with the Directors about the writing of the book, they did not even know it was being published until Rutherford released it to the "Bethel Family," the headquarters staff. Later Watch Tower publications, including the book *Jehovah's Witnesses in the Divine Purpose* (pp. 70, 71), give the impression that this was the initiating and primary cause of the objections of the four Directors. This distorts the facts, since Rutherford announced the dismissal of these four men as Directors the same day (July 17, 1917) that he presented the book *The Finished Mystery* to the headquarters staff. The announcement of the dismissal of the Directors was, in fact, made *before* the book was presented.

22 A. H. MacMillan, *Faith on the March* (Englewood Cliffs: Prentice-Hall, Inc., 1957), p. 80. The Foreword to the book is by N. H. Knorr.

What of the Editorial Committee? The *Watchtower* of June 15, 1938, page 185, shows that in 1925 the majority of this Committee "strenuously opposed" the publication of an article titled "The Birth of The Nation" (meaning "the kingdom had begun to function" in 1914). The *Watchtower* states the result to those who disagreed with the president:

> ". . . but, by the Lord's grace, it [the article] was published, and that really marked the beginning of the end of the editorial committee, indicating that the Lord himself is running his organization."

The Editorial Committee was now eliminated. Rutherford had effectively excised any opposition to his full control of the organization.

An interesting feature about all this is that during this entire time, not only *The Finished Mystery* book (a major bone of contention in 1917), but also the *Watch Tower* magazine had been forcefully teaching that Pastor Russell was indeed the "faithful and wise servant" foretold in Scripture, whom the Master would make "ruler over his household."[23] The way in which this teaching was used to insist upon everyone's full conformity is well illustrated in these statements from the *Watch Tower* of May 1, 1922, page 132:

FAITHFULNESS IS LOYALTY

To be faithful means to be loyal. To be loyal to the Lord means to be obedient to the Lord. To abandon or repudiate the Lord's chosen instrument means to abandon or repudiate the Lord himself, upon the principle that he who rejects the servant sent by the Master thereby rejects the Master.

There is no one in present truth today who can honestly say that he received a knowledge of the divine plan from any source other than by the ministry of Brother Russell, either directly or indirectly. Through his prophet Ezekiel Jehovah foreshadowed the office of a servant, designating him as one clothed with linen, with a writer's inkhorn by his side, who was delegated to go throughout the city (Christendom) and comfort those that sighed by enlightening their minds relative to God's great plan. Be it noted that this was a favor bestowed not by man, but by the Lord himself. But in keeping with the Lord's arrangement he used a man. The man who filled that office, by the Lord's grace, was Brother Russell.

---

23 See *The Finished Mystery*, p. 11; the *Watch Tower*, March 1, 1922, pp. 72, 73; May 1, 1922, p. 131; March 1, 1923, pp. 67, 68.

Again, in the March 1, 1923, *Watch Tower*, pages 68 and 71, in an article titled "Loyalty the Test," conformity to Russell's teachings and methods was equated with conformity to the Lord's will:

> [8] We believe that all who are now rejoicing in present truth will concede that Brother Russell faithfully filled the office of special servant of the Lord; and that he was made ruler over all the Lord's goods.

> [36] Every fellow servant has shown his ability or capacity and has increased the same in proportion as he has joyfully submitted to the Lord's will by working in the harvest field of the Lord *in harmony with the Lord's way*. which way the Lord used Brother Russell to point out, because Brother Russell occupied the office of that "faithful and wise servant." He did the Lord's work according to the Lord's way. If, then, Brother Russell did the work in the Lord's way, any other way of doing it is contrary to the Lord's way and therefore could not be a faithful looking after the interests of the Lord's kingdom.

The issue was quite clear. Either one could loyally line up with and conform to the teachings and way of this 'ruler over the Master's household' (Russell) or he could become guilty of repudiation of Christ Jesus, hence, an apostate. Rarely has appeal to human authority been more strongly stated.

That is what makes it so notable that, within a few years of Russell's death, and during the very time these claims about him were made, the provisions he made in life and his personal selections of men for the office of supervision were set aside by the new president. His expressions contained in his "Will" were discounted as having no legal force and, evidently, no moral force either. The *Watchtower* of December 15, 1931, page 376, says of it:

> [24] The facts which are well known to exist and which apply to the prophetic words of Jesus are these: In 1914 Jehovah placed his King upon his

throne. The three and one-half years immediately
following afforded the opportunity to test those who
had responded to the call to the kingdom, as to whether or not they were selfish or unselfish. In 1916 the
president of the Watch Tower Bible and Tract Society died. A paper writing was found which he had
signed and which was called his "last will and testament", but which in fact was not a will. It then
appeared that Brother Russell, some years before his
death, had concluded that he could not make such a
will. The work of God's organization is not subject
to the control of man or to be controlled by the will
of any creature. It was therefore not possible to carry
on the work of the Society to the Lord's glory and
honor as outlined in that paper writing, called a
"will".

Just eight years before, the *Watch Tower*, the "Lord's channel," had
insisted that Russell "did the Lord's work according to the Lord's way"
and therefore "any other way of doing it is contrary to the Lord's way."
Now, eight years later, any who objected to Rutherford's setting aside
of the directions given by the one the *Watch Tower* had so adamantly
argued was the "faithful and wise servant" were portrayed as motivated by ill will and malice, as workers of iniquity:

This gathered out or rejected
class, however, do weep and wail, and they gnash
their teeth against their brethren, because, they say,
"Brother Russell's will is being ignored, and *The
Watchtower* is not being published as he directed";
and they hold up their hands in holy horror and shed
crocodile tears because the Lord's organization on
earth is not being used according to the will of a
man. In other words, they make these pretenses as a
cause for weeping and wailing and sorrow. They
wail, complain and weep because they have not charge
of the Society. They gnash their teeth against those
who are engaged in the Lord's work, and they give
expression to all manner of ill will, malice and lying
statements against those whom they once claimed to
be their brethren. Jude mentions the same class, and
his words definitely fix the time when this wailing
and weeping begins, to wit, at the time the Lord Jesus Christ comes to the temple of Jehovah for judgment. He says: "These are murmurers, complainers,

walking after their own lusts [selfish desires]; and their mouth speaketh great swelling words [claiming themselves to be God's favored ones], having men's persons in admiration because of advantage [in other words, they express their admiration for the person of man and desire admiration for themselves, and their conduct and course of action exactly fit the words of the apostle]." They make great pretense of love and devotion to a man, namely Brother Russell, but it is manifest they do so with a view of gaining some selfish advantage. The purpose, therefore, of mentioning these matters, and manifestly the purpose of the Lord in permitting his people to understand them, is that they might avoid such workers of iniquity.

It is difficult to explain such fickle, unstable, erratic course. Yet this was supposedly the channel the Lord Jesus Christ had found so worthy of being made his sole means of direction to people on earth.

In actuality, by 1925 J. F. Rutherford exercised unquestioned direction of the Society and the years that followed only strengthened his control over all organization functions.[24]

This included full control of what would be published through the channel of the *Watch Tower* and other publications used to provide spiritual food for the congregations earthwide. I recall my uncle's telling me one day in his office of an occasion when Rutherford presented a certain issue, a new viewpoint, to the Bethel Family for discussion.[25] My uncle related that in the discussion he expressed himself negatively about the new view being advanced, doing so on the basis of Scripture. Afterward, he said, President Rutherford personally assigned him to prepare material *in support of* this new view, although he, Fred Franz, had made clear that he did not consider it Scriptural.

On another occasion he related that the "Judge" (Rutherford) later

24 A. H. MacMillan in *Faith on the March*, p. 152, says: "Russell had left it much to the individual as to how we were to fulfill our responsibilities. . . . Rutherford wanted to unify the preaching work and, instead of having each individual give his own opinion and tell what he thought was right and do what was in his own mind, gradually Rutherford himself began to be the main spokesman for the organization. That was the way he thought the message could best be given without contradiction."

25 The point at issue was either the new view that the "higher powers" of Romans 13:1 were not the governmental authorities of earth but were Jehovah God and Jesus Christ, or the decision regarding the elimination of Bodies of Elders, which of the two I do not now recall.

in his presidency made it a firm policy that the *Watch Tower* magazine would carry only articles that stressed prophecy or the preaching work. For that reason a period of years passed in which articles on subjects such as love, kindness, mercy, longsuffering and similar qualities simply did not appear in the magazine.

Thus, during the nearly sixty-year period of the presidencies of Russell and Rutherford, each man acted according to his own prerogative in exercising his presidential authority, with no hint of a governing body.

When Judge Rutherford died on January 8, 1942, Nathan H. Knorr was unanimously elected president by the Board of Directors. The organizational structure continued basically the same, though with some adjustments, as Knorr did field out some responsibility. (Circumstances actually made this a necessity, for the number of Witnesses grew from only 108,000 at the time of Rutherford's death to more than two million during Knorr's presidency.) Not a writer nor particularly a student of Scripture, Knorr relied on Fred Franz (the vice president) as more or less the final arbiter on Scriptural matters and the principal writer of the organization. Questions such as those discussed at Governing Body sessions (related earlier in this chapter) were, for decades, submitted to Fred Franz for decision. If President Knorr felt that the decision might have some critical effect on the Society's operation in certain countries of the world, he would usually discuss it personally with Fred Franz and would not hesitate to make known what he felt the circumstances made advisable in a pragmatic way, overruling the vice president if necessary. As has been noted earlier, this basic relationship continued up into the 1970's as illustrated in the decision to return to having bodies of elders in the congregations. That particular decision hinged largely upon the view and opinion of one person, the vice president, and when he changed his mind and favored the return to bodies of elders, the president acceded.

The same was basically the case with all published material. The president selected the main articles for the *Watchtower* from material submitted by various writers and he then passed these on to the Writing Department for proofreading and any necessary editing or polishing. Then these were finally read by the vice president and the president and, if approved, were published. Karl Adams, who was in charge of the Writing Department when I entered it in 1965, explained to me that the president by then had given the department considerable latitude as to the reworking of such material. He pointed out the one exception, namely, any material written by the vice president, stating that "what comes from Brother Franz is viewed as 'ready for publication,' with no adjustments to be made."

Here again, nonetheless, the president could overrule. As an example, in 1967, President Knorr sent to Karl Adams, Ed Dunlap and myself, copies of a "Questions from Readers" that Fred Franz had prepared and turned in for publication.[26] Just the year before, a book had been published, authored by Fred Franz, in which it was pointed out that the year 1975 would mark the end of 6,000 years of human history. Likening those 6,000 years to six days of a thousand years each, he had written:

> So in not many years within our own generation we are reaching what Jehovah God could view as the seventh day of man's existence.
>
> [48] How appropriate it would be for Jehovah God to make of this coming seventh period of a thousand years a sabbath period of rest and release, a great Jubilee sabbath for the proclaiming of liberty throughout the earth to all its inhabitants! This would be most timely for mankind. It would also be most fitting on God's part, for, remember, mankind has yet ahead of it what the last book of the Holy Bible speaks of as the reign of Jesus Christ over earth for a thousand years, the millennial reign of Christ. Prophetically Jesus Christ, when on earth nineteen centuries ago, said concerning himself: "For Lord of the sabbath is what the Son of man is." (Matthew 12:8) It would not be by mere chance or accident but would be according to the loving purpose of Jehovah God for the reign of Jesus Christ, the "Lord of the sabbath," to run parallel with the seventh millennium of man's existence.[27]

Not for many decades had there been such a sense of excitement among Jehovah's Witnesses as these statements generated. A tremendous surge of expectation developed, far surpassing the feeling of the end's nearness that I and others had experienced in the early 1940's.

That is why we were amazed to see that the "Question from Read-

---

26 Of the three receiving copies, I was the only one professing to be of the "anointed" class, having made such profession since 1946.

27 *Life Everlasting in Freedom of the Sons of God*, published in 1966, pp. 29, 30.

ers" Fred Franz had worked up now argued that the end of 6,000 years would actually come *one year earlier* than had just been published in the new book, namely that it would come in 1974 instead of 1975. As Knorr told Karl Adams, when he received this material he went to Fred Franz and asked why the sudden change. Franz replied with definiteness, "This is the way it is. *It's 1974*."

Knorr did not feel at ease with the change and that is why he sent the three of us copies with his request that we submit our individual observations. The vice president's argumentation was built almost entirely upon the use of a cardinal and an ordinal number in the account of the Flood at Genesis, chapter seven, verses 6 and 11 ("six hundred years" and the "six hundred*th* year"). The argument endeavored to show that the count of time set out in the new book was off one year as to the time of the Flood and that one more year needed to be added, with the result that the end of 6,000 years would come up one year earlier, in 1974 instead of 1975.

Each of the three of us respectfully wrote that we did not think the material should be published, that it would have an extremely unsettling effect on the brothers.[28] The president evidently agreed, since the material prepared by the vice president was never published and this was quite a rare occurrence.

It was during Knorr's presidency that the term "governing body" began to be used with a measure of frequency.[29] The literature now began to tie such a body in with the Board of Directors of the Watch Tower Society. In the Society's book, *Qualified to Be Ministers*, published in 1955, page 381, the statement appears:

> "During the years since the Lord came to his temple the visible governing body has been closely identified with the board of directors of this corporation."

Thus the seven members of the Board of Directors were considered to be the seven members of the "governing body."

The fact is, however, that their situation was much as had been the case with the Directors in Russell's and Rutherford's day.

Marley Cole, a Witness who wrote a book (with the full coopera-

---

28 I pointed out that the argument rested heavily on a portion of Scripture that is difficult to be definite about, and that the reasons given for the change were, at best, tenuous.

29 In the *Watchtower* of June 1, 1938, p. 168, in an article on "Organization" the expressions "central body" and "central authority" are used but only with reference to the body of apostles and those who were their immediate associates, with no modern application made.

tion of the Society) entitled *Jehovah's Witnesses—The New World Society*, points this out.[30] In a section headed "Internal Rebellion," he first describes the controversy in 1917 between Rutherford and the Board, saying:

> "Four directors wanted a reorganization. . . . As things stood the president was the administration. He was not consulting them. He was letting them know what he was doing only after it was done. He was putting them in the position of advisers on legal corporate matters.
>
> "Rutherford made no bones about 'going ahead.' The Pastor before him had worked that way. The Pastor made decisions. The Pastor issued administrative orders without the Board's prior sanction."

Then, in a footnote, Cole states:

> "That the president of the Society thereafter continued to exercise such unrestricted freedom may be seen by the following account of N. H. Knorr's actions in relation to bringing forth a new Bible translation."[31]

The *Watchtower* of September 15, 1950, pages 315 and 316, is then quoted. It reveals that the Directors of the Board were first informed by the president of the existence of the *New World Translation* (probably one of the biggest projects ever engaged in by the organization) only after the translation of the Greek Scripture portion had already been completed and was ready for printing.

Right up until 1971 when the "tail wagging the dog talk" was given, the Board of Directors did not meet on any regular schedule but only as the president decided to convene them. Sometimes months went by without any meetings, the most frequent agenda evidently being such corporate matters as the purchase of property or of new equipment. As a rule, they had nothing to say about what Scriptural material would be published, nor was their approval sought. Vice President Franz made this clear when testifying before a court in Scotland in 1954 in a case known as the Walsh Case. Questioned as to what was done if some major change in doctrine was made and whether such had to be first approved by the Board of Directors, the vice president replied (the material here being reprinted from the official court transcript

---

30 Marley Cole, *Jehovah's Witnesses—The New World Society* (New York: Vantage Press, 1955), pp. 86–89. Cole wrote the book as if he were a non-Witness writing an objective account. The idea was that by having the book published by an outside publishing firm it might reach persons who normally would not take Society literature. Thus it was a form of public relations tactic.

31 Ibid., p. 88.

with "Q" representing the question of the counselor and "A" the response given by Fred Franz):

> "Q. In matters spiritual has each member of the Board of Directors an equally valid voice? A. The president is the mouthpiece. He pronounces the speeches that show advancment of the understanding of the Scriptures. Then he may appoint other members of the headquarters temporarily to give other speeches that set forth any part of the Bible upon which further light has been thrown. Q. Tell me; are these advances, as you put it, voted upon by the Directors? A. No. Q. How do they become pronouncements? A. They go through the editorial committee, and I give my O.K. after Scriptural examination. Then I pass them on to President Knorr, and President Knorr has the final O.K. Q. Does it not go before the Board of Directors at all? A. No."[32]

I personally knew that presentation of matters to be true as regards the Board of Directors. Before 1971, I was in a meeting with several Writing Staff members called by Karl Adams, and the question arose as to how to get the president's approval of certain proposed improvements in the *Watchtower* magazine. Someone suggested that Lyman Swingle, who was present as one of the writers, broach the matter to Knorr. Swingle's reply was brief but spoke volumes as to the reality of the situation. He said: "Why me? What can I do? I'm only a Director."

The situation remained the same even after the enlargement of the Governing Body to include more than the seven Directors. In 1975 during one session some material the vice president had prepared for use as a convention talk came up for discussion. It dealt with the parable of the mustard seed and the parable of the leaven (found in Matthew chapter 13) and argued in detail that the "kingdom of the heavens" Jesus referred to in these parables was actually a "fake" kingdom, a counterfeit. One member of the Body who had read the material felt unconvinced by the argumentation. After discussion, of the fourteen members present only five (including Knorr and Fred Franz) voted in favor of using the material as a convention talk, the other nine did not. So it was not used—as a talk, but the material appeared in a book released at the convention and within a few months

---

32 Although the vice president makes reference to an "editorial committee" he later identifies only himself and President Knorr as on that committee from among the Board members. In actuality there was no *official* "editorial committee" aside from these two. In 1965 Karl Adams was the only other one whose signature was regularly required on material to be published and he was not on the Board of Directors nor does he profess to be of the "anointed" class.

also appeared in the *Watchtower* magazine.[33] The fact that nearly two-thirds of the Body members present had expressed at least some lack of confidence in the material did not affect the president's decision to go ahead with publishing it.

Not only the contents of the magazines and other literature, but every other feature of the world-wide activity of Jehovah's Witnesses—the direction of the 90 or more Branch Offices (each Overseer of a Branch being described as the "presiding minister of Christianity for and within the territory to which he has been appointed"), the supervision of all the work of all traveling representatives, the direction of the missionary School of Gilead and the assignment and work of all missionaries, the planning of conventions and convention programs—all this and much more were the sole prerogative of one person: the president of the corporation. Whatever the Governing Body discussed or did not discuss in any of these areas was strictly as the result of his decision and at his discretion.

All this was difficult to reconcile with the articles published after the vice president's "tail wagging the dog talk." The language there had been so forceful, so conclusive:

> "Thus, too, even though there were no apostles of Christ on hand in the nineteenth century, God's holy spirit must have been operative toward the formation of the governing body for his anointed remnant of the 'faithful and discreet slave' class. The facts speak for themselves. There came on the scene a body of anointed Christians who accepted and undertook the responsibilities of governing the affairs of Jehovah's dedicated, baptized, anointed people who were following in the footsteps of Jesus Christ and endeavoring to fulfill the work stated in Jesus's prophecy at Matthew 24:45–47. Facts speak louder than words. The governing body is there. Thankfully Jehovah's Christian witnesses know and assert that this is no one-man religious organization, but that it has a governing body of spirit-anointed Christians."[34]

Unfortunately the picture presented simply was not true. The *facts*, already presented from the Watch Tower Society's own approved publications and from statements of Directors, clearly show there was no governing body in any factual sense in the nineteenth century during Russell's presidency, none in the twentieth century during Rutherford's presidency, and there had been none in the sense described in this same *Watchtower* article during Knorr's presidency. It was an im-

---

33 See the book *Man's Salvation Out of World Distress At Hand!*, published in 1975, pp. 206–215; also the *Watchtower*, October 1, 1975, pp. 589–608.

34 The *Watchtower*, December 15, 1971, p. 761.

ONE LEADER

pressive-sounding picture presented but it was illusory, fictional. The fact is that a monarchical arrangement prevailed from the very inception of the organization (the word "monarch" being of Greek origin and meaning "one who governs alone," also defined in dictionaries as "one holding preeminent position and power"). That the first president was benign, the next stern and autocratic, and the third very business-like, in no way alters the fact that each of the three presidents exercised monarchical authority. The great majority of Witnesses forming what the *Watchtower* article had referred to as the "rank and file"—and including most of the "anointed" composing the "faithful and discreet slave class"—were totally unaware of this. Those in positions close enough to the seat of authority knew it to be the case; the closer they were the more they were aware of the facts.

This was particularly true of the members of the Governing Body and in 1975 the "dog" decided it was time to "wag the tail." Most of the members felt that it was time that the facts finally started matching the words being spoken and published.

Interestingly, what was done was essentially *the same as what the four Directors in 1917 had proposed*, a reorganization, an effort on their part that had consistently been described thereafter in the Watch Tower publications as an 'ambitious plot' and 'a rebellious conspiracy,' one that, 'by God's grace, did not succeed!' Fifty-five years later basically the same proposition did succeed, but only after months of turmoil for the Governing Body.

4

INTERNAL UPHEAVAL AND RESTRUCTURE

"So never make mere men a cause for pride."
"There is nothing to boast about in anything human."
—1 Corinthians 3:21, *New English Bible* and *Jerusalem Bible*.

THE information the book *Aid to Bible Understanding* presented about elders doubtless began the process. Till then congregations had been under the supervision of a single person, the "Congregation Overseer." His replacement by a body of elders of necessity raised questions about Branch organizations where one man was the "Overseer" for a whole country, much as a bishop or archbishop has under his supervision a large region composed of many congregations. And the central headquarters had its president, to whom I had personally referred (in addressing a seminar for Branch Overseers in Brooklyn) as "the Presiding Overseer for all congregations earthwide."[1]

Evidently the apparent anomaly, the contrast between the situation in the congregations and that at the international headquarters is what led to the "tail wagging the dog" talk and *Watchtower* articles, since these endeavored to explain away the difference existing between the situation in the congregations and that at the central headquarters. It is almost certain that at the same time these articles were meant to send out a signal to voting members of the corporation that they should not try to express themselves through vote to effect some change in the headquarters structure or to express themselves as regards the membership of the Governing Body and its administration.

---

1 President Knorr was sitting on the platform at the time and expressed no disagreement with the description.

67

The year of that talk, 1971, President Knorr decided to allow the Governing Body to review and pass judgment on a book entitled *Organization for Kingdom-Preaching and Disciple-Making*, a form of church manual setting out organizational structure and policy governing the entire arrangement, from the headquarters through to the Branches, Districts and Circuits, and on to the congregations. The Governing Body was not asked to supply the material for the book. The president had assigned the project of the book's development to Karl Adams, the overseer of the Writing Department (not a Governing Body member nor one professing to be of the "anointed"). He in turn had assigned Ed Dunlap and myself to collaborate with him in the manual's development, each of us writing about one-third of the material.[2]

The material we developed presented the relationship of the Governing Body and the corporations in harmony with the "tail wagging the dog" articles. When certain points relating to this came before the Body, they provoked rather heated discussion. President Knorr expressed himself clearly as feeling that there was an effort to "take over" his responsibility and work. He stressed that the Governing Body was to concern itself strictly with the "spiritual matters" and that the corporation would handle the rest. But, as the Body members knew, the "spiritual matters" allotted to them at that stage consisted almost entirely of the near ritual of approving appointments of largely unknown persons to traveling overseer work and the handling of the constant flow of questions about "disfellowshiping matters."

At certain points in the discussion I expressed my understanding that other matters of a spiritual nature were likewise the responsibility of the Body. (I could not personally harmonize the existing monarchical arrangement with Jesus' statement that "all you are brothers" and "your Leader is one, the Christ"; that "the rulers of the nations lord it over them and the great men wield authority over them," but "this is not the way among you."[3] It simply did not seem honest to say what had been said in the 1971 *Watchtower* articles and then not carry it out.)

In each case of my doing so, however, the president took the remarks very personally, speaking at great length, his voice tense and forceful, saying that 'evidently some were not satisfied with the way he was handling his job.' He would go into great detail as to the work

---

2   I was assigned chapters on "Your Service to God," "Safeguarding the Cleanness of the Congregation," and "Endurance That Results in Divine Approval."

3   Matthew 23:8, 10; 20:25, 26.

he was performing and then would say, "now apparently some don't want me to handle things anymore" and that perhaps he should "bring it all down here and turn it over to Ray Franz and let him handle it."

I found it hard to believe that he could so totally miss the whole point of my comments, that I was expressing myself in favor of a *body* arrangement, not in favor of a transferral of authority from one individual administrator to another individual administrator. Each time I would explain this to him, making plain that what was said was never meant as any kind of personal attack, that I did not feel that ANY one individual should take on the responsibilities under discussion, but rather that my understanding from the Bible and from the *Watchtower* was that they were matters for a body of persons to deal with. I said again and again that if it were a matter of one person handling every-thing, then he would be my choice; that I felt he had simply been doing what he felt he should do and what had always been done in the past; that I had no complaint about his doing so. This did not seem to make any impression, however, and, realizing that anything I said along this line would simply provoke anger, after a few attempts I gave up. On these occasions the remainder of the Body members sat, observed and said nothing. What happened a few years later therefore came as a surprise.

In 1975, two Bethel Elders (one a senior member of the Service Department and the other the Assistant Bethel Home Overseer) wrote letters to the Governing Body expressing concern over certain condi-tions prevalent within the headquarters staff, specifically referring to an atmosphere of fear generated by those having oversight and a growing feeling of discouragement and resultant discontent.

At that time anyone applying for service at headquarters ("Bethel Service") had to agree to stay a minimum of four years. Most of the applicants were young men, 19 and 20 years of age. Four years equalled one-fifth of the life they had thus far lived. When at the meal tables, I often asked the person next to me, "How long have you been here?" In the ten years I had by now spent at headquarters I had never heard one of these young men respond by saying in round figures, "About a year," or "about two years." Invariably the answer was, "One and seven," "two and five," "three and one," and so forth, always giving the year or years and the exact number of months. I could not help but think of the way men serving a prison sentence often follow a similar practice of marking off time.

Generally it was difficult to get these young men to express themselves about their service at headquarters. As I learned from friends who worked more closely with them, they were unwilling to say much in an open way since they feared that anything they said that was not positive would cause them to be classed as what was popularly called a "B.A.," someone with a "bad attitude."

Many felt like "cogs in a machine," viewed as workers but not as persons. Job insecurity resulted from knowing that they could be shifted at any time to another work assignment without any previous discussion and often with no explanation for the change made. "Management-employee" lines were clearly drawn and carefully maintained.

The monthly allowance of fourteen dollars often barely covered (and in some cases was less than) their transportation costs going to and from Kingdom Hall meetings. Those whose family or friends were more affluent had no problems as they received outside assistance. But others rarely could afford anything beyond bare necessities. Those from more distant points, particularly those from the western states, might find it virtually impossible to spend vacations with their families, particularly if they came from a poor family. Yet they were regularly hearing greetings passed on to the Bethel Family from members of the Governing Body and others as they traveled around the country and to other parts of the world giving talks. They saw the corporation officers driving new Oldsmobiles bought by the Society and serviced and cleaned by workers like themselves. Their work schedule of eight hours and forty minutes each day, and four hours on Saturday morning, combined with attendance at meetings three times a week, plus the weekly "witnessing" activity, seemed to many to make their lives very cramped, routine, tiring. But they knew that to lessen up in any of these areas would undoubtedly put them in the "B.A." class and result in their being called to a meeting designed to correct their attitude.

The letters by the two Bethel Elders touched on these areas but without going into detail. The president again seemed to feel, unfortunately, that this constituted criticism of his administration. He expressed himself to the Governing Body as wanting a hearing to be held on the matter and on April 2, 1975, this was done. A number of Bethel Elders spoke and many of the earlier-mentioned specifics were there aired. Those speaking did not indulge in personalities and made no demands, but they stressed the need for more consideration of the individual, for brotherly communication and the benefit of letting those close to problems share in decisions and solutions. As the Assistant Bethel Home Overseer put it, "we seem more concerned about production than people." The staff doctor, Dr. Dixon, related that he frequently received visits from married couples distressed due to the inability of the wives to cope with the pressures and keep up with the demanding schedule, many of the women breaking into tears when talking to him.

A week later, April 9, the official "Minutes" of the Governing Body session stated:

> "Comments were made on the relationship of the Governing Body and the corporations and what was published in the *Watchtower* of December 15, 1971.[4] It was agreed that a committee of five made up of L. K. Greenlees, A. D. Schroeder, R. V. Franz, D. Sydlik, and J. C. Booth go into matters concerning this subject and the duties of the officers of the corporations and related matters and take into consideration the thoughts of N. H. Knorr, F. W. Franz and G. Suiter who are officers of the two societies, and then bring recommendations. The whole idea is to strengthen the unity of the organization."

At a session three weeks later, April 30, President Knorr surprised us by making a motion that thenceforth all matters be decided by a two-thirds vote of the active membership (which by then numbered seventeen). Following this, the official "Minutes" of that session relate:

> "L. K. Greenlees then began his report from the committee of five on Brother Knorr's request to tell him what he should do.[5] The committee considered the *Watchtower* of December 15, 1971, paragraph 29 very carefully, also page 760. The committee feels that today the Governing Body should be directing the corporations and not the other way around. The corporations should recognize that the Governing Body of seventeen members has the responsibility to administer the work in the congregations throughout the world. There has been a delay of putting the arrangement into effect at Bethel as compared to the congregations. There has been confusion. We do not want a dual organization.
>
> "There followed a lengthy discussion of questions relating to the Governing Body and the corporations and to the president, with comments by all members present. At the close of the day a motion was proposed by N. H. Knorr, followed by a comment by E. C. Chitty. L. K. Greenlees also presented a motion. It was agreed that the three should be Xeroxed and copies given to all members and meet again the next day at 8 a.m. There would be time to pray over the matter which is so important."

---

4 The articles in this issue were on the relationship between the Governing Body and the corporations and contained the "tail wagging the dog" expression.

5 At the first meeting of the "Committee of Five" it was voted, on my motion, that Leo Greenlees serve as Chairman.

The Xeroxed motions referred to read as follows:

"N. H. Knorr: 'I move the Governing Body take over responsibility of looking after the work directed in the Charter of the Pennsylvania Corporation and assume the responsibilities set out in the Charter of the Pennsylvania Corporation and all other corporations throughout the world used by Jehovah's Witnesses.'"

"E. C. Chitty said: 'To "take over" means relieve the other party. I believe for my part responsibility stays as it is. Rather it would be right to say "supervise the responsibility."'"

"L. K. Greenlees said: 'I move that the Governing Body undertake in harmony with the Scriptures the full responsibility and authority for the administration and supervision of the world wide association of Jehovah's Witnesses and their activities; that all members and officers of any and all corporations used by Jehovah's Witnesses will act in harmony with and under direction of this Governing Body; that this enhanced relationship between the Governing Body and the corporations go into effect as soon as can reasonably be done without hurt or damage to the Kingdom Work.'"

On the next day, May 1, there was again a long discussion. The vice president (who had written the *Watchtower* articles referred to) in particular objected to the proposals made and to any change in the existing setup, any reduction of the president's authority. (This brought to mind, and was in harmony with, his remarks to me back in 1971 that he thought Jesus Christ would direct the organization through a single person on down to the time when the New Order came.) He made no comment on the evident contradiction between the presentation made in the *Watchtower* articles (and their bold statements about the Governing Body using the corporations as mere instruments) and the three motions made, each of which showed that the makers (including the president himself) recognized that the Governing Body did not at that time supervise the corporations.

Discussion went back and forth. A turning point seemed to come with remarks made by Grant Suiter, the crisp-speaking secretary-treasurer of the Society's principal corporations. Different from the comments made till then by those favoring a change, his expressions were quite personal, seemingly the release of a long pent-up feeling about the president, whom he directly named. While discussing the authority structure he made no specific charges, except as regards the right to make a certain change in his personal room that he had requested and had been denied, but as he went on his face became flushed, his jaw muscles flexed and his words became more intense. He closed with the remark:

> "I say if we are going to be a Governing Body, then let's get to governing! I haven't been doing any governing till now."

Those words hit me hard enough that I am satisfied that I have remembered and recorded them as said. Whether they were meant to convey the sense they did is, of course, beyond my knowing and they may well have been merely a momentary outburst, not indicative of any heartfelt motive. At any rate they served to make me think very seriously about the matter of right motivation and I felt considerable concern that whatever should come of this whole affair might be the result of a sincere desire on the part of all involved to hold more closely to Bible principles and patterns and not for any other reason. I found the whole session disturbing, mainly because the general spirit did not seem to conform to what one would expect of a Christian body.

However, shortly after these last-mentioned comments by the secretary-treasurer, Nathan Knorr evidently reached a decision and made a lengthy statement, taken down in shorthand by Milton Henschel, who had made certain suggestions himself and who acted as secretary for the Body.[6] As recorded in the official "Minutes" the president's statement included these expressions:

> ". . . I think it would be a very good thing for the Governing Body to follow through along the lines that Brother Henschel has mentioned and design a program having in mind what the *Watchtower* says, that the Governing Body is Governing Body of Jehovah's Witnesses. I am not going to argue for or against it. In my opinion it is not necessary. The *Watchtower* has stated it.
>
> ". . . It will be the Governing Body who will have overall guiding power and influence. They will take their responsibility as Governing Body and direct through different divisions they will set up and they will have an organization."

At the end he said, "I make that a motion." Somewhat to my surprise, his motion was seconded by F. W. Franz, the vice president. It was adopted unanimously by the Body as a whole.

The bold language of the *Watchtower* of four years previous seemed about to change from mere words into fact. From the expressions made

---

6 Milton Henschel, tall and of generally serious mien, spoke fairly seldom in discussions but when he did it was usually with considerable firmness, definiteness. In his younger years he had been President Knorr's personal secretary; at the time here being discussed, he was in his middle fifties.

by the president it appeared that a smooth transition lay ahead. It was, instead, only a lull preceding the stormiest period of all.

In the months that followed, the appointed "Committee of Five" met with all members of the Governing Body individually and with thirty-three other long-time members of the headquarters staff. By far the majority favored a reorganization. The Committee drew up detailed proposals for an arrangement of Governing Body Committees to handle different facets of the worldwide activity. Eleven of the seventeen Governing Body members when personally interviewed indicated basic approval.

Of the remaining six, George Gangas, a warm and effervescent Greek, and one of the oldest members of the Body, was very uncertain, changeable in his expressions according to the mood of the moment. Charles Fekel, an eastern European, had been a Society Director many years before but had been removed under the charge of having compromised his integrity by the oath he took when obtaining American citizenship. He was now among the recent appointees to the Body and, of a very mild nature, rarely shared in the discussion, consistently voting whichever way the majority went, and he had little to say on this issue. Lloyd Barry, a New Zealander and also a recent addition to the Body, had come to Brooklyn after a number of years as Branch Overseer of Japan, where Witness activity had seen phenomenal growth. He expressed strong misgivings about the recommendations, particularly the decentralizing effect it would have as regards the presidency; in a letter dated September 5, 1975, he referred to the recommended change as "revolutionary." Bill Jackson, a down-to-earth, unassuming Texan (not as rare as some would make it appear), had spent most of his life at headquarters, and, like Barry, he felt that things should be left very much as they were, especially since such good numerical increases had come under the existing administration.

The strongest voices of opposition were those of the president and vice president, the maker and seconder of the motion earlier quoted!

During the period the appointed "Committee of Five" was interviewing long-time staff members to get their viewpoint, the president's turn to preside at the head of the Bethel table for one week came up. For several mornings he used the opportunity to discuss before the 1,200 or more "Bethel Family" members in the several dining rooms (all tied in by sound and television) what he called the "investigation" going on (the Committee of Five's interviews), saying that "some persons" favored changing things that had been done a certain way for the whole life of the organization. He asked again and again, "Where is their proof that things aren't working well, that a change is needed?" He said that the "investigation" was endeavoring to "prove this family is bad," but said he was confident that "a few complainers" would not "overwhelm the joy of the majority." He urged all to "have faith in the Society," pointing to its many accomplishments. At one point he said with great force and feeling that the changes some wanted to make as to the Bethel Family and its work and organization "will be made over my dead body."[7]

In all fairness to Nathan Knorr, it must be said that he undoubtedly believed that the then-existing arrangement was the right one. He knew that the vice president, the organization's most respected scholar and the one he relied upon to handle Scriptural matters, felt that way. Knorr was basically an affable, often warm, person. When he was not in his president's "uniform" or role, I genuinely enjoyed my association with him. However, his position, as is so often the case, did not generally let that side of him be seen and (again, doubtless due to his feeling that the role he carried out was according to God's will) he inclined to react very quickly and forcefully to any apparent infringement upon his presidential authority. People learned not to do this. For all that, I seriously doubt that Nathan would have gone along with some of the harsh actions that were later to come from the collective body that inherited his presidential authority.

I can empathize with his feelings and reaction, having served for many years as a Branch Overseer in both Puerto Rico and the Dominican Republic where I was to be, according to the prevailing organizational viewpoint, the "top man" in the country, the president's personal representative. My efforts to act in accord with this viewpoint made me constantly aware of "position" and the need to uphold that "position." I found by hard experience, however, that trying to live up to that organizational concept did not contribute to pleasant relations with others and that it made my own life unpleasant; the confrontations it produced were not something I felt at all suited for by nature and, after a while, I simply gave up trying to emulate what I had seen at headquarters. My life became much more enjoyable as a result and I found the overall effect far more productive and beneficial.

The president's last-mentioned words nearly proved prophetic. At the time of saying them he evidently had already developed a malig-

---

7 Words in quotations are from notes written down at the time the words were spoken; they were, of course, heard by over a thousand persons in each case.

nant tumor on his brain, though this did not become known until after the reorganization was definitely a *fait accompli*, its completion taking place officially on January 1, 1976, and Knorr's death occurring a year and a half later, on June 8, 1977.

The president's quite vocal opposition was matched, perhaps even surpassed, by that of the vice president. At the September 7, 1975, Graduation Program for the missionary School of Gilead, attended by the Bethel Family members and invited guests (largely relatives and friends of the graduating class), the vice president gave a talk, a customary feature of each graduation program.

Fred Franz had an inimitable, often dramatic (even melodramatic) speaking style. What follows is from an exact copy of his talk, but the written words cannot convey the inflections, the spirit, the "flavor," even the occasional sarcasm, that came through in the talk itself.

His opening words gave a clear indication as to where the talk was headed. Having in mind that a committee duly appointed by the Governing Body was at that very time making a proposal that the training, assignment and supervision of missionaries be directed by the Governing Body rather than by the corporations, we may note his opening expression. He began saying:

> "This class is being sent forth in collaboration with the Watchtower Bible and Tract Society of New York, Incorporated, by the Watch Tower Bible and Tract Society of Pennsylvania. Now the question is raised today, What right does the Watch Tower Bible and Tract Society have to send missionaries out into the field? . . . Who authorized the Watch Tower Bible and Tract Society of Pennsylvania to send missionaries all around the globe?
>
> "Now, such a challenging question may be raised with an earlier circumstance. And that is based on the fact that the Watch Tower Bible and Tract Society was founded by a man who became an evangelizer of world note, one of the most eminent evangelizers of this twentieth century and who especially attained global fame when he made his trip around the world in the year 1912. That man was Charles Taze Russell of Allegheny, Pennsylvania."

The focus was clearly on the corporation; the Governing Body was not mentioned. Of course no one had raised the "challenging question" he was here raising; the real issue in the Governing Body was whether the talk he had given four years before about the relationship between the Body and the corporation was to be taken seriously. However, he went on to say in his distinctive manner:

> "Now I've wondered about this matter. Maybe you have too. Just how did Russell become an evangelizer? Who made him an evangelizer? . . . the var-

ious religious establishments of Christendom were in operation. For instance, there was the Anglican Church with its ruling body, and the Protestant Episcopal Church with its ruling body. There was the Methodist Church with its Conference; there was also the Presbyterian Church, to which Russell used to belong, with its Synod. There was also the Congregational Church, which Russell joined, with its Central Congregation.

"But by none of these controlling organizations . . . was Russell made an evangelizer or missionary."

Without directly or openly referring to the Governing Body he had managed to introduce it into the discussion indirectly by referring to these "ruling bodies," under various names. (He could also have mentioned the Jesuits, who have an administration bearing this name: Governing Body.) But the point made was that no such a Governing Body had anything to do with or exercised any authority toward this founder of the Watch Tower corporation. Russell was an "independent," not subject to any of them.

The Governing Body had appointed the "Committee of Five" and that committee was recommending that permanent committees be formed to care for the direction of the work worldwide. Thus these following words of the vice president's talk take on added significance as, after speaking of the seventy disciples Jesus sent out, he told the graduating class:

"Now we're not to imagine that by sending the seventy evangelizers . . . by sending them forth by twos the Lord Jesus Christ was not making each two a committee, so that for the seventy evangelizers there were thirty-five committees of two. . . . You're being sent forth today after your graduation as missionaries . . . two being sent to Bolivia, and then there are others who are being sent, maybe four or six or eight, to a different country as assignment for work. Now, don't you missionaries think because you are being sent forth two together, or maybe four or six or maybe eight, that you are being sent forth as a committee to take over the work for the land to which you are assigned. No such thing! You are being sent forth as individual missionaries to cooperate together and to cooperate with the Branch of the Watch Tower Bible and Tract Society which is operating and directing the work in the land to which you are assigned to act as an evangelizer. So don't get this committee idea into your head. . . ."

In all this, the Governing Body remained "conspicuous by its absence," eclipsed by the corporation. Not a single person had suggested that the missionaries be sent out as "committees" or that they "take over the work" in their assigned lands, but this served as a means for introducing the idea of committees and discrediting the concept.

The talk then went on to discuss Philip "the evangelizer," raising once more the question as to "who made him an evangelizer or missionary?"[8] The vice president referred to the account in Acts, chapter six, where the apostles as a body found it necessary to appoint seven men, including Philip, to care for food distribution so as to end complaints being made of discrimination against certain widows. He then said:

> "Well, now, if you look up the *McClintock and Strong's Cyclopedia of Religious Knowledge* you'll find that the work that the apostles assigned to these seven men is called a 'semi-secular work.' But the apostles didn't want that semi-secular work; they unloaded it onto these seven men and said 'you take care of that. Well, *we're* going to specialize on prayers and teaching.' Now were these twelve apostles of the Lord Jesus Christ, by unloading this responsibility for taking care of tables, were they making of themselves mere *figureheads* in the congregation of God and of Jesus Christ? They certainly were not making themselves figureheads because they specialized on spiritual things."

To those Governing Body members who had heard the president emphasize that the Governing Body should care for the "strictly spiritual things" and leave the rest to the corporation, the vice president's words had a familiar ring. Strangely, however, about half of the men on the Body were spending their eight hours and forty minutes of each day in just such "semi-secular work." Dan Sydlik and Charles Fekel worked in the factory; Leo Greenlees handled insurance and related matters for the Secretary-Treasurer's Office; John Booth had oversight of the Bethel kitchen; Bill Jackson handled legal matters and documents; Grant Suiter was daily occupied in financial matters, investments, stocks, wills; and Milton Henschel and the president himself (who controlled all these assignments of work) were engaged in much of the "semi-secular" administrative work that the vice president said should be "unloaded" for others to care for.

The history of Paul, the converted Saul, was now related; that after his conversion when he went to Jerusalem he saw only two of the apostles, not the whole body of them; how he eventually came to Antioch in Syria. In relating the holy spirit's calling of Paul and Barnabas to missionary activity, the vice president continually empha-

8   See Acts 8:5–13; 21:8.

sized that all this was done through the *Antioch* congregation (hence *not* through Jerusalem where the apostolic body was located).[9] He said:

> "And then, all of a sudden as he [Paul] was serving in Antioch, in Syria, not in Israel but in Syria, why God's spirit spoke to that congregation there in Antioch and said, 'Now of all things, you set aside, YOU, this congregation in Antioch, you set aside these two men, namely Barnabas and Saul for the work for which I have commissioned them.' And so the Antioch congregation did that and they laid their hands upon Paul (or Saul) and Barnabas and sent them forth . . . and they went forth by the holy spirit operating through the Antioch congregation and they went out on their first missionary assignment.
>
> "So, you see the Lord Jesus Christ was acting as the Head of the congregation and taking action directly, without consulting anybody here on earth what he could do and what he could not do. And he acted in that way in regard to Saul and Barnabas and they were both apostles of the Antioch congregation."

At this point of the talk I recall sitting there and saying to myself, "Does the man realize what he is saying? I know what his goal is, to de-emphasize the Governing Body so as to maintain the authority of the corporation and its president, but does he realize the implication of what he is saying? In the process of attaining his goal he is undermining the whole teaching and claim about the existence of a centralized, first-century governing body operating out of Jerusalem with earthwide authority to supervise and direct all congregations of true Christians everywhere in all matters, a concept that the Society's publications have built up in the minds of all of Jehovah's Witnesses and to which the vast majority hold today."

But the vice president had by no means finished and he drove the idea home with even greater force. Describing the completion of Paul and Barnabas' first missionary tour, he continued with growing intensity and dramatization:

> ". . . and where did they go, where did they report? There's the record, you read it for yourself in the closing verses of the fourteenth chapter of Acts. They went back to Antioch, to the congregation there, and the account says that they related things in detail to them, to this congregation that had committed them to the undeserved kindness of God for the work they had performed. So there's where they reported.

9 It should be remembered that the whole basis for the Witnesses' teaching of a "governing body" arrangement and authority is that there was such an arrangement operating from Jerusalem in Bible times.

"So the record also says they stayed in Antioch not a little time. Now, what happened? All of a sudden something occurred and Paul and Barnabas, they go up to Jerusalem. Well, what's the matter? What brings them up to Jerusalem?

"Well, is it the body of apostles and of other elders of the Jerusalem congregation that summoned them up there and say, 'Look here! We have heard that you two men have gone out on a missionary tour and finished it and you haven't come up here to Jerusalem to report to us. D'YOU KNOW WHO WE ARE? We are the council of Jerusalem. DON'T YOU RECOGNIZE THE HEADSHIP OF THE LORD JESUS CHRIST? If you don't come up here in a hurry, we're going to take disciplinary action against you!'

"Is that what the account says? Well, if they had acted that way toward Paul and Barnabas because they reported to the congregation by means of which the holy spirit had sent them out, then this council of apostles at Jerusalem and other elders of the Jewish congregation would have put themselves above the headship of the Lord Jesus Christ."

His points were completely valid. They were also completely contrary to the view presented in the Society's publications, which present a picture of Jerusalem as the seat of a governing body exercising full authority and direction over all Christians as Christ's agency, acting with divine authority. That is doubtless why, unlike other talks the vice president has given, this one was never used as the basis for articles in the *Watchtower* magazine. For any individual Witness to present such an argument today would be counted as heretical, rebellious speech. If actually applied as stated, his words would mean that any congregation on earth could send out its own missionaries if they believed Christ Jesus and holy spirit so directed, doing so without consulting anyone else, whether in Brooklyn or in a Branch Office. There was no question in my mind as to the quick and adverse reaction this would provoke from the Society's headquarters and its offices. It would be viewed as a threat to their centralized authority and any congregation doing this would in so many words be asked, "Do you know who we are? Don't you recognize the headship of the Lord Jesus Christ operating through us?" All that he said in the talk was true, perfectly true. but it was evidently no more meant to be applied in full force than the points that had been made about four years earlier in the "tail wagging the dog" talk, *except* that, by the references to Antioch, he was endeavoring to establish a parallel with the corporation as operating apart from the Governing Body.

The talk went on to show that the real reason Paul and Barnabas went to Jerusalem, as recorded in Acts, chapter fifteen, was because *Jerusalem itself* had been the source of a serious problem for the Antioch congregation, men coming down from Jerusalem and stirring up trouble over the issue of lawkeeping and circumcision. Hence the trip to Jerusalem was to overturn the effect of the teaching of these Jerusalem troublemakers.

Continuing the argument, he dealt with the second missionary tour of Paul and his new partner Silas and emphasized again that it was from the *Antioch* congregation that they went forth, so that "again, the Antioch congregation was being used to send out missionaries of great eminence in Bible history." That they returned to *Antioch* and that from *Antioch* Paul embarked on his third tour. Winding up the account from the book of Acts, the vice president said:

pg.76

> "And so as we examine this account of these two most outstanding among the missionaries recorded in Bible history, we find that they were sent out especially by the Lord Jesus Christ, the Head of the church, a fact which the Watch Tower Bible and Tract Society has upheld and accepted ever since the Society was formed. So, we see how the Lord Jesus Christ is the Head of the church and has a right to act direct, without whatever other organizations in view, no matter who they are. He is the Head of the church. We can't challenge what HE DOES."

Those last three sentences spoken by the vice president represent the position taken today by a number of Witnesses. For taking that identical position, they are now labeled "apostates." Again, however, those statements were clearly not meant the way they sounded. For the vice president was at the very same time saying that to challenge the authority of the Watch Tower Bible and Tract Society and the authority of its president was to challenge the Lord Jesus Christ. He did not believe the thinking or action of the Governing Body-appointed "Committee of Five" could in any way be representative of the direction of the Head of the church, for the simple reason that He, Jesus Christ, had caused the corporation to be formed and was dealing through it. This seemed to me to be a case of mixed-up reasoning.

That this was the whole thrust of his talk could be seen in that, coming to the crux of the matter, he now applied all these points to modern times. He spoke of the raising up of Charles Taze Russell, his starting a new religious magazine, the *Watch Tower*, and, "Who authorized this man to do that?" Then, on to Russell's incorporating Zion's Watch Tower Bible and Tract Society, and here he added:

"And mind you, friends, when he founded that Society, the Watch Tower Bible and Tract Society, he was not founding a DO-NOTHING society or organization."

The Lord Jesus Christ and God's spirit had raised Russell up, he said, and also backed the formation of the corporation, "this active, *do-something* Society." The vice president then described the origin of the Gilead School; that it had been the corporation president's idea; that, when informed, the Board of Directors had given its backing and that the president was to have supervision of the School. Nathan Knorr was sitting on the platform while the vice president gave his talk and Fred Franz gestured toward him in the course of these following remarks:

"So you see, dear friends, that the Boards of Directors of the New York corporation and of the Pennsylvania, as constituted back there, they had *respect* for the office of the president and they did not treat the president of these organizations as a *poker-faced, immobilized figurehead* presiding over a society, a *do-nothing* society."

From the start of the talk I had thought this was the goal aimed at and so it came as no surprise to me, though the language used did. From this stage of the presentation, the tone of the talk softened and he went on to highlight that particular day, September 7, 1975, saying:

"And do you know what that means? According to this diary, Hebrew diary, from the land of Israel [referring now to a small booklet he held in his hand], why this is the *second day* of the month Tishri of the lunar year 1976, and do you know what that means? That here on this day of your graduation, why it is the *second day of the seventh millenium* of man's existence here on earth. Isn't that something? Isn't that something grand [applause here] that the opening day of the seventh millenium of mankind's existence is signalized by the operation of the Watch Tower Bible and Tract Society in full compliance of the terms of its charter sending out the 59th class of the Gilead School for missionaries.

"Jehovah God certainly has blessed it, and by its fruit, why it has become known as an approved agency in the hand of Jehovah God and so that there is no need to challenge the right and the authority of this Society to send out missionaries.

"And, friends, notice this, that just as God used the Antioch congregation to send out the two of the most outstanding missionaries of the first century, Paul and Barnabas, so today Jehovah God is using the Watch Tower Bible and Tract Society of Pennsylvania, in collaboration with the New York corporation, to send out further missionaries and they are determined to keep on in that course. That's something very, very gratifying."[10]

There could be no question but that in the vice president's mind someone had "thrown down the gauntlet" in a challenge to the presidency. By this talk the battle lines had been carefully and emphatically drawn. The corporation had its sovereign terrain and it was off limits to the Governing Body. The sad effect of all this was that many of his fellow members of the Governing Body were distinctly cast in the role of aggressor and openly displayed as disrespectful of the authority of the Lord Jesus Christ vested in this "approved agency," the corporation.

The guests present, parents and friends of the graduating class, were generally mystified by many of the things said and by the whole thrust of the talk, the biting language at times employed. The Bethel Family members, though having a vague idea of difficulties because of comments made by the president and vice president when acting as head of the table, now had reinforced their suspicion that there was indeed a quarrel going on in the Governing Body, apparently a power struggle.

The contrast between this talk and the "tail wagging the dog" talk of four years previous could hardly have been greater. They were given by the same man, yet they seemed to go in totally opposite directions. I would be less than honest if I did not admit that I left the auditorium that day feeling not only deeply disturbed but also somewhat ill. It seemed that God's Word was something that could be made to fit one argument when circumstances made it advisable, and an opposite argument when circumstances were different. This disturbed me more than any other aspect of the matter.

As in Nathan Knorr's case, so, too, certain factors help in understanding Fred Franz's actions. In late 1941, when Judge Rutherford lay on his deathbed at Beth Sarim, he had called three men to his side: Nathan Knorr, Fred Franz and Hayden Covington. He told them that he wanted them to carry on after his death and that they should "stick together" as a team. That action was reminiscent of Pastor Russell's "Will," though here given orally rather than in writing. Twenty years later, 1961, in writing the book *"Let Your Name Be Sanctified,"* Fred Franz alluded to that occasion when discussing the account of the

---

10 Following the talk, President Knorr spoke, visibly moved and almost choked with emotion. He expressed great appreciation for what had been said, and I am sure he was thoroughly sincere in his feelings. He then gave a pleasant talk on "Wholesomeness of Speech."

passing on of Elijah's prophetic mantle ("official garment" in the *New World Translation*) to his successor Elisha.[11] He presented this as a prophetic drama and stated:

> [4] Rutherford was abed on the Pacific Coast when the United States of America was plunged into World War II Sunday, December 7, 1941. Two men of the anointed remnant (one since 1913 and one since 1922) and one of the "other sheep" (since 1934) were summoned from Brooklyn headquarters out to Rutherford's bedside at the home called "Beth-sarim," San Diego, California. On December 24, 1941, he gave these three his final instructions. For years he had been hoping to see the faithful prophets, including Elijah and Elisha, resurrected from the dead and installed as Kingdom "princes in all the earth" in God's new world. (Psalm 45:16) But on Thursday, January 8, 1942, Rutherford died at seventy-two years of age, as a faithful witness of Jehovah God, completely devoted to the interests of God's kingdom. He had proved himself fearless in support of Jehovah's side of the paramount issue of Universal Domination.
>
> [5] As viewed from our present time, it appears that there the Elijah work passed, to be succeeded by the Elisha work. It was as when Elijah and Elisha had crossed the Jordan River by means of a dividing of the waters to the east shore and were walking along, awaiting the removal of Elijah.[12]

When the Governing Body discussed the proposed reorganization, the vice president made direct reference to this assignment from the dying Judge Rutherford. I have no doubt that Fred Franz felt that a certain "mantle-izing" had occurred at that time. As has been stated, Nathan Knorr succeeded Rutherford to the presidency. Hayden Covington, the big Texas lawyer who defended Jehovah's Witnesses in many cases before the U.S. Supreme Court, was asked by Knorr to become vice president, this despite the fact that Covington made no profession then of being of the "anointed" class. (This shows that neither Judge Rutherford nor, initially, Nathan Knorr felt that being of the "anointed" was essential for directing the work worldwide.) Covington's own testimony, given during the Walsh case in Scotland, in-

---

11   2 Kings 2:8, 11–14.
12   *"Let Your Name be Sanctified,"* published in 1961, pp. 335, 336.

dicates that it was not until some correspondence came in a couple of years later asking how this could be, that he and Knorr talked about his not being of the "anointed" and Covington decided he should resign.[13] Relations between the two deteriorated as time went on and Covington eventually left the headquarters staff to go into private practice.[14] Fred Franz was elected as vice president following Covington's resignation in 1944.

Though the three heirs to Rutherford's deathbed transference of responsibility (which, incidentally shows there was no "governing body" in operation) had now become two, there was evidently still a definite feeling that a role in fulfilling prophecy was in effect. In 1978, at a large convention in Cincinnati, Ohio, when Fred Franz, now the Society's president, was asked to speak to the audience of over 30,000 persons about his life experience as a Witness, he chose to spend the bulk of the time discussing his relationship with the now deceased Nathan Knorr, particularly emphasizing Judge Rutherford's dying words to them. It can very truthfully be said that the talk took on the aspect of a eulogy as Fred Franz described Knorr's qualities and stressed that he had stuck by Nathan Knorr right to the end "just as the Judge had urged" and that he was proud of having done so.

Perhaps even more illuminating as regards this view of being "mantleized" was an expression made that same year during a session of what was now the Writing Committee of the Governing Body. Present were Lyman Swingle, Ewart Chitty, Lloyd Barry, Fred Franz and myself. A commentary on the Letter of James was being written by Ed Dunlap, and Fred Franz had asked for an adjustment on Dunlap's discussion of James, chapter three, verse 1, where the disciple says:

> "Not many of you should become teachers, my brothers, knowing that we shall receive heavier judgment."

The material Dunlap had prepared said that this evidently was a warning against unqualified individuals seeking to serve as teachers simply because of a desire for prominence. Fred Franz asked for the elimination of most of the material but gave no particular explanation for his objections except to ask in writing:

---

13 From the official court record, pp. 387, 388.
14 Covington had had a severe struggle with alcoholism and had undergone one 'drying out' treatment while still in headquarters service. He went through another at Speers Hospital in Dayton, Kentucky, after being disfellowshiped in the 1970's, and finally conquered the problem. He was reinstated and continued association until his death.

"If Jesus gave some to be teachers, how many was he to give? And since Jesus does the giving, how could James tell the men 'not *many* of you should become teachers'? How did James himself become a teacher?"

Since I had been assigned to oversee the project of the commentary's development, at the Committee hearing I asked Fred Franz to clarify his objection and tell us just what *he* thought was meant by this text. He stated that he believed it meant that it was God's will that there be just a few men in the entire Christian congregation who could rightly be called "teachers." I inquired who such would be in our time. Speaking very calmly his reply was:

"Well, I believe that I am. I have been here at headquarters for over fifty years and have been involved in the field of writing and research during most of that time, so I believe that I am. And—there are some other brothers throughout the earth who are."

This response was another occasion when the effect was so startling that the words were, in effect, burned into my memory. I was not the only witness to them since they were spoken before the other three members of the Writing Committee. By his remark we had had identified for us only one teacher on earth by name: Fred Franz. Who the others were, we were left to speculate. As I told Lyman Swingle on more than one occasion thereafter, I regretted not having pursued the matter further by asking for names of the other "teachers" of our time. But the response left me momentarily speechless.

In the same material in which he presented his objection to Dunlap's material, President Franz had also suggested the addition of the following points in the forthcoming commentary (quoting now from page 2 of his writeup):

"How James himself became a teacher we do not know except that his half brother, Jesus Christ, appeared to him after his resurrection. (1 Cor. 15:7; Acts 1:14) Not every dedicated, baptized Christian man who may want to 'become a teacher' does so out of selfish, ambitious motive. Such a rightly motivated teacher was seen in the case of the 27-year-old 'Editor and Publisher' of the magazine Zion's Watch Tower and Herald of Christ's Presence in July of 1879 [Pastor Russell]."

This brought memories of his Gilead Graduation talk in 1975 when he had made clear his conviction that Christ Jesus had personally raised up Pastor Russell to carry out a special role. This material three years later indicated that he felt such personal, individual selection by Christ was continuing in other cases, with the result that only a few select persons were raised up as special "teachers" for the congregation.[15]

The above-suggested material bringing Russell into the picture was not used, however, and the information found on pages 99 to the top of 102 in the *Commentary on the Letter of James* is a replacement of Dunlap's material which I wrote so that President Franz's objections would be met. It was in a certain sense a refutation of his view since Jesus' words at Matthew, chapter twenty-three, verse 8, "But you, do not you be called Rabbi, *for one is your teacher, whereas all you are brothers*," seemed to be completely contrary to the idea of a very small number of men forming a somewhat exclusive group of specially selected "teachers," the chosen few. The rewrite I submitted was approved in committee and published.

There is another reason why there was such an evident contradiction between certain bold, forceful statements made in print (as in the "tail wagging the dog" articles) and the comparatively timid, puny reality actually existing. The reason is that the officers of the corporation could rationalize that a small, representative change or reform would suffice as substitution for, or a "token" of, a larger, genuinely meaningful change.

As an example of this, the mere fact that in 1971 President Knorr had decided to relinquish his monopoly of the chairmanship at the Bethel dining tables, sharing it with the other members of the Board of Directors and also had decided to allow them to serve on a rotational basis as chairmen of the Governing Body sessions was viewed as all that was needed to demonstrate that the corporations (and their officers) were in fact directed by and submissive to the Governing Body and that the 'dog was indeed wagging the tail.' No other tangible action or significant change had taken place in the authority structure, nor was it viewed as necessary to fulfill the impressive picture painted.

That Fred Franz could so view matters seems evident, particularly so since, surprisingly, over twenty years earlier, back in 1944 he had written articles for the *Watchtower* that contained all the *basic* points on elders and overseers that appeared in the *Aid* book.[16] Despite this,

---

15 Karl Klein on several occasions during Governing Body sessions referred to Fred Franz as having been the "oracle" of the organization for many years. Though generally said with a smile, his repetitious use of the term implied more than mere jesting.

16 The *Watchtower*, October 15, 1944.

no change whatsoever took place back then in the congregational arrangement. But it had been *said*, it had been *published*, and this was viewed as enough.

In those articles, 1944 was presented as a marked year in Bible prophecy, and this mainly because an amendment had been passed whereby voting rights in the corporation would no longer be based on a $10 donation as previously. Instead a maximum number of 500 persons, selected by the corporation's Board, would be the only ones with a right to vote. Anyone who has attended an annual meeting of the Watch Tower Society where elections of Directors take place knows that it is extremely routine and that voting is mainly a mere formality. The bulk of the voting members know virtually nothing of the inner workings of the organization and have neither influence, voice or control as to the policies and programs of the organization. The actual *business* part of the meeting usually takes no more than one hour; then it is over until another year passes.

Yet the adoption of this amendment as to voting members was presented in articles in the *Watchtower* of December 1, 1971 (written by Fred Franz) as being an occasion of such significance and magnitude that it became a focal point in the explanation of the prophecy of Daniel 8:14, regarding the 2,300 prophetic days connected with the 'bringing of the sanctuary into its proper condition.' I doubt that one Witness in a thousand, if shown that verse today, would ever connect it up with 1944 and the corporation amendment made then. Yet that remains the official explanation of that prophecy to this day. It was another example of the ability to take an event of relatively minor effect and then to clothe it with symbolic value as being of great significance.

On August 15, 1975, the Committee of Five finally presented its findings and recommendations. On behalf of the committee I prepared a document of 45 pages, setting out the historical and, particularly, the Scriptural reasons for recommending that the basically monarchical structure should change, plus 19 pages outlining a system of Governing Body Committees for directing the different areas of activity. The initial document ended with this paragraph:

"All the deliberations of the committee of five have been made with much prayer and careful thought. We sincerely hope that God's spirit has guided in the results and pray that they will be of some assistance to the body in reaching a decision. It is hoped that the adjustments recommended, if approved, will contribute toward an even more pleasant, peaceful relationship among the members of the Governing Body, helping to eliminate the tension that at times has surfaced in our meetings. (Ps. 133:1; Jas. 3:17, 18) It is also hoped that the recommended adjustments will, if accepted, serve to enhance and make yet more prominent the headship of Christ Jesus and the spirit of genuine brotherhood found among his disciples.—Mark 9:50."

Those words expressed my sincere feelings and hope. I could not see how they could be viewed as a challenge to Christ Jesus' direction of his congregation.[17]

The material came before the Governing Body, and in the session on September 10, 1975, it was now obvious that by far the majority favored the basic change recommended. However, a second Committee of Five was assigned to make final adjustments.[18] The Body did not select either the president or vice president to serve on this committee since their opposition had been clearly stated.

The president's comments at this point mainly expressed doubt as to the practicality of the change. The vice president, however, made plain that he viewed the presentation as an "attack on the presidency." When the president's own motion was read out to him, he replied that Brother Knorr had made that statement "under duress."

Lyman Swingle expressed himself as feeling that all members of the Body had respect for the president and did not view him as a "poker-faced, immobilized figurehead of a do-nothing Society," here using the vice president's language at the graduation exercises. He stressed that the president could still use his energy, drive and initiative within the proposed arrangement. Later in the discussion, the vice president insisted that the Committee of Five's document did just what he had said was being done. He stated that at the coming annual meeting his vote would be for the corporation powers to continue and said that his talk at the Gilead Graduation owed to a feeling of obligation to let the brothers know this so that they would not feel that a "hoax" had been practiced on them.

After the second committee completed its recommendations and submitted these on December 3, 1975, the matter came down to a final

17 A covering letter, written by Leo Greenlees, accompanied the document and included this statement: "Our recommendations are not motivated by dissatisfaction with the work as it has been administered heretofore, but mainly out of concern for the direction indicated by the Bible and *Watchtower* articles. We believe that once the Scriptural principles are brought to bear on the matter, then the direction we should take is evident."

18 This second committee was composed of Milton Henschel, Ewart Chitty, Lyman Swingle, Lloyd Barry and Ted Jaracz.

vote.[19] The Chairman called for a show of hands. All but two raised their hands in favor of the motion to implement the recommendations. The two who did not raise their hands were the president and the vice president.

The following day the Body met again. The vice president said he had taken no part in the discussion the day before since he "didn't want to have anything more to do with it"; to participate would mean he was in favor and he "conscientiously could not do so." He referred repeatedly to Nathan Knorr as the "chief executive" of the Society, the "chief executive of the Lord's people on earth," and said that "Jesus Christ is not down here on earth and so is using agents to carry out his will."

Dan Sydlik, a square-built, deep-voiced man of Slavic descent, said he would have been "happy to see Brother Knorr or Brother Franz turn to the Scriptures or even to the *Watchtower* publications to support their position but that was not the case." Leo Greenlees remarked that if all the congregations were glad to submit to the direction of the Governing Body, why not the corporations also?

The president basically confined his remarks to saying that he thought the corporation would act "parallel" to the Governing Body but that, instead, the proposed arrangement subordinated the corporation, adding, "which is probably correct." The vice president said he too thought the two organizations were going to run parallel (perhaps like Antioch and Jerusalem?) and said: "I never had in mind what the Governing Body wants to do now."

It was obvious that the president and vice president were maintaining their opposition. Lloyd Barry, his voice strained and shaking with emotion, now pleaded with them that they make the matter unanimous since it was obvious that it would pass anyway.

Another vote was taken and this time President Knorr raised his hand and the vice president followed suit.

Four years later, in 1979, in a Governing Body session, Fred Franz, now president, stated that his vote for the change back then was made "under duress." I would agree. When Nathan Knorr conceded, Fred Franz felt compelled to join him. He went on to say that he had not been in favor of the change then and that from that point forward he had "just been watching" to see what would result.

---

19 About the only major change the second committee made in the recommendations of the first committee was that, in addition to a rotating chairmanship of each proposed Governing Body Committee, there should be a permanent "Coordinator" of the Committee.

The accompanying chart, prepared by the second Committee of Five, shows the arrangement that went into effect on January 1, 1976.

x - Chairman
* - Coordinator

John Booth, a member of the first Committee of Five, and in early life a farmer from upstate New York, a gentle man who thought deeply but normally had difficulty in expressing those thoughts well, seemed to have best described what now became the case with the corporation. In one of the Committee of Five's first meetings, he had said:

> "A corporation is just a legal tool. It's like a pen lying on the desk. When I want to use the pen I pick it up. When I'm finished I just lay it down until I want to use it again."

That now became the position of the Watch Tower Bible and Tract Society of Pennsylvania and its subsidiary corporations. Inevitably that meant that the power of the presidency was decimated and virtually disappeared, that office now serving an almost purely legal function.

When Nathan Knorr died, the Governing Body considered the matter of his successor. The most likely candidates were Vice President Franz and Milton Henschel, who had worked closely with Knorr in Administration. Henschel moved that Fred Franz become president and this was unanimously approved. When replacement for Knorr's position as "Coordinator" of the Publishing Committee came up, Henschel seemed the logical successor, but Fred Franz, now president, spoke in favor of Lloyd Barry. Relations between Knorr and Henschel had been poor in recent years and in one interview with the first Committee of Five, Knorr had implied that he felt Barry could take over his job (his presidential work) if necessary. Evidently Fred Franz viewed this somewhat in the light of Judge Rutherford's deathbed instructions and felt that some transfer of "mantle" to Barry was thus in order, but the Body voted Henschel into the position.

An article in *Time* magazine, reporting the election of Fred Franz as the new president, stated:

> "Though few people know his name, he has acquired more-than-papal power over 2.2 million souls around the world."[20]

That statement could hardly have been more wrong. It would have been true a year or so earlier, but the office of president, though still carrying a measure of prestige and prominence, was no longer the earthwide power base it had been. Few persons outside the Body could appreciate how drastic a change had taken place.

If the president had indeed had power of papal scope, though with none of the trappings and pomp of the papacy, the Branch Overseers had been equivalent in domain to archbishops, each being the "presiding minister of Christianity for and within the territory to which he has been appointed."[21] Here, too, a change entered as Branch Committees took on this responsibility.

The years of 1976 and 1977 brought some pleasant moments. A very different climate seemed to be in evidence at the international headquarters, a spirit of greater brotherliness, openness and equality. Some compared it to the "window" that Pope John XXIII had opened in the Catholic Church to 'let a breath of fresh air in.'

The new Governing Body Committees put into effect a number of changes to improve Bethel Family circumstances, both in Brooklyn and among the more than ninety Branches. Greater consideration was given to financial needs of the so-called "rank and file" members, to the special needs of women and to those who were older. During 1976 a series of meetings was held with respected and esteemed men in

---

20 *Time*, July 11, 1977, p. 64.
21 Quoted from pages 5 and 6 of the *Branch Office Procedure* book, a manual for all Branch Offices in effect at the time.

various categories: representatives from the Branches around the world were first brought in; then traveling representatives across the United States; finally congregation elders representing the different sectors of the country were invited to Brooklyn.[22] In all cases there was a freedom of discussion and expression that most found refreshingly different from any experienced in the past.

On the congregational level, I doubt that much of this was felt, since the many suggestions made by these men were not implemented to any major extent. Still, many Witnesses expressed appreciation that, for a time at least, published material gave stronger emphasis to the authority of the Scriptures and the headship of Jesus Christ and less to the authority of a human organization. They felt overall that a more moderate, balanced, compassionate approach was being taken. As one long-time Witness put it, "I used to feel like I *had* to do things; now I'm beginning to feel like I *want* to do them."

The sessions of the Governing Body manifested this changed atmosphere in some measure. The passing of the much publicized year of 1975 without the hoped-for arrival of a millennial jubilee doubtless had a somewhat humbling effect, as dogmatism diminished perceptibly. More caution as to imposing new rulings on the lives of people and less inclination to categorize specific actions as "disfellowshiping offenses" were reflected in the voting, though never in a complete sense.

During this year (1976), Nathan Knorr's health began to deteriorate. Yet, as long as he was able to attend, he shared in discussions and, though clearly not happy with changes made, showed a generally cooperative and helpful attitude. His expressions at times helped to overcome extreme points of view. Though rarely based on Scriptural argument, they reflected his common sense approach to matters. Throughout most of this period Vice President Franz preferred to sit and listen, only occasionally participating in discussions and, almost without fail, what he had to say would come toward the close of the discussion, just before voting took place. By that point the general consensus of thinking was fairly evident (based on the individual comments made) and often his remarks were opposite to the trend of the majority. Perhaps nothing illustrates more strikingly the changed thinking of the Body during this period as does the fact that the voting, while sometimes showing a shift due to the influence of the vice president's

---

22 Peter Gregerson of Gadsden, Alabama, was one of these invited. It was my having a meal with Peter some years later that led to my being disfellowshiped.

last-minute remarks, often went contrary to his expressions. In the main, however, during this period he gave no indication of his thinking until the customary show of hands was called for and, as the official "Minutes" record, there were numerous cases where the vote read "Sixteen [or whatever the figure might be] in favor; one abstention," that one being the vice president. This was generally where issues involved changes of policy regarding so-called "disfellowshiping matters." Matters in the secular or semi-secular field (such as purchases of property, office procedures) or appointments to membership in Branch Committees were usually unanimous.

When the new arrangement was voted in, I found it hard to believe that such a major change in the authority structure had actually taken place, particularly in view of the intense opposition it had met from the most prominent men in the organization, as well as from some of their close associates outside the Body. My earnest hope was that the "leveling" and equalizing effect of the change would allow for greater moderation, a reduction of dogmatism, a greater concern for individuals and their individual circumstances and problems, and perhaps, some day, the elimination of the authoritarian approach that produced so many rules and assumed such great control over the personal lives of people.

As has been noted, some of that came. It came for a while. Then, within about two years, like a chilling breeze in autumn that signals the approach of greater coldness, evidence of a very clear swing back to earlier approaches began surfacing again and again.

5

TRADITION AND LEGALISM

"Thus you nullify the word of God for the sake
of your tradition. . . . their teachings are but
rules made by man." —Matthew 15:6, 9,
New International Version.

M OST of Jehovah's Witnesses envision Governing Body sessions
as meetings of men who spend a great amount of their time in
intense study of God's Word. They think of them as meeting together
to consider humbly how they can better help their brothers understand
the Scriptures, to discuss constructive and positive ways to build them
up in faith and love, the qualities that motivate genuine Christian works,
doing all this in sessions where Scripture is always appealed to as the
only valid and final and supreme authority.

As has been noted, the Governing Body members, better than anyone, knew that the *Watchtower* articles describing the relationship between the corporation and the Governing Body presented a picture
that did not accord with reality. So, too, members of the Governing
Body know, better than anyone else, that the picture described in the
preceding paragraph differs measurably from reality.[1]

Going over the records of meeting after meeting after meeting, the
most prominent, constant and time-occupying feature found is the discussion of issues ultimately coming down to this question: "Is it a
disfellowshiping matter?"

I would liken the Governing Body (and in my mind I often did) to
a group of men backed up against a wall with numerous persons toss-

---

1 Since all Governing Body sessions are completely private, only its members are witnesses
of what actually occurs in those sessions.

ing balls at them for them to catch and throw back. The balls come so frequently and in such number that there is little time for anything else. Indeed, it seemed that every ruling made and sent out only brought additional questions thrown at us from new angles, leaving little time for truly positive, constructive thought, study, discussion and action.

Over the years I sat through many, many sessions where issues that could seriously affect the lives of people were discussed, yet where the Bible did not come into the hands or even on the lips of practically any of those participating. There were reasons, a combination of reasons, for this.

Many Governing Body members admitted that they found themselves so occupied with various matters that there was little time for Bible study. It is no exaggeration to say that the average Member spent no more time, and sometimes less, in such study than many Witnesses among the so-called "rank and file." Some of those on the Publishing Committee (which included the Officers and Directors of the Pennsylvania corporation) were notable in this regard, for a tremendous amount of paper work came their way and they evidently felt that they could not or should not delegate this to anyone else to review and present conclusions or recommendations.

On the few occasions when some purely Scriptural discussion was programmed it was generally to discuss an article or articles for the *Watchtower* that an individual had prepared and to which there was some objection. In these cases it regularly occurred that, even though notified a week or two in advance of the matter, Milton Henschel, Grant Suiter or another member of this Committee felt obliged to say, "I only had time to look this over briefly, I've been so busy." There was no reason to doubt that they were truly busy. The question that came to mind was, How then can they vote in good conscience on approval of the material when they have not been able to meditate on it, search the Scriptures to test it out? Once published it is to be viewed as "truth" by millions of people. What paper work could equal this in importance?

But these brothers were by no means alone, for the discussions themselves clearly demonstrated that by far the majority of the Body had done little else than read the material written. The subject was often one that had originated and developed in the mind of the writer without consultation with the Body, even though it represented some "new" understanding of Scripture, and often the writer had then worked up all his arguments and put the material in final form without having talked things over, tested his thinking, with even one other person.[2] The argumentation was frequently complex, involved, of a kind that no superficial reading could ever allow for sufficient analysis to test its validity and determine if it was Scripturally solid or just a case of 'acrobatical logic,' a skillful juggling of texts that made them say something other than what they really said. Those who had only read the material usually voted in favor; those who had done extra study and research were those most likely to raise serious questions.

Thus, after one discussion of an article which presented the view that the "festival of the harvest ingathering" (celebrated, according to the Bible, at the *close* of the harvest season) pictured a circumstance in the history of the Witnesses at the *start* of their spiritual harvesting, sufficient members voted in favor for it to be accepted.[3] The member serving at the time as Coordinator of the Writing Committee then said: "All right, if that's what you want to do I'll send it over to the factory for printing. But that does not mean that I believe it. It is just one more stone piled on the enormous monument of testimony that the *Watchtower* is not infallible."

A second reason for lack of real Bible discussion, follows obviously, I believe, from the preceding one. And that is that most of the Body were actually not that well versed in the Scriptures, for their "busyness" was not something of recent origin. In my own case, right up until 1965 I had been on such a "treadmill" of activity that I found little time for truly serious study. But I think the matter goes deeper than that. I believe that the feeling prevailed that such study and research were really not all that essential, that the policies and teachings of the organization—developed over many decades—were a reliable guide in themselves, so that, whatever motion might be made in the Body, as long as it conformed satisfactorily to such traditional policy or teaching, it must be all right.

The facts point to this conclusion. At times a long discussion on some "disfellowshiping" issue would suddenly be resolved because one member had found a statement related to the matter in the Society's *Organization* book, or, more likely, in the book called "Aid to Answering Branch Office Correspondence," a compendium of policies

---

2 Even during Nathan Knorr's lifetime this was the normal procedure followed by the Society's principal writer, Fred Franz. Only when put in completed form did anyone else—and usually only the president—have opportunity to consider and discuss the ideas or interpretations developed.

3 See the *Watchtower* of February 15, 1980, pp. 8–24.

arranged alphabetically on a broad range of subjects—employment, marriage, divorce, politics, military matters, labor unions, blood and scores of others. When such statement was found, even though no Scripture was cited in support of the particular point of policy, this seemed to settle the matter for most of the Body members and they would usually vote without hesitation in favor of any motion that conformed to the printed policy. I saw this happen on several occasions and I never ceased to be impressed by the way that kind of printed policy statement could effect such a sudden transformation in the progress and resolution of a discussion.

A final reason for the Bible's playing little part in such discussion is that in case after case the issue involved something on which the Scriptures themselves were silent.

To cite specific examples, the discussion might be to decide whether the injection of serums should be viewed the same as blood transfusions, or whether platelets should be considered just as objectionable for acceptance as packed red blood cells. Or the discussion might center on the policy that a wife who committed one act of unfaithfulness was obliged to confess this to her husband (even though he was known to be extremely violent in nature) or else her claim of repentance would not be considered valid, leaving her liable for disfellowshiping. What scriptures discuss such matters?

Consider this case that came up for discussion and decision by the Governing Body. One of Jehovah's Witnesses, driving a truck for the Coca-Cola Company, had as his route a large military base where numerous deliveries were made. The question: Could he do this and remain a member in good standing or is this a disfellowshiping offense? (The crucial factor here being that *military* property and personnel were involved.)

Again, what scriptures discuss such matters—in a way that can be clearly and reasonably seen, in a way that obviates the need for involved reasonings and interpretations? None were brought forward, yet the majority of the Body decided that this work was not acceptable and that the man would have to obtain another route to remain in good standing. A similar case came up involving a Witness musician who played in a "combo" at an officers' club on a military base. This, too, was ruled unacceptable by the majority of the Body. The Scriptures being silent, human reasoning supplied the answer.

Generally, in discussions of this type, if any appeal *was* made to Scripture by those favoring condemnation of the act or conduct, that appeal was to very broad statements such as, "You are no part of the world," found at John, chapter fifteen, verse 19. If a Governing Body member personally scrupled against the action or conduct under discussion and could think of no other argument against it, often he would fall back on this text, extending it and applying it to fit whatever the circumstances were. The need to let the rest of the Scriptures define what such a broad statement means and how it applies often seemed to be considered unnecessary or irrelevant.

A major factor in Governing Body decisions was the two-thirds majority rule. This produced some strange effects at times.

The rule was that a two-thirds majority (of the active membership) was needed to carry a motion. I personally appreciated the opportunity this allowed for a member to "abstain" without feeling that he was exercising "veto power." On minor matters, even when not in complete agreement, I generally voted with the majority. But when issues came up that genuinely affected my conscience I frequently found myself in the minority—seldom alone but often with only one, two or three other members expressing conscientious objection by not voting for the motion.[4] This was not so often the case during the first two years or so after the major change effected in the authority structure (officially put in motion on January 1, 1976). In the final two years of my membership, however, a strong trend toward a "hard line" approach obliged me to abstain with greater frequency.

But consider now what sometimes happened when the Body was quite divided in its viewpoint, not nearly so uncommon an occurrence as some might think.

An issue might be under discussion involving conduct that had, somewhere in the Society's past, been designated a "disfellowshiping offense," perhaps a person's having a particular blood fraction injected to control a potentially fatal ailment; or possibly the case of a wife who had a non-Witness husband in military service and who worked in a commissary on her husband's military base.

At times in such discussions the Body might be quite divided, sometimes even split right down the middle. Or there might be a majority who favored removing the particular action, conduct or type of employment from the "disfellowshiping offense" category. Consider what might happen because of the two-thirds majority rule:

---

4 I can recall, and my records indicate, only a couple of occasions in over eight years where I found myself completely alone in abstaining.

If out of fourteen members present, nine favored removing the disfellowshiping offense "label" and only five favored retaining it, the majority was not sufficient to change the disfellowshiping label. Though a clear majority, the nine were not a *two-thirds* majority. (Even if there were ten of them favoring change this was still not enough, for though they would be two-thirds majority of the fourteen *present*, the rule was two-thirds majority of the *total active membership*, which during much of the time was seventeen or eighteen.) If someone from the nine favoring removal of the disfellowshiping category advanced a motion it would fail, because twelve votes were needed for it to pass. If someone from the five favoring retainment of the disfellowshiping offense category advanced a motion that the policy be maintained, the motion would, of course, fail also. But even the failure of the motion to retain the category would not result in the removal of that disfellowshiping category. Why not? Because the policy was that some motion had to *carry* before any change would be made in previous policy. In one of the first of these instances of such a divided vote, Milton Henschel had expressed the view that, where there was no two-thirds majority, then "status quo should prevail," nothing should change. It was quite uncommon in these cases for any member to change over on his vote and so a stalemate usually resulted.

That meant that the Witness taking the particular action or having the particular employment involved would still be subject to disfellowshiping, *even though a majority of the Body had made clear that he or she should not be!*

On more than one occasion when a sizeable minority or even a majority (though not two-thirds) felt that a matter should not be a disfellowshiping offense, I voiced my feelings that our position was unreasonable, even incomprehensible. How could we let things go on as before, with people being disfellowshiped for such things, when right within the Governing Body there were several of us, sometimes a majority, who felt that the action involved did not merit such severe judgment? How would the brothers and sisters feel to know that this was the case and yet they were being disfellowshiped?[5]

To illustrate, if five congregational Elders forming a "judicial committee" were to hear a case and three of the five did not believe that the person's action or conduct called for disfellowshiping, would the

---

5   The secret nature of Governing Body sessions, of course, allows little likelihood for any to come to know this. The "Minutes" of the meetings are never opened for other Witnesses to see them.

fact that they were only a three-fifths majority and not a two-thirds majority make their position invalid?[6] Would the person then be disfellowshiped? Surely not. How could we, then, let a mere rule of voting cause a traditional stand on disfellowshiping to prevail when most of the Body members felt otherwise? Should we not at least take the position that, *in all disfellowshiping matters*, when even a considerable minority (and especially a majority, however small) felt that there were not sufficient grounds for disfellowshiping, then no disfellowshiping ruling should be sustained?

These questions put to the Body brought no response, but again and again in such cases the previously-established traditional policy was kept in force, and this was done as a matter of course, as normal. The effect on people's lives somehow did not carry enough weight to make the members feel moved to set aside their "standard" policy in such cases. Somewhere in the past history of the organization a disfellowshiping policy had been formulated (often the product of one man's thinking, a man all too often pathetically isolated from the circumstances being dealt with) and that policy had been put into effect; a rule had been adopted and that rule controlled unless a two-thirds majority could overturn it.

Perhaps no other case so well illustrates this strange approach as does that involving the issue of alternative service.

"Alternative service" describes civil service offered by a government as an alternative for those who have conscientious objections to participation in military service. Quite a number of enlightened countries offer this alternative to such persons among their citizens.

The official position of the Watch Tower Society, developed during the Second World War, is that if one of Jehovah's Witnesses accepts such alternative service he has "compromised," has broken integrity with God. The reasoning behind this is that because this service is a "substitute" it therefore takes the place of what it substitutes for and (so the reasoning apparently goes) comes to stand for the same thing. Since it is offered in place of military service and since military service involves (potentially at least) the shedding of blood, then anyone accepting the substitute becomes "bloodguilty." This remarkable policy developed before the Governing Body became a reality and was evidently decided upon by Fred Franz and Nathan Knorr during the period when they produced all major policy decisions.

---

6   Three out of five is only 60%, not 66⅔% as in a two-thirds majority.

In obedience to this policy, over the years literally thousands of Jehovah's Witnesses in different countries around the world have gone to prison rather than accept provisions for alternative service. There are Witnesses in prison right now for this reason. Failure to adhere to the Society's policy would mean being viewed automatically as "disassociated" and being treated the same as if disfellowshiped.

In November 1977, a letter from a Witness in Belgium questioned the reasoning on which this policy was based. This led to the matter's being dealt with by the Governing Body, first on January 28, 1978, then on March 1, and again on September 26, October 11, October 18 and November 15. A worldwide survey was made and letters received from some ninety branch offices. A sizeable number indicated that the Witnesses in their respective countries had difficulty seeing where there was any Scriptural basis for the stand taken. Consider what took place in the Governing Body.

At the October 11, 1978, meeting, of thirteen members present, nine voted in favor of changing the traditional policy so that the decision to accept or reject alternative service would be left to the conscience of the individual, four did not vote for this. The result? Since there were then sixteen members in the Body and since nine was not two-thirds of sixteen, no change was made.

On November 15, all sixteen members were present and eleven voted for changing the policy so that the Witness who conscientiously felt he could accept such service would not be automatically categorized as unfaithful to God and disassociated from the congregation. This was a two-thirds majority. Was the change made?

No, for after a brief intermission, one of the Governing Body members announced that he had changed his mind. That destroyed the two-thirds majority. A subsequent vote taken, with fifteen members present, showed nine favoring a change, five against and one abstention.[7]

Even though in all of these votes a clear majority of the Governing Body favored removing the existing policy, that policy remained in force and as a result Witness men were still expected to risk imprisonment rather than accept alternative service—even though they conscientiously felt such was proper in God's sight. Incredible as it may seem, this was the position taken, and most members of the Body

---

7 According to my records, those voting in favor were: John Booth, Ewart Chitty, Ray Franz, George Gangas, Leo Greenlees, Albert Schroeder, Grant Suiter, Lyman Swingle and Dan Sydlik. Those voting against were: Carey Barber, Fred Franz, Milton Henschel, William Jackson and Karl Klein. Ted Jaracz abstained.

seemed to accept it all as nothing to be disturbed about. They were, after all, simply following the rules in force.

In all these controversial cases, the "disfellowshiping offense" was not something clearly identified in Scripture as sinful. It was purely the result of organizational policy. Once published, that policy became fixed on the worldwide brotherhood for them to bear, along with the consequences of the policy. Is it wrong in such circumstances to feel that Jesus' words apply: "They tie up heavy loads and put them on men's shoulders, but they themselves are not willing to lift a finger to move them"?[8] I leave that to the reader to decide. I only know what my conscience told me and the stand I felt compelled to take.

Nonetheless, I feel that the Governing Body members generally believed they were doing the right thing. What thinking could cause them to hold to a disfellowshiping stand in the face of objection from a sizeable minority or possibly from half or more of their fellow members?

In one case where prolonged discussion had made such a situation predictable, Ted Jaracz voiced a view that may well reflect the thinking of others. Of Slavic descent (Polish) like Dan Sydlik, Jaracz was different both in build and in temperament. Whereas Sydlik often was moved by a "gut" feeling as to the rightness or wrongness of an issue, Jaracz was of a more dispassionate nature. In this particular session he acknowledged that 'the existing policy might work a measure of hardship on some individuals in the particular situation being discussed' and said, "It is not that we don't feel for them in the matter, but we have to always keep in mind that we are not dealing with just two or three persons—we have a large, worldwide organization to keep in view and we have to think of the effect on that worldwide organization."[9]

This view, that what is good for the organization is what is good for the people in it, and that the interests of the individual are, in effect "expendable" when the interests of the large organization appear to require it, seemed to be accepted as a valid position by many members.

Additionally, some might advance the argument that any softening of position could "open the way" to a floodtide of wrongdoing. If one

8 Matthew 23:4, NIV.
9 These points may also have been substantially what Milton Henschel meant when he frequently commented on the need to "be practical" in our approach to such matters, for in voting his position and that of Ted Jaracz regularly coincided.

or more extreme examples of bad conduct were known that could be related to the issue under discussion, these were presented as strong evidence of the potential danger. The ominous spectre of such danger was usually brought forth in these cases where, even before a motion had been offered, it was fairly evident that a considerable number of the Body inclined toward a change. In one such case, Milton Henschel seriously urged caution, making the point that, "If we let the brothers do this, there is no telling how far they will go."

I believe that he, and others who made the same point on other occasions, doubtless felt sincerely that it was necessary to hold firmly to certain long-time policies in order to 'keep people in line,' to hold them within a protective "fence" so that they would not stray off.

If the protective "fence" of these policies had actually been one plainly outlined in God's Word, I would have had to agree and would gladly have done so. But so often that was not the case, and that it was not was clearly indicated by the fact the elders (often men on Branch Committees) who had written in about the subject had found nothing in Scripture dealing with the matter, and by the fact the Body itself had not found anything either. Thus the members had to resort to their own reasoning in a prolonged discussion, in many respects, a debate.

On the occasion last mentioned, following Milton Henschel's expression, my comment was that I did not believe that it was up to *us* to "let" the brothers do anything. Rather, I believed that God is the One who "lets" them do certain things, either because his Word approves it or because it is silent on the matter, and that He is the One that prohibits, when his Word clearly condemns the action, either explicitly or by clear principle. That I did not believe that as imperfect, error-prone men we were ever authorized by God to decide what should be allowed or disallowed for others. My question before the Body was, "When the matter is not clear in Scripture, why should we try to play God? We do so poorly at it. Why not let Him be the Judge of these people in such cases?" I repeated that view on other occasions when the same line of argument was being advanced, but I do not feel that the majority saw it in that light and their decisions indicated that they did not.

To paint a foreboding picture of potential unrestrained wrongdoing on the part of the brothers simply because we, as a Governing Body, removed some existing regulation, appealed to me as saying that we suspected our brothers of lacking true love of righteousness, of inwardly *wanting* to sin and being held in check only by organizational regulations.

An article published some years earlier in the Society's magazine *Awake!* came to mind. It described a police strike in Montreal, Canada, and showed that the absence of the police force for a day or so led to all kinds of lawless deeds by usually law-abiding citizens.

The *Awake!* article pointed out that genuine Christians did not have to be subject to law enforcement in order to act in a lawful manner.[10]

Why, then, I wondered, was the position taken by the Governing Body that it was dangerous to remove a traditional regulation, in the belief that this could "open the way" for widespread immorality and misconduct on the part of the brothers? What did that say about our attitude toward, and our confidence in, those brothers? How different did we feel that these brothers were from those individuals who violated laws during the police strike in Montreal, and how deep and genuine did we believe their love of righteousness really was? At times it seemed that the prevailing sentiment within the Body was, trust no one but ourselves. That, too, did not seem to reflect commendable modesty to me.

Another clue to the thinking in such cases was the emphasis often placed on the long-standing nature of a particular policy. Hence, through the years thousands had abided by the Society's policy even though it created a severe burden for them, perhaps leading to imprisonment or other suffering. To change now, it was argued, might make such ones feel that what they had undergone had been unnecessary and, whereas they had found personal satisfaction in suffering in such way, viewing it as 'suffering for righteousness sake,' now they might feel disillusioned, possibly even feel it unfair that they had endured a form of martyrdom while others now could escape such.

I found that hard to equate with the spirit the Scriptures encourage. It seemed that such ones ought instead to rejoice in knowing that others would not be called upon to undergo that burden in order to stay in good standing in the organization. If, as an illustration, a person had lost a farm due to heavy taxation, should he not rejoice on behalf of friends, faced with a similar loss, if he learned that the heavy tax was lifted? Should not a miner suffering with a lung ailment be happy if conditions in mines improved, even though he could no longer benefit from this? It seemed that a genuine Christian would.

10 See *Awake!*, December 8, 1969, pp. 21–23.

The attitude over which some Body members expressed grave concern appeared to reflect more the spirit of the men in Jesus' account of the vineyard, those men who had endured the heat and hard work over long hours and who felt it unfair that the eleventh-hour workers did not have to undergo such to receive the same recompense they did. Or, that of the prodigal son's older brother who said to his father, "Here it is so many years I have slaved for you and *never once did I transgress your commandments*," and who felt it unfair that his younger brother should not have to do the same to gain his father's approval.[11] Again, it seemed to me that to expect brothers to be anything but happy if others did not have to suffer what they had suffered would be to impute wrong motives to them. It appeared to me that we needed to ask ourselves how much of the concern expressed might not be traceable to a concern over the Governing Body's own "image," its credibility, and its hold on people's confidence, being affected by fear that admitting error could weaken this.

The results that came out of these divided decisions were by no means inconsequential. Failure to conform to a Governing Body decision once published or made known could, and did, bring disfellowshiping, being cut off from congregation, family and friends. To conform, on the other hand, might require giving up a certain employment, sometimes when jobs were scarce and costs of caring for a family were great. It could mean taking a stand against a marriage partner's wishes, a stand that could, and sometimes did, lead to divorce, the breaking up of marriage, home and family, separating children from father and mother. It could mean feeling compelled to refuse to obey a certain law and then being arrested and sent away from family and home to a place of imprisonment. It could, in fact, mean loss of life itself, or what can be even more difficult to bear, to see loved ones lost in death.

To illustrate the difficulties that might arise even when a change *was made* in some earlier ruling, consider the organizational position taken regarding hemophiliacs and the use of blood fractions (generally platelets or Factor VIII) to control against fatal bleeding.

For many years inquiries sent by hemophiliacs to the headquarters organization (or its Branch Offices) received the reply that to accept such blood fraction *one time* could be viewed as not objectionable, as, in effect, "medication." But to do so *more than once* would constitute

11 Matthew 20:1–15; Luke 15:25–32.

a "feeding" on such blood fraction and therefore be considered a violation of the Scriptural injunction against eating blood.[12]

Years later, this ruling changed. Those staff members who worked at answering correspondence knew that in the past they had sent out letters to the contrary and that hemophiliacs who had taken their "one time" injection were still under the impression that to do so again would be counted as a violation of Scripture. They could bleed to death because of holding to such a stand.

The administration was not in favor of publishing the new position in print since the old position had never been put in print but only conveyed to the particular individuals inquiring. To publish something would require first explaining what the old position had been and then explaining that it was now obsolete. This did not seem desirable. So the staff workers made a diligent search through their files to try to find the names and addresses of all such persons and another letter was sent to each advising of the change. The staff workers felt better about this.

Then they realized that many of the inquiries had come in by phone and that they had no record of such phone calls and absolutely no way of determining who such inquiring hemophiliacs were. Whether, in the interim between the old ruling and the new, some had died, they did not know; whether some whom they had not been able to contact would yet die because of holding to the old ruling, they did not know. They only knew that they had followed instructions, being loyally obedient to their superiors in the organization.

Listening to some of the arguments presented in the Governing Body sessions brought to mind the many cases that Jehovah's Witnesses had carried before the Supreme Court of the United States. Opposing lawyers had used arguments similar in many respects to those used on the Governing Body. Such lawyers stressed *potential* dangers. They claimed that there was a strong danger that door-to-door visitation might become a serious nuisance or a blind for thievery and other criminal activity and that this justified placing restrictions on the Witnesses' freedom to carry on this activity. They said that to allow the Witnesses freedom to carry on their public activity or to give talks in parks in certain communities could lead to mob violence, due to the adverse and hostile attitude of the community as a whole, and therefore that restrictions should be placed. They argued that to allow the Witnesses

12 Texts referred to included Genesis 9:3, 4; Leviticus 17:10–12; Acts 15:28, 29.

to express their views on such subjects as saluting the flag, or their attitude toward worldly governments as being "part of the Devil's organization," could be detrimental to the interests of the larger community, could tend to create widespread disloyalty, hence be seditious; restrictions were necessary.

The Supreme Court justices in many cases showed remarkable insight and clarity of mind in cutting through such arguments, demonstrating them to be specious. They did not agree that the rights of the individual or of a small unpopular minority could properly be curtailed just because the fear of *possible* or imagined danger or the claimed interests of the larger majority made this appear desirable. They held that before any rightful restriction could be applied limiting such freedoms, the danger must be more than a "fear," something *presumed* to be likely to develop. It must be proven a *"clear* and *present* danger," one actually existing.[13]

How many favorable decisions would the Witnesses have received if the Supreme Court justices had not shown such judicious wisdom, such ability to see where the real issue lay, such concern for the individual? Their decisions were applauded in the Society's publications. Sadly, however, their high standards of judgment and their approach to emotionally charged issues often appeared to be on a higher level than that manifested in many Governing Body sessions. The expression of one Supreme Court justice in a particular Witness case comes to mind. He stated:

"The case is made difficult not because the principles of its decision are obscure but because the flag involved is our own. Nevertheless, we apply the limitations of the Constitution with no fear that freedom to be intelligently and spiritually diverse or even contrary will disintegrate the social organization. . . .freedom to differ is not limited to things that do not matter much. That would be a mere shadow of freedom. The test of its substance is the right to differ as to things that touch the heart of the existing order."[14]

The confidence that the justice expressed in the 'existing social order' and the freedoms it espoused seemed considerably greater than the confidence expressed by some Governing Body members in their fellow Witnesses and the effect their freedom of conscience, if exercised, could have on the existing "Theocratic order." If the Supreme Court justices had reasoned as some of the Governing Body members reasoned, the Witnesses would likely have lost case after case.

---

13 See the Society's publication *Defending and Legally Establishing the Good News*, p. 58.
14 Ibid., p. 62.

Court decisions are judged by history. The Scriptural declaration that, on a day certain to come, each Christian elder will "render an account" to the Supreme Judge regarding his dealings with, and treatment of, God's sheep, should surely give those exercising great authority among Christians a serious reason for weighing carefully what they do.[15]

Because of the power the organization exercises over its members through its decisions, and because of the enormous effect that these can have on people's lives, it seems proper here to review what I consider one of the greatest examples of inconsistency experienced in my nine years on that Body. It still seems difficult to believe that men who voiced such strong concern for "an uncompromising stand," "keeping the organization clean," avoiding any taint of "worldliness," could simultaneously gloss over a circumstance that can only be described as shocking. You may judge the appropriateness of that term by what follows.

15 Hebrews 13:17.

6

DOUBLE STANDARDS

*"The doctors of the law and the Pharisees sit
in the chair of Moses; therefore do what they
tell you; pay attention to their words. But do
not follow their practice; for they say one thing
and do another."*
—Matthew 23:2, 3, *New English Bible.*

MANY worthwhile and helpful discussions can be found in the
publications of the Watch Tower Society. Frequently articles
supply support for belief in a Creator, encourage wholesome family
life, exhort to honesty, stress the importance of humility and other
virtues, doing this on the basis of Scripture. Other articles speak out
strongly against religious deception and hypocrisy. Consider, for example, the portion of an article published in the *Watchtower* magazine
reproduced on the following page.

The Watch Tower Society has, throughout its entire history, never
been guilty of "condoning and 'whitewashing' the wrongdoing and
violation of God's righteous standards and way" on the part of the
various religious organizations and their leaders. The Watch Tower
publications have taken the lead in boldly publicizing worldwide any
misconduct or evidence of hypocrisy within these organizations. They
have pointed out the parallel between the deceptiveness of such religious leaders and the Pharisees of Jesus' day. They have made clear
their own declared position of strict adherence to righteous standards,
moral integrity and upright and honest dealings with all.

It is precisely this that made so disturbing certain information that
came to light at the same time the issue of alternative service was
being debated within the Governing Body of Jehovah's Witnesses.

Can You Be True to God,
YET HIDE THE FACTS?

WHAT results when a lie is let go unchallenged? Does not silence help the lie to pass as truth, to have freer sway to influence many, perhaps to their serious harm?

What happens when misconduct and immorality are allowed to go unexposed and uncondemned? Is this not like covering over an infection without any effort to cure it and keep it from spreading?

When persons are in great danger from a source that they do not suspect or are being misled by those they consider their friends, is it an unkindness to warn them? They may prefer not to believe the warning. They may even resent it. But does that free one from the moral responsibility to give that warning?

If you are among those seeking to be faithful to God, the issues these questions raise are vital for you today. Why? Because God's servants in every period of his-

**WOULD YOU RATHER HAVE
THE TRUTH COVERED OVER . . . ?**

THE WATCHTOWER — JANUARY 15, 1974

tory have had to face up to the challenge these issues present. They have had to expose falsehood and wrongdoing and warn people of dangers and deception— not just in a general way, but in a specific way, in the interest of pure worship. It would have been far easier to keep silent or say only what people wanted to hear. But faithfulness to God and love of neighbor moved them to speak. They realized that "better is a revealed reproof than a concealed love."—Prov. 27:5.

THE CONTINUING PATTERN

Consider the situation in ancient Israel and the example that God's prophets then set. Wrongdoing became rampant in that nation. Dishonesty, violence, immorality and hypocrisy disgraced the name of the God whom the Israelites claimed to worship. Did the people welcome divine correction? To the contrary, the Bible shows that they said this to God's prophets:

" 'You must not see,' and to the ones having [inspired] visions, 'You must not envision for us any straightforward things. Speak to us smooth things; envision deceptive things. Turn aside from the way; deviate from the path.' "—Isa. 30:9-11.

The majority of the religious leaders sought popularity by doing just that, condoning and "whitewashing" the wrongdoing and violation of God's righteous standards and ways. But God's instructions to his true prophets are exemplified by what he said to the prophet Ezekiel:

"Now as regards you, O son of man, a watchman is what I have made you to

**. . . OR DO YOU
WANT TO KNOW
THE FACTS?**

35

The information came from Mexico. As startling as the information itself was, what I found far more disquieting was the stark contrast it revealed between the organizational position adopted toward that country as compared with that adopted in another country—the East African country of Malawi (formerly Nyasaland).

To appreciate this it is important to know certain background. Beginning in 1964, Jehovah's Witnesses in Malawi began to experience persecution and violence on a scale rarely equalled in modern times. Successive waves of vicious countrywide attacks and brutality by savage mobs swept over them in 1964, 1967, 1972 and again in 1975. In the first attack, 1,081 Malawian families saw their little homes burned or otherwise demolished, 588 fields of crops destroyed. In the 1967 attacks Witnesses reported the rapings of more than one thousand of their women, one mother being sexually violated by six different men, her thirteen-year-old daughter by three men. At least forty of the women were reported to have suffered miscarriages due to this. In each wave of violence, beatings, torture and even murder went virtually unchecked by the authorities and reached such intensity that thousands of families fled their homes and fields to neighboring countries. In 1972 authoritative estimates were that 8,975 fled to Zambia, 11,600 to Mozambique. When violence subsided, in time the families filtered back to their homeland. Then a new wave forced them to flee again. Adding to the tragedy of all this were the reports coming out of the camps of small children dying because of lack of medicine and medical treatment.[1]

What was the issue around which this recurrent storm of violence revolved? It was the refusal of the Witnesses to purchase a party card of the ruling political party. Malawi is a one-party state, ruled by the Malawi Congress Party through its head, Dr. H. Kamuzu Banda, who is "president for life" of the country. Jehovah's Witnesses who inquired were informed by the Society's Branch Office that to buy such a party card would be a violation of their Christian neutrality, a compromise, hence, unfaithfulness to God. The Branch position was upheld by the world headquarters organization and presented in detail in the Watch Tower Society's publications. The vast majority of Malawian Witnesses held firm to that position even though at enormous cost to themselves.

1 Details of these attacks and the conditions in the refugee camps are found in the *1965 Yearbook of Jehovah's Witnesses*, p. 171; *Awake!* magazine, February 8, 1968, pp. 16–22; the *Watchtower*, February 1, 1968, pp. 71–79; *Awake!*, December 8, 1972, pp. 9–28; December 8, 1975, pp. 3–13.

The brutality that was practiced upon defenseless people in Malawi can never be justified. There is no question in my mind about that. The government and party officials were determined to attain a state of total conformity to their policy that all persons should possess a party card; it was viewed as tangible evidence of loyalty to the governmental structure. The methods used to attain that goal were depraved, criminal.

There is, however, a serious question in my mind about the position taken by the Branch Office and supported by the central headquarters in Brooklyn. There are a number of reasons for such question.

In 1975 I was assigned to write material on the latest campaign of terror being carried on against the Malawian Witnesses. In explaining why Jehovah's Witnesses viewed the purchase of the party card so seriously, I presented information that had been published earlier, tracing a parallel between their stand and that of Christians in early centuries who refused to put a pinch of incense on an altar as a sacrifice to the "genius" of the Roman emperor.[2] At the time of doing so, I felt a sense of uncertainty—was the parallel *completely true*? There was no question but that the placing of the incense on the altar was viewed as an act of worship. Was purchasing a party card just as clearly an act of *worship*? I could not really see any strong argument in that direction. Was it, then, a violation of Christian neutrality, a breaking of integrity with God?

I cannot say that my thinking on the matter fully crystallized at that time, nor am I dogmatic on the point today. But the following thoughts came to mind, making me wonder how solid a basis the organization, of whose Governing Body I was now a member, had for taking a positive, unbending position of condemnation of such card purchase as an act of unfaithfulness to God:

The issue hinged on the fact that the card was a "political" card representing membership in a "political" party. To many, and particularly to Jehovah's Witnesses, the word "political" is viewed as describing something inherently bad. Corrupt politicians have, over the centuries, contributed toward the unsavory connotation the term often carries today. The same might be said, however, of such terms as "pious," which frequently calls up visions of sanctimoniousness and feigned holiness due to the hypocrisy of some religious persons. Yet the term "pious" actually relates to dutiful reverence and earnest de-

---

2 This argument was presented in the *Awake!* magazine of December 8, 1972, p. 20. The articles I wrote appeared in the December 8, 1975, issue of same publication.

votion to God; that is its *basic* meaning. Similarly, the word "political" carries this basic definition:

> "Having a fixed or regular system or administration of government; relating to civil government and its administration; concerned in state affairs or national measures; pertaining to a nation or state, or to nations or states, as distinguished from *civil* or *municipal*; treating of politics or government; as, *political* parties."[3]

I knew that the word "political" as well as "politics" came from the Greek word *polis* meaning simply a *city*. In Greek *politēs* meant a "citizen" (this English word being drawn from the Latin term for "city"), and the adjective *politikos* (from which our English "political" is derived) meant "of the citizens, of the state." The English language received these terms through Latin and the Latin term *politia* means simply "citizenship, government, administration." Such words as "police," and "policy" all derive from the same source.

Obviously, all government is *political* in this fundamental sense of the word. Every government on earth is a political entity; every people organized under a particular form of government form a "polity" (from Greek *politeia*). To be a *citizen* of any country is to be a *member* of such a political state, enjoying the benefits and bearing the responsibilities this membership brings. The *extent* to which one may submit to the demands of such a political state may vary; but the membership is still a fact.

It is of such political states and their rulers that the apostle Paul writes at Romans chapter thirteen, exhorting Christians to be submissive to these as unto "God's servant" or "minister." True, political activity may become corrupt—and there is no question but that the political state of Rome became extremely corrupt—yet that of itself does not make everything political inherently evil. Nor does it make national citizenship—membership in a political state or nation—something inherently bad. Political parties in their competition for power are largely responsible for the added, subordinate (not the *basic* or fundamental) meaning which the word "politics" may have, that of "the plotting or scheming of those seeking personal power, glory, position, or the like." This *is* evil, but not because everything related to political activity is evil, for the absence of political activity is, in its secular sense, the absence of government.

Which leads to the second reason for my questioning. I can under-

---

3 *New Webster's Dictionary*, Deluxe Encyclopedic Edition.

stand why a person could conscientiously desire to be separate from the political strife and fierce competition that generally characterize *party* politics. The factors that made me think seriously about the situation in Malawi, however, was that it was, and is, a *one-party state*. The Malawi Congress Party is the country's ruling party with no other parties allowed. It thus becomes, in a *de facto* sense, equivalent to the government itself, the "superior authority." If a person could be a citizen, and hence a member of the national political community, without violating integrity to God, where was the evidence to show that being submissive to the government's insistence (expressed from the head of state on down) that *everyone* purchase a card of the ruling party would constitute such a violation of integrity to God? I wondered then, and I still wonder, how major is the difference?

Most of all I ask myself whether, if found in a similar circumstance in Bible times, Abraham, Daniel, Jesus and his apostles, or early Christians, would have viewed submission to such government demands in the way the organization has presented it? Granted, there was no actual *law* passed in Malawi requiring the purchase of the card, but would such a technicality have been viewed by Christ Jesus as crucial in the face of the statements made nationwide by the ruling authorities?[4] How would Christians of the first century have viewed it in the light of the apostle's exhortation, "Render to all their dues, to him who calls for the tax, the tax; for him who calls for the tribute, the tribute; to him who calls for fear, such fear; to him who calls for honor, such honor"?[5]

To submit to such demands, then as now, would certainly be condemned by some as "compromise," a "caving in" to the demands of the political authorities. But I am sure that in Jesus' day there were many devout Jews who felt that to accede to the demands of a military officer of the hated Roman Empire that one carry certain baggage for a mile would be just as detestable; many would have suffered punishment and mistreatment rather than submit. Yet Jesus said to submit and to go, not just one mile, but two![6] To many of his listeners this counsel was doubtless repugnant, smacking of craven surrender instead of unbending adherence to a position of no collaboration with alien, Gentile powers.

Of one thing I eventually became certain and that was that I would

---

4 Compare Matthew 17:24–27, where Jesus states that a certain tax did not rightly apply to him, but he nevertheless tells Peter to pay it so as 'not to offend the authorities.'

5 Romans 13:7.

6 Matthew 5:41.

want to be very confident that the position adopted was solidly founded on God's Word, and not on mere human reasonings, before I could think of advocating it or promulgating it, particularly in view of the grave consequences it produced. I no longer felt confident that the Scriptures did give such *clear* and *unequivocal* support to the policy taken toward the situation in Malawi. I could see how one might feel impelled by conscience to refuse to purchase such a card and, if that were the case, then one *should* refuse, in harmony with the apostle's counsel at Romans, chapter fourteen, verses 1 to 3 and verse 23.[7] But I could not see the basis for anyone's imposing his conscience on another in this matter, nor of presenting such position as a rigid standard to be adhered to by others, particularly without greater support from Scripture and fact.

Against such background of circumstances relating to Malawi consider now the information that came to light during the Governing Body's discussion of the alternative service issue. Many of the statements made by members arguing this issue reflected the strict, unyielding attitude encouraged on the part of the Malawian Witnesses. Statements such as these were made:

> "Even if there is the slightest suggestion of compromise, or a doubt, we should not do it."
>
> "There must be no compromise. . . . Again, it needs to be made clear that a stand of neutrality, as 'no part of the world,' keeping clear of those arms of the world—religion, politics and the military—supporting them neither directly nor indirectly, is the stand that will be blessed by Jehovah. We want no grey areas, we want to know exactly where we stand as non-compromising Christians."[8]
>
> ". . . doing civilian work in lieu of military duty is . . . a tacit or implied acknowledgement of one's obligation to Caesar's war machine. . . . A Christian therefore cannot be required to support the military establishment either directly or indirectly."[9]
>
> "For one of Jehovah's Witnesses to tell a judge that he is willing to accept

---

7   These verses say: "Welcome the man having weaknesses in his faith, but not to make decisions on inward questionings. One man has faith to eat everything, but the man who is weak eats vegetables. Let the one eating not look down on the one not eating, and let the one not eating not judge the one eating, for God has welcomed that one." "But if he has doubts, he is already condemned if he eats, because he does not eat out of faith. Indeed, everything that is not out of faith is sin."

8   From the memorandum submitted by Governing Body member Lloyd Barry.

9   From the memorandum by Governing Body member Karl Klein.

work in a hospital or similar work would be making a 'deal' with the judge, and he would be breaking his integrity with God."[10]

"To accept the alternative civil service is a form of moral support to the entire arrangement."[11]

"We should have a united stand all over the world. We should be decisive in this matter. . . . If we were to allow the brothers this latitude we would have problems. . . .the brothers need to have their consciences educated."[12]

"If we yield to Caesar then there is no witness given."[13]

"Those who accept this substitute service are taking the easy way out."[14]

What I find amazing is that at the same time these strong, unyielding statements were made those making them were aware of the situation in Mexico. When I supplied each member of the Governing Body with a copy of the survey of Branch Committee reports on alternative service, I included material sent in by the Branch Committee of Mexico. It included this portion dealing with the "Identity Cartilla for Military Service" ("cartilla" means a certificate):

The "Identity Cartilla for Military Service" should be obtained by carrying out military service during one year. Those who have a Cartilla have the obligation to present themselves when the nation calls them, be it by movilization of forces or at least by effecting an act of presence. (Articles 136 to 139, page 6)

However, although the law prohibits the military or members of the Draft Offices to make out "Cartillas" by illegal means, such as payment, the great majority of the officials violate these laws. (Articles 50 and 51, page 21; Article 3, page 29; Instructive number 1, of September 16, 1977, page 2, paragraphs 3 and 4)

Almost any person, under any pretext, can avoid military service and pay an official to note down supposed attendances for the weekly instruction, (giving appearance of regular attendance) or paying at the same time so that

10 From statements made by Governing Body member Fred Franz and spelled out in a letter by William Jackson to Paul Trask.
11 From the Denmark Branch Committee letter, quoted in Lloyd Barry's memorandum.
12 From statements made by member Ted Jaracz.
13 From statement made by member Carey Barber.
14 From statement made by member Fred Franz.

the document is given to them correctly legalized. In Mexico this is very
common. The Mexican government is trying to stop the officials making
out documents of military service for persons not having rendered such
service, when there is no valid justification according to law. Recently
a general said, when the President of the Republic, Licenciado Jose Lopez
Portillo, was at the ceremony of pledging allegiance to the flag, on May
5, 1978, before close to 100,000 young men, draftees, that "the army will
not tolerate illegal operations to obtain Military Service 'Cartilla.'" The
general said: "we have made ourselves responsible, so that in a brief
period of time, the last protuberances of unlawfulness in the service will
be erradicated and we will succeed in that all young men can go to the
Municipal Draft Boards to obtain their 'Cartillas'." (See El Heraldo,
May 6, 1978)

What was the position of Jehovah's Witnesses as to such "illegal
operations" in connection with this law? The Branch Committee's letter goes on to say:

Young publishers in Mexico have had no difficulty in relation to
military service. Although the laws on military service are very specific,
generally they are not enforced strictly. If a publisher, upon arriving at
military age, does not present himself voluntarily before a draft board,
they do not call him to do so. On the other hand, those who have their
"cartilla" and are in one of the reserves have never been called. They only
have to go in order to have their "cartilla" stamped when they transfer
from one reserve to the other, but this does not involve any ceremony,
but only presenting themselves in an office having to do with the stamping
of the "cartilla."

The "cartilla" has become a document of identification. It is used
as identification when one requests employment, although it is not indispensable.

In order to obtain a passport, this document is indispensable. One cannot

leave the country without the "cartilla" unless a special permit is obtained

from the military authorities. Publishers who wish to obtain a "cartilla"

go to one of the Draft Boards, to register to receive immediately their

"cartilla" but of course this is not complete, that is, it is not legalized.

Then in order to legalize it they go to someone they know with influence or

directly to an official. For this they have to pay a certain amount of money

(according to what may be asked). In this way the publishers obtain their

"cartilla" or the majority of them that have it.

Put briefly, in Mexico men of draft age are required to undergo a specified period of military training during a period of one year. Upon registration the registrant receives a certificate or "cartilla" with places for noting down attendance at weekly military instruction classes. It is illegal and punishable for any official to fill in this attendance record if the registrant has not actually attended. But officials can be bribed to do so and many men in Mexico do this. According to the Branch Office Committee this is also a common practice among Jehovah's Witnesses in Mexico. Why? Note what the Branch statement goes on to say:

The position of the brothers in Mexico related to this matter was

considered years ago by the Society and we have information that we

have followed since then when the brothers have come to the Society

to inquire on this matter. (See the enclosed photostatic copy.)

What was the information provided by the Society that the Branch Office in Mexico had been following for years? How was it supplied? How did the information provided compare with the position taken in Malawi and with the strong, unbending statements made by Governing Body members against even "the slightest suggestion of compromise," against any form of "moral support," either "directly or indirectly," of the military establishment?

I made a trip to Mexico within a few days of the November 15, 1978, Governing Body session which had resulted in a stalemate on the alternative service issue. I was assigned to visit the Mexico Branch

Office as well as those of several Central American countries. During my meeting with the Mexico Branch Committee they brought up the practice described in their report. They said that the terrible persecution endured by Jehovah's Witnesses in Malawi due to their refusal to buy a party card had caused many Witnesses in Mexico to feel disturbed in their conscience. They made clear, however, that their counsel to the Mexican Witnesses was fully in accord with the counsel the Branch Office had received from the world headquarters. What was that counsel? It may be difficult for some to believe that the counsel given was actually given, but this is the evidence presented by the Branch Committee. First comes this letter:

February 4, 1960   No. 123

N. H. Knorr
124 Columbia Heights
Brooklyn 1, New York

Dear Brother Knorr:

We have two questions that we would like the Society's policy on. First we have a case where the father of the girl is congregation servant. The girl is married and her husband as well as she were publishers and living with the father who is congregation servant. The son-in-law is disfellowshiped because he had another woman. Over a period of some years this son-in-law raises two families — one by his legal wife and sister in the truth and lives with her in the home of his father-in-law who is congregation servant and at the same time has his other woman and raises a family by her. Of course he is disfellowshiped all this time. Because of the father-in-law of this wicked man permitting him to live with his daughter in his own house has caused much confusion and dissention in the congregation until the number of publishers has dropped over the years and the congregation (unit) is in a very bad condition. The question is, does the daughter have the right to live with this man? He is her legal husband it is true but at the same time retains another family. Is the father-in-law doing right to permit this man to live with his daughter (a sister) in his house? We would like the Society's policy in such a case so we can handle this case.

Another thing that has to be contended with here is the law to march as part of the military training program. After "marching" for 1 year you get a card showing you have marched your 1 year and this card is your basic document to secure a passport, driver's liscence and in fact many legal transactions. The brothers understand the Christian's position of neutrality with regard to such matters but many brothers pay money to certain officials and they arrange for their marching card. Is this action right? If a brother actually marches we apply the policy that they have comprimized and we will not appoint them as servants for at least 3 years. But here a brother who probably is a servant or circuit servant has his marching card which he uses now and then in such legal transactions but he has not marched. What is correct in this regard? It is and has been the custom amoung the brothers to pay this sum of money and secure their marching cards and many of them are now serving as circuit servants and congregation servants. Are they living a lie? Or is it just one of those things in this crookked system of things? Shall we pass it by or should something be done about it? There are so many irregularities in this country. A cop pulls you over for some traffic violation and works for his "mordida" or little bribe of 40 cents. Everyone knows he has no right to do it but they give him the 5 pesos in order to avoid going to the police station and be charged 50 pesos and waste much time. It is a habit here, common practice. Is the marching card the same? Your counsel on this will be appreciated.

With you serving Jehovah,

What you have just read is a copy of a letter from the Mexico Branch to the president of the Society, the second paragraph of which shows the question the Branch presented for answer on the paying of bribes for a falsified military document. (The copy is of the carbon copy retained by the Branch which, unlike the original, customarily did not bear a signature.)

What reply did their inquiry receive? The Society's answer came in a two-page letter dated June 2, 1960. The second page dealt with the military issue written about. This is the page of the letter the Branch Committee presented to me, containing the Society's counsel on their questions.

```
La Torre Del Vigia
Calzada Melchor Ocampo No. 71
Mexico 4, D.F.
Mexico

June 2, 1960 (157) Page Two
```

course as that described above would not be necessary. The major stumblingblock, namely, the man's adultery, would be removed. Consequently the matter will have to be presented very straight and unmistakenably to both the congregation servant and his daughter. The congregation servant will have to make the first move in the right direction in the interests of the congregation to which he by his course is a stumblingblock now if he refuses to eject the adulterous son-in-law and continues to furnish offense to the congregation, disturbing its unity and peace of heart and mind. If he chooses not to follow this course, then he must be removed from his position as congregation servant.

As to those who are relieved of military training by a money transaction with the officials who are involved therewith, this is on a par with what is done in other Latin American countries where brothers have paid for their relief through some military official in order to retain their freedom for theocratic activities. If members of the military establishment are willing to accept such an arrangement upon the payment of a fee then that is the responsibility of these representatives of the national organization. In such a case the money paid does not go to the military establishment, but is appropriated by the individual who undertakes the arrangement. If the consciences of certain brothers allow them to enter into such an arrangement for their continued freedom we have no objection. Of course, if they would get into any difficulties over their course of action then they would have to shoulder such difficulties themselves, and we could not offer them any assistance. But if the arrangement is current down there and is recognized by the inspectors who do not make any inquiries into the veracity of the matter then the matter can be passed by for the accruing advantages. Should a military emergency arise and confront these brothers with their marching card it would oblige them to make a decision by which they could not extricate themselves by a money payment and their mettle would be tested and they would have to demonstrate outright where they stand and prove that they are in favor of Christian neutrality in a determinative test.

Faithfully yours in the Kingdom ministry,

Watch Tower B & T Society
OF PENNSYLVANIA

Although the Branch's letter was directed to President Knorr, the reply, bearing the stamped corporation signature, was evidently written by Vice-President Fred Franz, who, as stated earlier, was regularly called upon by President Knorr to formulate policy on matters of this type. The language is typically that of the vice president.

The expressions this letter contains are worth noting. It would be worthwhile to take the time to go back and compare them with the earlier listed statements by Governing Body members arguing the alternative service issue, statements made then that neither minced words nor sought nicety of language but which were often blunt, even hard-hitting.

In this Society reply to the Mexico query, the word "bribe" is avoided, replaced by reference to "a money transaction," the "payment of a fee." Emphasis is placed on the fact that the money goes to an individual rather than to the "military establishment," apparently indicating that this somehow improves the moral character of the "transaction." The letter speaks of the arrangement being "current down there" and says that as long as inspectors do not inquire about the "veracity of matters" it can be "passed by" for the "accruing advantages." It ends with mention of maintaining integrity in some possible future "determinative test."

If this same message were put in the kind of language heard from Governing Body members in the sessions debating alternative service, I believe it would read more like the following:

"Paying bribes to corrupt officials is done by Jehovah's Witnesses in other Latin American countries. If the men of the war machine are willing to be bribed the risk is theirs. At least you are not paying the bribe to the actual war machine itself—only to a colonel or other officer who pockets the bribe for himself. If brothers' consciences will let them make a 'deal' with some official who is 'on the take,' we will not object. Of course, if there is trouble they should not look to us for help. Since everyone down there is doing it and inspectors make no issue about the faked documents, then you at the Branch Office can just look the other way too. If war comes that will be time enough to worry about facing up to the issue of neutrality.

Faithfully yours in the Kingdom ministry,"

It is not my intent to be sarcastic and I do not believe what is set out constitutes sarcasm. I believe it to be a fair presentation of the

Society's counsel to the Mexican Branch Office put in down-to-earth language, free from euphemisms—language more like that used in the Governing Body sessions mentioned.

One reason why this information is so personally shocking to me is that, at the very time the letter stating that the Society had "no objection" if Witnesses in Mexico, faced with a call to military training, chose to "extricate themselves by a money payment," there were scores of young men in the Dominican Republic spending precious years of their life in prison—because they refused the identical kind of training. Some, such as Leon Glass and his brother Enrique, were sentenced two or three times for their refusal, passing as much as a total of nine years of their young manhood in prison. The Society's president and vice president had visited the Dominican Republic during those years and visits had even been made to the prison where many of these men were detained. How the situation of these Dominican prisoners could be known and yet such a double standard be applied is incomprehensible to me.

Four years after that counsel was given to Mexico the first eruption of violent attacks against Jehovah's Witnesses in Malawi took place (1964) and the issue of paying for a party card arose. The position taken by the Malawi Branch Office was that to do so would be a violation of Christian neutrality, a compromise unworthy of a genuine Christian. The world headquarters knew that this was the position taken. The violence subsided after a while and then broke out again in 1967, so fiercely that thousands of Witnesses were driven into flight from their homeland. The reports of horrible atrocities in increasing number came flooding in to the world headquarters.

What effect did it have on them and on their consciences as regards the position taken in Mexico? In Malawi Witnesses were being beaten and tortured, women were being raped, homes and fields were being destroyed, and entire families were fleeing to other countries—determined to hold to the organization's stand that to pay for a party card would be a morally traitorous act. At the same time, in Mexico, Witness men were *bribing* military officials to complete a certificate falsely stating that they had fulfilled their military service obligations, and when they went to the Branch Office, the staff there followed the Society's counsel and said nothing to indicate in any way that this practice was inconsistent with organizational standards or the principles of God's Word. *Knowing this*, how were those in the position of highest authority in the organization affected? Consider:

Nine years after the Mexico Branch wrote their first letter they wrote a second letter, dated August 27, 1969, also addressed to President Knorr. This time they emphasized a particular point they felt had been overlooked. Set out is material from pages three and four of the letter provided me by the Branch Committee. I have underlined the main point the Branch focuses on.

        Question. During the branch meetings in June the matter was discussed which is presented on pages 34 and 35 of the "Aid to Answering." Due to the way the military question has been handled over the years here I brought the matter to the attention of some of the brothers there but since I thought I might not have some of the details of the matter in mind it was thought best to wait and write from here and then get an answer. After checking back in the files we have found a letter dated February 4, 1960, No. 123, in which the question was asked as to what to do because many were paying a sum of money to obtain the legal document given to those of draft age. However, it was not mentioned in the question that when this document is obtained it places the receiver in the first reserve subject to being called if and when an emergency should arise which the army in uniform could not handle. So our question is this: Does this change the policy set out in your letter of June 2, 1960 (157) Page Two which answered our letter mentioned above? Your letter said this: "As to those who are relieved of military training by a money transaction with the officials who are involved therewith, this is on a par with what is done in other Latin American countries where brothers have paid for their relief through some military official in order to retain their freedom for theocratic activities. If members of the military establishment are willing to accept such an arrangement upon the payment of a fee then that is the responsibility of these representatives of the national organization. In such a case the

Watch Tower Bible and Tract Society
Office of the President
124 Columbia Heights
Brooklyn, New York 11201

August 27, 1969   Page 4 , No. 182

money paid does not go to the military establishment, but is appropriated by the individual who undertakes the arrangement. If the consciences of certain brothers allow them to enter into such an arrangement for their continued freedom we have no objection. Of course, if they would get into any difficulties over their course of action then they would have to shoulder such difficulties themselves, and we could not offer them any assistance. But if the arrangement is current down there and is recognized by the inspectors who do not make any inquiries into the veracity of the matter then the matter can be passed by for the accruing advantages. Should a military emergency arise and confront these brothers with their marching card it would oblige them to make a decision by which they could not extricate themselves by a money payment and their mettle would be tested and they would have to demonstrate outright where they stand and prove that they are in favor of Christian neutrality in a determinative test." What has been quoted from your letter is what has been followed but it seems that there would be some modification in this when it is considered that these brothers are in the first reserves. Of course, it appears that Jehovah's blessing has been on his servants here because the work has progressed very well over the years and this even though the majority of the circuit and district servants and those in the Bethel family have followed this procedure. We would very much appreciate having some information from you on this matter if a change should be made or not. If a change is made and this procedure is not followed then the brothers could not obtain a passport but they can always attend an assembly in the country. If a change is made what will be the position of those in the first reserves? How should this be handled? We will await your answer on the matter.

The construction of our new building is progressing very well and we look forward to seeing it finished and in use to Jehovah's praise and to build up the brothers by the assemblies to be held there. Be assured of my love and best wishes.

Your brother and fellow servant,

The reply sent, dated September 5, 1969, bears the stamp of the New York Corporation but the symbol before the date indicates that it was written by the president through a secretary ("A" is the symbol for the president, "AG" is the symbol held by one of his secretaries). Keeping in mind that the world headquarters was fully informed of the horrible suffering Jehovah's Witnesses in Malawi had already undergone in 1964 and in 1967 because they steadfastly refused to pay for the party card being pushed by the government of their country, consider the reply of September 5, 1969, sent to the Mexico Branch's inquiry.

TELEPHONE (212) 625-1240   WATCHTOWER   CABLE WATCHTOWER
BIBLE AND TRACT SOCIETY OF NEW YORK, INC.
117 ADAMS STREET, BROOKLYN, NEW YORK 11201, U.S.A.

A/AG September 5, 1969

Mexico Branch

Dear Brothers:

We have your letter of August 27 (182) in which you ask a question about brothers who had registered in Mexico and are now in the first reserves.

The letter that you quoted of February 4, 1960 (123) covers the whole matter. There is nothing more to be said. The responsibility will be upon these individuals if they are ever called up as to what they are going to do and that is soon enough to take any action. In the meantime these brothers who have registered and who have paid a fee are free to go ahead in the service. Not that we are giving our approval in this matter, but it is their conscience, not ours, that has allowed them to take the course of action that they have taken. If their conscience allows them to do what they have done and they are not compromising in any way then you just lay the

matter on the shelf. There is no reason for you to answer any
questions or give comment to individuals, nor to enter into a
discussion. Someday we may have to face the issue and they
may have to make a decision, as the letter points out, and
then it will be for them to decide. We cannot decide the lives
of everyone in the world. If the consciences of these persons
allowed them to do what they did and to be registered in the
reserves that is for them to worry about, if they are worried.
It is not for the Society's office to be worried about it.

The Society has always said that people should comply with
the law and if the individual has done what you have described
in your letter and it does not hurt his conscience then we
leave the matter just as it is. There is no reason for us to
decide another man's conscience, nor to get into an argument
or controversy over the matter. If the individuals are not
compromising in the sense of taking up arms, and what they
are doing continues to allow them to beat their swords into
pruning shears, then the decision rests with them. If they
change that position in their lives that is soon enough for
the overseers in the congregation to take action. So leave
things stand as they are and have been since February of 1960
with no further comment.

May Jehovah's rich blessing go with you.

Your brothers,

Watchtower B. & Society
OF NEW YORK, INC.

What makes all this so utterly incredible is that the organization's
position on membership in the military has always been identical to
its position on membership in a "political" organization. In both cases
any Witness who enters such membership is automatically viewed as
"disassociated." Yet the Mexico Branch Committee had made crystal
clear that all these Witnesses who had obtained the completed certificate of military service (by means of a bribe) were now placed *in the
first reserve of the military*. The Witnesses in Malawi risked life and
limb, homes and lands, to adhere to the stance adopted by the organization for their country. In Mexico there was no such risk involved,
yet a policy of the utmost leniency was applied. There, Witness men
could be members of the first reserves of the army and yet be Circuit
or District Overseers, members of the Bethel family! The report from
the Branch Committee makes this clear (as well as showing how common the practice of bribing to get the certificate was among the Witnesses). It goes on to say:

As indicated in the above mentioned letter from Brooklyn, the brothers

have to use their own conscience on this matter. Something that nevertheless

would be good to clarify is that it has become so common in the organization

in Mexico to obtain the "cartilla" in this way (paying). The inconveniences caused by not obtaining the "cartilla" are that one cannot leave the country

(which the brothers of this country frequently do going to the United States

to assemblies) or having a little difficulty obtaining work when this document

is required. Aside from that young men would have no strong reason

to try to obtain the document. But it is so easy to obtain it and consulting

with other young men who have obtained it, they tell them how it can be

done, and these young men do not even think if it is all right for them

in itself, individually, to obtain this document in the above mentioned way.

Literally thousands of Witnesses in Mexico know the truth of the situation as described. All the members of the Mexico Branch Committee know it. And all the members of the Governing Body of Jehovah's Witnesses know what the stated position of the world headquarters was on the matter. Yet outside of Mexico very few people have any idea of what was said. Probably no one among the Witnesses in Malawi does.

I cannot imagine a more obvious double standard. Nor can I conceive of more twisted reasoning than that which allows for the position taken in Mexico and at the same time argues so strenuously and so dogmatically that to accept alternative service is condemnable because it is "viewed by the government as fulfillment of military service, is a "tacit or implied acknowledgement of Caesar's war machine." The same men who made those statements in Governing Body sessions and insisted that "we want no grey areas" and that "the brothers need to have their consciences educated," said this knowing that the common practice among Jehovah's Witnesses in Mexico for over twenty years had been to pay a bribe for a certificate saying they had fulfilled their military service, a practice that the world headquarters had officially stated was 'up to their conscience.'

Despite this, some members (and, happily, in several of the sessions it was only a minority) argued for the traditional position labeling a man as "disassociated" if he answers a judge's question about working in a hospital by giving the simple and truthful response that his conscience would allow this. They favored that policy while knowing that in Mexico men who are Elders, Circuit Overseers, District Overseers and Branch Office staff personnel, bribed officials to get their completed military service certificate stating that they were now in the first reserves of the military, the "war machine."

One Governing Body member, arguing for the traditional stand, had quoted a member of the Denmark Branch Committee, Richard Abrahamson, as having said regarding alternative service, "I shudder to think of putting these young men on their own choice." Yet the official counsel sent by the headquarters organization to the Mexico Branch was that young brothers' paying a bribe for a falsified document placing them in the first reserves was "for them to worry about, if they are worried. It is not for the Society's office to be worried about." Later the letter states that, "There is no reason to decide another man's conscience."

Why was not the same position taken toward those in Malawi? I seriously doubt that the majority of Witnesses there would have arrived at the same conclusions as the Branch Office personnel did. It is equally doubtful that there was a single native of Malawi (then Nyasaland) among those making such policy decision.

Is there no responsibility resting upon those in authority within the organization for what amounts to a grotesque disparity of direction given?

Notably, as regards the failure of the Malawian authorities to uphold the high principles of their Constitution, the Watch Tower Society stated that the "ultimate responsibility" must be placed on President Banda, saying:

"If he knows and allows it [the mistreatment of the Witnesses] to continue, then surely he as the leader of the country and the Malawi Congress Party must bear the responsibility for what is happening in his country and in the name of the party.

"Likewise, members of Parliament and party members who have either incited the young people to violence or turned a blind eye to what is happening cannot be exempted from responsibility. Can civil servants, police officers, the legal profession and other responsible officials who because of concern for their security of position condone by silence what is happening in Malawi absolve themselves from responsibility?"[15]

The same standard by which the organization judged the actions of the Malawian authorities should certainly apply to the organization also. If the Governing Body, not only knowing what had been said about the Malawian authorities and their responsibility, but also knowing of the organization's stand taken in Mexico, really believed that the position promulgated among the brotherhood in Malawi was the

15   Quoted from *Awake!*, February 8, 1968, pp. 21, 22; compare Matthew 7:1–5.

right one, then they should certainly have felt impelled to reject the position taken in Mexico. To uphold the rigid position taken in Malawi they should have been positively convinced of the rightness of that stand, with no doubts about it as being the only stand for a true Christian to take, one soundly and solidly based on God's Word. To countenance in any way the position taken in Mexico would be to deny that they held such a conviction. If on the other hand they believed the position taken in Mexico, allowing men to exercise their personal conscience as to obtaining the military certificate (even by illegal means), was right or at least acceptable, then they certainly should have accorded to the brotherhood in Malawi the same right to exercise their conscience in a matter that involved *no bribing, no illegality, no falsification.* Any fence-straddling, and 'turning of a blind eye to the facts,' 'condoning by silence' a double standard, perhaps out of "concern for their security of position," would mean following the same course they condemned on the part of Malawian officials, from top to bottom.

What was actually said by the Governing Body during the sessions in which the information from Mexico was called to their attention? The policy for Mexico had been developed primarily by only two men, but now the entire Body knew of it.[16] What responsibility did they feel and how did they react to the obvious disparity between this position and that taken in Malawi?

When I brought up the matter, not one word of disapproval or of moral indignation was heard from those who argued in such forceful, uncompromising terms against alternative service. There was no call for some action to change the existing policy in Mexico for one boldly declaring against even the "suggestion" of compromise. Though the third and fourth waves of violence had hit Malawian Witnesses (in 1972 and 1975), I heard no expression of dismay at the disparity in the standard there and the one applied in Mexico. Most of the members apparently found they could accept the Mexico policy while simultaneously insisting upon a totally different standard for people elsewhere.

Once more, I do not think the matter simply resolves down to personalities, the individual members involved. I have come to the conclusion that this outlook is in reality a typical product of any authority structure that takes a legalistic approach to Christianity, enabling those

---

16 By this time (1978) Nathan Knorr had died; Fred Franz, now president, was at all the sessions involving the discussion of alternative service.

sharing in the authority structure to see double standards exist without feeling strong qualms of conscience. To their credit, brothers in Mexico were disturbed in their consciences at learning of the intense suffering of Witnesses in Malawi who refused to pay a legal price in a lawful way for a party card of the government running the country, while they themselves were illegally obtaining a military certificate through bribes. Those at the "top," in the so-called "ivory tower," however, seemed strangely detached from such feelings, insensitive to the consequences to people from such double standard. This, too, I believe is an effect of the system, which is one reason why I find such a system so personally repelling.

All Governing Body members were fully aware of the policy in Mexico by the fall of 1978. Almost *a year later*, in September of 1979, the Governing Body again resumed discussion of the undecided issue of alternative service, this time brought to the fore by a letter from Poland.

Warning that alternative service could be a "trap for indoctrinating the brothers," Milton Henschel urged extreme caution, speaking in favor of the practice of many Polish Witnesses who take the expedient course of going to work in coal mines to avoid induction. Lloyd Barry again urged that we hold to the position that Witnesses "should keep free from the entire military organization." Ted Jaracz said that "our brothers are going to have problems and they look to Jehovah's organization for direction," that there was need to avoid diversity of opinions, that we should not give the brothers the idea that the Governing Body was saying, 'go ahead and submit' to alternative service orders. Carey Barber voiced the view that "there is no room here for exercising conscience, it is something where we just have to go right on through" without yielding. Fred Franz said our "conscience has to be Bible trained" and stated again his support for the traditional position against any acceptance of alternative service.

By now, Ewart Chitty was no longer a member of the Body, having submitted his resignation in accord with the Governing Body's wishes. Grant Suiter was absent from the session, both he and Chitty having voted for a change in policy at the November 15, 1978, meeting. But there were two new members on the Body, Jack Barr (from England) and Martin Poetzinger (from Germany), and they were present at the September 15, 1979, session. When a motion was finally presented, the vote was split right down the middle, eight in favor of changing the policy, eight against doing so (including the two new members).

In 1980, on February 3, the subject was once more placed on the agenda. By this time more than a year had elapsed since my visit to Mexico and Albert Schroeder had made another annual visit there. The Mexico Branch Committee members again expressed their concern about the practice of bribing to obtain falsified documents of military service, and Schroeder related this continuing situation to the Body after his return. Remarks by the various members during the session made it evident that no two-thirds majority would be attained either way on the alternative service issue and there was not even a motion made.

The matter was "shelved." From the time the letter from Michel Weber, the elder in Belgium, was received in November 1977, until February, 1980, the Governing Body of Jehovah's Witnesses had tried on *six separate occasions* to resolve the issue without success.

What, though, of the *people* affected by the policy that continued in force, those of what the *Watchtower* had called "the rank and file"? Could they also "shelve" the issue? To the contrary, the inability of the Body to achieve that indispensable two-thirds majority meant that male Jehovah's Witnesses in any country of the world who acted according to their conscience and accepted alternative service as a proper government requirement, could still do so only at the cost of being viewed as outside the organization, equivalent to expelled persons. It also meant that the Governing Body as a whole was willing for the twenty-year-old policy in effect in Mexico to continue in effect while a totally different policy in Malawi remained unchanged.

TWO SORTS OF WEIGHTS FOR MEASURING

"Two sorts of weights are something detestable to Jehovah, and a cheating pair of scales is not good." —Proverbs 20:23.

It may help to understand the reasoning of some Members if other circumstances prevailing among Jehovah's Witnesses in Mexico are reviewed. As a result of the Mexican revolution, and because of the Catholic Church's long history of holding immense quantities of land and other property in the country, the Mexican Constitution forbids any religious organization the right to own property. Churches and church property are, in effect, held in custody by the government, which allows the religious organizations to use these. Due to past exploitation by foreign clergy, no foreign missionaries or ministers are allowed to function as such in Mexico. What has this resulted in for the Witness organization?

The administration of the headquarters organization of Jehovah's Witnesses long ago decided that, because of Mexican law, Jehovah's Witnesses there would present themselves, not as a religious organization, but as a "cultural" organization. The local corporation there formed, La Torre del Vigia, is so registered with the government of Mexico. So, Jehovah's Witnesses in Mexico do not speak of having religious meetings or Bible meetings but of having "cultural" meetings. At these meetings they have no prayers or songs, and this is also true of their larger assemblies. When they engage in door-to-door activity they only carry Watch Tower literature (which they say the Watch Tower Society provides as an "aid to them in their cultural activity"). They do not carry the Bible while in such activity since that would identify them as engaging in religious activity. A group of Witnesses in a given area is not called a "congregation" but a "company." They do not speak of having baptisms but do the same thing under the name of performing the "symbol."

This "double talk" is not done because of living in some totalitarian country that takes repressive measures against freedom of worship.[17] It is done largely to avoid having to comply with government regulations regarding ownership of property by religious organizations. Nor should it be thought that the arrangement is something originating with the Mexican Witnesses themselves; it is an arrangement worked out and put into effect by the international headquarters at Brooklyn.

It is interesting to contrast the deliberate elimination of prayers and songs at Witness meetings in Mexico with the action of the Society in the United States, where they were willing to fight case after case all the way up to the Supreme Court of the country rather than give up certain practices, such as offering literature from door to door without a license and without having to register with the police, the right to use sound cars, distribute literature on street corners, and many other such practices which are covered by Constitutional rights. The organization did not want to relinquish any of these things. It fought to hold on to them, even though these particular practices are certainly not things that were done by early Christians in the first century and hence cannot be counted as among primary Christian practices.

---

17 The government of Mexico has, in fact, shown considerable leniency toward Jehovah's Witnesses, for it must be known that their presentation of themselves as a non-religious "cultural" organization is simply a subterfuge.

But congregational or group prayer *was* a primary religious practice in early Christian meetings and has been among servants of God from time immemorial. The Mexican government says nothing against prayer at religious meetings. Jehovah's Witnesses, however, are instructed to say that their meetings are *not* religious. Few things could be viewed as more completely related to worship of God, as more purely spiritual, than prayer. When an imperial decree in Persia prohibited prayer to anyone except to the king for a period of thirty days, the prophet Daniel considered the issue so crucial that he risked position, possessions and life itself in violating the decree.[18]

The headquarters organization, however, considered it expedient to sacrifice congregational prayer among Jehovah's Witnesses throughout Mexico. With what benefit, what "accruing advantage"? By giving up congregational prayer and song and the use of the Bible in public witnessing activity, the organization can retain ownership of Society property in Mexico and operate free from the governmental regulations that other religions comply with. They are willing to say that their organization is not a religious organization, that their meetings are not religious meetings, that their witnessing activity is not religious activity, that baptism is not a religious act—when in every other country of the world Jehovah's Witnesses are saying just the opposite.

Since they know of this arrangement, some Governing Body members may have been inclined to accept the paying of bribes for falsified documents as being not far out of line with the overall policy for Jehovah's Witnesses in that country. This may explain in part how they could at the same time speak so adamantly for "no compromise" in other lands. It seems evident that in the minds of some members it is not a question of a double standard. In their minds there is just the one standard. That standard is: *doing whatever the organization decides and approves*. The organization made decisions regarding Mexico and the practice of bribing there, leaving it to the individual conscience, and so that is acceptable and a man can pay such bribe for a military certificate and still be used in the most responsible way, with no need for particular concern before God on the part of those directing the work there. The organization decided otherwise regarding alternative service (as it also did regarding the situation in Malawi), and so any man who fails to follow that decision is unworthy of occupying

18 Daniel 6:1–11.

any position at all in the congregation, is in fact a breaker of integrity with God.

I could not understand then how Christians could adopt such a viewpoint and I can not understand it now. For me it made all the bold, almost strident, calls of some for 'staying clean from the world' sound hollow, like mere rhetoric, as impressive language that did not fit reality. I could not relate in any way to the reasoning that allowed for such expressions in the face of facts that were well known to all members speaking and hearing those expressions.

I lived in Latin American countries for nearly twenty years and paid no bribes. But I know full well that there are some places, not just in Latin America but in various parts of the earth, where, although the law is on your side and what you seek is perfectly legitimate, it is almost impossible to get certain things done without money being paid to an official who has no right to such. It is not hard to see that a person confronted with this situation may view this as a form of extortion, even as in Bible times tax-collectors and also military men might exact more than was due and thus practice extortion. It does not seem fair to me to judge adversely persons who feel obliged to submit to such extortion. More than that, I am not presuming to judge those in Mexico who, not having the law on their side, acted against the law, who did not simply submit to extortion but instead deliberately *solicited* the illegal actions of an official through an offer of money to get a falsified, illegal document. This is *not* what I find so shocking and even frightening about the whole affair.

It is instead the way that men in high authority can allow supposed "organizational interests" to be counted as of such enormous importance as compared to the interests of ordinary people, people with children and homes and jobs, individuals many of whom give evidence of being every bit as conscientious in their devotion to God as any man among those men who sit as a court to decide what is and what is not within the realm of conscience for such people.

It is men in authority who accord to *themselves* the right to be of divided opinion, but who exact uniformity from all others; men who express mistrust of others' use of Christian freedom of conscience, but who expect such others to put implicit trust in them and their decisions, while they grant to themselves the right to exercise their conscience to condone illegal maneuvering and obvious misrepresentation of fact.

It is men in authority who, because the change of one vote reduces a majority down from 66⅔% to 62½%, are willing to allow this to keep in force a policy that can cause other men to undergo arrest, be separated from family and home for months, even sent to jail for years, when those men do not understand the Scriptural basis for the policy they are asked to follow and, in some cases, believe that the policy is wrong.

It is men in authority who can apply a policy that calls on ordinary people, men, women and children, to face loss of home and lands, beatings, torture, rape and death because of refusal to pay a legal fee for the card of the organization that is, to all intents and purposes, the ruling power of their country, while at the same time telling men in another country that it is acceptable for them to bribe military officers for a card that falsely says they fulfilled their military service and are in the first reserves of the army.

All *this* is what I find shocking. And, however sincere some may be, I still find it frightening.

I could not personally comprehend how grown men could fail to see inconsistency in all of this, could fail to be repelled by it, could not be deeply moved by its effect on people's lives. In the end it simply convinced me that "organizational loyalty" can lead people to incredible conclusions, allow them to rationalize away the grossest of inequities, relieve them from being particularly affected by any suffering their policies may cause. The insensitizing effect that organizational loyalty can produce is, of course, well documented, having been demonstrated again and again throughout the centuries, both in religious and political history, as in the extreme cases of the Inquisition and during the Nazi regime. But it can still produce a sickening effect when seen at close quarters in an area where one never expected it. To my mind, it illustrates forcefully the reason why God never purposed that men should exercise such excessive authority over fellow humans.

7

PREDICTIONS AND PRESUMPTION

"When the prophet speaks in the name of Je-
hovah and the word does not occur or come
true, that is the word that Jehovah did not speak.
With presumptuousness the prophet spoke it.
You must not get frightened at him."
—Deuteronomy 18:22.

WHEN it comes to attitudes about the promised return of Christ Jesus, eagerness is certainly to be preferred to apathy. Early Christians were definitely not apathetic about that hoped-for event.

Recently I watched a television broadcast in which a public relations representative of the Canadian Branch Office of Jehovah's Witnesses, Walter Graham, responded to questions about the failure of certain predictions regarding Christ's return. He said that if any fault was to be found with Jehovah's Witnesses in this respect, then it was only due to "our enthusiasm of seeing God's name vindicated and his Kingdom rule the earth."

Most persons, I think, will agree that it is only human to make the mistake of saying things on the spur of the moment, to let wishful thinking or perhaps strong desire and enthusiasm sway our judgment, causing us to jump to hasty conclusions. Somewhere in our lives we have all done that. Surely if that were all that is involved, no one should have cause for great concern.

Personally I do not believe that that is all that is involved here, however. The issues go deeper and the factors related have far greater significance than some common, incidental mistake that we all commit at times. This is particularly so because of the way the predictions involved have affected people's most vital interests.

A factor that cannot be treated lightly is that the Governing Body views Jehovah's Witnesses, at least those of the "anointed class" (to which the Governing Body members all belong), as cast in the role of a "prophet," assigned to that awesome responsibility by God.

Thus, the April 1, 1972, issue of the *Watchtower* magazine, page 197, carried an article titled, "'They Shall Know that a Prophet Was Among Them.'" It raised the question as to whether in modern times Jehovah God has had a prophet to help the people, "to warn them of dangers and declare things to come." The answer given was, yes, that the record showed there was such a prophet.

IDENTIFYING THE "PROPHET"

These questions can be answered in the affirmative. Who is this prophet?

This "prophet" was not one man, but was a body of men and women. It was the small group of footstep followers of Jesus Christ, known at that time as International Bible Students. Today they are known as Jehovah's Christian witnesses. They are still proclaiming a warning, and have been joined and assisted in their commissioned work by hundreds of thousands of persons who have listened to their message with belief.

Of course, it is easy to say that this group acts as a "prophet" of God. It is another thing to prove it. The only way that this can be done is to review the record. What does it show?

The "record" is worth reviewing. That it reveals mistakes even the headquarters organization will acknowledge. One morning in 1980, when serving as chairman for the daily text discussion at the Brooklyn Bethel home, the Society's president, Fred Franz, recounted to the headquarters family his recollections of expectations held regarding the year 1925, forecast to be the time for the start of the millennium. He quoted Judge Rutherford as having said afterward about his own predictions: "I know I made an ass of myself."[1]

---

1 Talking to a large audience in Australia in 1975, Fred Franz related the same remark.

The organization, however, treats these mistakes as mere evidence of human imperfection and also as evidence of great desire and enthusiasm to see God's promises fulfilled.

I believe that the "record" shows there is more to it than that. It is one thing for a man to make an "ass" of himself because of wanting to see something happen. It is quite another thing for him to urge others to share his views, to criticize them if they do not, even to question their faith or impugn their motives if they do not see the matter as he sees it.

It is still more serious for an organization representing itself as God's appointed spokesman to all mankind to do this—and to do it, not for a few days or months, but for years, even decades, repeatedly, on an earthwide basis. The responsibility for the results can surely not be shrugged off with simply saying, "Well, nobody's perfect."

No one is, but every one of us bears a responsibility for what we do. And that is especially so when our actions dramatically affect something as important and personal as others' relationship with God.

No less serious is it when a group of men have divided views on predictions related to a certain date and yet present to their adherents an outward appearance of united confidence, encouraging those adherents to place unwavering trust in those predictions.

I suppose I must credit my experience with the Governing Body for also bringing home to me the reality of these matters. During the first twenty years or so of my active association with Jehovah's Witnesses, I had at most a hazy idea about any failures in past predictions and simply did not attach any great importance to them. I had no interest in literature attacking our teachings on this point. From the late 1950's onward, certain Society publications, such as *Jehovah's Witnesses in the Divine Purpose* (a history of the organization), and the Society-sponsored book *Faith on the March*, did mention these failures, but they did so in a way that made them appear as of minor consequence and I viewed them in that same light.

It was not until the late 1970's that I learned just how far the matter went. I learned it then, not from so-called "opposition literature," but from Watch Tower publications themselves and from active respected Witnesses, including fellow members of the Governing Body of Jehovah's Witnesses.

1914 is a pivotal date on which a major portion of the doctrinal and authority structure of Jehovah's Witnesses rests. Jehovah's Witnesses today hold the following beliefs tied in with that date:

> That in 1914 Christ Jesus became "present," invisible to human eyes, but now beginning a judgment period for all his professed followers and for the world.
>
> That in 1914 Christ Jesus now began active rulership toward all the world, his kingdom officially taking power.
>
> That 1914 marks the start of the "last days" or the "time of the end" foretold in Bible prophecy.
>
> That the generation of persons living in 1914 and having the ability to understand what they saw occurring then would be the 'generation that will not pass away until all things are fulfilled,' including the destruction of the existing system of things.
>
> That three and a half years after 1914 (in 1918) the resurrection of Christians sleeping in death, from the apostles onward, began.
>
> That about that same time (in 1918) Christ's true followers then living went into spiritual captivity to Babylon the Great, being released the following year, 1919, at which time Christ Jesus acknowledged them collectively as his "faithful and discreet slave," his approved agency for directing his work and caring for his interests on earth, his sole channel for communicating guidance and illumination to his servants earthwide.
>
> That from that time forward the final "harvest" work has been in progress, resulting in all people being divided into two classes as "sheep" and "goats," with salvation or destruction as their respective destinies.

To weaken belief in the significance of the foundation date of 1914 would weaken the whole doctrinal superstructure (described above) that rests on it. It would also weaken the claim of special authority for those acting as the official spokesman group for the "faithful and discreet slave" class.

To *remove* that date as having such significance could mean the virtual collapse of all the doctrinal and authority structure founded on it. That is how crucial it is.

Yet few Witnesses today know that for nearly half a century—from 1879 to the late 1920's—the time prophecies published in the *Watch Tower* magazine and related publications were essentially *contrary to all the beliefs just outlined*. I for one did not realize it until recent years. Then I found that for nearly fifty years the "channel" of the *Watch Tower* had assigned different times and dates for every one of the things just listed, and that it was only the failure of all the original expectations regarding 1914 that led to an assigning of new dates to those claimed fulfillments of prophecy.

As discussed in a previous chapter, the research I had to do in connection with the book *Aid to Bible Understanding* brought home to me that the Society's date of 607 B.C.E. for Jerusalem's destruction by Babylon was contradicted by all known historical evidence. Still, I continued to put trust in that date in spite of the evidence, feeling that it had Scriptural backing. Without 607 B.C.E. the crucial date of 1914 would be placed in question. I took the view that the historical evidence was likely defective and argued that way in the *Aid* book.

Then, in 1977, one of Jehovah's Witnesses in Sweden, named Carl Olof Jonsson, sent to the Brooklyn headquarters a massive amount of research he had done on Biblically related chronology and on chronological speculation. Jonsson was an elder and had been actively associated with Jehovah's Witnesses for some twenty years.

Having had experience researching chronology myself, I was impressed by how deeply he had gone into the matter, also by the completeness and factualness of his presentation. Basically he sought to draw the Governing Body's attention to the weakness in the Society's chronological reckonings leading to the 1914 date as the end point of the "Gentile Times," referred to by Jesus at Luke, chapter twenty-one, verse 24 (called "the appointed times of the nations" in the *New World Translation*).

Briefly stated, the 1914 date is arrived at by the following process:

In the fourth chapter of Daniel's prophecy, the expression "seven times" occurs, applied there to the Babylonian king Nebuchadnezzar and describing a period of seven years of insanity the king would experience.[2] The Society teaches that those "seven times" are prophetic of something greater, namely, of the period of time extending from Jerusalem's destruction (placed by the Society at 607 B.C.E.) down to the end of the "Gentile Times," explained as meaning the period during which the Gentile nations exercise "uninterrupted" dominion over all the earth.

The "seven times" are interpreted as meaning seven years with each year consisting of 360 days. Seven multiplied by 360 gives 2,520 days. However, other prophecies are referred to that use the expression "a day for a year."[3] Employing this formula, the 2,520 days become 2,520 years, running from 607 B.C.E. to the year 1914 C.E.

As noted earlier, the Society's present teachings about the beginning of Christ's kingdom rule, the "last days," the start of the resur-

---

2 Daniel 4:17, 23–33.
3 Numbers 14:34; Ezekiel 4:6.

rection and related matters are all tied in with this calculation. Not many Witnesses are able to explain the rather intricate application and combination of texts involved, but they accept the end product of this process and calculation.

Most of Jehovah's Witnesses understand that this explanation leading to 1914 is more or less unique with their organization, that it was initially published by the Society's first president, Pastor Russell. On its inside cover, the Society's publication *Jehovah's Witnesses in the Divine Purpose* contains these statements:

"1870   Charles Taze Russell begins his study of the Bible with a small group of associates

"1877   The book 'Three Worlds' is published identifying the date 1914 as the end of 'Gentile Times'"

The impression given here, as well as that presented within the book, is that this book "The Three Worlds" (of which Russell was a co-author) was the first publication to contain this teaching about 1914.

This is what I had thought, until the material from the Swedish elder came in to the world headquarters. Then I realized how many facts had been either ignored or glossed over by the Society's publications.

Jonsson first traced the long history of chronological speculation. He showed that the practice of arbitrarily applying the "year for a day" formula to various time periods found in the Bible was initially done by Jewish rabbis dating back to the first century C.E. In the ninth century C.E. a "string of Jewish rabbis" began making calculations and predictions utilizing this day-year formula in connection with the time periods of 1,290, 1,335 and 2,300 days found in Daniel's prophecy, in each case applying their results to the time for the appearance of the Messiah.[4]

Among professed Christians, the practice first surfaces in the twelfth century, beginning with a Roman Catholic abbot, Joachim of Floris. Not only the periods of days found in Daniel's prophecy, but also the period of 1,260 days mentioned in Revelation, chapter eleven, verse 3, and chapter twelve, verse 6, were now interpreted by employing the "year for a day" method. As time went along, a remarkable

---

4 Daniel 8:14; 12:11, 12. The complete text of Carl Olof Jonsson's research has since been published under the title *The Gentile Times Reconsidered* (Lethbridge: Hart Publishers, 1983).

succession of dates was arrived at by the different interpreters, their predictions including the year 1260, then 1360 and later various dates in the sixteenth century. Changes and new interpretations were regularly made necessary as one date after another eventually passed without the foretold event taking place.

In 1796, George Bell, writing in a London magazine, predicted the fall of the "Antichrist" (according to his view, the Pope). This was to come in "1797 or 1813," his prediction being based on an interpretation of the 1,260 days, but using a different starting point than other interpreters (some had begun their count from the birth of Christ, others from the fall of Jerusalem, others from the start of the Catholic Church). His prediction was written during the French Revolution. Not long after he made it, a shocking event took place—the Pope was taken captive by French troops and forced into exile.

Many took this as a most remarkable fulfillment of Bible prophecy and 1798 was accepted by them as the end of the prophetic 1,260 days. From this developed the view that the following year, 1799, marked the beginning of the "last days."

Further upheavals in Europe produced a spate of new predictions. Among the predictors was a man in England named John Aquila Brown. In the early 1800's he published an explanation of the 2,300 days of Daniel, chapter twelve, showing these as ending in 1844 C.E. This understanding was also adopted by the American pioneer of the Second Advent movement, William Miller.

We will see how these calculations later came to play a role in the history of Jehovah's Witnesses.

But John Aquila Brown developed another explanation that is intimately related to the year 1914 as that date figures in the beliefs of Jehovah's Witnesses. How so?

The evidence is that Brown was the real originator of the interpretation of the "seven times" of Daniel chapter four, the interpretation that produces the 2,520 years by means of the day-year formula.

Brown first published this interpretation in 1823 and his method converted the "seven times" into 2,520 years in *exactly the same way found today in Watch Tower publications.*

This was twenty-nine years before Charles Taze Russell was born, forty-seven years before he began his Bible study group and more than a half century before the book "The Three Worlds" appeared.

I was totally unaware of this before reading the material sent to the Society from Sweden.

John Aquila Brown, however, started his 2,520-year period in 604 B.C.E. and therefore had it ending in 1917 C.E. He foretold that then "the *full glory* of the kingdom of Israel shall be perfected."

Where, then, did the emphasis on the date of 1914 originate?

After the failure of expectations surrounding the year 1844, a split up of various Second Advent groups resulted, most of them setting up new dates for Christ's return. One of these groups formed around N. H. Barbour of Rochester, New York.

Barbour studied John Aquila Brown's works, adopted much of his interpretation, but changed the starting point of the 2,520 years to 606 B.C.E. and came up with the ending date of 1914 C.E. (Actually this was a miscalculation since that would only be 2,519 years.)

Barbour published a magazine for his Second Adventist adherents first titled *The Midnight Cry* and later the *Herald of the Morning*. On the next page is a copy of the title page of the *Herald of the Morning* of July, 1878, the year before the publication of the first issue of the *Watch Tower* magazine. Note the statement found at the lower right-hand corner, "'Times of the Gentiles' end in 1914".

This copy was made from one kept on file at the Brooklyn headquarters, though not accessible for general use. Its existence there shows that some persons of the headquarters staff must have known that the *Watch Tower* magazine was clearly *not* the first magazine to publicize and advocate the 1914 date as the end of the Gentile Times. That teaching was actually adopted from the Second Adventist publication of N. H. Barbour.

It may also be noted that at that time, July, 1878, C. T. Russell had become "assistant editor" of this Second Adventist magazine, the *Herald of the Morning*. Russell himself explains how he came to be associated with N. H. Barbour and how he came to adopt Barbour's chronology, much of which, including the interpretation of the "seven times" of Daniel chapter four, Barbour had in turn adopted from John Aquila Brown. Russell's explanation is published in the July 15, 1906, issue of the *Watch Tower*.

It was about January, 1876, that my attention was specially drawn to the subject of prophetic time, as it relates to these doctrines and hopes. It came about in this way: I received a paper called *The Herald of the Morning*, sent by its editor, Mr. N. H. Barbour. When I opened it I at

HERALD OF THE MORNING
GOD IS LOVE

" All nations whom thou hast made, shall come and worship before thee,"

| Vol. 7. | ROCHESTER, N. Y., July, 1878. | No. 1. |

THREE WORLDS

N. H. BARBOUR, Editor.

ASSISTANT EDITORS,

C. T. Russell, Pittsburg, Pa.   Eld. J. H. Paton, Almont, Mich.

| WORLD BEFORE THE FLOOD. | WORLD THAT NOW IS | WORLD TO COME OR AGE OF AGES. |
| Patriarchal Age | Jewish Age   Gospel Age. | Millennial Age |

PLAN OF THE AGES:

" Both the Cherubim of one measure and one size."

PLANE OF THE FLESH		PLANE OF THE SPIRIT
Earthly Jerusalem.		Heavenly Jerusalem.
Earthly Sacrifice.		Spiritual Sacrifice.
Earthly Kingdom.		Heavenly Kingdom.
This one looking forward to the sacrifice.		This one looking back to the sacrifice.
TWELVE TRIBES.		TWELVE APOSTLES.
From the end of the Patriarchal age, at the death of Jacob, to the end of the Jewish age, at the death of Christ, was 1845 years.	1841½ 1841½	From the end of the Jewish age, at the death of Christ, to the end of the Gospel age, should, if of equal measure, be 1845 years.
Birth of Jesus—		2300 days ended in 1843–4.
		1335 days ended in
Baptism of Jesus—	3½ HARVEST 3½ HARVEST	1874, also Jubilee cycles
Crucifixion, A. D. 33—	3½ 3½	1878, the double complete.
	TIME OF TROUBLE 33½ TIME OF TROUBLE 33½	"Times of the Gentiles"
Jerusalem destroyed— A. D. 70.		end in 1914.

TERMS--Six Months, 25 Cents; One Year, 50 Cents.

once identified it with Adventism from the picture on its
cover, and examined it with some curiosity to see what time
they would next set for the burning of the world. But
judge my surprise and gratification, when I learned from
its contents that the Editor was beginning to get his eyes
open on the subjects that for some years had so greatly
rejoiced our hearts here in Allegheny—that the object of
our Lord's return is not to destroy, but to bless all the
families of the earth, and that his coming would be thief-
like, and not in flesh, but as a spirit-being, invisible to men;
and that the gathering of his church and the separation of
the "wheat" from the "tares" would progress in the end
of this age without the world's being aware of it.

I rejoiced to find others coming to the same advanced
position, but was astonished to find the statement very
cautiously set forth, that the editor believed the prophecies
to indicate that the Lord was already *present* in the world
(unseen and invisible), and that the harvest work of gathering the wheat was already due,—and that this view was
warranted by the time-prophecies which but a few months
before he supposed had failed.

Here was a new thought: Could it be that the *time
prophecies* which I had so long despised, because of their
misuse by Adventists, were really meant to indicate when
the Lord would be *invisibly present* to set up his kingdom
—a thing which I clearly saw could be known in no other
way? It seemed, to say the least, a reasonable, a very reasonable thing, to expect that the Lord would inform his
people on the subject—especially as he had promised that
the faithful should not be left in darkness with the world,
and that though the day of the Lord would come upon all
others as a thief in the night (stealthily, unawares), it
should not be so to the watching, earnest saints.—1 Thes.
5:4.

I recalled certain arguments used by my friend Jonas
Wendell and other Adventists to prove that 1873 would
witness the burning of the world, etc.—the chronology of
the world showing that the six thousand years from Adam
ended with the beginning of 1873—and other arguments
drawn from the Scriptures and supposed to coincide. Could
it be that these *time* arguments, which I had passed by as
unworthy of attention, really contained an important truth
which they had misapplied?

Note that up to this point Russell states that he had no regard for
time prophecies, had in fact "despised" them. What did he now do?

Anxious to learn, from any quarter, whatever God had
to teach, I at once wrote to Mr. Barbour, informing him of
my harmony on other points and desiring to know particu-.
larly why, and upon what Scriptural evidences, he held
that Christ's *presence* and the harvesting of the Gospel age
dated from the Autumn of 1874. The answer showed that
my surmise had been correct, viz.: that the *time arguments*,
chronology, etc., were the same as used by Second Adventists
in 1873, and explained how Mr. Barbour and Mr. J. H. Paton,
of Michigan, a co-worker with him, had been regular Second

Adventists up to that time; and that when the date 1874 had passed without the world being burned, and without their seeing Christ in the flesh, they were for a time dumbfounded. They had examined the time-prophecies that had seemingly passed unfulfilled, and had been unable to find any flaw, and had begun to wonder whether the *time* was right and their *expectations* wrong,—whether the views of restitution and blessing to the world, which myself and others were teaching, might not be the things to look for. It seems that not long after their 1874 disappointment, a reader of the *Herald of the Morning*, who had a copy of the *Diaglott*, noticed something in it which he thought peculiar,—that in Matt. 24:27, 37, 39, the word which in our common version is rendered *coming* is translated *presence*. This was the clue; and, following it, they had been led through prophetic *time* toward proper views regarding the object and manner of the Lord's return. I, on the contrary, was led first to proper views of the object and manner of our Lord's return and then to the examination of the *time* for these things, indicated in God's Word. Thus God leads his children often from different starting points of truth; but where the heart is earnest and trustful, the result must be to draw all such together.

But there were no books or other publications setting forth the time-prophecies as then understood, so I paid Mr. Barbour's expenses to come to see me at Philadelphia (where I had business engagements during the summer of 1876), to show me fully and Scripturally, if he could, that the prophecies indicated 1874 as the date at which the Lord's *presence* and "the harvest" began. He came, and the evidence satisfied me. Being a person of positive convictions and fully consecrated to the Lord, I at once saw that the special times in which we live have an important bearing upon our duty and work as Christ's disciples; that, being in the time of harvest, the harvestwork should be done; and that *present truth* was the sickle by which the Lord would have us do a gathering and reaping work everywhere among his children.

Thus, the visit of the Second Adventist, N. H. Barbour, changed Russell's mind about time prophecies. Russell became an assistant editor of Barbour's magazine, the *Herald of the Morning*. From this time forward, time prophecies formed a prominent feature of Russell's writings and of the *Watch Tower* magazine he soon founded.[5]

The "seven times" interpretation and the 1914 date that Russell picked up were all tied in with the date of 1874, given primary importance

---

5 It was *after* the meeting with Barbour that Russell wrote an article for *The Bible Examiner*, published by George Storrs, another Adventist, in which article Russell set forth the 1914 date Barbour had arrived at. Like so many of the Second Adventist magazines, the magazine that Russell began included the term "Herald" in its title, *Zion's Watch Tower and Herald of Christ's Presence* (believed to have begun in 1874).

by Barbour and his adherents (1914 was still decades away whereas 1874 had just passed). They believed that 1874 marked the end of 6,000 years of human history and they had expected Christ's return in that year. When it passed they felt disillusioned. As the earlier-quoted material shows, a Second Adventist contributor to Barbour's magazine named B. W. Keith later noticed that a certain New Testament translation, *The Emphatic Diaglott*, used the word "presence" in place of "coming" in texts relating to Christ's return. Keith advanced to Barbour the idea that Christ had indeed returned in 1874 but *invisibly* and that Christ was now invisibly "present" carrying on a judging work.

An "invisible presence" is a very difficult thing to argue against or disprove. It is something like having a friend tell you that he knows that a dead parent invisibly visits him and comforts him, and then trying to *prove* to your friend that this is not really so.

The "invisible presence" concept thus allowed these Second Adventists associated with Barbour to say that they had, after all, had the "right date [1874] but had just expected the wrong thing on that date."[6] That explanation was also accepted and adopted by Russell.

Today the more than two million Jehovah's Witnesses believe and teach that Christ's invisible presence began in 1914. Very few realize that *for nearly fifty years* the Watch Tower Society announced and heralded, in their role as prophet, that such invisible presence began in 1874. As late as 1929, fifteen years *after* 1914, they were still teaching this.[7]

Jehovah's Witnesses today believe that Christ officially began his Kingdom rule in 1914. The *Watch Tower* taught for decades that this took place in 1878.[8]

Jehovah's Witnesses today believe that the "last days" and the "time of the end" also began in 1914. The *Watch Tower* magazine taught for *half a century* that the "last days" began in 1799 (accepting the interpretation by George Bell published in 1796).

They believe today that the resurrection of anointed Christians who

6 The July 15, 1906, *Watch Tower*, earlier quoted, shows that they did advance that very argument.

7 See the book *Prophecy*, published in 1929, pp. 64, 65. The August 15, 1974, *Watchtower* makes mention of this belief, but gives no indication that it continued to be taught after 1914.

8 This view began to be changed in 1922 at the Cedar Point Convention, eight years *after* 1914.

died from Christ's time forward began to take place in 1918. For more than forty years the *Watch Tower* taught that it began in 1881.

Their present belief is that from and after 1914 and particularly from 1919 onward the great "harvest" work is under way, to be climaxed by the destruction of the present system and all those who have not responded to their preaching activity. From its beginning, the *Watch Tower* magazine taught instead that the "harvest" would run from 1874 to 1914, and that by 1914 the destruction of all human institutions of this world would take place.

The organization today places the fall of "Babylon the Great" (the "world empire of false religion") in 1919. For at least four decades the *Watch Tower* placed it in 1878, with Babylon's complete destruction due in 1914 or 1918.

What was responsible for the change in all these major prophetic teachings held to for so many decades and by so many people?

It was the same as in the case of all the long line of predictions from the thirteenth century onward—the failure of their published expectations to be realized.

Some may incline to discount this as a mere assertion. After all, hardly any of Jehovah's Witnesses now have access to older issues of the *Watch Tower* and today, even when discussing the organization's past history, the Society's publications either ignore or present only a partial, sometimes altered, view of these teachings advocated for so long a time. They give little idea of how positively and confidently these views were advanced.

Consider then a portion of the evidence from "the record" of this organization that claims the role of modern-day prophet.

In reviewing the earliest issues of the *Watch Tower* magazine, from 1879 onward, a notable feature is that they were expecting major things to happen *right then*. Though believing that 1914 would mark the end of the "Gentile Times," that date figured relatively little in their thinking. They were thinking far more of 1874 and the belief that Christ had begun his invisible presence then, had thereafter entered his Kingdom rule. So they expected to experience their transferral to heavenly life very soon. With this, the opportunity to become part of the "bride of Christ" would be closed. They expected, as well, that long before 1914 the world would enter into a time of great trouble that would worsen and develop into a state of chaos and anarchy. By 1914 everything would be over, finished, and Christ Jesus would have taken full charge of earth's affairs, his Kingdom completely replacing all human systems of rule.

This is aptly illustrated in the following material from the January, 1881, issue of the *Watch Tower*, certain points being underlined here for the reader's convenience:

> We see too that not only are the harvest of Jewish and Gospel ages parallel in point of beginning, but also in length of duration; theirs being in all 40 years from the time of Jesus anointing [at beginning of their harvest, A. D. 30.] to destruction of Jerusalem, A. D. 70. So, ours, beginning in 1874 closes with the end of the "day of wrath" and end of the "times of the Gentiles," 1914—a similar and parallel period of 40 years.. The first seven years of the Jewish harvest was especially devoted to the gathering of ripe wheat from that church; three and one-half of it was while he was present as the Bridegroom and three and a half of it after he had come to them as king and had entered into glory, but it was all under his supervision and direction.
>
> As John had said he purged his flood, gathered his wheat and burned the chaff. So here the parallel is being fulfilled: We find, [as heretofore shown—see "Day Dawn"] *the law and the prophets* declaring him present at the culmination of the "Jubilee cycles" in 1874. And the parallels show us that then the *harvest* began, and that the gathering of the bride into the place of safety, will occupy a parallel of seven years of time, ending in 1881. But how. when. and why did the "house of servants" stumjle over Christ? If we can ascertain this it should give us a clue to how, when, and why, the Gospel house stumbles, especially in view of the fact that in so many particulars the closing work of that age is the *exact pattern* of this.

> We believe that Christ is now present, in the sense of having commenced the work of taking to himself his great power and reigning. The work begins with the separating of tares from wheat in the living church and the association of the wheat of all ages with himself in the authority of his kingdom. "To him that overcometh will I grant to sit with me in my throne," and "to him will I give power over the nations," to continue until all things are subdued under him. It seems proper, too, that the work should begin thus, by taking his bride and the twain becoming one.

The real "anchor" date for the *Watch Tower* then was clearly 1874. As of that date, Christ was present. Within the following 40 years he would accomplish all his harvest work. Because of believing this, it was felt that dramatic events should be taking place very quickly, perhaps in that very year of 1881, as argued in the additional article headed "How Long, O Lord?" Note these points:

> This is a question doubtless that many ask themselves, viz:
> "How soon will our change come?" This change many of us
> have looked forward to for years, and we yet with much
> pleasure, think of the time when we shall be gathered unto
> Jesus and see him as he is.   In the article concerning our
> change, in December paper, we expressed the opinion that it
> was nearer than many supposed, and while we would not
> attempt to prove our change at any particular time, yet we
> propose looking at some of the evidences which *seem* to show
> the translation or change from the natural to the spiritual
> condition, due this side or by the fall of our year 1881.   The
> evidence that our change will be by that time, increases since
> we have seen that the change to spiritual bodies is not the
> marriage.   While we thought the marriage to be the change,
> and knowing there was three and a half years of special
> favor to the nominal church (now left desolate) from 1878, we
> could not expect any translation this side of 1881, or during
> this three and a half years.   But since we recognize that going
> into the marriage is not only being made ready (by recognizing
> his presence) for the change, but also, that going in includes
> the change itself, then the evidences that we go in (or will
> be changed) inside of the time mentioned are strong, and
> commend themselves to all interested as worthy of investiga-
> tion.   Aside from any direct proof that our change is near, the
> fact that the manner of the change can now be understood,
> is evidence that we are near the time of the *change*, for truth
> is "meat in due season," and understood only as due.   It will
> be remembered that after the spring of 1878, (when we under-
> stand Jesus was due as King) that the subject of holiness or
> the wedding garment, was very much agitated.   And aside
> from the parallel to the end of the Jewish age, and favor at
> that time being shown to the Jewish nation, which implied the
> presence of the King, the consideration of the wedding gar-
> ment, was also proof of the correctness of the application. for
> "the King had come in to see the guests," [Matt. xxii. 11.]
> and hence all were interested in knowing how they stood
> before him.   Now as the inspection of guests is the last thing
> prior to our change, which precedes the marriage and we are
> all now considering *the change,* it would seem that the time
> for it, is nigh.
> We shall now present what we adduce from the types and
> prophetic points as seeming to indicate the translation of the
> saints and closing of the door to the high calling by 1881.

Detailed argumentation followed, with emphasis on the fall of 1881 as the likely time for their change to heavenly life and the time "when the door—opportunity to become a member of the bride—will close." This would be *35 years before 1914*, which to them was simply a terminal point, the time by which all things would wind up.

The expectation that the anointed Christians of the "Bride class" would undergo a transition to heavenly life by the fall of 1881 obviously did not materialize. As the years passed, the span of attention began to lengthen and 1914 began to receive somewhat greater emphasis. It was still the *terminal* point, however, when the elimination of earthly rulerships and the destruction of "nominal Christendom" would be complete, for it was believed that Christ began to exercise his full Kingdom power in 1878, as shown in the book Russell published in 1889, titled *The Time Is At Hand*.

Parallel Dispensations. **239**

house he came as Bridegroom and Reaper in the beginning of their harvest (the beginning of his ministry); and just before his crucifixion he presented himself as their King, exercising kingly authority in pronouncing judgment against them, in leaving their house desolate, and in the typical act of cleansing their temple. (Luke 19:41-46; Mark 11:15-17.) Just so it has been in this harvest: Our Lord's presence as Bridegroom and Reaper was recognized during the first three and a half years, from A. D. 1874 to A. D. 1878. Since that time it has been emphatically manifest that the time had come in A. D. 1878 when kingly judgment should begin at the house of God. It is here that Rev. 14:14-20 applies, and our Lord is brought to view as the Reaper *crowned*. The year A. D. 1878, being the parallel of his assuming power and authority in the type, clearly *marks the time* for the actual assuming of power as King of kings, by our present, spiritual, invisible Lord—the time of his taking to himself his great power to reign, which in the prophecy is closely associated with the resurrection of his faithful, and the beginning of the trouble and wrath upon the nations. (Rev. 11:17, 18.)

THEY KNEW NOT THE TIME OF THEIR VISITATION.
LUKE 19:44; MATT. 24:38, 39.
OUR LORD PRESENTED IN THREE CHARACTERS—AS BRIDEGROOM, REAPER AND KING.
JOHN 3:29; 4:35, 38; MATT. 21:5,9,4; 2 COR. 11:2; REV. 14:14,15; 17:14.

AN ADVENT MOVEMENT AT THE TIME OF JESUS' BIRTH, THIRTY YEARS PRIOR TO HIS ADVENT AND ANOINTING, AS MESSIAH, AT BAPTISM. MATT. 2:1-16; ACTS 10:37,38.	AN ADVENT MOVEMENT IN 1844, THIRTY YEARS PRIOR TO THE ACTUAL TIME OF HIS PRESENCE, TO AWAKEN AND TEST THE CHURCH. MATT. 25:1.
ACTUAL PRESENCE OF THE LORD AS BRIDEGROOM AND REAPER—OCTOBER, A. D. 29.	ACTUAL PRESENCE OF THE LORD AS BRIDEGROOM AND REAPER—OCTOBER, A. D. 1874.
POWER AND TITLE AS KING ASSUMED THREE AND A HALF YEARS LATER—A. D. 33.	POWER AND TITLE OF KING ASSUMED THREE AND A HALF YEARS LATER—A. D. 1878.

FIRST WORK OF THE KING, JUDGMENT.

NOMINAL JEWISH HOUSE REJECTED; LITERAL TEMPLE CLEANSED.—MATT.20:18; 21:5-15; 23:37; 24:1.	NOMINAL CHRISTIAN HOUSE REJECTED; SPIRITUAL TEMPLE CLEANSED.—1 PET.4:17; REV.3:16; MAL 3:2.
ENTIRE DESTRUCTION OF JEWISH POLITY, ACCOMPLISHED IN 37 YEARS AFTER BEING CAST OFF—OR 40 YEARS FROM THE BEGINNING OF THE HARVEST—A. D. 70.	ENTIRE DESTRUCTION OF NOMINAL CHRISTENDOM, ACCOMPLISHED IN 37 YEARS AFTER BEING CAST OFF—OR 40 YEARS FROM THE BEGINNING OF THE HARVEST—A. D. 1914.

Even after the turn of the century, in the early 1900's, the focus was still largely on 1874 and 1878 as the key dates to which all thinking was geared. They were *in* the "last days" since 1799, *in* the "harvest" period since 1874, Christ had been exercising his kingly power since 1878 and the resurrection had then begun. The passing of the years did not change these claims. They all related to *invisible* events, unlike the prediction about the 'translation to heaven of the living saints' expected in 1881. With no visible evidence to discredit them, these claims could be, and were, maintained.

Within three years of 1914, in 1911, the *Watch Tower* still proclaimed the importance of 1874, 1878 and 1881. "Babylon the Great" had fallen in 1878 and her "full end" would come in October 1914. An 'adjustment' was made, however, as regards the "closing of the door" to the opportunity to be part of the heavenly Kingdom class, earlier placed in 1881. Now the *Watch Tower* readers are informed that the "door" still "stands ajar," in this material from the June 15, 1911, issue:

> Noting these parallels, we find 1874 as the beginning of this "harvest" and the gathering together of the "elect" from the four winds of heaven; 1878 as the time when Babylon was formally rejected, Laodicea spewed out—the time from which it is stated, "Babylon is fallen, is fallen"—fallen from divine favor. The parallel in 1881 would seem to indicate that certain favors were still continued to those in Babylon up to that date, notwithstanding the rejection of the system; and since that date we would understand that that relationship has been in no sense an advantageous one, but has been in many senses of the word a distinct disadvantage, from which only with difficulty could any free themselves, the Lord's grace and truth assisting. And in harmony with this parallelism, October, 1914, will witness the full end of Babylon, "as a great millstone cast into the sea," utterly destroyed as a system.
>
> Coming back: We concede it reasonable to infer that the close of the favors upon fleshly Israel represent the close of the special favor of this Gospel age, viz., the invitation to the high calling; accordingly, our understanding is that the open or general "call" of this age to kingdom honors ceased in October, 1881. However, as already shown in SCRIPTURE STUDIES, we make a distinction between the end of the "call" and the closing of the "door"; and believe that the door into the kingdom class is not yet closed; that it stands ajar for a time, to permit those who had already accepted the "call" and who fail to use its privileges and opportunities in self-sacrifice to be thrust out, and to permit others to enter to take their crowns, in harmony with Rev. 3:11. The present time, therefore, from 1881 until the door of opportunity for sacrifice in the Lord's service shall fully

close, is a period of ''sifting'' as respects all who are already in divine favor, in covenant relationship with God.

The windup date of 1914 was now at hand. With its arrival the harvest would be over, the last days would have reached their culmination, their hopes would be fully realized. Exactly what did the Watch Tower publications teach would take place by the time 1914 came?

The book *The Time Is At Hand*, published twenty-five years before 1914, set out seven points, as follows:

In this chapter we present the Bible evidence proving that the full end of the times of the Gentiles, *i. e.*, the full end of their lease of dominion, will be reached in A. D.

Times of the Gentiles. 77

1914; and that that date will be the farthest limit of the rule of imperfect men.   And be it observed, that if this is shown to be a fact firmly established by the Scriptures, it will prove:—

Firstly, That at that date the Kingdom of God, for which our Lord taught us to pray, saying, ''Thy Kingdom come,'' will have obtained full, universal control, and that it will then be ''set up,'' or firmly established, in the earth.

Secondly, It will prove that he whose right it is thus to take the dominion will then be present as earth's new Ruler; and not only so, but it will also prove that he will be present for a considerable period before that date; because the overthrow of these Gentile governments is directly caused by his dashing them to pieces as a potter's vessel (Psa. 2:9; Rev. 2:27), and establishing in their stead his own righteous government.

Thirdly, It will prove that some time before the end of A. D. 1914 the last member of the divinely recognized Church of Christ, the ''royal priesthood,'' ''the body of Christ,'' will be glorified with the Head; because every member is to reign with Christ, being a joint-heir with him of the Kingdom, and it cannot be fully ''set up'' without every member.

Fourthly, It will prove that from that time forward Jerusalem shall no longer be trodden down of the Gentiles, but shall arise from the dust of divine disfavor, to honor; because the ''Times of the Gentiles'' will be fulfilled or completed.

Fifthly, It will prove that by that date, or sooner, Israel's blindness will begin to be turned away; because their "blindness in part" was to continue only " *until* the fulness of the Gentiles be come in " (Rom. 11: 25), or, in other words, until the full number from among the Gentiles, who are to be members of the body or bride of Christ, would be fully selected.

Sixthly, It will prove that the great " time of trouble such

78   *The Time is at Hand.*

as never was since there was a nation," will reach its culmination in a world-wide reign of anarchy ; and then men will learn to be still, and to know that Jehovah is God and that he will be exalted in the earth. (Psa. 46:10.) The condition of things spoken of in symbolic language as raging waves of the sea, melting earth, falling mountains and burning heavens will then pass away, and the "new heavens and new earth" with their peaceful blessings will begin to be recognized by trouble-tossed humanity.   But the Lord's Anointed and his rightful and righteous authority will first be recognized by a company of God's children while passing through the great tribulation—the class represented by *m* and *t* on the Chart of the Ages (see also pages 235 to 239, VOL. I.); afterward, just at its close, by fleshly Israel ; and ultimately by mankind in general.

Seventhly, It will prove that *before that date* God's Kingdom, organized in power, will be in the earth and then smite and crush the Gentile image (Dan. 2:34)—and fully consume the power of these kings. Its own power and dominion will be established as fast as by its varied influences and agencies it crushes and scatters the "powers that be"—civil and ecclesiastical—iron and clay.

These statements are from the pre-1914 edition. Note how some of its statements were 'adjusted' in a post-1914 edition (1924).

As can be noted in the material quoted, the pre-1914 edition clearly stated that 1914 "will be the *farthest limit* of the rule of imperfect men." It said that at that date the Kingdom of God "*will have obtained* full, universal control, and that it will then be 'set up,' or firmly established, in the earth."

The post-1914 edition covers this up by saying:

In this chapter we present the Bible evidence proving that the full end of the times of the Gentiles, *i. e.*, the full end of their lease of dominion, will be reached in A. D.

1914; and that that date will see the disintegration of the
rule of imperfect men. And be it observed, that if this is
shown to be a fact firmly established by the Scriptures,
it will prove:—

Firstly, That at that date the Kingdom of God, for which
our Lord taught us to pray, saying, "Thy Kingdom
come," will begin to assume control, and that it will
then shortly be "set up," or firmly established, in the
earth, on the ruins of present institutions.

In point three, the pre-1914 edition stated that previous to the end
of 1914 the last member of the "body of Christ" would be glorified
with the Head. Here, also, the post-1914 edition changed the wording
and eliminated any reference to the year 1914:

Thirdly, It will prove that some time before the end of
the overthrow the last member of the divinely recognized
Church of Christ, the "royal priesthood," "the body of
Christ," will be glorified with the Head; because every
member is to reign with Christ, being a joint-heir with him
of the Kingdom, and it cannot be fully "set up" without
every member.

Thus, in later editions a clear effort was made to cover up the more
obvious failures of the very positive claims made regarding 1914 once
that date had passed without the predicted events occurring. Few Jehovah's Witnesses today have any concept of the magnitude of the
claims made for that year or the fact that not a single one of the original seven points was fulfilled as stated. Those expectations now receive only the briefest of mention in the Society's publications; some
are totally passed over.[9]

In fact, by reading the Society's recent publications one might gather
that Russell, the Watch Tower president, did not speak specifically
about just what 1914 would bring. They imply that any strong expectations or dogmatic claims were the responsibility of others, the readers. An example of this is found in the official history *Jehovah's Witnesses in the Divine Purpose*, page 52.

There is no doubt that many
throughout this period were overzealous
in their statements as to what could be ex-

---

9 So, too, with the claims made about the years 1878 and 1881, which, along with those
about 1799 and 1874, were all eventually discarded as in error.

> pected. Some read into the *Watch Tower*
> statements that were never intended, and
> while it was necessary for Russell to call
> attention to the certainty that a great
> change was due at the end of the Gentile
> times, he still encouraged his readers to
> keep an open mind, especially as regards
> the time element.

The book quotes excerpts from *Watch Tower* magazines but when examined they simply do not support the statement made. The only one dealing with a specific "time element" is from a *Watch Tower* of 1893, which says:

> A great storm is near at hand. Though one may
> not know exactly when it will break forth, it
> seems reasonable to suppose that it cannot be
> *more* than twelve or fourteen years yet future.

This does nothing to prove the claim made; it merely confirms what other writings of Russell show, that he definitely expected worldwide trouble to break out *before* 1914 arrived, not later than 1905 or 1907 according to the quoted material, and that this outbreak would lead up to the eventual destruction of all earth's governments by that terminal date.

Two years before 1914 arrived, the *Watch Tower* did urge some caution on the part of its reader.

The book *Jehovah's Witnesses in the Divine Purpose* (page 53) quotes Russell's statement in a 1912 *Watch Tower* as follows:

> There surely is room for slight differences of
> opinion on this subject and it behooves us to
> grant each other the widest latitude. The lease
> of power to the Gentiles may end in October,
> 1914, or in October, 1915. And the period of
> intense strife and anarchy "such as never was
> since there was a nation" may be the final
> ending of the Gentile times or the beginning
> of Messiah's reign.
> But we remind all of our readers again, that
> we have not prophesied anything about the
> Times of the Gentiles closing in a time of trou-
> ble nor about the glorious epoch which will
> shortly follow that catastrophe. We have mere-
> ly pointed out what the Scriptures say, giving
> our views respecting their meaning and asking

> our readers to judge, each for himself, what
> they signify. *These prophecies still read the
> same to us.* ... However, *some* may make posi-
> tive statements of what they know, and of
> what they do not know, *we never indulge in
> this;* but we merely state that we believe thus
> and so, for such and such reasons.[u]

This, then, is the picture the organization seeks to convey. Compare
that with other statements made in the *Watch Tower* magazine and
other publications, statements to which the Society's publications today make no reference whatsoever. Ask whether it is true that the
responsibility for any dogmatic claims rests outside the Society, rests
instead with those who "read into" the publications a certainty never
intended, particularly as regards what 1914 would bring.

From *The Time Is At Hand* (pages 98 and 99), published in 1889,
we read the following:

> True, it is expecting great things to claim, as we do, that
> within the coming twenty-six years all present governments
> will be overthrown and dissolved; but we are living in a
> special and peculiar time, the "Day of Jehovah," in which
> matters culminate quickly; and it is written, "A short work
> will the Lord make upon the earth." (See Vol. I., chap. xv.)

> In view of this strong Bible evidence concerning the
> Times of the Gentiles, we consider it an established truth
> that the final end of the kingdoms of this world, and the
> full establishment of the Kingdom of God, will be accom-
> plished by the end of A. D. 1914.   Then the prayer of tne
> Church, ever since her Lord took his departure—"Thy
> Kingdom come"—will be answered; and under that wise and
> just administration, the whole earth will be filled with the
> glory of the Lord—with knowledge, and righteousness, and
> peace (Psa. 72:19; Isa. 6:3; Hab. 2:14); and the will
> of God shall be done *"on earth, as it is done in heaven."*

If you say, not merely that something is true, but that you consider
it an "*established* truth," is that not the same as saying that you *know*
it to be so? Is that not 'indulging in positive statements'? If there is
any difference, how much of a difference is it?

In the same publication, on page 101, this statement appears:

and the living saints, as well as many of the world, are now being used as the Lord's soldiers in overthrowing errors and evils.   But let no one hastily infer a *peaceable conversion* of the nations to be here symbolized ; for many scriptures, Such as Rev. 11 : 17, 18 ; Dan. 12 : 1 ; 2 Thes. 2 : 8 ; Psalms 149 and 47, teach the very opposite.

Be not surprised, then, when in subsequent chapters we present <u>proofs</u> that the <u>setting up</u> of the <u>Kingdom of God</u> is <u>already begun</u>, that it is pointed out in prophecy as due to begin the exercise of power in A. D. 1878, and that the ''<u>battle of the great day of God Almighty</u>'' (Rev. 16:14.), which <u>will end</u> in A. D. <u>1914</u> with the <u>complete overthrow</u> of <u>earth's</u> present <u>rulership</u>, is already commenced.   The gathering of the armies is plainly visible from the standpoint of God's Word.

If our vision be unobstructed by prejudice, when we get the telescope of God's Word rightly adjusted we may see with clearness the character of many of the events due to take place in the ''Day of the Lord''—that we are in the very midst of those events, and that '' <u>the Great Day of His Wrath is come.</u>''

Two years after this book was published, another book by Russell, *"Thy Kingdom Come"* was published in 1891, and on page 153 we find the following:

The fall, plagues, destruction, etc., foretold to come upon mystic Babylon, were foreshadowed in the great trouble and national destruction which came upon fleshly Israel, and which ended with the complete overthrow of that nation in A. D. 70.   And the period of falling also corresponds ; for from the time our Lord said, '' Your house is left unto you desolate,'' A. D. 33, to A. D. 70 was 36½ years ; and so from A. D. 1878 to the end of A. D. 1914 is 36½ years.   <u>And, with the end of A. D. 1914, what God calls Babylon, and what men call Christendom, will have passed away, as already shown from prophecy.</u>

The next year, 1892, in the January 15 issue, the *Watch Tower* stated that the final "battle" had already begun, its end to come in 1914:

While it was an agreeable surprise to us (in view of the contrary sensational accounts so often published) to find the situation in Europe as we here describe it—in harmony with what the Scriptures had led us to expect—yet so great is our confidence in the Word of God and in the light of present truth shining upon it, that we could not have doubted its testimony whatever had been the appearances. The date of the close of that "battle" is definitely marked in Scripture as October, 1914. It is already in progress, its beginning dating from October, 1874. Thus far it has been chiefly a battle of words and a time of organizing forces—capital, labor, armies and secret societies.

Never was there such a general time of banding together as at present. Not only are nations allying with each other for protection against other nations, but the various factions in every nation are organizing to protect their several interests. But as yet the various factions are merely studying the situation, testing the strength of their opponents, and seeking to perfect their plans and power for the future struggle, which many, without the Bible's testimony, seem to realize is the inevitable. Others still delude themselves, saying, Peace! Peace! when there is no possibility of peace until God's kingdom comes into control, compelling the doing of his will on earth as it is now done in heaven.

This feature of the battle must continue with varying success to all concerned; the organization must be very thorough; and the final struggle will be comparatively short, terrible and decisive—resulting in general anarchy. In many respects the convictions of the world's great generals coincide with the predictions of God's Word. Then "Woe to the man or nation who starts the next war in Europe; for it will be a war of *extermination*." It will be abetted not only by national animosities, but also by social grievances, ambitions and animosities, and if not brought to an end by the establishment of God's kingdom in the hands of his elect and then glorified Church, it would exterminate the race.—Matt. 24:22.

This short item appearing in July, 1894, in the *Watch Tower* reveals how they viewed world conditions of that time as clear proof that the world was then about to enter its final throes, with its last gasp coming in 1914:

CAN IT BE DELAYED UNTIL 1914?

Seventeen years ago people said, concerning the time features presented in MILLENNIAL DAWN, They seem reasonable in many respects, but surely no such radical changes could occur between now and the close of 1914: if you had proved that they would come about in a century or two, it would seem much more probable.

What changes have since occurred, and what velocity is gained daily?

"The old is quickly passing and the new is coming in."

> Now, in view of recent labor troubles and threatened anarchy, our readers are writing to know if there may not be a mistake in the 1914 date. They say that they do not see how present conditions can hold out so long under the strain.
>
> We see no reason for changing the figures—nor could we change them if we would. They are, we believe, God's dates, not ours. But bear in mind that the end of 1914 is not the date for the *beginning*, but for the *end* of the time of trouble. We see no reason for changing from our opinion expressed in the view presented in the WATCH TOWER of January 15, '92. We advise that it be read again.

It is true that the word "opinion" is here used, but how meaningful is this when at the same time God is brought into the picture as backing up the dates set forth? Who would be inclined to doubt "God's dates"?

Today, the organization would say that these matters are all peripheral, minor when compared to what they would present as a major truth, namely that the Society was right about the "end of the Gentile times" as coming in 1914, the *one* early belief concerning 1914 that they still retain. But in saying this they commit probably the greatest misrepresentation of all. For the fact is that all that has been retained is the *phrase*: "the end of the Gentile times." The *meaning* they now assign to that phrase is *totally different* from the meaning assigned to it by the Watch Tower Society during the forty years up to 1914.

During all those forty years those associated with the Watch Tower Society understood that the "end of the Gentile times" would mean the complete overthrow of all earthly governments, their total elimination and replacement by the rule of the whole earth by Christ's kingdom. No human rule would remain. Recall the statement on pages 98 and 99 of *The Time Is At Hand*, that "within the coming twenty-six years [from 1889] *all present governments will be overthrown and dissolved.*" That, "In view of this strong Bible evidence concerning the Times of the Gentiles, we consider it an *established truth* that the *final end of the kingdoms of this world*, and the full establishment of the Kingdom of God, will be accomplished by the end of A.D. 1914."

Today the meaning assigned to the phrase "end of the Gentile Times" (or "the appointed times of the nations") is quite different. It is not the *actual* end of rulership by human governments as a result of their destruction by Christ. Now it is said to be the end of their "uninterrupted rule" of the earth, the 'interruption' resulting from Christ's invisibly having taken Kingdom power and begun reigning in 1914 and directing his attention in a 'special way' toward the earth, (which actually is what had been earlier taught about the year 1874).

Since, again, the realm of the invisible is where this is said to have occurred, it is difficult to argue with such a theory. The fact that nothing whatsoever has changed since 1914 as regards the earthly governments' dominion of the earth does not seem to be viewed as of any consequence. Their "lease" of power has expired, it is now said, being invisibly cancelled by the invisible King, and thus the "end" of their appointed time has come.

All of which is something like proclaiming for forty years that on a certain date the undesirable occupant of a property is going to be completely expelled, removed for all time, and then, when that date comes and goes and the undesirable occupant is still there carrying on as usual, explaining this away by saying, "Well, I cancelled his lease and as far as I'm concerned it's the same as if he were actually moved out. And, besides, I'm keeping a much closer watch on things now."

Admittedly, the closer 1914 came, the more cautious the forecasts became. Whereas Russell had argued that the storm of trouble and universal anarchy would take place before October of 1914, later, in a 1904 issue of the magazine he said:

UNIVERSAL ANARCHY—JUST BEFORE OR AFTER OCTOBER, 1914 A. D.

What seems at first glance the veriest trifle and wholly unrelated to the matter, has changed our conviction respecting the time when universal anarchy may be expected in accord with the prophetic numbers. We now expect that the anarchistic culmination of the great time of trouble which will precede the Millennial blessings will be after October, 1914, A. D. —very speedily thereafter, in our opinion—"in one hour," "suddenly." [10]

And, whereas in 1894 he had affirmed that the figures expounded were "God's dates, not ours," in the October 1, 1907, *Watch Tower*, seven years before 1914, he now said:

---

10 *Watch Tower*, July 1, 1904.

A dear Brother inquires, Can we feel absolutely sure that the Chronology set forth in the DAWN-STUDIES is correct?—that the harvest began in A. D. 1874 and will end in A. D. 1914 in a world wide trouble which will overthrow all present institutions and be followed by the reign of righteousness of the King of Glory and his bride, the church?

We answer, as we have frequently done before in the DAWNS and TOWERS and orally and by letter, that we have never claimed our calculations to be infallibly correct; we have never claimed that they were *knowledge,* nor based upon indisputable evidence, facts, knowledge; our claim has always been that they are based on *faith.*

This same article, however, goes on to imply that those doubting such calculations were lacking in faith. It says:

We remind you again that the weak points of chronology are supplemented by the various prophecies which interlace with it in so remarkable a manner that *faith* in the chronology almost becomes *knowledge* that it is correct. The changing of a single year would throw the beautiful parallels out of accord; because some of the prophecies measure from B. C., some from A. D., and some depend upon both. We believe that God meant those prophecies to be understood "in due time"; we believe that we do understand them now—and they speak to us through this chronology. Do they not thereby seal the chronology? They do to *faith,* but not otherwise. Our Lord declared, "The wise shall understand"; and he told us to "Watch" that we might know; and it is this chronology which *convinces us* (who can and do receive it by faith) that the Parable of the Ten Virgins is now in process of fulfilment—that its first cry was heard in 1844 and its second cry, "Behold the Bridegroom"—present—was in 1874.

How beneficial is it—or, for that matter, how much humility does it demonstrate—to acknowledge fallibility while at the same time implying that only those who accept one's views are showing faith, are among 'the wise who shall understand'? Would not those failing to heed these "cries" of 1844 and 1874 be classed logically with the "foolish virgins" of the parable?

Earlier the same article had said:

God's times and seasons are given in such a way as to be convincing only to those who, by acquaintance with God, are able to recognize his characteristic methods.

Thus, if any expressed doubts about the Society's chronology, the very quality of their relationship with God was subtly placed in question—along with their faith and wisdom. This is a form of intellectual intimidation, a practice that increased manyfold once 1914 had passed by, failing to fulfill the expectations published worldwide.

8

JUSTIFICATION AND INTIMIDATION

*"When men talk too much, sin is never far
away; common sense holds its tongue."*
—Proverbs 10:19, *New English Bible*.

CHARLES Taze Russell, who had referred to himself as "God's mouthpiece," died in 1916. He left behind a legacy of time prophecies not one of which had brought the results foretold. He also left behind thousands of confused followers.

The book *Light I*, published in 1930, page 194, describes the situation in this way:

> All of the Lord's people looked forward to 1914 with joyful expectation. When that time came and passed there was much disappointment, chagrin and mourning, and the Lord's people were greatly in reproach. They were ridiculed by the clergy and their allies in particular, and pointed to with scorn, because they had said so much about 1914, and what would come to pass, and their 'prophecies' had not been fulfilled.

With the passage of both 1914 and 1915 and no complete overthrow of all kingdoms and human institutions, no takeover of all earth's rule by Christ's kingdom, no transition of the anointed to heavenly life, no destruction of "Babylon the Great," no conversion of Israel to Christianity—all foretold to take place by 1914—serious doubts arose among Watch Tower adherents. True, there had been the outbreak of World War I but it had not resulted in the worldwide anarchy predicted.

In October, 1916, shortly before his death, Russell, in writing a foreword to a new edition of *The Time Is At Hand*, endeavored to play down the significance of the inaccuracy of what had been predicted for 1914. What follows is illustrative of the approach he took:

> The author acknowledges that in this book he presents the thought that the Lord's saints might expect to be with Him in glory at the ending of the Gentile Times. This was a natural mistake to fall into, but the Lord overruled it for the blessing of His people. The thought that the Church would all be gathered to glory before October, 1914, certainly did have a very stimulating and sanctifying effect upon thousands, all of whom accordingly can praise the Lord—even for the mistake. Many, indeed, can express themselves as being thankful to the Lord that the culmination of the Church's hopes was not reached at the time we expected; and that we, as the Lord's people, have further opportunities of perfecting holiness and of being participators with our Master in the further presentation of His Message to His people.

Involving God and Christ with the mistakes made, with God 'overruling' certain predictions, provides a very convenient escape from having to shoulder the true responsibility for having falsely presented as "God's dates" things that were not God's dates but simply the product of unauthorized human speculation. Merit is found even in false predictions because of the "stimulating and sanctifying effect" produced, so that one may "praise the Lord—even for the mistake." That approach allowed for still more false predictions with their "stimulating" effect. One is reminded of the true prophet's presentation of God's words, saying:

> "Woe to those who are saying that good is bad and bad is good, those who are putting darkness for light and light for darkness, those who are putting bitter for sweet and sweet for bitter!"[1]

While he remained alive and for a few years after his death, Russell's followers remained hopeful. When the war ended and things began to normalize, the passing of each year caused more questions to surface about the chronology advanced.

That is the situation Judge Rutherford inherited. (He had been elected as president of the Society in January, 1917, at the annual corporation meeting.) He was faced with two choices: rectifying by frank admis-

---

1 Isaiah 5:20.

sion of error, or trying to justify the predictions of his predecessor. He chose the course of justification.

Acting quickly to revive any flagging confidence on the part of *Watch Tower* readers, Rutherford arranged for a book called *The Finished Mystery* to be published in 1917, the year following Russell's death.

This book endeavored to move some of the things expected in 1914 up to 1918, doing this by drawing a parallel with the smashing of the Jewish revolt by the Romans. The Roman destruction of Jerusalem came in the year 70 C.E., but the end of the struggle did not come until three and a half years later, in the year 73 C.E. So, that same amount of time was added to the autumn of 1914 and *The Finished Mystery* now pointed to the spring of 1918 as a new date of great significance.

The portions of the book here underlined show what was now foretold to occur. On reading them, note the language used and ask whether it would be 'reading into the book things that are not there' to say that it contained outright predictions and aroused expectations that were never fulfilled:

---

62   *The Finished Mystery*   REV. 8

Mark 1:5; Luke 1:5, 65; 3:1; 7:17; Acts 11:29; Rom. 15:31, and *especially* John 7:1-3 and 1 Thes. 2:14-16.
  The data presented in comments on Rev. 2:1 *prove* that the conquest of Judea was not completed until the day of the Passover, A. D. 73, and in the light of the foregoing Scriptures, *prove* that the Spring of 1918 will bring upon Christendom a spasm of anguish greater even than that experienced in the Fall of 1914. Reexamine the table of the Parallel Dispensations in STUDIES IN THE SCRIPTURES, Vol. 2, pages 246 and 247; change the 37 to 40, 70 to 73 and 1914 to 1918, and we believe it is correct and will be fulfilled "with great power and glory." (Mark 13:26.) It was entirely impossible to foresee whether our Lord meant that A. D. 70 or A. D. 73 should serve as our guide to the time when the Jewish polity came to an end, until after October, 1915, had passed. Moreover, we have seen the promised signs, "upon the earth distress of nations, with perplexity; men's hearts failing them for fear, and for looking after those things which are coming on the earth," and we have the Lord's words for it that having seen those things "the Kingdom of God is nigh at hand," "even at the doors," and our "redemption draweth nigh." (Luke 21:25-36; Mark 13:27-30.) It is possible that A. D. 1980 marks the regathering of all of Fleshly Israel from their captivity in death. It is just 70 years beyond 1910, the date when Pastor Russell gave his great witness to the Jewish people in the New York Hippodrome. See page 551 (1).

> But if the time of nominal Zion's travail (Isa. 66:8) is due to occur in the Spring of 1918, and if we are now but the "one day" (one year) distant from that event which the Prophet mentions, what should be our expectation regarding the experience of the "little flock" meantime? "The symbolic travail, in the above prophecy, is a reference to the great Time of Trouble—the travail that is to come upon the nominal Gospel church, Great 'Babylon,' from which some are to be counted worthy to escape.

1918 was thus to see the nations of Christendom suffer a "spasm of anguish" greater than that experienced in 1914 when World War I started. In reality, that year saw the end of the war in an armistice. The book also foretold that the remnant of "anointed ones," the "last of the Elijah class," would experience their transition to heaven in that year, as page 64 states:

> Forty days after Christ's resurrection His ascension occurred. This confirms the hope of the Church's glorification forty years' (a year for a day) after the awakening of the sleeping saints in the Spring of 1878. The ·seven days before the Deluge may represent seven years, from 1914 to 1921, in the midst of which "week of years" the last members of the Messiah pass beyond the veil. The Great Company class shall be cut off at its end—the fact that we see the first half of this week so distinctly marked would lead us to expect three and one-half years more of witnessing by the Great Company class; for it seems to be the Heavenly Father's way to accomplish His work by weeks and half weeks, from the very beginning of creation until now. The covenant with Abraham, 2045 B. C., was half way (2081 years each way) between the fall of Adam, 4127 B. C., and the conversion of Cornelius, A. D. 36. The last observance of a typical Jubilee by Israel, 626 B. C., was half way (2500 years each way) from the end of Adam's Day, 3127 B. C., and the beginning of the Times of Restitution, A. D. 1874. The captivity, 606 B. C., marks the beginning of the Times of the Gentiles, half way (2520 years each way) between the end of Adam's 1000-year day, 3127 B. C., and the end of Gentile Times, A. D. 1914. The captivity, 606 B. C., marks a point half way (3520 years each way) between the fall of man, 4127 B. C., and his full restoration to Divine favor, A. D. 2914. Christ's death, A. D. 33, marks a point half way (1845 years each way) between the death of Jacob, 1813 B. C., and the restoration of favor to ·Israel in 1878 A. D. The death of Christ, A. D. 33, was half way (three and one-half years each way) between His baptism, A. D. 29, and the conversion of Cornelius, A. D. 36.
> The awakening of the sleeping saints, A. D. 1878, was just half way (three and one-half years each way) between the beginning of the Times of Restitution in 1874 and the close of the High Calling in 1881. Our proposition is that the glorification of the Little Flock in the Spring of 1918 A. D. will be half way (three and one-half

years each way) between the close of the Gentile Times
and the close of the Heavenly Way, A. D. 1921.

As with the similar prediction regarding 1881, this also failed. Perhaps the most forceful language used was in the predictions of a terrible destruction due to come on Christendom's churches and their
members in 1918, with their dead bodies strewn about unburied. Pages
484 and 485 contain two of several examples of this prophecy:

THE CHURCHES TO CEASE TO BE

24:20, 21. Then I answered them, The word of the Lord
came unto me, saying, Speak unto the house of Israel.
Thus saith the Lord God; Behold, I will profane My Sanctuary, the excellency of your strength, the desire of your
eyes, and that which your soul pitieth; and your sons and
your daughters whom ye have left shall fall by the sword.
—God gives the reason. It was as a picture or parable of
what is to happen to Christendom. Until 1878 the nominal
church had been in a sense God's sanctuary or Temple:
but He was from then on, culminating in 1918, to remove it
with a stroke or plague of erroneous doctrines and deeds
Divinely permitted. The Church was the strength of Christendom, that about which its life centered, and around
which its institutions were built. It was the desire of the
eyes of the people, that which all Christians loved. Nevertheless, God was to make manifest the profanation which
ecclesiasticism had made of the Christian Church, and to
cause the church organizations to become to Him as one
dead, an unclean thing, not to be touched, or mourned.
And the "children of the church" shall perish by the
sword of war, revolution and anarchy, and by the Sword
of the Spirit be made to see that they have lost their hope
of life on the spirit plane—that "the door is shut."
24:22. And ye shall do as I have done: ye shall not
cover your lips, nor eat the bread of men.—So universal
and dreadful will be the troubles that the dead will literally lie unburied and unwept. There can be no mourning
for the dead in a period when the living are overwhelmed
by troubles worse than death.

PASTOR RUSSELL DEAD, BUT SPEAKING AGAIN

24:25, 26. Also, thou son of man, shall it not be in the
day when I take from them their strength, the joy
of their glory, the desire of their eyes, and that whereupon
they set their minds, their sons and their daughters. That
he that escapeth in that day shall come unto thee, to cause
thee to hear it with thine ears?—Also, in the year 1918,
when God destroys the churches wholesale and the church
members by millions, it shall be that any that escape shall
come to the works of Pastor Russell to learn the meaning
of the downfall of "Christianity."
24:27. In that day shall thy mouth be opened to him
which is escaped, and thou shalt speak, and be no more
dumb: and thou shalt be a sign unto them; and they shall
know that I am the Lord.—Pastor Russell's voice has been

stilled in death; and his voice is, comparatively speaking, dumb to what it will be. In the time of revolution and anarchy he shall speak, and be no more dumb to those that escape the destruction of that day. Pastor Russell shall "be a sign unto them," shall tell them the truth about the Divine appointment of the trouble, as they consult his books, scattered to the number of ten million throughout Christendom. His words shall be a sign of hope unto them, enabling them to see the bright side of the cloud and to look forward with anticipation to the glorious Kingdom of God to be established. Then "they shall know the Lord."

Not only Christendom's churches but her governments as well would meet up with catastrophe and oblivion:

Christendom Not to Endure   513

31:14. To the end that none of all the trees by the waters exalt themselves for their height, neither shoot up their top among the thick boughs, neither their trees stand up in their height, all that drink water; for they are all delivered unto death, to the nether parts of the earth, in the midst of the children of men, with them that go down to the pit.—No other earthly system may follow her proud example; for all of them are delivered, as systems, into death, to a dishonored place among the lowest in society.

31:15. Thus saith the Lord God; In the day when he went down to the grave I caused a mourning: I covered the deep for him, and I restrained the floods thereof, and the great waters were stayed: and I caused Lebanon to mourn for him, and all the trees of the field fainted for him. —In the year 1918, when Christendom shall go down as a system to oblivion, (Sheol) to be succeeded by revolutionary republics, God will cause mourning. He will restrain and defer for a brief period the threatening waves of anarchy. He will cause the nations to mourn for Christendom, and all the man-made systems (trees) of the world (field) to become weak on account of her fall.—E392, 372.

31:16. I made the nations to shake at the sound of his fall, when I cast him down to hell (Sheol) with them that descend to the pit: and all the trees of Eden, the choice and best of Lebanon, all that drink water, shall be comforted in the nether parts of the earth.—God will cause the nations to shake with gigantic revolutions, when He shall cast worldly Christendom, as an organized system, down to oblivion (as He did the Jews in the Dives parable).

31:17. They also went down into hell (Sheol) with him, unto them that be slain with the sword; and they that were in his arm, that dwelt under his shadow in the midst of the heathen.—But they also shall go down to oblivion (Sheol) (E392, 372), with Christendom, as well as those that were her power, that dwelt under her defense among the people.

All these things were foretold for the year 1918. None of them took place. But the book also predicted stupendous events for the year 1920. The gigantic revolutions that were to begin in 1918 would reach a

culmination in 1920 with the disappearance of all orderly government
of any kind:

258   *The Finished Mystery*   REV. 16

To give unto her the cup of the wine of the fierceness of
[His] THE wrath.—The wine of the vine of the earth.—Rev.
14:17-20; Jer. 8:14; Isa. 51:17-20; Jer. 25:26-28; Rev. 18:6.
16:20. And every island fled away.—Even the republics
will disappear in the fall of 1920.
And the mountains were not found.—Every kingdom of
earth will pass away, be swallowed up in anarchy.
16:21. And there fell upon men.—Greek "The Men," the
worshipers of the beast and his image, i. e., the clergy.
A great hail out of heaven.—Truth, compacted, coming with crushing force. A concluding statement
of how the seventh volume of *Scripture Studies* ap-
pers to the worshipers of the beast and his image.—Rev.
11:19; Isa. 28:17; 30:30; Ezek. 13:11; Joshua 10:11.
Every stone about the weight of a talent.—113 lbs. (Mal.
3:10.) Another view of the seventh volume of *Scripture
Studies*, as it appears to the worshipers of the beast and
his image, is found in the last of the Egyptian plagues,
the death of the first-born, Exodus 11th. and 12th. chapters.
As soon as this plague came the Egyptians, from Pharaoh
down, were anxious to speed the parting guest, and willing
to give up all the jewels of silver (the Great Company) and
the jewels of gold (the Little Flock). In connection with
the statement that "there was not a house where there
was not one dead," it is admitted that if any sects were
overlooked in the lists cited in comments on Rev. 8th and
9th chapters the omission was unintentional and will be
corrected in later editions. The three days in which Pharaoh's host pursued the Israelites into the wilderness represent the three years from 1917 to 1920 at which time all
of Pharaoh's messengers will be swallowed up in the sea of
anarchy. The wheels will come off their chariots—organizations.

Thus, even the radical elements that would produce the revolutions
in Christendom in 1918 and give birth to the laborite and socialist
governments were to see those movements meet their demise. This
would be because, even as those movements were to bring about the
downfall of Christendom's existing governments, they themselves would
be brought down by anarchists in 1920:

542   *The Finished Mystery*   EZEK. 35

upon ecclesiasticism and Christianity in anger and fury
and with hateful envy, so God will do to the Socialistic,
laborite order of things. As they aid in smiting down
Christianity, so will the anarchists smite them down.
35:12. And thou shalt know that I am the Lord, and
that I have heard all thy blasphemies, which thou hast
spoken against the mountains of Israel, saying, They are

laid desolate, they are given us to consume.—The laborites, etc., will learn that God rules in the affairs of men, and that the Almighty will pay attention to their utterances against the nations (mountains) of Christendom (Israel), when, after ecclesiasticism's fall, the laborites shall say, "The nations have been desolated, and are given to us working people to divide up for ourselves."

35:13. Thus with your mouth ye have boasted against Me, and have multiplied your words against Me: I have heard them.—The Socialistic and kindred movements, while speaking savagely against capitalism, and covertly against Christianity, have in reality been speaking against an order permitted by God, and in which God was—in the indwelling of His Holy Spirit, in such true Christians as were in the systems. In expressing the determination to lead the world out of the darkness of evil economic, social and political conditions, they unwittingly boast against God by presuming to perform what God previously planned to be done by His faithful Church, and which by any lesser agency is absolutely impossible of accomplishment, God will not pass by unnoticed the words of Socialists, syndicalists, laborites, etc. He will hear them, and remember them for just recompense.

35:14. Thus saith the Lord God; When the whole earth rejoiceth, I will make thee desolate.—When the Times of Restitution of all things come, one of the things not to be restored is the Socialist, laborite movement. When all society rejoices in the new order of things ordained of God, the Socialistic state will have been utterly and forever desolated.

35:15. As thou didst rejoice at the inheritance of the house of Israel, because it was desolate, so will I do unto thee; thou shalt be desolate, O mount Seir, and all Idumea, even all of it: and they shall know that I am the Lord.—As the fleshly-minded apostates from Christianity, siding with the radicals and revolutionaries, will rejoice at the inheritance of desolation that will be Christendom's after 1918, so will God do to the successful revolutionary movement; it shall be utterly desolated, "even all of it." Not one vestige of it shall survive the ravages of world-wide all-embracing anarchy, in the fall of 1920. (Rev. 11:7-13.)

"World-wide, all-embracing anarchy, in the fall of 1920." Despite all the striking, stirring language and the positiveness of the claims, none of it came. Like 1914, the new dates of 1918 and 1920 passed without the foretold "spasm of anguish" upon Christendom, the overthrow of her governments and destruction of her churches or the transferral of the anointed to heaven.

Instead, 1918 saw President Rutherford and six other principal officers of the Society tried and sentenced to prison on wartime charges that *The Finished Mystery* book and other publications contained seditious statements. The following year, 1919, they were released and exonerated of all charges.

Thus, they were free to observe 1920, the year in which, by autumn time, all republics and "every kingdom of earth" would be "swallowed up in anarchy," according to *The Finished Mystery*. By that year, however, new predictions were developed and proclaimed. Without even allowing 1920 to pass, a new date was now set forth to be anticipated.

"MILLIONS NOW LIVING WILL NEVER DIE"

"I did not send the prophets, yet they themselves ran. I did not speak to them, yet they themselves prophesied." —Jeremiah 23:21.

In 1920, Watch Tower president Rutherford published a booklet titled *Millions Now Living Will Never Die*. That catchy phrase is still used by the organization to this day. Back there, however, it was based on a new prediction that the Watch Tower president had developed. The whole thrust of the claim that millions then living would never die was tied to a new date: 1925. Note what the underlined portions of the booklet say of that year on pages 88, 89, 90 and 97:

---

88   *Millions Now Living Will Never Die*

seventy jubilees kept. (Jeremiah 25:11; 2 Chronicles 36:17-21) A simple calculation of these jubilees brings us to this important fact: Seventy jubilees of fifty years each would be a total of 3500 years. That period of time beginning 1575 before A. D. 1 of necessity would end in the fall of the year 1925, at which time the type ends and the great antitype must begin. What, then, should we expect to take place? In the type there must be a full restoration; therefore the great antitype must mark the beginning of restoration of all things. The chief thing to be restored is the human race to life; and since other Scriptures definitely fix the fact that there will be a resurrection of Abraham, Isaac, Jacob and other faithful ones of old, and that these will have the first favor, we may expect 1925 to witness the return of these faithful men of Israel from the condition of death, being resurrected and fully restored to perfect humanity and made the visible, legal representatives of the new order of things on earth.

Messiah's kingdom once established, Jesus and his glorified church constituting the great Messiah, shall minister the blessings to the people they have so long desired and hoped for and prayed might come. And when that time comes, there will be peace and not war, as the prophet beautifully states: "In the last days it shall come to pass, that the mountain of the house of the Lord shall be established in the top of the mountains, and it shall be exalted above

---

the hills; and people shall flow unto it. And many nations shall come, and say, Come, and let us go up to the mountain of the Lord, and to the house of the God of Jacob; and he will teach us of his ways, and we will walk in his paths: for the law shall go forth of Zion, and the word *of the Lord from Jerusalem. And he shall judge* among many people, and rebuke strong nations afar off; and they shall beat their swords into plowshares, and their spears into pruninghooks; nation shall not life up a sword against nation, neither shall they learn war any more. But they shall sit every man under his vine and under his fig tree; and none shall make them afraid; for the mouth of the Lord of hosts hath spoken it." —Micah 4:1-4.

EARTHLY RULERS

As we have heretofore stated, the great jubilee cycle is due to begin in 1925. At that time the earthly phase of the kingdom shall be recognized. The Apostle Paul in the eleventh chapter of Hebrews names a long list of faithful men who died before the crucifixion of the Lord and before the beginning of the selection of the church. These can never be a part of the heavenly class; they had no heavenly hopes; but God has in store something good for them. They are

to be resurrected as perfect men and constitute
the princes or rulers in the earth, according to
his promise. (Psalm 45:16; Isaiah 32:1; Matthew 8:11)   Therefore we may confidently expect that 1925 will mark the return of Abraham,

90   *Millions Now Living Will Never Die*

Isaac, Jacob and the faithful prophets of old,
particularly those named by the Apostle in
Hebrews chapter eleven, to the condition of
human perfection.

Millions Now Living Will Never Die   97

in due time after the establishment of the kingdom.   Then it shall come to pass that every one
who will keep the saying of the Lord shall never
see death.   This promise would not have been
made by Jesus if he did not intend to carry it
into full force and effect in due time.

Again he said: "Whosoever liveth and be-
lieveth in me shall never die". (John 11:26)
Do we believe the Master's statement?   If so,
when the time comes for the world to know, then
they who believe and, of course, render themselves in obedience to the terms have the absolute and positive statement of Jesus that they
shall never die.

Based upon the argument heretofore set forth,
then, that the old order of things, the old world,
is ending and is therefore passing away, and
that the new order is coming in, and that 1925
shall mark the resurrection of the faithful
worthies of old and the beginning of reconstruc-
tion, it is reasonable to conclude that millions

> of people now on the earth will be still on the earth in 1925. Then, based upon the promises set forth in the divine Word, we must reach the positive and indisputable conclusion that millions now living will never die.
>
> Of course, it does not mean that every one will live; for some will refuse to obey the divine law; but those who have been evil and turn again to righteousness and obey righteousness shall live and not die. Of this we have the positive statement of the Lord's prophet, as follows:

This formed the basis for what was called the "Millions Campaign," a worldwide effort to call attention to the message of this booklet during a two-year period. As the book *Jehovah's Witnesses in the Divine Purpose* states, "large billboard advertisements were erected in all the big cities with streaming letters, "Millions Now Living Will Never Die."

That publicity was buttressed by newspaper advertisements. All public talks given by Watch Tower representatives focused on this theme.[2] The Society relates these features of this all-out, worldwide effort. It even occasionally uses the spectacular slogan today. What it does not inform its readers is that the *prime foundation* and the *whole strength* of the claim that "Millions Now Living Will Never Die" rested on the predictions about 1925, predictions that proved utterly false.

In 1921, Rutherford published his first full-sized book, *The Harp of God*. It reaffirmed the Society's confidence and faith in 1799 as the start of the "last days" and 1874 as the time when Christ began his "invisible presence." In the portions that follow, with key points underlined, note the way the developments that were distinctive of those times and world conditions were used as "indisputable" testimony in support of those dates:

236   *The Harp of God*

> *Scriptures.* The purpose here is to call attention to certain important dates and then see how much, if any, prophecy has been fulfilled within these dates. Chronology, to some extent at least, depends upon

---

2 *Jehovah's Witnesses in the Divine Purpose*, pp. 98, 100, 104.

accurate calculations and there is always some possibility of mistakes. Fulfilled prophecy is the record of physical facts which are actually existent and definitely fixed. Physical facts do not stultify themselves. They stand as silent witnesses whose testimony must be taken as indisputable.

⁴⁰⁰ There are two important dates here that we must not confuse, but clearly differentiate, namely, the beginning of "the time of the end" and of "the presence of the Lord". "The time of the end" embraces a period from 1799 A. D., as above indicated, to the time of the complete overthrow of Satan's empire and the establishment of the kingdom of the Messiah. The time of the Lord's second presence dates from 1874, as above stated. The latter period is within the first named, of course, and in the latter part of the period known as "the time of the end".

---

⁴⁰⁴ From that time forward there has been a great corresponding increase of knowledge in all the sciences; and in fact, in all lines of learning. The common school, always opposed by the Papacy, has afforded a means of general education and increase of knowledge for people in all walks of life. Colleges and universities have sprung up throughout the world. With the increase of knowledge on various lines have come the numerous inventions that man now has, time and labor-saving machines, etc.

⁴⁰⁵ Before 1799 the means of transportation were such that a man could travel only a short distance in a day. He must go either by a vehicle drawn by horses or oxen, or afoot; and when he would cross the sea he must go in a sailboat that made little progress. In 1831 the first locomotive steam engine was invented. Such wonderful progress has been made in this regard that now one can travel through almost any part of the earth at a rapid rate upon a railway train. Later came the electric engines and electric motor cars and gas engines; and now there is a tremendous amount of travel in every part of the earth. It is no uncommon thing for one to travel at the rate of 75 and 100 miles an hour; and particularly is this true by means of the flying machine, which is a very modern invention.

[406] The aforementioned inventions are related to 'the day of God's preparation' during Christ's presence.—Nahum 2:1-6.

[407] In 1844 the telegraph was invented, and later the telephone. These instruments were first used with wires, and by electricity messages were conveyed throughout the earth; but now by later invention wires are dispensed with and messages are flashed through the air by the use of instruments all over the earth.

[408] This great increase of knowledge and the tremendous running to and fro of the people in various parts of the earth is without question a fulfilment of the prophecy testifying as to "the time of the end". These physical facts can not be disputed and are sufficient to convince any reasonable mind that we have been in "the time of the end" since 1799.

[409] The latter part of "the time of the end" Jesus designates as a time of harvest, because he says: "The harvest is the end of the world [age]." He stated that he would be present at that time. From 1874 forward is the latter part of the period of "the time of the end". From 1874 is the time of the Lord's second presence, as above stated. The Apostle Paul, enumerating many things done concerning Israel, states that "they are written for our admonition, upon whom the ends of the world [ages] are come". (1 Corinthians 10:11) It must be presumed, then, that these things would be understood at "the time of the end".

---

[410] The laboring classes have always been downtrodden and kept in subjection to the financial, ecclesiastical, and political princes. It was in the year 1874, the date of our Lord's second presence, that the first labor organization in the world was created. From that time forward there has been a marvelous increase of light, and the inventions and discoveries have been too numerous for us to mention all of them here, but mention is made of some of those that have come to light since 1874, as further evidence of the Lord's presence since that date, as follows: Adding machines, aeroplanes, aluminum, antiseptic surgery,

artificial dyes, automatic couplers, automobiles, barbed wire, bicycles, carborundum, cash registers, celluloid, correspondence schools, cream separators, Darkest Africa, disk plows, Divine Plan of the Ages, dynamite, electric railways, electric welding, escalators, fireless cookers, gas engines, harvesting machines, illuminating gas, induction motors, linotypes, match machines, monotypes, motion pictures, North Pole, Panama Canal, pasteurization, radium, railway signals, Rœntgen rays, shoe-sewing machines, skyscrapers, smokeless powder, South Pole, submarines, subways, talking machines, telephones, television, typewriters, vacuum cleaners, and wireless telegraphy.

Note particularly that, after describing the development of such things as Bible Societies, increase of colleges and universities; steam, electric and gasoline modes of transportation; telegraph and telephone—all resulting in a great increase in knowledge and movement—the book, on page 239, states:

"[This] is without question a fulfilment of the prophecy testifying to the 'time of the end.' These physical facts can not be disputed and are sufficient to convince any reasonable mind that we have been in 'the time of the end' since 1799."

That which is "without question" is logically infallible. The word "infallible" is not used—but to all intents and purposes the claim is made. And if any doubt or are not convinced, well, they simply do not come within the category of those having a "reasonable mind." This is also intellectual intimidation, a weapon that solid truth never needs to employ.

Despite whatever "stimulating and sanctifying" effect these new forecasts and strong affirmations about some of the old dates may have had, by the year 1922, with 1914 now eight years in the past, the confidence that many had placed in the Society's time prophecies was wearing thin. The methods the headquarters organization resorted to in trying to overcome this problem are revealing. They also form a pattern seen again in recent times, since 1975.

Instead of becoming more moderate in its claims about its interpretations or taking a more modest view of its authority, the organization became far more insistent upon conformity, the claims about the accuracy of its chronology became more dogmatic. "Loyalty" to the teachings of the "faithful and wise servant" (then argued as applying definitely to Pastor Russell) was the watchword. Those who questioned the chronology based on his teachings (which chronology was in turn based on the teachings of N. H. Barbour, John Aquila Brown and others) were depicted as not only lacking in faith but also overly impressed with their own wisdom, as proud, egotistical, ambitious, self-willed, misled by the adversary and guilty of repudiating the Lord. To give any weight to the testimony of ancient historians in contradiction of the organization's dates was to put confidence in "agents of Satan's empire."

If that seems difficult to believe, consider the statements made in a steady stream of *Watch Tower* articles during 1922 and 1923. Note the repeated use of terms such as "indisputable," "correct beyond a doubt," "divinely corroborated," "absolutely and unqualifiedly correct," "incontestably established," "proven certainty," "of divine origin"—terms applied to the whole chronological scheme including 1799 (the start of the last days), 1874 (the start of Christ's invisible presence), 1878 (the start of the resurrection of the anointed), 1881 (the time when Russell was fully appointed as the Lord's steward), as well as 1914, 1918 and the most recent prophetic date of 1925, said to have 'as much Scriptural support as 1914.' For the reader's convenience, sections are underlined.

From the March 1, 1922, *Watch Tower*:

THE TIME OF THE HARVEST

Jesus said that the age would end with a harvest. at which time he would be present, and that he would then send forth his messengers to gather together his elect. (Matthew 13: 24-30; 24: 31) It is to be expected that the Lord would have some witness in the earth at the time of the harvest to make announcement of the fact of his presence and of the harvest. Here is some more circumstantial evidence which is proof conclusive; some more physical facts that speak louder than audible words, to wit: It was Brother Russell who announced the time of the harvest and the presence of the Master of the harvest. It was he who first went forth throughout the land crying out, 'The harvest is here; go ye into the field and labor'. And thousands of others taking up the slogan joined in the proclamation of the message.

Jesus plainly said that during the time of his presence

he would have a faithful and wise servant whom he would use to give meat to the household (of faith) in due season. Every one today who has a knowledge of the divine plan of the ages must truthfully answer that he derived that knowledge from studying his Bible in connection with what Brother Russell wrote; that before such time he did not even know that God had a plan of salvation. Every person who today is rejoicing in the light of the truth of God's Word realizes that the Lord brought to him that truth, unfolding it through the ministrations and work begun by Brother Russell shortly following the presence of the Lord.

Under the heading "Wise Toward God" (referring to Russell), the article speaks disparagingly of those who "believe they have greater wisdom than others" and says such typically "make statements in dogmatic form." A few paragraphs later it begins setting forth the "indisputable facts" about 1799 and 1874. What is "dogmatism" in others, is evidently considered "sincere conviction" when practiced by the writers of the magazine.

WISE TOWARD GOD

Was he wise? As the world understands that word, particularly as defined by worldly clergymen, *he was not*. And thank God he was not. Had he possessed great worldly wisdom, such as that employed by his defamers, the Lord would never have used him. Be it noted that these so-called learned clergymen charge against him that he was not learned in the Greek and Hebrew. That charge is true. The facts demonstrate beyond a doubt that the majority of men who possess a knowledge of Greek and Hebrew take themselves too seriously. They begin to think they know so much that they must bring forth something startling to upset what somebody else has done. They depart from the Lord's way and lean to their own understanding, contrary to his Word. (Proverbs 3:5, 6) They usually speak and write in such phrase that the ordinary mind cannot grasp it; and this they do hoping to magnify their own wisdom in the eyes of others. Because they believe they have greater wisdom than others they make statements in a dogmatic form, regardless of whether right or wrong, depending on the matter being swallowed by others because not able to fathom this supposed wisdom.

The indisputable facts, therefore, show that the "time of the end" began in 1799; that the Lord's second presence began in 1874; that the harvest followed thereafter and greater light has come upon the Word of God. In this connection, then, let us note the words of Jesus: "Who then is a faithful and wise servant, whom his lord hath made ruler over his household, to give them meat in due season? Blessed is that servant, whom his lord when he cometh shall find so doing." (Matthew 24:

Two months later the May 1, 1922, issue continued the campaign to rout out any thought of questioning the organization's teachings, using the same tactic:

AMBITION'S FRUITAGE

Ever and anon there arises some one who has been following the Lord, for a time at least, who possesses a measure of beauty of mind and character, and possibly of person—one who takes himself too seriously. He succeeds in convincing himself that the Lord has appointed him to look after things divine and to lead God's people out of the wilderness. As he goes on in this way, he becomes convinced in his own mind that the Lord made a mistake in selecting Brother Russell as that servant; and this doubt leads to the conclusion later on that Brother Russell was not "that servant" at all. He begins to doubt what Brother Russell wrote, and so expresses himself. Now he disregards the Lord's Word, which says: "Trust in the Lord with all thine heart; and lean not unto thine own understanding. In all thy ways acknowledge him, and he shall direct thy paths."

Thus disregarding this admonition, and being led on by the subtle influence of the adversary, he convinces himself that it is his solemn duty to undo all the things that Brother Russell taught and to turn the church's vision in the right way. He prepares a manuscript and charts in support of same, setting forth his views. Submitting it to others and being advised that his thoughts are wrong, he construes this to mean a desire to prevent him from permitting his light to shine,

and disregards such advice. So thoroughly is he impressed that he must thus teach the people and undo
that which has been taught, that he begins the publication of his thoughts and to send these forth to the
consecrated. His arguments seem plausible to those who
make only a superficial examination, and especially to
those who have forgotten what they were taught. Doubt
arises in the minds of some who thus read. Now the
test is on.

Loyalty to the Society's teachings, received from Russell, was equated
with loyalty to God and Christ. To deny Russell's teachings was to
deny Christ. This amazing claim is plainly stated in the same issue of
the *Watch Tower*:

Jesus clearly indicated that during his second presence he would have amongst the church a faithful and
wise servant, through whom he would give to the household of faith meat in due season. The evidence is overwhelming concerning the Lord's second presence, the
time of the harvest, and that the office of "that servant"
has been filled by Brother Russell. This is not man-
worship by any means. It matters not who Charles T.
Russell was—whether he was a doctor, a hod-carrier or
a seller of shirts. St. Peter was a fisherman; St. Paul
a lawyer. But these matters are immaterial. Above
all, these men were the chosen vessels of the Lord. Regardless of his earthly avocation, above all, Brother Russell was the Lord's servant. Then to repudiate him and
his work is equivalent to a repudiation of the Lord,
upon the principle heretofore announced.

This line of argument is precisely the same as that used half a century later, in the 1980's, in condemning those called "apostates." Then
as now, chronology was a major factor, made a "Test of Faith" as to
the genuineness of one's Christianity. This same issue of the *Watch
Tower* also warned that doubting the Society's date system, including
1799, 1874, 1914 and 1925, would lead eventually to a "repudiation
of God and our Lord Jesus Christ and the blood with which we were
bought." It said:

Again the test is on.. This time it is on chronology. And following this lead, it will be found that the road of doubt and opposition will carry one into doubting the second presence of the Lord, the time of the harvest, the office of "that servant" and the one who filled it, the evidences of the end of the world. the inauguration of the kingdom, the nearness of the restoration of man, and finally to a repudiation of God and our Lord Jesus Christ and the blood with which we were bought.

Now, issue after issue focused on the Society's chronology, speaking deprecatingly of any contrary evidence, and exalting the accuracy of the organization's own date system. 1914 was only one feature of that date system, and the *Watch Tower* argued insistently that *all* the dates (and the accompanying claims about them) were right, the product of divine guidance; hence there was no need to doubt any of them. From the May 15, 1922, *Watch Tower*:

CHRONOLOGY

WE HAVE no doubt whatever in regard to the chronology relating to the dates of 1874, 1914, 1918, and 1925. Some claim to have found new light in connection with the period of "seventy years of desolation" and Israel's captivity in Babylon, and are zealously seeking to make others believe that Brother Russell was in error.

The apostle James assures us that "if any of you lack wisdom, let him ask of God, that giveth to all men liberally, and upbraideth not; and it shall be given him". We believe that promise and daily petition for heavenly wisdom and grace to be guided aright. We also believe that the prayers of the saints ascend daily to the throne of heavenly grace for divine guidance as to what shall appear in THE WATCH TOWER, and we are very appreciative of that fact.

Readers were warned not to be easily swayed in favor of evidence from secular history that contradicted the Society's chronology. Note the closing statement of this paragraph:

Some of their best "authorities" are found at times to be unreliable; as, for instance, Josephus and Ptolemy.

These men lived during the first two centuries after Christ. They had difficulty in compiling their records; for complete data were not accessible to them. No doubt they did the best they could under their limited circumstances. They are accepted as among the best that secular history can produce. From these and from others, certain dates have been generally accepted by historical writers; but to be generally accepted does not necessarily imply absolute accuracy. However, to impress the weight of their wisdom upon their readers, these conclusions are often stated in positive language, and the student is inclined to accept them at their face statement without further investigation.

Compare that final statement with the kind of language the *Watch Tower* thereafter uses in urging acceptance of its system of dates:

STAMPED WITH GOD'S APPROVAL

It was on this line of reckoning that the dates 1874, 1914, and 1918 were located; and the Lord has placed the stamp of his seal upon 1914 and 1918 beyond any possibility of erasure. What further evidence do we need?

Using this same measuring line, beginning with the entry of the children of Israel into Canaan, and counting the full 70 cycles of 50 years each, as clearly indicated by Jehovah's sending of the Jews into Babylon for the full 70 years, it is an easy matter to locate 1925, probably the fall, for the beginning of the antitypical jubilee. There can be no more question about 1925 than there was about 1914. The fact that all the things that some looked for in 1914 did not materialize does not alter the chronology one whit. Noting the date marked so prominently, it is very easy for the finite mind to conclude that all the work to be done must center about it, and thus many are inclined to anticipate more than has been really foretold. Thus it was in 1844, in 1874, in 1878 as well as in 1914 and 1918. Looking back we can now easily see that those dates were clearly indicated in Scripture and doubtless intended by the Lord to encourage his people, as they did, as well as to be a means of testing and sifting when all that some expected did not come to pass. That all that some expect to see in 1925 may not transpire that year will not alter the date one whit more than in the other cases.

Once again the failed expectations resulting from earlier time prophecies are all charged up to the Lord's account, as of his doing, used by him, "doubtless intended by the Lord to encourage his people." Nothing strange is seen in this concept that God and Christ would use falsehood as a means of encouragement for their servants. Yet in Scripture we read that "God is light and there is no darkness at all in union with him."[3] The idea that God or his Son employ error in their guidance of Christians is foreign to Scripture. It is clearly an attempt to put the questioning one on the defensive, cast him in the role of complainer against God.

Great stress was laid on the claim that to change the chronology presented by *even one year* would be disastrous, "would destroy the entire system of chronology" advanced by the Society.[4] The fact is that most of the dates used for the B.C.E. period have been changed substantially by the Society in more recent times.

No adjective seemed too extreme and no claim too extravagant to be used in insisting on the rightness of what was then called "present-truth chronology." Keeping in mind that the great bulk of it has since been rejected, consider these claims made in the June 15, 1922, *Watch Tower*:

FURTHER PROOF OF PRESENT-TRUTH CHRONOLOGY

There is a well known law of mathematics called "the law of probabilities". Applications of this law are frequent in everyday life in settling matters of doubt. In a family of children, if a certain kind of mischief is committed, the probabilities— indeed, the certainty— are that it was done by a certain one, and that the others assuredly did not do it. If some peculiar damage is done by night to a single house, then by the law of probabilities it may have been a pure accident; if done to two houses in the same manner it probably was not accidental but by design of some person; but if done to three or more houses in the same manner it passes out of the possibility of accident into the *certainty* of design.

The chronology of present truth might be a mere happening if it were not for the repetitions in the two great cycles of 1845 and 2520 years, which take it out of the realm of chance and into that of certainty. If there were only one or two corresponding dates in these

3   1 John 1:5.
4   *Watch Tower*, June 15, 1922, p. 187.

cycles, they might possibly be mere coincidences, but where the agreements of dates and events come by the dozens, they cannot possibly be by chance, but must be by the design or plan of the only personal Being capable of such a plan—Jehovah himself; *and the chronology itself must be right.*

In the passages of the Great Pyramid of Gizeh the agreement of one or two measurements with the present-truth chronology might be accidental, but the correspondency of dozens of measurements proves that the same God designed both pyramid and plan—and at the same time proves the correctness of the chronology.

The agreement of the chronology with certain measurements of the Tabernacle and the Temple of Ezekiel further stamps the chronology as true.

It is on the basis of such and so many correspondencies—in accordance with the soundest laws known to science—that we affirm that, *Scripturally, scientifically, and historically, present-truth chronology is correct beyond a doubt.* Its reliability has been abundantly confirmed by the dates and events of 1874, 1914, and 1918. Present-truth chronology is a secure basis on which the consecrated child of God may endeavor to search out things to come.—1 Peter 1: 11, 12 ; John 16 : 13.

The chronology stood "firm as a rock, based upon the Word of God," the article said, stressing that belief in it was a "matter of faith in Jehovah and in his inspired Word."[5] The "divine" nature of the now largely rejected chronology was insisted upon, not for certain parts or elements of it, but for *all of it*, "absolutely." It bore the "stamp of approval of Almighty God." Thus the July 15, 1922, *Watch Tower*, under the heading "The Strong Cable of Chronology," said:

> The chronology of present truth is, to begin with, a string of dates, like other chronologies. That is to say, the dates are each known to be so many years before and after the succeeding and preceding dates, each step being proved by the most reliable evidence in existence. But if this were all the proof of the trustworthiness of the chronology, it could not truthfully be claimed to be more reliable than are the secular chronologies. Thus far, it is a chain, and no stronger than its weakest link.

5 *Watch Tower*, June 15, 1922, p. 187.

There exist, however, well established relationships among the dates of present-truth chronology. These internal connections of the dates impart a much greater strength than can be found in other chronologies. Some of them are of so remarkable a character as clearly to indicate that this chronology is not of man, but of God. Being of divine origin and divinely corroborated, present-truth chronology stands in a class by itself, absolutely and unqualifiedly correct.

INCONTESTABLY ESTABLISHED

When a date is indicated by several lines of evidence it is strongly established. The scientific law of probabilities imparts a united strength to the strands of the cable of chronology far greater than the sum of the individual lines of evidence. This is a law which is implicitly relied upon in important affairs: viz., that when a thing is indicated in only one way it may be by chance; if it is indicated in two ways, it is almost certain to be true; and if in more than two ways, it is usually impossible that it is by chance, or that it is not true; and the addition of more proofs removes it entirely from the realm of chance into that of proven certainty.

This principle is applied daily in the weightiest matters in courts of law. The testimony of a single witness may be considered doubtful, but that of only two or three witnesses incontestably establishes the truth. "In the mouth of two or three witnesses shall every word be established."—2 Corinthians 13:1.

In the chronology of present truth there are so many inter-relationships among the dates that it is not a mere string of dates, not a chain, but a cable of strands firmly knit together—a divinely unified system, with most of the dates having such remarkable relations with others as to stamp the system as not of human origin.

PROOF OF DIVINE ORIGIN

It will be clearly shown that present-truth chronology displays indisputable evidence of divine foreknowledge of the principle dates, and that this is proof of divine origin, and that the system is not a human invention but a discovery of divine truth.

The proof resides in the many connecting inter-relationships among the dates. Without these relations
the chronology would not differ from secular systems,
but with them we believe that it bears the stamp of
approval of Almighty God.

"Parallelisms" were relied upon heavily as evidence of the divine
origin of the date system advanced, parallel periods of 1,845 years
and of 2,520 years being applied to a considerable number of dates
and events in history. Of this system of using parallelisms the article
in this issue of the *Watch Tower* stated:

Parallelisms of this nature are proof of divine origin
of present-truth chronology, because they show foreknowledge. In the instance cited, the division of Israel
and that of Christendom, 2520 years apart, are evidence
that when the first division was permitted, the latter
one was foreknown. This is true because of the relationship between the two events as regards both time and
nature.

When it is found that there is a series or system of
parallel dates composed of pairs of dates 2520 years
apart, the foreknowledge becomes obvious. It would
be absurd to claim that the relationship discovered was
not the result of divine arrangement. God alone has
such foreknowledge, and this proves that he so overruled
times and events that they should be knit together into
a beautiful and harmonious whole too sublime to be the
result of chance or of human invention.

Though described as so obviously the product of divine foreknowledge that to deny their reliability and significance would be "absurd,"
the whole system of using parallelisms has since been discarded by
the organization.

All of this material, hammering away at any tendency to question
the time prophecies that formed such a vital part of the doctrinal structure of the organization seems to have been preparing the *Watch Tower*
readers for a coming event. It apparently was designed to build up a
certain spirit and attitude before the holding of that year's convention
in Cedar Point, Ohio. Regularly referred to as a major milestone in
the organization's history, that 1922 convention had as its principal
talk a discussion that built on the foundation already laid by the earlier

Watch Tower articles. Today the organization quotes a small portion of that talk in support of 1914. It ignores the fact that 1799 and 1874 figured with equal strength in the argument advanced and in the conclusion the audience was then called upon to reach, as seen in the following portions published in the November 1, 1922, *Watch Tower*:

> Bible prophecy shows that the Lord was due to appear for the second time in the year 1874. Fulfilled prophecy shows beyond a doubt that he did appear in 1874. Fulfilled prophecy is otherwise designated the physical facts; and these facts are indisputable. All true watchers are familiar with these facts, as set forth in the Scriptures and explained in the interpretation by the Lord's special servant.
>
> Jesus himself declared that in the time of his presence he would conduct a harvest of his people, during which he would gather unto himself the true and loyal ones. For some years this work has been in operation and is nearing completion. He stated that during his presence he would have one who would fill the office of a faithful and wise servant, through whom the Lord would bring to his people meat in due season. All the facts show that those prophecies have been fulfilled.
>
> DAY OF PREPARATION
>
> Why has the King come? To set up his kingdom and reign as King. But he had a work to do before his reign began, and that is a preparatory work. Since there are to be associated with him in his reign his body members, these must be gathered together and prepared for the beginning of the reign. The gentile times under the supervision of the god of this world ended August 1, 1914. Before that date it would not have been consistent for the Lord, the King of glory, to take unto himself his great power and reign. (Ezekiel 21:27) Since he has been present from 1874, it follows, from the facts as we now see them, that the period from 1874 to 1914 is the day of preparation. This in no wise militates against the thought that "the time of the end" is from 1799 until 1914. The period from 1799 to 1874 could not be said to be a day of preparation, but a day of increasing light. It is not reasonable to think that the King began to make preparations until he was present.
>
> For six thousand years God has been preparing for this kingdom. For nineteen hundred years he has been gathering out the kingdom class from amongst men. Since 1874 the King of glory has been present; and during that time he has conducted a harvest and has gathered unto himself the temple class. Since 1914 the King of glory has taken his power and reigns. He has cleansed the lips of the temple class and sends them forth with the message. The importance of the message of the kingdom cannot be overstated. It is the message of all messages. It is the

message of the hour. It is incumbent upon those who are
the Lord's to declare it. The kingdom of heaven is at
hand; the King reigns; Satan's empire is falling; millions
now living will never die.

Do you believe it? Do you believe that the King of glory
is present, and has been since 1874? Do you believe that
during that time he has conducted his harvest work? Do
you believe that he has had during that time a faithful
and wise servant through whom he directed his work and
the feeding of the household of faith? Do you believe that
the Lord is now in his temple, judging the nations of
earth? Do you believe that the King of glory has begun
his reign?

Then back to the field, O ye sons of the most high God!
Gird on your armor! Be sober, be vigilant, be active, be
brave. Be faithful and true witnesses for the Lord. Go
forward in the fight until every vestige of Babylon lies
desolate. Herald the message far and wide. The world
must know that Jehovah is God and that Jesus Christ is
King of kings and Lord of lords. This is the day of all
days. Behold, the King reigns! You are his publicity
agents. Therefore advertise, advertise, advertise, the King
and his kingdom.

Despite the fierce calls for "loyalty" to Pastor Russell's teachings
and chronology, this talk is remarkable in that it reveals the first sign
of a gradual edging away from those very teachings. In *The Time Is
At Hand*, Russell had taught that "1878, being the parallel of his
[Christ's] assuming power and authority in the type, clearly marks the
time for the actual assuming of power as King of kings, by our present, spiritual, invisible Lord—the time of his taking to himself his
great power to reign." By Rutherford's talk at Cedar Point these acts—
invisible acts—were moved up from 1878 to 1914, a date that had
proved empty of all the things forecast and hoped for. It was the start
of what would later become an almost wholesale transferral of events
assigned to pre-1914 dates up to 1914 and post-1914 dates.

In harmony with the *Millions Now Living Will Never Die* booklet,
the organization was now teaching that the Jubilee cycle (which, according to God's law through Moses, involved consecutive periods of
fifty years, with a Jubilee year coming each fiftieth year) pointed to
1925 as the start of the millenium. It was to be marked by the return
of the prophets of old to earth. In 1924, the organization published a
booklet designed to be used by young people titled *The Way to Paradise*. Note how confidently these predictions were offered to those
young minds, including the description of earthly Jerusalem as the
world capital of restored mankind:

privilege of the heavenly invitation. God proved that he could easily find enough from the Gentiles to fill all the places of highest honor in his kingdom. This will be very humiliating to the Jews when they see what they have missed.

The Jewish legal year begins in the fall, about our October first. The year 1926 would therefore begin about October first, 1925. It would be very reasonable to expect to see some beginning of God's favor returning to the Jewish people, as a part of the world, shortly after that date. Many of the Jews are already looking longingly towards their old home-land, Palestine. God's limit of time to the Gentiles as nations expired in 1914, as we have already seen. Thus as the Jewish nation, as a nation, lost favor with God when they crucified Jesus, and the Gentile nations have no further recognition by God as nations, Christ will soon begin to deal with the world as individuals, commencing with the Jew first, through the ancient worthies. We should, therefore, expect shortly after 1925 to see the awakening of Abel, Enoch, Noah, Abraham, Isaac, Jacob, Melchisedec, Job, Moses, Samuel, David, Isaiah, Jeremiah, Ezekiel, Daniel, John the Baptist, and others mentioned in the eleventh chapter of Hebrews.

These will form a nucleus of the new kingdom on earth. One of the first things necessary will be to put Jerusalem in condition to be the capital of the world. This will necessitate a great deal of work, but there will be many willing

---

workers. Current news informs us that attention is already being centered upon Palestine, and thousands of Jews are trying to return there. Already considerable work has been done in the

way of building better roads and cultivating the
fields. However, we should not expect to see
much systematic work under way until these
"princes" have been awakened and placed in
charge.

The capital of every country should be in direct and quick communication with all parts of
its territory. If Jerusalem is to be the capital of
the world, it should be able to get into quick
touch with every locality. Christ's kingdom is
to undo in one thousand years all the evil
brought about in the previous six thousand
years. Old-fashioned methods will not suffice.
Already we see great changes coming in. The
wireless and radio can carry messages half way
around the world now; and by the time the
princes are brought forth these inventions will
be perfected to reach all the way around.

Everybody in the world will be "in one room,"
so to speak. The room will be a little larger than
we may have been accustomed to hold meeting
in; but what of that? Now when we read Isaiah
2:3 and Zechariah 14:16, 17 we see how easy
it will be for all the people to go "up to Jerusalem." The princes can easily radio their instructions to any part of the world. Think of
Prince Abraham having some general instructions to give, calling "Attention"; and all the

226   *The Way to Paradise*

people everywhere listening, and hearing every
word he speaks, as easily as though he were
addressing them from the platform of a public
hall!

Of course if any one desires to visit Jerusalem and personally interview the princes, or
if the princes should desire to make a personal
inspection of some public work, aeroplanes will

soon be so perfected that it will be a matter of but a few hours ride to any part of the earth to or from Jerusalem. This will indeed be a new world, made glorious in every way.—Zechariah 14:20, 21; Revelation 21: Psalms 72 and 145.

These ancient worthies will also have the power to use the "rod of iron," if necessary, to deal with the wilful and disobedient. All must learn that unrighteousness will not be permitted. Justice is the foundation law of the new kingdom.—Psalm 37:9, 10, 2, 38.

No doubt many boys and girls who read this book will live to see Abraham, Isaac, Jacob, Joseph, Daniel, and those other faithful men of old, come forth in the glory of their "better resurrection," perfect in mind and body. It will not take long for Christ to appoint them to their posts of honor and authority as his earthly representatives. The world and all the present conveniences will seem strange to them at first, but they will soon become accustomed to the new methods. They may have some amusing experiences at first; for they never saw telephones, radios, automobiles, electric lights, aeroplanes,

---

Princes in All the Earth   **227**

steam engines, and many other things so familiar to us.

What a privilege to be living just at this time and to see the ending of the old and the coming in of the new! Of all the times in earth's history, today is the most wonderful.

Needless to say, the boys and girls to whom this publication was addressed are now old men and old women, at least in their sixties or seventies.

Although the Society occasionally employs the catchy slogan "Millions now living will never die," and calls attention to the fact that Witness membership now surpasses the two million mark, they gloss over an obvious misrepresentation. The claim that "Millions now living will never die" was not made to people living in the 1980's. It was made to people in the first half of the 1920's. Only a fraction of the two-million-plus members of Jehovah's Witnesses were living then. Only if there were today more than two million Witnesses 63 years of age or older could there be any pretense that the prediction was in any way substantiated.

1925, on which the prediction and slogan were based, proved empty of all the things foretold. The teaching was without substance, mere fluff, prophetic fantasy.

Yet all of this material, appearing in the *Watch Tower* magazine and other publications, was supposedly "food in due season" being provided through God's channel of communication, a channel claiming the special approval and direction of Christ Jesus as the now reigning King. As they themselves say, they spoke as God's "genuine prophet."

The passing of 1925 and the failure of these latest predictions, however, proved that the predictors had not acted as a "faithful and discreet slave." They had not held faithfully and humbly to the inspired Word of God, which alone merits such terms as "indisputable," "absolutely and unqualifiedly correct," "incontestably established." Nor had they been discreet during all the years they published such dogmatic claims earthwide, that indiscretion being, in effect, acknowledged by Judge Rutherford's recognition that he had made an "ass" of himself.

The intimidating language used in the proclaimed "channel" of God, the *Watch Tower*, the insinuations of ambition, pride, and disloyalty to Christ it directed at any who did not want to take the same presumptuous course, doubtless influenced the majority to 'follow the leader' as he made admittedly asinine claims. Many, however, found they could not continue to support such an irresponsible course and the organization experienced a major loss in adherents after 1925.[6]

How do recent publications of the organization depict the 1925 situation? The *1975 Yearbook of Jehovah's Witnesses* attributed the problem, not to the organization that published the information, but to "the brothers" who read it, saying:

> The year 1925 came and went. Jesus' anointed followers were still on earth as a class. The faithful men

---

6 Among these was Alvin Franz, my father's brother and the youngest of the four Franz brothers.

> of old times—Abraham, David and others—had not been resurrected to become princes in the earth. (Ps. 45:16) So, as Anna MacDonald recalls: "1925 was a sad year for many brothers. Some of them were stumbled; their hopes were dashed. They had hoped to see some of the 'ancient worthies' [men of old like Abraham] resurrected. <u>Instead of its being considered a 'probability,' they read into it that it was a 'certainty,' and some prepared for their own loved ones with expectancy of their resurrection</u>.

Does a review of the published statements in the *Watch Tower*, as found in the preceding pages of this book, in any way justify this shifting of responsibility onto the "brothers" for having developed such high hopes and seeing those hopes dashed?

The 1980 *Yearbook* (published the same year that Rutherford's private remark was recounted to the headquarters family by President Franz) similarly gave this slant to the matter.

It tells of Judge Rutherford's visiting Switzerland in May of 1926 for a convention and his participation in a question meeting in which this interchange took place:

> "Question: Have the ancient worthies returned?
>
> "Answer [by Rutherford]: Certainly they have not returned. No one has seen them, and it would be foolish to make such an announcement. It was stated in the 'Millions' book that we might reasonably expect them to return shortly after 1925, but this was merely an expressed opinion."

Everyone has the right to express opinions. But men who claim to be God's spokesmen on earth surely do not have the right to express mere opinions while claiming that what they say is backed up by God's own Word and should be accepted as such. When statements are spread around the globe as God's message for mankind, as spiritual "food in due season," those publishing them are certainly neither "faithful" or "discreet" if they irresponsibly express fallacious opinions, argue tenaciously for them, belittle any who disagree or, worse, question their loyalty and humility before God.

In 1930, the house called Beth-Sarim was constructed by the organization in San Diego, California. Of this, the book *The New World*, written by Fred Franz, states:

were promptly thereafter defeated in battle
and cast out of heaven and down to the earth.
That wicked one and his demons now bring
great woes upon the earth and sea to drive all
nations into a totalitarian system and to turn
all people in bitterness against God. The
Lord Jesus has now come to the temple for
judgment, and the remnant of the members
of "his body" yet on earth he has gathered
into the temple condition of perfect unity
with himself (Malachi 3:1-3), and hence
those faithful men of old may be expected
back from the dead any day now. The Scriptures give good reason to believe that it shall
be shortly before Armageddon breaks.

In this expectation the house at San Diego,
California, which house has been much publicized with malicious intent by the religious
enemy, was built, in 1930, and named "Beth-
Sarim", meaning "House of the Princes".
It is now held in trust for the occupancy of
those princes on their return. The most recent facts show that the religionists of this
doomed world are gnashing their teeth because of the testimony which that "House
of the Princes" bears to the new world. To
those religionists and their allies the return
of those faithful men of old to rule with
judgment over the people shall not bring
any pleasure. [7]

As shown in an earlier chapter, it was in 1941, just sixteen years
after 1925, at a convention in St. Louis, Missouri, that the organization's head, President Rutherford, again was assuring young children
that very soon the faithful men and women of Bible times would return. They would direct the young people in their selection of mar-

---

7 A few years after this book was published (1942), the house was sold. At a large assembly
of Jehovah's Witnesses held in 1950 in Yankee Stadium, New York City, Fred Franz gave
a talk in which the predicted return of the "princes" before Armageddon was officially
abandoned, replaced with the view that the Society's appointees in the congregations already filled such princely role.

riage mates, making it advisable for them to postpone marriage until such time. The *Watchtower* describing the event then made its comment about the book *Children*, there released, as, "the Lord's provided instrument for most effective work *in the remaining months before Armageddon.*"

Approximately three hundred months later, in 1966, a new date came to the fore: 1975.

9

1975: 'THE APPROPRIATE TIME FOR GOD TO ACT'

"It is not for you to know the times or dates
the Father has set by his own authority."
—Acts 1:7, *New International Version*.

DURING the second half of Rutherford's presidency most of the older time prophecies so strenuously argued for in the first half, were gradually dropped or relocated.

The start of the "last days" was moved up from 1799 to 1914.

The 1874 presence of Christ was also moved up to 1914 (as had already been done in 1922 with the 1878 official start of Christ's active Kingdom rule).

The beginning of the resurrection was moved from 1878 to 1918.

For a time it was even claimed that 1914 had indeed brought the "end of the world" in the sense that God had 'legally' terminated the worldly nations' lease of power on the earth. This, too, was dropped and the "end," or "conclusion of the system of things" (as rendered in the *New World Translation*) is now held to be future.

All of the things claimed being *invisible*, the acceptance of them obviously depended entirely upon one's faith in the interpretations offered. After one Governing Body session in which these time prophecies and changes came up for discussion, Bill Jackson smilingly said to me, "We used to say, you just take the date from this shoulder and put it on the other shoulder."

It was not until after Rutherford's death in 1942 that a change was made regarding the year 606 B.C.E. as the starting point for the 2,520 years. Strangely, the fact that 2,520 years from 606 B.C.E. actually leads to 1915 C.E., and not 1914 C.E., was not acknowledged or dealt with for over 60 years.

Then, quietly, the starting point was moved back one year to 607 B.C.E., allowing for the retention of the year 1914 C.E. as the ending point for the 2,520 years. No historical evidence had come forward to indicate that the destruction of Jerusalem had occurred a year earlier than believed. The organization's desire to retain 1914 as a marked date pointed to by them for so many years (something they had not done with 1915) dictated moving Jerusalem's destruction back one year, a simple thing to do—on paper.

By the mid-1940's it had been decided that the chronology used during Russell's and Rutherford's presidencies was off some 100 years as regards the count of time back to Adam's creation. In 1966, the organization said that, instead of coming in 1874 as previously taught, the end of six thousand years of human history would arrive in 1975.

This was published in the summer of 1966 in a book written by Fred Franz, titled *Life Everlasting in Freedom of the Sons of God*. In its first chapter, the book drew upon the Jubilee arrangement, which had also featured prominently in the predictions relating to 1925, and it argued (as had also been done back then) in favor of belief in six "days" of a thousand years each, during which mankind was to experience imperfection, to be followed by a seventh "day" of a thousand years in which perfection would be restored in a grand Jubilee of liberation from slavery to sin, sickness and death. The book said on pages 28 and 29:

> [41] Since the time of Ussher intensive study of Bible chronology has been carried on. In this twentieth century an independent study has been carried on that does not blindly follow some traditional chronological calculations of Christendom, and the published timetable resulting from this independent study gives the date of man's creation as 4026 B.C.E.† According to this trustworthy Bible chronology six thousand years from man's creation will end in 1975, and the seventh period of a thousand years of human history will begin in the fall of 1975 C.E.
> [42] So six thousand years of man's existence on earth will soon be up, yes, within this generation. Jehovah God is timeless, as it is written in Psalm 90:1, 2: "O Jehovah, you yourself have proved to be a real dwelling for us during generation after generation. Before the mountains themselves were born, or you proceeded to bring forth

as with labor pains the earth and the productive
land, even from time indefinite to time indefinite
you are God." So from the standpoint of Jehovah
God these passing six thousand years of man's
existence are but as six days of twenty-four hours,
for this same psalm (verses 3, 4) goes on to say:
"You make mortal man go back to crushed matter, and you say: 'Go back, you sons of men.' For
a thousand years are in your eyes but as yesterday when it is past, and as a watch during the
night." So in not many years within our own
generation we are reaching what Jehovah God
could view as the seventh day of man's existence.

What would be the significance of this? The book goes on to make
this application of the points developed:

[43] How appropriate it would be for Jehovah God
to make of this coming seventh period of a thousand years a sabbath period of rest and release,
a great Jubilee sabbath for the proclaiming of
liberty throughout the earth to all its inhabitants!
This would be most timely for mankind. It would
also be most fitting on God's part, for, remember,
mankind has yet ahead of it what the last book
of the Holy Bible speaks of as the reign of Jesus
Christ over earth for a thousand years, the millennial reign of Christ. Prophetically Jesus Christ,
when on earth nineteen centuries ago, said concerning himself: "For Lord of the sabbath is
what the Son of man is." (Matthew 12:8) It
would not be by mere chance or accident but
would be according to the loving purpose of Jehovah God for the reign of Jesus Christ, the
"Lord of the sabbath," to run parallel with the
seventh millennium of man's existence.

Had the organization said 'flat out' that 1975 would mark the start
of the millennium? No. But the above paragraph was the climax to
which all of the involved, carefully constructed argumentation of that
chapter had been building.

No outright, unqualified prediction was made about 1975. But the
writer had been willing to declare it to be "appropriate" and "most
fitting on God's part" if God would start the millennium at that partic-

ular time. It would seem reasonable that for an imperfect man to say what is or what is not "fitting" for the Almighty God to do would call for quite a measure of certainty, surely not the mere 'expression of an opinion.' *Discretion* would require, rather, would *demand* that. Even stronger is the subsequent statement that "it would be according to the loving purpose of Jehovah God for the reign of Jesus Christ, the 'Lord of the sabbath,' to run parallel with the seventh millennium of man's existence," which seventh millennium had already been stated as due to begin in 1975.

That same year, the October 8, 1966, issue of *Awake!*, the companion magazine to the *Watchtower*, carried an article titled "How Much Longer Will It Be?" and under the subheading "6,000 Years Completed in 1975," it too reasoned that the millennium would be the last 1,000 years of a 7,000-year rest day of God. It went on to say (pages 19, 20):

> Hence, the fact that we are nearing the end of the first 6,000 years of man's existence is of great significance.
>
> Does God's rest day parallel the time man has been on earth since his creation? Apparently so. From the most reliable investigations of Bible chronology, harmonizing with many accepted dates of secular history, we find that Adam was created in the autumn of the year 4026 B.C.E. Sometime in that same year Eve could well have been created, directly after which God's rest day commenced. In what year, then, would the first 6,000 years of man's existence and also the first 6,000 years of God's rest day come to an end? The year 1975.* This is worthy of notice, particularly in view of the fact that the "last days" began in 1914, and that the physical facts of our day in fulfillment of prophecy mark this as the last generation of this wicked world. So we can expect the immediate future to be filled with thrilling events for those who rest their faith in God and his promises. It means that within relatively few years we will

>witness the fulfillment of the remaining
>prophecies that have to do with the "time
>of the end."

The May 1, 1968, *Watchtower* continued this stimulation of anticipation. Using much the same argument as the article last mentioned,
it then said (page 272):

>*"The immediate future is certain to be filled with climactic events*, for this
>old system is nearing its complete end. *Within a few years at most* the final
>parts of Bible prophecy relative to these "last days" will undergo fulfillment,
>resulting in the liberation of surviving mankind into Christ's glorious 1,000-
>year reign. What difficult days, but, at the same time, what grand days are just
>ahead!"[italics mine]

Fifteen years later, one may ask, What does the phrase "the *immediate* future" mean? How many years are a "few years at most"?

In an article titled "What Will the 1970s Bring?" the October 8,
1968, *Awake!* again emphasized the shortness of the remaining time,
saying at the start (page 13):

>"The fact that fifty-four years of the period called the 'last days' have already
>gone by is highly significant. It means that only a few years, at most, remain
>before the corrupt system of things dominating the earth is destroyed by God."

Later, drawing on the year 1975 as the close of six thousand years
of human history, the article said (page 14):

>"There is another way that helps confirm the fact that we are living in the
>final few years of this 'time of the end.' (Dan. 12:9) The Bible shows that we
>are nearing the end of a full 6,000 years of human history."

Again and again the Watch Tower publications quoted statements
made by people of prominence or "experts" in any field who made
some reference to 1975, for example, the statement made in 1960 by
former U.S. Secretary of State Dean Acheson, who said:

>"I know enough of what is going on to assure you that, in 15 years from
>today [hence, by 1975], this world is going to be too dangerous to live in."

The book *Famine—1975!*, by two food experts, was quoted repeatedly, particularly these statements:

>"By 1975 a disaster of unprecedented magnitude will face the world. Fa-
>mines, greater than any in history, will ravage the undeveloped nations."

"I forecast a specific date, 1975, when the new crisis will be upon us in all its awesome importance."

"By 1975 civil disorder, anarchy, military dictatorships, runaway inflation, transportation breakdowns and chaotic unrest will be the order of the day in many of the hungry nations."

Three years after the original focusing on 1975 in the book *Life Everlasting in Freedom of the Sons of God*, the author, Fred Franz, wrote another publication titled *The Approaching Peace of a Thousand Years.*[1] If anything, the language in it was even more definite and specific than in the previous publication. Released in 1969, it contained these statements on pages 25, 26:

> More recently earnest researchers of the Holy Bible have made a recheck of its chronology. According to their calculations the six millenniums of mankind's life on earth would end in the mid-seventies. Thus the seventh millennium from man's creation by Jehovah God would begin within less than ten years.

> In order for the Lord Jesus Christ to be "Lord even of the sabbath day," his thousand-year reign would have to be the seventh in a series of thousand-year periods or millenniums. (Matthew 12:8, *AV*) Thus it would be a sabbatic reign.

The argumentation here is quite clear and direct: As the sabbath was the seventh period following six periods of toil, so the thousand-year reign of Christ will be a sabbatical seventh millenium following those six milleniums of toil and suffering. The presentation is in no sense indefinite or ambiguous. As page 26 states:

"In order for the Lord Jesus Christ to be 'Lord even of the sabbath day,' his thousand-year reign would have to be the seventh in a series of thousand-year periods of milleniums."

Even as it had been determined what would be "appropriate" and "fitting" for God to do, so also a requirement is now set out for Jesus

---

1 This 32-page booklet is no longer published by the Society.

Christ. For him to be what he says he will be, 'Lord of the sabbath day,' then his reign "would have to be" the seventh millennium in a series of millenniums. Human reasoning imposes this requirement upon God's Son. Six thousand years would end in 1975; Christ's rule, according to the argument, "would have to be the seventh" thousand years following. The "faithful and discreet slave" had, in effect, outlined the program he expected his Master to adhere to if he was to be true to his own word.

Though the writing is more polished, the expressions more refined, this material in essence is remarkably like that set forth in Judge Rutherford's booklet *Millions Now Living Will Never Die*, in which he admittedly made asinine claims. Aside from the date being publicized, it was as if the clock had now been turned back about a half a century to the pre-1925 days. The difference was that the things said then were now being said of 1975.[2]

When the 1970's arrived, the buildup of expectation kept on. The October 8, 1971, *Awake!*, spoke yet again of six periods of toil and labor followed by a seventh (sabbath) period of rest and said:

"So, as we draw close to the completion of six thousand years of human existence during this decade, there is the thrilling hope that a grand Sabbath of rest and relief is indeed at hand."

Beneath this there was the following chart:

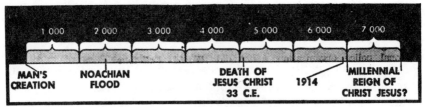

As we near the end of 6,000 years of human history in the
mid-1970's there is the thrilling hope of a grand relief

All these statements are clearly designed to foment and build up hope, anticipation. They are not designed to calm or defuse a spirit of excited expectation. True, most were accompanied by some qualify-

2   It is true that (on page 25) the less specific phrase "the mid-seventies" is used, but the year 1975 had already been presented as a Biblically marked date and that date was now firmly imprinted on the minds of all of Jehovah's Witnesses earthwide.

ing statement to the effect that 'we are not saying positively' or are not 'pointing to a specific date,' and that 'we do not know the day and the hour.' But it must be remembered that the organization was not a novice in this field. Its whole history from its very inception was one of building up people's hope in certain dates only to have those dates pass with the hope unrealized. In past cases the publications of the Society subsequently sought to place the responsibility for any disillusionment on the receivers, not the givers, of the information, as inclined to expect too much. Surely, then, the responsible men of the organization should have realized the danger, realized what human nature is, realized how easily great hopes can be excited.

Yet, while carefully avoiding any *explicit* prediction that a *specific* date would see the start of the millennium, those responsible men approved the use of the phrases, "within relatively few years," "the immediate future," "within a few years at most," "only a few years, at most" "the final few years" all used in the *Watchtower* and *Awake!* magazines with reference to the beginning of the millennial reign and *all in a context that included the date 1975.* Do such words mean anything? Or were they used loosely, carelessly? Are people's hopes and plans and feelings something to be toyed with? Yet the *Watchtower* of August 15, 1968, even implied that one should be careful about putting too much weight on Jesus Christ's own cautionary words.

[35]One thing is absolutely certain, Bible chronology reinforced with fulfilled Bible prophecy shows that six thousand years of man's existence will soon be up, yes, within this generation! (Matt. 24:34). This is, therefore, no time to be indifferent and complacent. This is not the time to be toying with the words of Jesus that "concerning that day and hour *nobody* knows, neither the angels of the heavens nor the Son, but only the Father." (Matt. 24:36) To the contrary, it is a time when one should be keenly aware that the end of this system of things is rapidly coming to its violent end. Make no mistake, it is sufficient that the Father himself *knows* both the "day and hour"!

How could a "faithful and discreet slave" possibly say this—in effect, say that, "True, my master said thus and so, but don't make too much of that; to the contrary, realize that what I am telling you should be the guiding force in your life"?

Some of the most direct statements came from the international headquarters' Service Department, which produces a monthly paper called "Kingdom Ministry," a paper which goes only to Witnesses and not to the public. The March, 1968, issue urged getting into full-time preaching activity ("pioneer service") saying:

> In view of the short period
> of time left, we want to do this as often as
> circumstances permit. Just think, brothers,
> there are only about ninety months left be-
> fore 6,000 years of man's existence on earth
> is completed.

The May, 1974, issue of *Kingdom Ministry*, having referred to the "short time left," said:

> Reports are heard
> of brothers selling their homes and property
> and planning to finish out the rest of their
> days in this old system in the pioneer service.
> Certainly this is a fine way to spend the short
> time remaining before the wicked world's
> end.—1 John 2:17.

Quite a number of Witnesses did just that. Some sold their businesses, gave up jobs, sold homes, farms and moved with their wives and children to other areas to 'serve where the need was greater,' counting on having sufficient funds to carry them through 1975.

Others, including some older persons, cashed in insurance policies or other valuable certificates. Some put off surgical operations in the hope that the millennium's entrance would eliminate the need for these.

When 1975 passed and their funds ran out or their health worsened seriously, they now had to try to cope with the hard realities and rebuild as best they could.

What was the thinking within the Governing Body during this time?

Some of the older men on the Body had personally experienced the failed expectations of 1914, 1925, as well as the hopes excited in the early 1940's. The majority, from my observation, took a 'wait and see' attitude. They were reluctant to call for restraint. Big increases were taking place. Consider the record of baptisms for the period from 1960 on up to 1975:

Year	Number Baptized	Year	Number Baptized
1960	69,027	1968	82,842
1961	63,070	1969	120,805
1962	69,649	1970	164,193
1963	62,798	1971	149,808
1964	68,236	1972	163,123
1965	64,393	1973	193,990
1966	58,904	1974	297,872
1967	74,981	1975	295,073

From 1960 up until 1966, the rate of increase had diminished to a near standstill. But following 1966, when 1975 was highlighted, there came a phenomenal period of growth, as the chart reveals.

During the years 1971 to 1974 while I was serving on the Governing Body I do not recall hearing any strong expressions of concern from Body members about the excited expectations that had been generated. I would not pretend that I did not initially feel stirred myself in 1966 when the book *Life Everlasting in Freedom of the Sons of God* came out with its glowing picture of the nearness of a millennial jubilee. Nor would I claim to have had no part whatsoever in the early part of the campaign to focus attention on the target date of 1975. But each passing year from 1966 on made the idea seem more and more unreal. The more I read the Scriptures the more the whole concept seemed out of line; it did not square with the statements of Jesus Christ himself, statements such as:

> "Concerning that day and hour nobody knows, neither the angels of the heavens nor the Son, but only the Father."
>
> "Keep on the watch, therefore, because you do not know on what day your Lord is coming."
>
> "On this account you too prove yourselves ready, because at an hour that you do not think to be it, the Son of Man is coming."
>
> "Keep looking, keep awake, for you do not know when the appointed time is."
>
> "It does not belong to you to get knowledge of the times or seasons which the Father has placed in his own jurisdiction."[3]

As part of a headquarters organization that was flushed with joy because of riding a crest of remarkable growth, there was not much that could be done, however. Some articles on the subject that came to me for editing I tried to moderate but that was about all. In my personal activity I did try to draw attention to the scriptures just mentioned, both in private conversations and in public talks.

One Sunday evening in 1974, after my wife and I had returned from a speaking engagement in another part of the country, my uncle, then vice president, came over to our room. (His eyesight being extremely poor, we usually read the *Watchtower* study material out loud to him each week.) My wife mentioned to him that in my talk that weekend I had cautioned the brothers about becoming unduly excited over 1975. His quick response was, "And why *shouldn't* they get excited? It's something to be excited about."

---

3 Quoted from Matthew 24:36, 42, 44; Mark 13:33; Acts 1:7.

There is no question in my mind that, of all the Governing Body members, the vice president was most convinced of the rightness of what he had written, and on which writing others had built. On another evening in the summer of 1975, an elderly Greek brother named Peterson (originally Papagyropoulos) joined in our reading, as was his custom. After the reading, my uncle said to Peterson, "You know, it was very much like this in 1914. Right up into the summer months everything was quiet. Then all of a sudden things began to happen and the war broke out."

Earlier, toward the start of 1975, President Knorr had made a trip around the world, taking Vice President Franz with him. The vice president's speeches in all countries visited centered on 1975. Upon their return, the other members of the Governing Body, having heard reports from many countries of the stirring effect of the vice president's talk, asked to hear a tape recording of it, made in Australia.[4]

In his talk, the vice president spoke of 1975 as a "year of great possibilities, tremendous probabilities." He told his audience that, according to the Hebrew calendar, they were "already in the fifth lunar month of 1975," with less than seven lunar months remaining. He emphasized several times that the Hebrew year would close with Rosh Hashanah, the Jewish New Year, on September 5, 1975.

Acknowledging that much would have to happen in that short time if the final windup was to come by then, he went on to talk about the possibility of a year or so difference due to some lapse of time between Adam's creation and Eve's creation. He made reference to the failure of expectations in 1914 and 1925 and quoted Rutherford's remark, "I made an ass of myself." He said that the organization had learned not to make "very bold, extreme predictions." Toward the close, he urged his listeners not to take an improper view, however, and assume that the coming destruction could be "years away," and focus their attention on other matters, such as getting married and raising families, building up a fine business venture or spending years at college in some engineering course.

After hearing the tape, a few of the Governing Body members expressed concern that if indeed no "very bold, extreme predictions" were being made, some subtle predictions were, and the effect was palpably evident in the excitement generated.

This was the first time that concern was expressed in the Governing Body discussions. But no action was taken, no policy decided upon.

4 This was in the session of February 19, 1975.

The vice president repeated many of the points of the same talk on March 2, 1975, at the following Gilead School graduation.[5]

1975 passed—as had 1881, 1914, 1918, 1920, 1925 and the 1940's. Much publicity was given by others as to the failure of the organization's expectations surrounding 1975. There was considerable talk among Jehovah's Witnesses themselves. In my own mind, most of what was said did not touch upon the major point of the matter.

I felt that the real issue went far beyond that of some individual's accuracy or inaccuracy or even an organization's reliability or untrustworthiness or its members' sensibleness or gullibility. It seemed to me that the really important factor is how such predictions ultimately reflect on God and on his Word. When men make such forecasts and say that they are doing it on the basis of the Bible, build up arguments for these from the Bible, assert that they are God's "channel" of communication—what is the effect when their forecasts prove false? Does it honor God or build up faith in Him and in the reliability of his Word? Or is the opposite the result? Does it not give added inducement for some to feel justified in placing little importance upon the Bible's message and teachings? Those Witnesses who made major changes in their lives in most cases could, and did, pick up the pieces and go on living in spite of being disillusioned. Not all could. Whatever the case, however, serious damage had been done in more ways than one.

In 1976, a year after the passing of that widely publicized date, a few members of the Governing Body began urging that some statement should be made acknowledging that the organization had been in error, had stimulated false expectations. Others said they did not think we should, that it would "just give ammunition to opposers." Milton Henschel recommended that the wise course would be simply not to bring the matter up and that in time the brothers would stop talking about it. There was clearly not enough support for a motion favoring a statement to carry. That year, an article in the July 15 *Watchtower* did refer to the failed expectations but the article had to conform to the prevailing sentiment within the Governing Body and no clear acknowledgement of the organization's responsibility was possible.

In 1977, the subject again surfaced in a session. Though the same objections were raised, a motion passed that a statement should be

5 See the *Watchtower*, May 1, 1975.

included in a convention talk that Lloyd Barry was assigned to prepare. I understand that afterward Governing Body members Ted Jaracz and Milton Henschel talked with Lloyd about their feelings on the matter. Whatever the case, when the talk was prepared, no mention of 1975 was included. I recall asking Lloyd about this and his reply was that he had just not been able to make it fit in with his subject. Almost two years went by and then in 1979 the Governing Body again considered the matter. By then everything indicated that 1975 had produced a serious "credibility gap."

A number of members of the headquarters staff expressed themselves in that vein. One described 1975 as an "albatross" hanging around our necks. Robert Wallen, a Governing Body secretary, wrote as follows:

"I have been associated as a baptized Witness well over 39 years and with Jehovah's help I will continue to be a loyal servant. But to say I am not disappointed would be untruthful, for, when I know my feelings regarding 1975 were fostered because of what I read in various publications, and then I am told in effect that I reached false conclusions on my own, that, I feel, is not being fair or honest. Knowing that we are not working with infallibility, to me it is but proper that when errors are made by imperfect, but God-fearing men, then corrections will be made when errors are found."

Raymond Richardson of the Writing Department said:

"Are not persons drawn to humility, and more willing to place confidence where there is *candor*? The Bible itself is the greatest example of candor. This is one of the most outstanding reasons why we believe it to be truthful."

Fred Rusk, also of the Writing Department, wrote:

"Despite any qualifying statements that might have been made along the way to admonish the brothers not to say that Armageddon would come in 1975, the fact is there were a number of articles in the magazines and other publications that more than hinted that the old system would be replaced by Jehovah's new system in the mid-1970's."

Merton Campbell of the Service Department wrote:

"A sister called the other day on the phone from Massachusetts. She was at work. Both the sister and her husband are working to pay up bills that have accumulated because of sickness. She expressed herself as feeling so confident that 1975 would bring the end that they both were having trouble facing up to the burdens of this system. This example is typical of many of the brothers we meet."

Harold Jackson, also of the Service Department, said:

> "What is needed now is not a statement to the effect that we were wrong about 1975 but rather a statement as to why the whole matter has been ignored so long in view of the fact that so many lives have been affected. Now it is a credibility gap we are faced with and that can prove to be disastrous. If we are going to say something at all, let us speak straightforwardly and be open and honest with the brothers."

Howard Zenke, of the same department, wrote:

> "We certainly do not want the brothers to read something or listen to something and then say in their own mind that the approach that we have taken amounts to a 'Watergate.'"

Others made similar comments. Ironically, some who now spoke the strongest criticism had themselves been among the most vocal before 1975 in stressing that date and the extreme "urgency" it called for, had even written some of the articles earlier quoted, had approved of the *Kingdom Ministry* statement commending those who were selling homes and property as 1975 drew near. Many of the most dogmatic statements about 1975 were made by traveling representatives (Circuit and District Overseers) all of whom were under the direct supervision of the Service Department.

In the March 6, 1979, session of the Governing Body, the same arguments against publishing anything were advanced—that it would lay the organization open to further criticism from opposers, that at this late date there was no need to make an apology, that nothing really would be accomplished by it. However, even those so arguing were less adamant than in previous sessions. This was because of one factor in particular: the worldwide figures had registered serious drops for two years.

The yearly reports on the total number participating in witnessing activity reveal this:

Year	Total Number Reporting Activity	% Increase Over Previous Year
1970	1,384,782	10.2
1971	1,510,245	9.1
1972	1,596,442	5.7
1973	1,656,673	3.8
1974	1,880,713	13.5
1975	2,062,449	9.7

1976	2,138,537	3.7
1977	2,117,194	− 1.0
1978	2,086,698	− 1.4

This drop, more than any other factor, seemed to carry weight with the Governing Body members. There was a vote of 15 to 3 in favor of a statement making at least some acknowledgement of the organization's share in the responsibility for the error. This was published in the March 15, 1980, *Watchtower*.

It had taken nearly four years for the organization through its administration finally to admit it had been wrong, had, for an entire decade, built up false hopes. Not that a statement so candid, though true, could be made. Whatever was written had to be acceptable to the Body as a whole for publishing. I know, because I was assigned to write the statement and, as in similar cases before, I had to be governed by—not what I would have liked to say or even what I thought the brothers needed to hear—but by what could be said that would receive approval of two-thirds of the Governing Body when submitted to them.

Today, all the decade-long buildup of hopes centered on 1975 is discounted as being of any particular importance. The essence of Russell's word in 1916 is again expressed by the organization: It "certainly did have a very stimulating and sanctifying effect upon thousands, all of whom can praise the Lord—even for the mistake."

1914 AND "THIS GENERATION"

"For the couch has proved too short for stretching oneself on, and the woven sheet itself is too narrow when wrapping oneself up." —Isaiah 28:20.

The Governing Body of Jehovah's Witnesses feels a fair degree of discomfort as regards what remains as the organization's major time prophecy. The time-frame allotted for its fulfillment is proving quite short and narrow as to covering the things foretold. The passing of each year only serves to accentuate the discomfort felt.

1914, for more than three decades the *terminal* point for the organization's time prophecies, is now the *starting* point for the time prophecy that constitutes the major stimulus to "urgency" in the activity of Jehovah's Witnesses. The words of Jesus Christ, "Truly I say to you that this generation will by no means pass away until all these things occur," are stated to have commenced applying with that year, 1914. Note the statements here underlined.

Jesus was obviously speaking about those who were old enough to witness *with understanding* what took place when the "last days" began. Jesus was saying that some of those persons who were alive at the appearance of the 'sign of the last days' would still be alive when God brought this system to its end.

Even if we presume that youngsters 15 years of age would be perceptive enough to realize the import of what happened in 1914, it would still make the youngest of "this generation" nearly 70 years old today. So the great majority of the generation to which Jesus was referring has already passed away in death. The remaining ones are approaching old age. And remember, Jesus said that the end of this wicked world would come *before* that generation passed away in death. This, of itself, tells us that the years left before the foretold end comes cannot be many.

When the *Awake!* magazine of October 8, 1968 (pages 13, 14) discussed this fifteen years ago in the pre-1975 days the stress was on how *soon* the generation of 1914 would be running out, *how little time* was left for that generation's lifespan. For any of Jehovah's Witnesses then to have suggested that things might go on for another twenty or thirty years would have been viewed as manifesting a poor attitude, one not indicative of strong faith.

When 1975 passed, the emphasis changed. Now the effort was made to show that the 1914-generation's span was not as narrow as one might think, that it could stretch for quite a long ways yet.

Thus, the October 1, 1978, *Watchtower* spoke, not of those witnessing "with *understanding* what took place" in 1914, but of those who "were able to *observe*" the events beginning that year. Mere observation is quite different from understanding. This could logically lower the minimum age limit of the ones forming "this generation."

Continuing this trend, two years later, the *Watchtower* of October 15, 1980, cited an article in the *U. S. News & World Report* magazine which suggested that ten years of age could be the point at which events start creating "a lasting impression on a person's memory." The article said that, if such be true, "then there are today more than 13 million Americans who have a recollection of World War I."

'Recollecting' also allows for a more tender age than does understanding (suggested as being found among "youngsters 15 years of age" in the 1968 *Awake!* quoted earlier). Actually, World War I continued up into 1918, with American involvement beginning only in

1917. So the suggested 10-year-old age given in the news magazine quoted does not necessarily apply to 1914.

Though different systems of measuring may gain a year or so here and there, the fact is that the generation of the 1914 period is shrinking with great rapidity, since the death rate is always highest among those of older age. The Governing Body is aware of this, for the matter came up for discussion a number of times.

The issue arose during the June 7, 1978, session of the Body. Earlier factors led to this. Governing Body member Albert Schroeder had distributed among the members a copy of a demographic report for the United States. The data indicated that less than one percent of the population who were out of their teens in 1914 were still alive in 1978. But a more attention-getting factor had to do with statements Schroeder had made while visiting certain countries in Europe.

Reports drifted back to Brooklyn that he was suggesting to others that the expression "this generation" as used by Jesus at Matthew chapter twenty-four, verse 34, applied to the generation of "anointed ones," and that as long as any of these were still living such "generation" would not have passed away. This was, of course, contrary to the organization's teaching and was unauthorized by the Governing Body.

When the matter was brought up, following Schroeder's return, his suggested interpretation was rejected and it was voted that a "Question from Readers" be run in a forthcoming issue of the *Watchtower* reaffirming the standard teaching regarding "this generation."[6] Interestingly, no rebuke or reproof whatsoever was directed to Governing Body member Schroeder for having advanced his unauthorized, contradictory view while in Europe.

The issue emerged again in both the March 6 and November 14, 1979, sessions. Since attention was being focused on the subject, I made Xerox copies of the first twenty pages of the material sent in by the Swedish elder which detailed the history of chronological speculation and revealed the actual source of the 2,520-year calculation and the 1914 date. Each member of the Body received a copy. Aside from an incidental comment, they did not see fit to discuss the material.

Lyman Swingle, as head of the Writing Department, was already familiar with this material. He directed the Body's attention to some of the dogmatic, insistent statements published in the 1922 *Watch Towers*, reading portions of these aloud to all the members. He said

6 See the *Watchtower*, October 1, 1978.

that he had been too young in 1914 (only about four years old then) to remember much about it, but that he did remember the discussions that took place in his home regarding 1925.[7] That he also knew what had happened in 1975. He said he personally would not want to be misled regarding another date.

In the course of the session, I pointed out that the Society's 607 B.C.E. starting date had no historical evidence whatsoever for support. As for 1914 and the generation then living, my question was: If the organization's traditional teaching is valid, how can we possibly apply Jesus' *accompanying* words to the people living in 1914? He said: "When you see all these things, know that he is near at the doors," and "as these things start to occur, raise yourselves erect and lift your heads up, because your deliverance is getting near." The publications regularly stated that those words began applying from 1914 onward, to those Christians living in 1914. But if so, then to *whom* among them could this apply? To those who were then 50 years old? But such ones if still alive would now be 115 years old. The 40-year-olds? They would be 105. Even the 30-year-olds would be 95 and those just out of their teens would already be 85 in 1979. (They would have reached 90 if still living today.)

If then those stirring words 'lift up your heads because your deliverance *is getting near*, it's *at the doors*' indeed applied to people in 1914 and meant that they could hope to see the final windup, reasonably that exciting announcement would need to be qualified by saying: "Yes, *you* may see it—that is, provided you are now quite young and live a very, very long life." As an example, I pointed to my father who, born in 1891, was just a young man of twenty-three in 1914. He lived, not just three score years and ten, or four score years, but reached eighty-six years of age. He had now been dead for two years and died without seeing the predicted things.

So I asked the Body how meaningful the application of Jesus' words in Matthew chapter twenty-four, verses 33 and 34, could have been in 1914 if the only ones who could hope to see them fulfilled were children just in their teens or younger? No specific reply was given.

A number of members, however, did voice their support for the organization's existing teaching about "this generation" and the 1914

---

7 Of the current Governing Body members, only Fred Franz was out of his teenage years in 1914, being 21 years old then. George Gangas was 18, John Booth 12, Martin Poetzinger 10, Karl Klein and Carey Barber were 9, Grant Suiter 6, Lloyd Barry and Lyman Swingle 4, Albert Schroeder and Leo Greenlees 3, and Dan Sydlik, Milton Henschel and Ted Jaracz had not yet been born, their births coming after the War had ended.

date. Lloyd Barry expressed personal dismay that doubts existed within the Body regarding the teaching. Referring to Lyman Swingle's reading of statements from the 1922 *Watch Towers*, he said that he saw nothing to be concerned about in these, that they were "present truth" for the brothers at that period.[8] As to the oldness of the 1914 generation, he pointed out that in some parts of the Soviet Union there are regions where people live to be 130 years old. He urged that a united position be expressed to the brothers so that they would maintain their sense of urgency. Others expressed concurring views.

When later recognized by the Chairman, my comment was that it seemed we would need to keep in mind that what is today taught as "present truth" may also in time become "past truth," and that the "present truth" that replaces such "past truth" may itself become replaced by "future truth." I felt that the word "truth" used in such a manner became simply meaningless.

A couple of the Body members said that if the current explanation was not the right one, then what *was* the explanation of Jesus' statements? Since the question seemed aimed at me, my response was that I felt there was an explanation that harmonized with Scripture and fact, but that anything presented should surely not be some "spur-of-the-moment" idea, but something carefully researched and weighed. I said that I thought there were brothers capable of doing that work but that they would need the Governing Body's authorization. Was the Governing Body interested in having this done? There was no response and the question was dropped.

At the discussion's end, with the exception of a few members, the Body members indicated that they felt that 1914 and the teaching about "this generation" tied to it should continue to be stressed. The Writing Committee Coordinator, Lyman Swingle, commented, "All right, if that is what you want to do. But at least you know that as far as 1914 is concerned, Jehovah's Witnesses got the whole thing—lock, stock and barrel—from the Second Adventists."

Perhaps one of the most disturbing things to me was knowing that, while the organization urged the brothers to maintain unwavering trust in the interpretation, there were men in responsible positions within the organization who had themselves manifested that they did not have full confidence in the predictions based on the 1914 date.

---

8 The expression "present truth" was popular in the time of Russell and Rutherford and was based on a faulty translation of 2 Peter 1:12. The *New World Translation* there reads more accurately, "the truth that is present in you."

As a notable example, at the time of the February 19, 1975, session, in which the Governing Body listened to Fred Franz's taped talk on 1975, there followed some discussion about the uncertainty of time prophecies. Nathan Knorr, then the president, spoke up and said:

> "There are some things I know—I know that Jehovah is God, that Christ Jesus is his Son, that he gave his life as a ransom for us, that there is a resurrection. Other things I'm not so certain about. 1914—I don't know. We have talked about 1914 for a long time. We may be right and I hope we are."[9]

At that session the date under discussion was 1975, so it came as a surprise that the far more fundamental date of 1914 should be referred to in such context. As stated, the president's words were spoken, not in private conversation, but before the Governing Body in session.

Previous to the major discussion of 1914 (in the November 14, 1979, full Governing Body session), the Body's Writing Committee in a committee meeting had discussed the advisability of continuing to stress 1914.[10] In the committee discussion it was suggested that we might at least refrain from "pushing" the date. As I recall, Karl Klein reminded us of the practice sometimes followed of simply not mentioning a certain teaching for a time, so that if any change came it would not make such a strong impression.

Remarkably, the Writing Committee voted unanimously to follow basically that very policy in the publications with regard to 1914. This position, however, was short-lived, since the November 14, 1979, full session of the Governing Body made clear that the majority favored emphasizing the date as usual.

That questions about this teaching were not limited to Brooklyn was brought home to me by an incident occurring while I was on a trip to West Africa in the fall of 1979. In Nigeria, two members of the Nigerian Branch Committee and a long-time missionary, took me to see a property the Society had purchased for constructing a new Branch headquarters. On the return trip I asked when they expected to be able to move to the new site. The reply was that, with the clearing of the land, obtaining approval of plans and getting necessary permits, and

---

9   This does not seem to have been just a momentary thought on President Knorr's part, for the same viewpoint was expressed in virtually the same words by one of his closer associates, George Couch. Knowing the two, it seems more likely that Couch acquired the view from Knorr than vice versa.

10 The Writing Committee membership was then composed of Lloyd Barry, Fred Franz, Raymond Franz, Karl Klein and Lyman Swingle.

then the actual construction, it might well be in 1983 before the move was made.

Because of this, I asked, "Do you get any questions from the local brothers as to the length of time that has passed since 1914?" There was a momentary silence, and then the Branch Coordinator said, "No, the Nigerian brothers seldom ask questions of that kind—but WE do." Almost immediately the long-time missionary said, "Brother Franz, could it be that Jesus' reference to 'this generation' applied only to persons back there who saw the destruction of Jerusalem? If that were the case, then everything would seem to fit."

Quite evidently not everything did seem to fit in his mind, the way the existing teaching had it. My reply was simply that I supposed that such was a possibility but that there was not much more that could be said for the idea. I repeated this conversation to the Governing Body after my return, for it gave evidence to me of the questions existing in the minds of men throughout the world, respected men in positions of considerable authority. The comments the men in Nigeria made and the *way* that they made them indicated clearly that they had discussed the question among themselves before ever my visit took place.

Shortly after my return from Africa, in a Governing Body session on February 17, 1980, Lloyd Barry again voiced his feelings about the importance of the teaching regarding 1914 and "this generation." Lyman Swingle said that the "Questions from Readers" material published in 1978 had not settled the matter in the brothers' minds. Albert Schroeder reported that in the Gilead School and in Branch Committee seminars, brothers brought up the fact that 1984 was now being talked about as a possible new date, 1984 being seventy years from 1914 (the figure seventy evidently being looked upon as having some special import). The Body decided to discuss the matter further in the next session.

The Chairman's Committee, consisting of Albert Schroeder (Chairman), Karl Klein and Grant Suiter, now produced a most unusual document. They supplied a copy to each member of the Governing Body. Briefly put, these three men were suggesting that, rather than applying to people living in 1914, the expression "this generation" would begin applying as of 1957, forty-three years later!

This is the material exactly as these three members of the Governing Body supplied it to us:

To Members of the Governing Body -- On Agenda for Wednesday Mar.5 '80

Question: What is "this generation (genea')?"(Mt. 24:34; Mr. 13:30;
                                            Luke 21:32)

TDNT (many Commentaries) say: genea' "mostly denotes the sense of
   contemporaries." Vol. 1, p. 663

   Most all say genea' differs from genos; genos means offspring,
      people, race. See TDNT Vol. 1 p. 685 (genos at 1 Pet. 2:9)

Answer may be tied to question on Mt. 24:33. What is meant by: "When
   you see all these things"?

   Lange's Commentary (Vol. 8) suggests that "these things" do not
   refer to C.E. 70, nor the parousia 1914 but to vss. 29,30 the
   celestial phenomina that we now see began with the space age
   1957 onward. In that case it would then be the contemporary
   generation of mankind living since 1957.

Three Sections

   Lange's Commentary divides Matthew 24th chapter into "three cycles."
   His 1st cycle-- Matt. 24:1-14
        2nd cycle-- Matt. 24:15-28
        3rd cycle-- Matt. 24:29-44 (synteleia or conclusion)
   (See Vol. 8 pp 421, 424 and 427)
   Based on Matt. 24:3 question in three parts.

   The Watchtower and God's Kingdom of a Thousand Years (ka)
   Have now also divided Matthew 24 into three parts so to speak

   (1) Matt. 24:3-22 Has parallel fulfillments in 1st century
      and today since 1914. (See w 75 p. 273, ka p. 205)

   (2) Matt. 24:23-28 Period into Christ's parousia of 1914.
      (See w 75 p. 275)

   (3) Matt. 24:29-44 "Celestial Phenomina"have literal application
      since the space age began in 1957 and onward to include
      Christ's erkhomenon (coming as the executioner at the
      beginning of the "great tribulation.")
      (See w 75 p 276 par. 18; ka pp 323 to 328)

"All these things" would have to throw back in the context to the nearest
   items listed in the composite sign, namely, the celestial phenomina
   of verses 29 and 30.*

If this is true: to
   Then "this generation" would refer/contemporary mankind living
   as knowledgeable ones from 1957 onward.

*Confirmed in thought by C.T.Russell in Berean Commentary, p. 217:
   "Genea, people living contemporaneously which witness the signs
   just mentioned." Vol. 4 p. 604.

                              Chairman's Committee,3/3/80

1957 marked the year when the first Russian Sputnik was launched
into earth's outer space. Evidently the Chairman's Committee felt that
that event could be accepted as marking the start of the fulfillment of
these words of Jesus:

". . . the sun will be darkened, and the moon will not give its light, and
the stars will fall from heaven, and the powers of heaven will be shaken."[11]

Based on that application, their conclusion would be as they stated:

11 Matthew 24:29.

"Then 'this generation' would refer to contemporary mankind living as knowledgeable ones from 1957 onward."

The three men were not suggesting that 1914 be dropped. It would stay as the "end of the Gentile Times." But "this generation" would not begin applying until 1957.

In view of the swiftly diminishing numbers of the 1914 generation, this new application of the phrase could undoubtedly prove even more helpful than some person allegedly living to be 130 years old in a certain section of the Soviet Union. As compared with starting in 1914, this new 1957 starting date would give *an additional 43 years* for the period embraced by the expression "this generation" to reach.

Governing Body standards required that for any Committee to recommend something there should be unanimous agreement among the Committee members (otherwise the divided viewpoint should be presented to the Body for settlement). The presentation of the novel idea regarding 1957 was therefore one upon which the three members of the Chairman's Committee must have agreed.

I would think that, if asked about this presentation today, the response would be, "Oh, that was just a suggestion." Possibly, but if so it was a suggestion seriously made. And for Albert Schroeder, Karl Klein and Grant Suiter to bring such a suggestion to the Governing Body *they must have been willing in their own minds to see the suggested change made.* If, indeed, their belief and conviction as to the Society's long-time teaching about "this generation" (as applying from 1914 onward) had been strong, firm, unequivocal, they certainly would never have come forward with the new interpretation they offered.

The Governing Body did not accept the new view proposed by these members. Comments made showed that many considered it fanciful. The fact remains, however, that Governing Body members Schroeder, Klein and Suiter presented their idea as a serious proposition, revealing their own lack of conviction as to the solidity of the existing teaching on the subject.

To this day, however, bold, positive, forceful statements regarding 1914 and "this generation" continue to be published as Biblically established fact by the "prophet" organization and all of Jehovah's Witnesses are urged to put full trust in this and carry the message about it to other people earthwide. In an apparent effort to calm concern about the diminishing ranks of the 1914 generation, the same *Watchtower* that implied that the age limit for that generation's members could be lowered to ten years of age, also said:

"And if the wicked system of this world survived until the turn of the century [the year 2000], which is highly improbable in view of world trends and the fulfillment of Bible prophecy, there would still be survivors of the World War I generation."

By the turn of the century, the ten-year-olds of 1914 would be ninety-six years old. Still, there might be a few of them yet around and evidently that was viewed as all that was necessary for Jesus' words to be fulfilled—depending, of course, on the acceptance of the idea that Jesus was directing his words particularly to ten-year-old children.

I have no idea what the future may bring as to the Governing Body's position on this matter. By their emphasizing 1914 with renewed vigor they have, in effect, "made their bed" and seem to feel compelled to lie in it. But the span of the 1914 generation is proving like a couch that is too short for comfort, and the reasonings used to cover that doctrinal "couch" are like a woven sheet that is too narrow, not able to shut out, in this case, the cold facts of reality.

It is possible, of course, that somewhere down the line they will feel obliged to make some adjustment. As long as the world figures show at least some increase, however, I would doubt that they would do this. It is hard for me to believe that they would take up the 1957 starting date for "this generation" proposed by members Schroeder, Klein and Suiter.

They have other options nonetheless. They could acknowledge the historical evidence placing Jerusalem's destruction twenty years later than the Society's 607 B.C.E. date. This would make the Gentile Times run out (using their 2,520-year interpretation) about 1934. But such enormous importance has been placed on 1914 and, as has been shown, so much of the doctrinal superstructure is linked to it, that this also seems an unlikely step.

Perhaps Albert Schroeder's idea of applying the phrase to the "anointed" class (an idea that has been floating around the organization for many, many years) might prove more attractive. There are always additional persons (some fairly young) who each year decide for the first time that they are of that "anointed" class. So this would offer an almost limitless extension of time for the teaching about "this generation."

The one thing I can say with positiveness is that I personally found the reasoning employed within the Governing Body to be incredible. I found it tragic that a time prophecy could be proclaimed to the world as something solid upon which people could and *should* confidently rely, build their hopes, form their life plans—when the very ones publishing this knew that within their own collective body there did not exist a unanimity of genuine, firm conviction as to the rightness of that teaching. It may be that when viewed against the whole background of the organization's decades of date-fixing and shifting of dates, their attitude becomes more understandable.

Perhaps more incredible to me is that the Chairman's Committee members, Albert Schroeder, Karl Klein and Grant Suiter, within about *two months* of their submission of their new idea on "this generation," listed the teaching about the start of Christ's presence in 1914 as among the decisive teachings for determining whether individuals (including headquarters staff members) were guilty of "apostasy" and therefore merited disfellowshipment. They did this knowing that just months before they themselves had placed in question the corollary, companion doctrine regarding "this generation." But that is a matter that will be dealt with in the following chapter.

10

POINT OF DECISION

"But whatever was to my profit I now consider loss for the sake of Christ. What is more, I consider everything a loss compared to the surpassing greatness of knowing Christ Jesus my Lord, for whose sake I have lost all things."
—Philippians 3:7, 8, *New International Version.*

B Y the end of 1979 I had arrived at my personal crossroads.
I had spent nearly forty years as a full-time representative, serving at every level of the organizational structure. The last fifteen years I had spent at the international headquarters and the final nine of those as a member of the worldwide Governing Body of Jehovah's Witnesses.

It was those final years that were the crucial period for me. Illusion there met up with reality. I have since come to appreciate the rightness of a quotation I recently read, one made by a statesman, now dead, who said:

> "The great enemy of the truth is very often not the lie—deliberate, contrived and dishonest—but the myth—persistent, persuasive and unrealistic."

I now began to realize how large a measure of what I had based my entire adult life course on was just that, a myth—"persistent, persuasive and unrealistic." It was not that my view toward the Bible had changed. If anything, my appreciation of it was enhanced by what I experienced. It alone gave sense and meaning to what I saw happening, the attitudes I saw displayed, the reasonings I heard advanced, the tension and pressure I felt. The change that did come was from the realization that my way of looking at the Scriptures had been from such a thoroughly sectarian viewpoint, a trap that I thought I had been protected against. Letting the Scriptures speak for themselves—without being first funneled through some fallible human agency as a "channel"—I found they became immensely more meaningful. I was frankly astonished at how much of their import I had been missing.

The question was, what should I now do? My years on the Governing Body, the things I heard said in and out of sessions, the basic spirit I saw displayed, steadily brought me to the awareness that, as regards the organization, the 'wineskin had grown old,' had lost whatever flexibility it might have had, and that it was stiffening its resistance to any Scriptural correction either as to doctrinal beliefs or its methods of dealing with those who looked to it for guidance.[1] I felt, and still feel, that there were many good men on the Governing Body. In a long-distance phone call, a former Witness said to me, "We have been followers of followers." Another said, "We have been victims of victims." I think both statements are true. Charles Taze Russell followed the views of certain men of his time, was victimized by some of the myths they propagated as "revealed truth." Each successive part of the organizational leadership has followed along, at times contributing additional myth in support of or in elaboration of, the original myth. In place of rancor, I feel only pity for those men I know, for I too was such a "victim of victims," a "follower of followers."

Though each year on the Governing Body, particularly from 1976 onward, became increasingly difficult and more stressful for me, I clung to the hope that things would improve. In time I was obliged to recognize that that was a hope which the evidence did not support.

I was not opposed to authority. I was opposed to the extremes to which it was carried. I could not believe that God ever purposed for men to exercise such all-pervading authoritarian control over the lives of fellow members of the Christian congregation. My understanding was that Christ grants authority in his congregation only to serve, never to dominate.[2]

Similarly, I did not object to "organization" in the sense of an orderly arrangement, for I understood the Christian congregation itself

---

1   Compare Jesus' words at Luke 5:37–39.
2   Matthew 20:25–28; 23:8–12; 2 Corinthians 4:5; 1 Peter 5:3.

to involve such an orderly arrangement.[3] But I believed that, whatever the arrangement, its purpose and function, its very existence, was only as an aid for the brothers; it was there to serve their interests, not the other way around. Whatever the arrangement, it was to build men and women up so that they would not be spiritual babes, dependent on men or on an institutionalized system, but able to act as full-grown, mature Christians. It was not to train them to be simply conformists to a set of organizational rules and regulations, but to help them to become persons "having their perceptive powers trained to distinguish both right and wrong."[4] Whatever arrangement there was, it must contribute toward a genuine sense of brotherhood with the freeness of speech and mutual confidence true brotherhood brings—not a society composed of the few who are the governors and the many who are the governed. And finally, whatever the arrangement, the way to 'take the lead' therein must be by example, by holding firmly to the Word of God, passing on and inculcating the instructions of the Master the way he gave them, not "adjusting" these to fit what seemed to be in the interests of a humanly created organization, not by 'making people feel the weight of one's authority' in the way the great men of the world do.[5] It must result in the exaltation of Christ Jesus as the Head, never in the exaltation of an earthly authority structure and its officers. As it was, I felt that the role of Christ Jesus as active Head was overshadowed and virtually eclipsed by the authoritarian conduct and constant self-commendation and self-praise of the organization.

Furthermore, I did not deny the value and need for teaching. But I could not accept that organizational interpretations, based on shifting human reasonings, could ever be made equal in authority to the actual statements found in God's unchangeable Word. The great importance given to traditional views, the bending and slanting of God's Word to accommodate it to those views, and the inconsistencies that resulted in double standards were a source of serious emotional upset to me. What I found unacceptable was, not teaching, but dogmatism.

The convictions I held I tried to reflect during my years of service on the Governing Body. From the beginning I found that this brought me difficulty, animosity. In the end it brought rejection, expulsion.

3   1 Corinthians 12:4–11, 25; 14:40.
4   Hebrews 5:14; 1 Corinthians 8:9; 16:13, 14.
5   Matthew 20:25.

In the autumn of 1979 I had an assignment to go on a "zone visit" to certain Branch Offices in West Africa. Some were in countries where the government had placed an official ban on the activity of Jehovah's Witnesses. Knowing how easily something could happen that might result in my being detained, possibly imprisoned, I felt an obligation to discuss some of my concerns with my wife. (In view of her previous health problems, including a blood condition that nearly caused her death in 1969, I felt it best to make the trip alone.) Though she could not help but be aware of the emotional strain I felt, I had never discussed with her the actual circumstances that produced that strain, what the real issues were that affected me. I had not felt free to do so. Now I felt not only that it was proper but that I had an obligation to consider with her what I had become aware of, particularly in the light of the Scriptures. How could I let men hold me back from discussing with my own wife truths that I saw in the Word of God?

By that time we concluded that the advisable course for us was to terminate our activity at the international headquarters. We felt that our peace of mind and heart, as well as our physical health, required it. We also had faint hopes that it might yet be possible to have a child and we had, in fact, talked to two doctors about this, including one of the staff doctors, Dr. Carlton, on a confidential basis.[6] I was fifty-seven and I knew that it would be very difficult to find secular employment due to that factor. But I trusted that somehow things would work out.

The decision was not easy. I felt torn between two desires. On the one hand, I felt that by remaining on the Body at least I could speak up on behalf of others' interests, on behalf of the truth of the Scriptures, on behalf of moderation and balance, even though my voice was heard with irritation or ignored. I sensed that the time-span in which I could do that was rapidly shortening, that whatever voice I had in Governing Body discussions would soon be shut out, silenced. The desire to be free from the suspicious atmosphere I saw developing, to be free from participation in an authority structure I could not Scripturally defend and decisions I could not morally condone, weighed equally heavy with me.

If security and comfort were my aim, I certainly would have opted for staying where I was, for all our physical needs would have been

---

6 My wife is thirteen years younger than I. We recognized the risks the doctors brought to our attention but were willing to face these.

provided us as part of the headquarters staff. Our long years of "seniority" would give us the choice of some of the better rooms that periodically became available in the Society's many large buildings.[7] Our vacation time would increase to the equivalent of some six weeks a year and, because of being a Governing Body member, it would always be possible to combine this with speaking engagements that carried one to points all over the United States and Canada, or with zone visits that took one to points all over the earth. (Governing Body members can regularly take their vacations in places most people could only afford to dream about.) In 1978, my wife and I found ourselves boarding planes over fifty times in that one year, and over the years we had traveled to Central and South America, Asia, Europe, Africa and the Middle East.

If prestige or prominence were what was sought, I could not reasonably have asked for more. I was already declining, on a monthly basis, about three or four invitations for speaking engagements for every one that I accepted. Internationally, if traveling to Paris, Athens, Madrid, Lisbon, Mexico City, Sao Paulo, or almost any other major city, it was only necessary to advise the Branch Office and a meeting would be arranged to which thousands of Jehovah's Witnesses would flock. It became almost commonplace to address audiences ranging in size anywhere from five thousand up to thirty thousand persons. Practically anywhere a Governing Body member goes he is the guest of honor among his fellow Witnesses.[8]

As for the Governing Body itself, it was quite evident to me that esteem from one's peers on the Body could be assured simply by regularly voicing total support for the organization and, with rare exceptions, by noting which way the majority inclined in discussions and speaking and voting that way. I am not being cynical in saying this. Those few others on the Body who on occasion felt compelled to voice conscientious objections to certain traditional positions, policies or teachings, know—even if they do not express it—that this is so.

Even as it was, I had been assigned to membership on what might be called two of the more influential Governing Body committees, the Writing Committee and the Service Committee. The Writing Commit-

7 The Society had not long before purchased the fifteen-story Towers Hotel, complementing other ten-story residences already owned in the Brooklyn Heights area. Since then the Society has purchased (through agents) the Standish Arms Hotel and the Bossert Hotel, both in Brooklyn.
8 I found Jesus' words at Matthew 23:6 brought to mind by all this.

tee saw fit to assign me to oversee the development (not to do the actual writing thereof) of a number of publications printed eventually in many languages in the millions of copies.[9]

The "formula," if it may be called that, for maintaining a position of prominence in the organization was easily discernible. But I could not find it conscientiously acceptable.

I would have had to have been blind not to have seen that my expressions on certain issues, motivated by what I felt were clear Scriptural principles, did not please many on the Body. There were times when I went to Governing Body sessions having decided simply not to speak rather than see animosity build. But when issues arose that could seriously affect the lives of people, I found I could not hold back from making some expression. I would have felt guilty not to have done so. I had no illusions that what I said would carry particular weight—in fact I knew from experience that it would more probably only make my own situation more difficult, more precarious. But I felt that if I did not stand for something, for certain principles that I felt were crucial to Christianity, then there was no purpose in being there, for that matter, not much real purpose in life.

It has been mentioned that from about 1978 onward a changed climate began to manifest itself in the Body. The initial euphoria that accompanied the dramatic change in the administration had faded. The spirit of brotherly "comradeship" that seemed to prevail for a time, along with its accompanying expressions of moderation, greater flexibility in viewpoint, had also noticeably diminished. The members had settled into their respective positions on the various Committees and after a time there seemed to be some "muscle flexing" shown on the part of certain ones. Fairly discernible lines began to be evident within the membership, so that it was often not difficult to foresee what the vote was likely to be on an issue.

If, for example, the hands of Milton Henschel, Fred Franz, Ted Jaracz and Lloyd Barry went up, one could *generally* be sure that the hands of Carey Barber, Martin Poetzinger, William Jackson, George Gangas, Grant Suiter and Jack Barr would go up as well. If the hands

---

9 These included the books *Is This Life All There Is?* (actual writing by Reinhard Lengtat); *Life Does Have a Purpose* (by Ed Dunlap); *Making Your Family Life Happy* (written principally by Colin Quackenbush); *Choosing the Best Way of Life* (by Reinhard Lengtat); and *Commentary on the Letter of James* (by Ed Dunlap). At the time of resigning I was assigned to oversee the development of a book on the life of Jesus Christ that Ed Dunlap was assigned to write.

of the former stayed down, the hands of the latter would generally stay down also. Some others would *likely* vote with these but their vote was not as predictable. With rare exceptions, this pattern prevailed.

The pattern held particularly true if any traditional policy or position was under discussion. One could know beforehand those members who would almost certainly vote in favor of maintaining that traditional policy and against any change therein. Even in the case of the "alternative service" issue, already discussed in a previous chapter, though here outnumbered, these members were still able to prevent a two-thirds majority vote from altering the position on that issue.

In certain controversial cases there seemed to be at least some evidence of "lobbying" on the part of some members. I felt that if anyone wanted to present information apart from the actual session, the better way was to put it in writing and submit copies to all members. Then at least everyone heard the same thing and, in effect, the 'cards were all on the table.' But such written submissions were usually quite rare and, when made, were seldom discussed to any extent.

The Governing Body session of November 14, 1979, was, I believe, a precursor of the traumatic events that violently shook the headquarters in the spring of 1980, resulting in a number of members of the staff being disfellowshiped for "apostasy," and also my own resignation from the Body and from the headquarters staff.

That day we handled four minor issues; each motion carried unanimously. Any sense of harmony that might have existed was quickly broken by a jarring note, however. Grant Suiter said he wished to bring up a matter about which he stated there was "considerable gossip." He said that he had heard reports that some members of the Governing Body and the Writing Department had given talks in which they made comments not in accord with Society teaching and that this was causing confusion. He had also heard, he said, that within the headquarters family staff some were making expressions such as, "When King Saul dies then things will change."[10]

I had never heard anyone in the headquarters family make such a remark. Grant Suiter did not say where he obtained his information or who was the source of the "gossip" he referred to, but he became very intense and both his words and facial expressions reflected strong and

10 Presumably the reference was to the corporation president, some apparently believing (mistakenly so) that the presidency still represented the power base it had up until 1976.

heated emotion. And, for the first time, the term "apostasy" surfaced in a Governing Body session.

Considerable discussion followed, with most members indicating they were hearing such things for the first time. In my own expression, I stated that I had given talks all over the United States and in many countries and that in not one of them had I ever made statements contradicting published teachings of the organization. It was rare that talks by a Governing Body member would not be taped by at least someone and, had anything out of line been said, the evidence would be there. In that case, I pointed out, the Body would surely not have to rely on rumor to know about it, for someone would certainly write in about it, asking questions. I asked if Grant Suiter knew personally of any such case on the part of any member of the Body or of the Writing Department? His comment was simply that 'these matters were being talked about,' and that some Branch Committee members attending seminars at the headquarters had said they were "confused" because they had heard some conflicting views from those conducting classes.

The decision was that the Teaching Committee (which had oversight of the seminars) should investigate. At a later session, they reported that they had found no evidence of the things spoken of, that the only "confusion" among the Branch men was about a point developed in a class conducted by Governing Body member Carey Barber. He dealt with Christ's kingdom having commenced in 33 C.E. upon his ascension to heaven and some had difficulty in reconciling this with the teaching about 1914.[11] The resolution of the matter was an agreement that all Governing Body members would exercise care when speaking on assignments; it was clearly stated in the session, however, that this did not imply any attempt to control private conversations by the members, as among personal friends. This latter stand did not hold up under test.

I found the discussion significant. Although Grant Suiter had not indicated knowing of any case where a Governing Body member had, when on assignment, made comments contrary to published teachings, I knew that some could have been cited. The Body had already considered the occasion of Albert Schroeder's visit to some European branches and his advancing the view that the expression "this generation" might have a meaning different from the published one. Word

---

11 The official teaching is that upon his ascension Christ began ruling as king toward his congregation only; that in 1914 he took full power to reign toward all the earth.

had reached us about this from more than one place. It was also known that the president, Fred Franz, had introduced a new view regarding the "keys of the kingdom" (referred to at Matthew, chapter sixteen, verse 19) when teaching certain classes in the Gilead School, a view that contradicted published teachings of the organization. This had been done without previous consultation with the Body and the view was presented, not as a suggestion, but as the *correct* view.[12] Entire classes of Gilead graduates went to their assignments with this new view that none of the rest of the brotherhood had even heard about.

None of these cases were brought up in the Governing Body session, however, and I felt no inclination to do so.[13] But I sensed that a definite undercurrent was running that sooner or later would come into the open. And I had no doubt that when it did its force would be directed, not against any such persons, but against myself and, outside the Body, Edward Dunlap.

Due to the sentiment that I could discern on the part of several members, I had already been weighing the advisability of resigning from the Service Committee, thus limiting my participation in committee membership to just the Writing Committee. One day in conversation with Robert Wallen, who acted as Secretary for the Service Committee (not himself a Governing Body member), I mentioned that I had about decided to drop off that committee.[14] His response was, "You can't do that. There has to be some balance on the committee." He urged me to change my mind.

However, the same adverse sentiment expressed in the November 14, 1979, session, surfaced in another session and, as I had thought, I now came in for specific mention. In the course of the session, Lloyd Barry, who had the responsibility of seeing that each issue of the *Watchtower* magazine was put together and ready for publishing, voiced strong concern over the fact that I had not placed my signature on a

---

12 Eventually this came before the Body and, after much debate, was finally approved (*not* unanimously) and published in the *Watchtower* of October 1, 1979, pp. 16–29.

13 At a meeting (in Chicago I believe) of Witness attorneys and doctors, another Governing Body member had invited them to express themselves as to the rightness of the Society's then current position on the use of the term "ordained minister." Though no open statement of disagreement was expressed at that meeting by him, he had made such before the Body, and the response that followed his invitation indicated clearly that those hearing it felt free to criticize that current position. This issue is one that has been widely discussed among Witnesses, seldom with any knowledge of the facts. For those interested in further information, details are set forth in the Appendix.

14 The other Committee members then were Ted Jaracz (Coordinator), Milton Henschel, Albert Schroeder, William Jackson and Martin Poetzinger.

considerable number (he gave the number) of *Watchtower* articles circulated in the Writing Committee. (Each article due to be published was first circulated among the five committee members and their signatures at the top indicated approval.) While not understanding his reason for bringing the matter up in a full session, rather than speaking first to me privately or at a Writing Committee meeting, I acknowledged that what he stated was true. (I was actually surprised to hear the exact number of articles I had not signed since I had kept no count; he had.)

I explained that I had not signed in those cases simply because I could not do so conscientiously. At the same time I had made no effort whatsoever to impede the publication of the particular articles (some of them being articles written by the president on the prophecy of Jeremiah and laying much stress on the 'prophetic role' of the organization and on certain dates, such as 1914 and 1919), nor had I made any effort to create an issue of the matter. My signature's absence represented abstention, not opposition. I stated before the entire Body that if this was viewed as a problem, if having someone refrain from signing for conscientious reasons was viewed as undesirable, then there was a simple solution. They could appoint someone else to serve on the Writing Committee who would not feel such conscientious restraint about approving material. I mentioned at that time my thoughts about resigning from the Service Committee so as to spend more time contributing to the needs of the Writing Department. So I placed the matter in their hands and made it clear that whatever disposition they chose to make would be acceptable to me.

After the session, Lyman Swingle, then the Coordinator of both the Writing Committee and the Writing Department, spoke to me in his office and said: "You can't do that to me. If they decide on their own to replace you on the Writing Committee, all right. But *don't you offer to resign*." He spoke with considerable force. I told him I was simply leaving it up to the Body, but that I was tired of controversy and would be happy for anything that would lessen some of the strain I felt. He repeated his urging.

The Body made no change in my assignment.

Nonetheless I had a strong presentiment of trouble brewing. But I had no way of knowing that within six months I would find myself in the midst of a storm of near fanatical intensity, with the Governing Body reacting with harsh measures to what it viewed as a "conspiracy" of serious proportions, one that threatened the very heart of the organization. Consider, now, what this "dangerous conspiracy" actually was, just how "massive" its proportions were, how great the "criminality" of those involved was, what the justification was for the state of "siege mentality" that developed within the organization and which continues to this day, the events that led up to the "purge" in the spring of 1980.

The day before I took off for Paris on the first leg of my trip to West Africa (November 16, 1979), the Society's president was presiding at the morning Bible text discussion (that being his week to serve as chairman). In his comments, he stated that some were questioning the Society's position (set forth in a recent *Watchtower*) that Jesus Christ is the mediator only for the "anointed" ones and not for the other two million of Jehovah's Witnesses.[15] He said of such ones:

"They would merge everyone together and make Jesus Christ the mediator for every Tom, Dick and Harry."

I could not help but think of all the Toms and Dicks and Harrys there present in the headquarters family and wondered how those words would sound to them. I knew that there was considerable discussion within the family on this subject, some of it definitely unfavorable.

The president went on to affirm that the Society's teaching was right. The one text he referred to in Scripture was Hebrews, chapter twelve, and the words:

"It is for discipline you are enduring. God is dealing with you as sons. For what son is he that a father does not discipline? But if you are without the discipline of which all have become partakers, you are really illegitimate children, not sons."

He then gave the illustration of a horse whose master uses discipline to teach it to walk around in a circle and he stated, "Sometimes it may take a few lashes with the whip to get it to do this." He urged anyone who had doubts about the Society's teaching on this point to hold on, take the discipline and "show that he has the *guts* to stick with it!"[16]

That evening I took off for Paris but for days I felt sickened, not merely by these words, but by the whole approach and spirit I had been witness to for the last few years.

For me it was evident from Scripture that Jesus Christ did offer his mediation to bring about reconciliation with God for every Tom, Dick

15 See the *Watchtower* of April 1, 1979, p. 31; November 15, 1979, pp. 21–27.
16 Ed Dunlap's comment on this afterward was, "I always thought that what enabled us to endure was faith, not 'guts'."

and Harry and that his laying down his life for all persons, his providing the ransom sacrifice and making its benefits available to any and all who might choose to accept them, was the very opposite of the attitude expressed in that headquarters discussion. It seemed that we were hearing "a different good news," not the good news as it was presented by the inspired writers of the first century.

In Africa, the next-to-the-last country I visited was Mali. Most of the missionaries there were French nationals. After working my way through a presentation in French of some points I was covering with missionaries in each country, I asked if they had any questions. The second question presented was, "The *Watchtower* says that Jesus is the mediator only for the anointed, not for the rest of us. Can you clear this up for us? Not even in prayer is he our mediator?"

If it had been my interest to sow doubts, this would have been an obvious opportunity. Instead I tried to calm them, pointing to the First Letter of John, chapter two, verse 1, which speaks of Jesus as the "Helper" of those for whom he is a "propitiatory sacrifice for sins," including those of "the whole world." I said that even if they were not to think of Jesus as their Mediator, they could surely think of him as their Helper. And, that of one thing they could be sure: that his interest in them was as great as his interest in any other persons on earth.

I felt that I had managed to keep the matter from becoming a serious issue with them, and I had said nothing that in any way placed in question the *Watchtower's* statements.

However, a few days later, on going to the airport to depart for Senegal, the missionaries came out to see me off. One of the women missionaries approached and asked me, "But not even in prayer is Jesus our mediator?" I could do nothing but repeat and reemphasize basically the same points I had presented earlier in their missionary home meeting.

I returned to Brooklyn after about three weeks, the only difficulty encountered in Africa being the derailment of the train on which I was making a twenty-hour, overnight trip from Ouagadougou, Upper Volta, to Abidjan in the Ivory Coast.

Upon my return, the following morning at the breakfast table a visiting Branch Committee member and his wife were seated next to me. Breakfast had barely begun when the wife wanted to know if she could ask me a question. I replied, "You can ask it. I don't know if I can answer it." She said that the previous night they had attended the study of a *Watchtower* dealing with the mediatorship of Christ, and she then asked virtually the same question that the French missionary in Mali had asked. I gave the same answer.

That weekend, I went to New Jersey on a speaking assignment and following the talk a woman in the audience came up (an active Witness) and said she had some questions. There were three questions and the second was about Christ's mediatorship. Once again I gave the same response.

These incidents are cited because they represent my standard practice when questions arose from such persons, questions involving published teachings of the organization. Any question as to the Scriptural backing for the organization's teachings that I myself had, I discussed only with personal acquaintances of long association, every one of them (in the case of men) being elders. Up until 1980, aside from my wife I do not believe there were more than four or five persons on earth who knew to any real extent the concerns I had, and none of these knew all the reasons that caused these concerns. It would have taken a book such as this for them to have known that.

I had not the slightest doubt, however, that many, many others among Jehovah's Witnesses had a number of the same concerns that I did.[17] From my years on the Governing Body I saw no evidence that those concerns would be frankly faced or given the consideration they merited by means of careful, thorough research of the Scriptures, and decided, not on the basis of traditional views long held, but on the basis of the Biblical proof or lack of it.

The evidence pointed instead to the conclusion that any open discussion of these difficulties was viewed as a great danger to the organization, as disloyal to its interests. Unity (actually uniformity) was apparently counted more important than truth. Questions about organizational teachings could be discussed within the inner circle of the Governing Body but nowhere else. No matter how heated the debate on an issue within that inner circle, the Body must present a face of

17 One day a long-time member of the Service Department approached me, raising a question about an article written by the president. I said I could not answer for the article and suggested he write in his query. He replied, "No, I did that before and got burned." I said that unless people did write in no one would know their concerns. His response was, "If you really want to know how people feel about these articles, tell the Circuit and District Overseers to write in how they feel about some of the articles. But you must tell them NOT to sign their names, otherwise they'll only write what they feel is wanted." He said the same would be true if Bethel Elders were invited to write.

unanimity toward all those on the outside, even though such "face" actually masked serious disagreement on the point in question.

I found nothing in the Scriptures to justify this pretense, for those Scriptures commended themselves as truthful by their very frankness, openness and candor in acknowledging the differences existing among early Christians, including apostles and elders. More importantly I found nothing in Scripture to justify the restricting of discussion to such a secretive, closed society of men, whose two-thirds majority decisions must then be accepted by all Christians as "revealed truth." I did not believe that truth had anything to fear from open discussion, any reason to hide from careful scrutiny. Any teaching that had to be shielded from such investigation did not deserve to be upheld.

From the time of the writing of the reference work called *Aid to Bible Understanding*, I had had close association with Edward Dunlap. I first met him in 1964 when attending a ten-month course at Gilead School. He was then the Registrar of the School and one of its four instructors. Our class (the 39th) was composed of about one hundred persons, the majority of them men from Branch Offices. It can be truthfully stated that most of them considered Dunlap's classes by far the most instructive as regards gaining understanding of the Scriptures.[18] Originally from Oklahoma, of somewhat rough-hewn appearance, Ed was of ordinary education but had the ability to take very difficult, complex subjects and put them in understandable language, whether it was the functions of the Mosaic Law or a scientific study of genetics. However, more important to me was his unpretentiousness. Aside from a penchant for loud ties, he was a basically low key, low profile person, in appearance, demeanor and speech. No matter what responsibility was assigned him, he stayed the same person.

One incident that typified for me his personality was a remark he made to me in connection with a semestral exam. We were going through the various letters of Paul in our classes and each week there was an exam on points studied. Among the points there were generally questions about the likely time and place of writing for each letter. Taken one letter at a time this was not difficult to remember. But when time came for exams at the end of the semester, I realized that now we would have ALL the thirteen Pauline letters involved, and how to remember the different suggested times and places of writing posed a

18 Lloyd Barry was also in this class and made such expression on more than one occasion while a Governing Body member. I doubt that any others of the students ever had any question as to Ed's deep love for, and knowledge of, the Scriptures.

fair-sized problem. They followed no chronological order in the Bible canon. I worked for a long time at it and finally came up with a mental system for recalling these.

The exam came, with a two-hour period for completing it. I finished somewhat early and on leaving the classroom I met Ed coming in. He asked, "How was it?" I replied, "Oh, it wasn't bad. But I'll never forgive you." He asked what I meant. I said, "I worked and worked and worked to develop a system for remembering the times and places of writing of each letter and then you didn't ask a *single* question on that." Taking my remark somewhat more seriously than it was intended, he said, "You know the reason I don't put questions on that in the semester exams? I can't keep that stuff in mind myself." There were four instructors for the school, Ulysses Glass, Bill Wilkinson, Fred Rusk and Ed Dunlap. I think it is fair to say that of the four only Ed would have made the reply he did. It was typical of his unassuming personality.

He had always been thoroughly devoted to the organization; his full-time service record equalled mine in length. Another circumstance that tells something about him relates to an illness he developed in the late 1960's. Commonly called *tic douleureux* (a French term meaning "painful spasm"), the medical name for it is trigeminal neuralgia, the inflammation of a large, three-branched facial nerve that produces one of the most painful ailments known to humans. The stabbing, blinding pain can be provoked by anything, a slight breeze, a touch, that excites the nerve, and as the ailment worsens the victim can hardly do such ordinary things as comb his hair, brush his teeth, or eat, without risking an attack. Some so afflicted are driven to suicide.

Ed suffered with this for seven years, having some temporary remissions and then worsening. During this time, the president, Nathan Knorr, somehow acquired the opinion (based perhaps on others' comments) that this was something emotional on Ed's part, not genuinely of physical origin. One day he talked with Ed, questioning him about his married life and other matters in relation to this ailment. Ed assured him that that had absolutely nothing to do with the problem, that he could be thoroughly enjoying himself on vacation and yet the attacks could strike without warning. The president did not give any weight to Ed's explanation, however, and informed him that he had decided to send him over to the factory for a while to give him more exercise. He was to work in the bindery department.

Ed was then in his sixties, for some time had been taking strong medication prescribed by the staff doctor designed to suppress the painful attacks, at times had been bedridden for days or a week with the ailment. But he was now sent to the bindery and was there assigned to feed a machine on the bindery line. He did this for months and quietly endeavored to make the best of this "theocratic" assignment. But as he confided to me, it made him realize for the first time the absolute control the organization exercised over his life. His attempts at explaining were ignored and, contrary to all good sense, he was placed in the least desirable situation for one with that kind of ailment.

It was some years later, when he was at the point of absolute despair, that he learned of a neurosurgeon in Pittsburgh who believed he had discovered the cause of this age-old ailment and had perfected microsurgery to remedy it. Ed had the operation (involving the removal of a portion of the skull and remedial operation in connection with the main artery to the brain, which artery runs parallel to the inflamed nerve). He was thus finally cured. He expected no apology from the organization for its serious error in judgment in its viewing and handling of his agonizing problem. He received none.

Since our places of work, both during the *Aid* project and thereafter, were never more than an office apart, we conversed regularly, sharing with each other any interesting items we came across in research. The Writing Committee of the Governing Body assigned us to work together on a number of projects, such as the *Commentary on the Letter of James*. In our conversations we did not always agree on all points, but this did not affect our friendship or mutual respect.

I mention all this because Edward Dunlap was one of the few persons who knew how deep my concerns ran as to what I saw in the organization and particularly within the Governing Body. He shared that concern. Like myself, he did so because he could not harmonize much of what he saw, heard and read with Scripture.

Though associated with the organization since the early 1930's, during most of that association he did not count himself as among the "anointed." I was talking to him about this one day in the late 1970's and he related that when he began associating the *Watch Tower* then taught that there were two classes who would inherit heavenly life: the "elect" (composed of the 144,000) and the "great company" (or "great crowd" of Revelation chapter seven). The "great company" were said to be Christians of *lesser faith* than the elect and hence, though likewise destined for heavenly life, the "great company" would not be among those who would reign with Christ as kings and priests. Since, of the two classes, one was clearly superior and the other inferior, Ed typically assumed that he must be of the inferior class, the "great company."

Came 1935 and Judge Rutherford, at the Washington D.C., assembly, announced the "revealed truth" that those of the "great company" were Scripturally destined to live, not in heaven, but on earth. As Ed stated, he had always had the hope of heavenly life, felt there could be nothing more wonderful than to serve in the presence of God and in company with his Son. But because of the announced change in organizational viewpoint, he subdued those hopes and accepted what he was told should be his hope as part of the "great company."

It was not until 1979 that he clearly arrived at the decision that no human organization could change the invitation found in Scripture, as by setting a date for a change in the hope the Bible presented as open to any person embracing that hope, whether his name was Tom, Dick, Harry or Ed. So, forty-four years after 1935 he began to partake of the emblems, the bread and the wine, at the Lord's Evening Meal, something only the "anointed" among Jehovah's Witnesses do.

When a Witness or any one else asks, "How does one know whether he or she is of the 'anointed' class with heavenly hopes?" the standard response is to refer to Paul's statement at Romans, chapter eight, verse 16, 17:

> "The spirit itself bears witness with our spirit that we are God's children. If, then, we are children, we are also heirs, heirs indeed of God, but joint heirs with Christ, provided we suffer together that we may also be glorified together."

The official teaching has been, and is, that only those of the 144,000 "anointed" can have such 'witness of the spirit,' and that this would tell them that they were of the select group of 144,000 who alone could hope for heavenly life. All others could only be classed as "prospective" children of God and their hopes must be earthly.

In reading the context, from the very start of the chapter, it was evident to Ed that the apostle Paul was indeed writing about two classes. But *not* two classes divided by their hope of either heavenly or earthly life in the future.

The two classes instead clearly were: those guided by God's spirit, on the one hand, and those ruled by the sinful flesh, on the other.

The contrast the apostle set forth was not between hope of life in heaven or of life on earth, but between life and death themselves, between friendship with God or enmity with God. As verses 6 through 9 state:

"For the minding of the flesh means death, but the minding of the spirit means life and peace; because the minding of the flesh means enmity with God, for it is not under subjection to God, nor, in fact can it be. So those who are in harmony with the flesh cannot please God."

"However, you are in harmony, not with the flesh, but with the spirit, if God's spirit truly dwells in you. But if anyone does not have Christ's spirit, this one does not belong to him."

There was no question about heavenly or earthly life in Paul's discussion but simply whether one was living by God's spirit or was instead living according to the sinful flesh. Paul made it clear that it was one thing or the other: Either one had God's spirit and produced its fruitage or he was at enmity with God and did not belong to Christ. Without that spirit there could be no "life and peace," only death. If the person *did* have God's spirit, then he was a son of God, for Paul states (verse 14):

"For all who are led by God's spirit, these are God's sons."[19]

As Ed noted, Paul says, not some, but "ALL who are led by God's spirit" are his sons, his children. Those led by that spirit would have the "witness" of the spirit to that effect, including the evidence of its fruitage in their lives, somewhat similar to the way the Bible says that Abel, Enoch, Noah and others had "witness borne to them" that they were pleasing to God.[20]

The relevance of these points will become evident as later developments are considered.

Suffice it to say here, that Ed Dunlap shared with me the same basic concerns and particularly the concern over the dogmatism and authoritarian spirit being manifested. His view, like mine, was that human authority, when pushed beyond its proper limits, inevitably detracts from the role of Christ Jesus as Head of the congregation.

Not long after my return from Africa, a long-time friend came by our room at the headquarters. His name was Rene Vazquez and I had known him for about thirty years. I had first met him in Puerto Rico, in the town of Mayaguez where he lived with his father, who had remarried. Rene was then a high school student in his teens. Both his

---

19 Compare the apostle's use of the same phrase "led by the spirit" in a similar contrast between sinful flesh and God's spirit at Galatians 5:18, where it is stated that those "led by spirit" are "not under law." To deny that this applies to *all* Christians, rather than to a select group, would be to leave all the others still under law and law's condemnation.

20 Hebrews 11:1–7.

father and his father's wife strongly opposed Rene's studying with Jehovah's Witnesses. Their opposition became so intense that one evening, after having studied at the home of some Witness missionaries, Rene felt he could not endure any more. He spent the night on a park bench in a public plaza. The following morning he went to the home of an uncle and aunt and asked to be allowed to live with them, to which they agreed. Though not in favor of Jehovah's Witnesses, they were tolerant people. Upon graduation from high school, Rene immediately took up full time "pioneer service."

Attending an assembly in New York in 1953, he decided to remain in the United States, met a young girl in Michigan, married, and they both "pioneered" together. They were invited into traveling work among Spanish congregations in the western United States, later attended Gilead School and were sent to Spain. Rene was soon assigned as District Overseer in that country. The work of Jehovah's Witnesses was under official ban and he and his wife Elsie traveled all over Spain, having to be on constant watch for the police and conscious of the danger of being discovered and arrested or deported. All meetings held were clandestine. After years of such "underground" activity, Rene's nerves had worn thin to the point of breaking. By now he and Elsie had been in Spain seven years. Due to his health and some needs within Elsie's family, they returned to the United States, paying their own way and arriving with virtually no funds.

On his return, the only job Rene could find was in a steel mill, lifting heavy loads. A small person, his frail frame gave way the second day, putting him in the hospital. He later found other work and once they had settled their financial problems he and his wife were right back into "pioneer" service, then into Circuit and District work and finally were asked to become part of the Brooklyn headquarters staff where Rene was given supervision of the Service Desk caring for all the Spanish congregations in the United States, composed of about thirty thousand Witnesses. He served there until 1969 when Elsie became pregnant, requiring them to give up their "Bethel service."

Rene told me he would try to remain in New York, not because he liked the city, but with the thought that, should his circumstances allow, he could be of some service to the headquarters organization. It turned out that way, and in a few years he was donating his time two days a week to help out, doing Spanish translation, directing the taping of Spanish-language dramas for conventions, doing part-time Circuit and District Overseer work among the scores of Spanish congregations in the New York area. He had spent some time in Portugal and when Portuguese congregations developed, he brushed up on the language and served them also.

In his thirty some years of association with the organization, I seriously doubt that anyone in Puerto Rico, Spain or the United States ever found cause for complaint about Rene's service. Of a quite gentle nature, he was at the same time a person of principle: he had learned the art, however, of being firm without being in any way hard or harsh. Even given his present situation, which will be presented later, I doubt that any of those persons who worked with Rene Vazquez in any of the places he served would deny that the above is an honest assessment of him as a person. If he had a notable fault, it was, as he himself acknowledges, that he was perhaps too compliant when asked to do something for others, particularly by the Society. He feels today that his family life suffered unnecessarily because of this.

As one example, he and his wife had gone for some years without a true vacation and he had lined up a trip that would take them back to Spain for a visit. Shortly before the time arrived, Harley Miller, then the head of the Service Department, called and asked Rene to do some Circuit work at that particular time. Rene felt that the right thing to do was to accept, for he had never turned down an assignment from "the Lord's organization." His wife made the trip to Spain, accompanied by her mother.

Rene lived near La Guardia airport and members of the Service Department, Harley Miller among them, when traveling by plane on weekend speaking engagements, regularly arranged for Rene to meet them and transport them to Bethel on their return. Some of the flights arrived near midnight, others even later. Rene had insisted on providing such service for me and I had accepted on the basis of our long friendship, until I learned to what extent others were making use of his willingness to be helpful. To my mind, his good nature was imposed upon and, with rare exceptions, I sought other means of transportation thereafter.

I would think that if the view of the Governing Body were obtainable as to whom they would list as the principal figures in the "conspiracy against the organization" that they took such radical action to wipe out, they would point to us three—Ed, Rene and myself. Yet there was never an occasion when the three of us spent any time together. During the period involved I had extended conversations with Rene on perhaps two occasions; the same was true of Ed and Rene.

What were the supposedly sinister activities we engaged in? Simply this, we discussed the Bible as friends and with friends of long standing.

The night Rene came by our room, he had been attending a seminar for elders arranged by the Society. We discussed his impressions, which were basically favorable. At one point in the conversation, however, he said, "It seems to me as if we almost worship *figures*. Sometimes I wish we would do away completely with reports." By reports he was referring to the system of having each Witness turn in report slips each month listing what "witnessing" activity was done, including hours spent, literature distributed, and so forth.[21]

I recalled some points made in the previous District Assembly program about "faith and works" and we talked about this and the apostle's statements in Romans on the subject. As I saw it, the apostle's teaching called first of all for building people up in faith; when that was done the works would follow—for genuine faith is productive and active in the same way that genuine love is. One can keep constantly at people to perform certain works and they may do this as a result of pressure. But where is the evidence that the works are generated by faith and love? And if not so motivated, how pleasing would they be to God anyway?

It seemed evident that deeds of faith had to be spontaneous, not systematized or made to conform to a certain mold, just as acts of love should be spontaneous, not something performed out of mere compliance with some scheduled activity programmed by others. Orderly arrangements are fine, but they should be for the purpose of convenience, not as a means of subtle compulsion, used to create a guilt complex in any not 'fitting into the mold.' The more closely men try to supervise the lives and activity of fellow Christians, the more they actually squeeze out the opportunity for faith and love to motivate and control. I acknowledged that it is more difficult and far harder work to build up people's faith and appreciation through Scripture than simply to give "pep talks" or make people feel guilty, but, from what the

---

21 The importance given to these reports is undeniable. Every Witness reports to the congregation, every congregation reports to the Branch Office of their country, every Branch Office sends a detailed monthly report to the international headquarters where these monthly reports are compiled, averages are figured, percentages of increase are noted. They are studied with the same avid interest that a large corporation would study the figures of its production records, its business growth; any fluctuations or downward trends in the number of Witnesses reporting time, the hours reported or the distribution of literature, become causes for concern. Branch representatives become uneasy if the monthly reports for their country fail to show increase or, worse, show a decrease.

apostle wrote, that harder way seemed to me to be the only Scripturally right and wise way.

That was the essence of the conversation. The subject of report slips sparked the conversation but thereafter did not figure therein. On meeting up with Rene in the lobby of one of the buildings sometime later, he said he found that approaching matters in the light of Paul's writings in Romans made his Circuit and District Overseer work far more enjoyable, his discussion with Elders more meaningful.

Some weeks later my wife and I went to his home for a meal. Though we two couples had been together in the same Spanish-speaking congregation in Queens, New York, during our first years in the city, since then our getting together had been quite sporadic. Both before and after the meal, Rene wanted to discuss the message of Romans. Though to a lesser degree than with my wife, I felt an obligation to respond to his questions rather than evade issues. I had known him for thirty years; I knew him to be a serious student of the Scriptures. I spoke to him as a friend, not as an organizational official, and in discussing the Word of God with him I felt my prime responsibility was to God, not to men, not to an organization. If I held back from speaking to persons like this on what I saw to be clear-cut teachings of Scripture, how could I say as Paul did in his words to the Ephesian elders, recorded at Acts, chapter twenty, verses 26 and 27:

> "I call you to witness this very day that I am clean from the blood of all men, for I have not held back from telling you all the counsel of God."

Paul knew that it was doing this that had resulted in his being spoken of injuriously within the synagogue of Ephesus.[22] I knew, as well, that my speech could produce similar results.

Among other sections, we discussed the first portion of the eighth chapter of Romans (considered earlier in this chapter of this book). I was interested to know how he viewed verse 14, as to the sonship relation to God, when considered in the light of the context. He had never examined it contextually (as is probably true of practically all of Jehovah's Witnesses). When he did, his reaction was both spontaneous and stirring. What to others might seem obvious, can strike one of Jehovah's Witnesses as if it were a revelation. Rene's comment was, "For years I have had the feeling that I was resisting holy spirit when reading the Christian Scriptures. I would be reading along and applying to myself everything I read, then suddenly I would stop and

22   Acts 19:8, 9.

say, 'But these things do not apply to me, they apply only to the anointed.'"

I know, he knows and God knows that I used no persuasion to cause him to see matters differently. It was the apostle's own words in the Bible, read contextually, that did the persuading. His expression on a later incidental contact was that the Scriptures as a whole came alive with far greater meaning to him from that point forward.

Though it may seem strange, for one of Jehovah's Witnesses (not of the 9,000-plus "anointed") to come to the conclusion that the words found from Matthew to Revelation *are* directed to him and *do* apply, not merely "by extension," but actually and directly, causes a door to open to a whole host of questions, questions that have often been longing for an answer but which did not dare to be asked.

When I review what has been done in recent times in an effort to uphold the organization's interpretations, the manipulation of Scripture and fact, I can only feel grateful that I did not let concern for an organization's favor hold me back from pointing at least some persons to the Scriptures on these points.

On March 4, 1980, I submitted a request to the Personnel Committee of the Governing Body for a leave of absence to extend from March 24 to July 24. My wife and I both felt that our health demanded an extended change. During that period I also hoped to investigate what possibility there was of finding employment and somewhere to live should we terminate our headquarters service. We had about $600 in a savings account and a seven-year-old car as our major assets.

One of our first steps was to get a complete physical examination. Mine indicated that I was approaching the high-risk level for cardiac problems.

When attending District Assemblies in Alabama, we had previously met and become acquainted with a Witness named Peter Gregerson. Later he had invited us to visit Gadsden, Alabama, on a couple of occasions so that I could speak to the local congregations. Peter had developed a small chain of supermarkets in the Alabama-Georgia area. In 1978, when a "zone trip" took my wife and me as far as Israel, Peter and his wife joined us there and we spent parts of two weeks touring that Bible land.

At that time Peter expressed serious concern about the effects the 1975 predictions ("hinted" predictions?) had had. He said he thought it would be a grave error if the Society pushed strongly on their 1914 date; that the disillusionment resulting from 1975 would be nothing as compared with what would come if the Society was forced to move away from that 1914 chronology. I acknowledged that his assessment was undoubtedly correct but we went no further into the matter.

When Peter learned of our proposed leave of absence, he urged us to spend some time with them and fixed up a mobile home belonging to one of his sons for us to stay in. He offered to let me do yard work on his property to help cover some of our expenses and at the same time get some of the vigorous exercise that was medically recommended for me.

Peter's father had become one of Jehovah's Witnesses when Peter was a small child, and from about the age of four he had been taken by his parents to meetings. As a young man he had become a full-time "pioneer" and even after marriage and the arrival of his first child he had struggled to keep on in that full-time activity, doing janitorial work for income.[23] He had been sent by the Society into "problem" areas in Illinois and Iowa to help solve difficulties and build up certain congregations. In 1976 he was one of a representative group of elders invited to Brooklyn for discussions with the Governing Body and a couple of years later was asked to serve as an Instructor for a seminar for elders in the Alabama area.

A year or so after this seminar, however, he decided to relinquish his congregational eldership. He had recently turned over the presidency of the grocery company to one of his brothers and had made use of his increased free time to do more Bible study. He was troubled by some of the organization's teachings and wanted to reaffirm his convictions as to the rightness of those beliefs, reestablish his confidence in his life-long religion. (He was now in his early fifties.)

The result was exactly the opposite. The more he studied the Scriptures, the more convinced he became that there were serious errors in the organization's theology. This led to his decision regarding eldership. As he put it in talking with me about it, "I just can't bring myself to stand before people and conduct studies on things that I cannot see have a Scriptural backing. I would feel like a hypocrite doing that and my conscience won't let me do it." Although when first hearing his decision, I had encouraged him to reconsider it, I could not deny the validity of his serious questions, and I had to respect his conscientiousness and his distaste for hypocrisy. He had reached his personal crossroads before I reached mine.

This was the man that organizational policy later categorized as a

---

23 He and his wife now have seven children and as many grandchildren.

"wicked man" with whom one should not even eat and my having a meal with him in a restaurant in 1981 resulted in my trial and banishment from the organization.

It was in April, 1980, while we were in Gadsden on leave of absence that I first began to hear of what seemed to me to be strange occurrences back in Brooklyn. The expected storm had begun to break upon us.

INQUISITION

"When he left the house, the scribes and the Pharisees began a furious attack on him and tried to force answers from him on innumerable questions, setting traps to catch him out in something he might say." — Luke 11:53, 54, *Jerusalem Bible*.

An inquisition, in the religious sense, is an *inquiry* into individuals' personal convictions and beliefs.

Historically, its aim has been, not to aid the individual or to provide basis for reasoning with him, but to incriminate, to convict as heretical.

The initiating cause for the inquiry often has nothing to do with the individual's being disruptive, malicious or even being particularly vocal about his beliefs. Mere suspicion is sufficient cause to set in motion the inquisitory action. The suspect is viewed as, in effect, having no rights: even his personal conversations with intimate friends are treated as something the inquisitors have full right to delve into.

It was not solely the atrocious acts of punishment meted out in the Spanish Inquisition that earned it such a despised name in history. It was also the authoritarian approach and arrogant methods of interrogation employed to gain the incrimination so often zealously pursued by the religious judicial court. The torture and the violent punishment meted out then are outlawed today. But the authoritarian approach and arrogant methods of interrogation can still be practiced with apparent impunity.

I am reminded here of an article in the January 22, 1981, issue of the *Awake!* magazine, titled "Searching Out Legal Roots." It emphasized the superb legal precedents found in the Mosaic Law and, among other things, said:

> "Since the local court was situated at the city gates, there was no question about the trial being public! (Deut. 16:18–20) No doubt the public trials helped

influence the judges toward carefulness and justice, qualities that sometimes vanish in secret star-chamber hearings."

This principle was praised in the Society's publication. In actual practice it was totally rejected. As Jesus said, "They say one thing and do another."[24] The "secret star-chamber hearings" were preferred, as the evidence clearly shows. Only fear of the power of truth prompts that kind of proceedings. Those methods serve, not the interests of justice or mercy, but the cause of those who seek incrimination.

Four weeks after starting my leave of absence, while in Alabama, a phone call came from Ed Dunlap. After some general conversation, he told me that two members of the Governing Body, Lloyd Barry and Jack Barr, had come into his office and had interrogated him about his personal beliefs for about three hours. At one point Ed asked, "What's the purpose of this 'third degree'?" They assured him that it was not a "third degree" but that they simply wanted to hear how he felt about some matters.

They gave him no explanation as to what motivated their interrogation. Despite their claim that the discussion was simply informative, Ed's distinct impression was that it was the start of an organizational action that would prove both inquisitorial and punitive. Their questions inquired into his view of the organization, the teachings about 1914, the two classes of Christians and the heavenly hope, and similar points.

As regards the organization, he told his interrogators that his major concern was the obvious lack of Bible study on the part of the members of the Governing Body, that he felt that they had an obligation to the brothers to make such study and research of the Scriptures a primary concern, instead of allowing themselves to become so preoccupied with paper work and other affairs that Bible study got crowded out. As to 1914, he frankly acknowledged that he felt it was something that one should not be dogmatic about, and he asked them if the Governing Body itself believed this was something completely solid, certain. The reply from the two men was that 'while there were one or two who had doubts, the Body as a whole supported the date fully.' He told them that if others in the Writing Department expressed themselves it would be evident that almost all had different views on certain points.

24 Matthew 23:3, NEB.

On another day, Albert Schroeder and Jack Barr began a person-by-person interrogation of each member of the Writing Department. None of these acknowledged the uncertainty they felt about specific teachings, though in personal conversation virtually every one had some point that he had expressed a different view on.

The ironical feature of this was the diversity of viewpoint existing within the Governing Body itself, something that the interrogators never mentioned or acknowledged to those they questioned.

I knew that Lyman Swingle, the Coordinator of the Writing Committee of the Governing Body and the Coordinator of the Writing Department was away on a zone trip. I found it puzzling that such an intensive investigation should be initiated in his absence. Yet the Governing Body members doing the investigating had given no indication that anything out of the ordinary had arisen that should call for such a full-scale inquiry. From experience with the organization, I felt that this absence of any explanation for their action was indicative, not of something innocuous or benign, but of something that, when it came into the open, could prove quite devastating to those affected by it. For that reason, on Monday, April 21, 1980, I phoned the Brooklyn headquarters from Alabama and asked to speak to Governing Body member Dan Sydlik. He was not available, the Society's telephone operator informed me. I then asked to speak to Governing Body member Albert Schroeder, who was acting Chairman of the Body that year. He likewise was not available. I left a message with the operator that I would appreciate it if one or the other would phone me.

The next day, a call came from Albert Schroeder.

Before considering the conversation and the way he, as the Chairman of the Governing Body answered my questions, consider what I eventually learned had already happened and was in the process of happening at the time he talked to me.

On April 14, eight days before Schroeder returned my call, a Witness in New York named Joe Gould phoned the Brooklyn Service Department and talked to Harley Miller, a member of the five-man Service Department Committee.[25] He told Miller that a fellow employee, a Cuban Witness named Humberto Godinez, had told him of a conversation in his home with a friend who was a Bethel family member. He said that the Bethel family member expressed himself on

---

25 This committee supervises the Service Department, at that time composed of a staff of about forty persons.

a number of points that differed from the organization's teachings. Miller recommended to Gould that he try to find out from Godinez the name of the Bethel family member. This was done and the name of Cris Sanchez was supplied. Godinez also said that my name and those of Ed Dunlap and Rene Vazquez came into the conversation. Miller did not recommend to Gould and Godinez that they endeavor to clarify matters with those involved nor to seek a solution through brotherly discussion. Miller did not speak to Ed Dunlap who was well known to him and in an office just across the street from him. He did not make a phone call to Rene Vazquez whom he had known for years and whose services as voluntary chauffeur he regularly employed. He did not endeavour to contact Cris Sanchez who worked in the Society's factory and was accessible by telephone.

He first spoke to the members of the Service Department Committee asking them if any of them could supply any similar information. He then went to the Chairman of the Governing Body, Albert Schroeder.

He was told to arrange for Godinez and his wife to come to the headquarters for an interview with Miller. Nothing was said to Cris Sanchez, Ed Dunlap or Rene Vazquez, nor was anything communicated to me. The Chairman's Committee of the Governing Body evidently felt that to have acted in such a friendly way, thereby endeavoring to keep the matter from becoming a major issue, was not the desirable way to proceed.

During Miller's interview with the Godinezes, he suggested to Godinez that he phone Rene Vazquez and "tactfully" see if he would express himself about the matter. Miller himself did not see fit to do so, nor did he consider it advisable to phone Ed Dunlap or walk across the street to talk to him about the matter. The phone call to Rene was made and the apparent goal was achieved, Rene responded in a way that could be viewed as incriminating. Another interview with the Godinez couple was arranged, this time with the Chairman's Committee, composed of Governing Body members Schroeder, Suiter and Klein, present. This was held on Tuesday, April 15. Still nothing had been said to Rene, Ed, Cris or myself. The interview ran two hours and was taped. Through Godinez' recollections and impressions, they heard of his conversation with fellow Cuban and long-time friend Cris Sanchez, following a meal in the Godinez home. A number of controversial points were discussed. Godinez' presentation included numerous references to Rene, Ed Dunlap and myself. At the close of the taping, each of the three Governing Body members, Schroeder, Suiter and Klein, commended the Godinez couple for their loyalty and expressed (on tape) their disapproval of those who had been implicated by the interview.

Like Miller, the Chairman's Committee of the Governing Body had made no effort to talk to Cris Sanchez, about whom they had heard only hearsay evidence. They had made no effort to talk with Rene Vazquez, Ed Dunlap or myself, about whom they had heard only third-hand information. Yet the next day, Wednesday, April 16, 1980, at the regular Governing Body session, the Chairman's Committee played the entire two-hour tape of the interview to the Body (Milton Henschel, Lyman Swingle and myself being absent).

All this had taken place *one week* before Schroeder spoke to me on the phone, a phone call that he made only at my request.

It was after this playing of the tape to the Governing Body that the questioning of Ed Dunlap and, subsequently, of the entire Writing staff took place. It was that tape that motivated the questioning. The Governing Body members who did the questioning, Barry, Barr and Schroeder, knew that was the case. Yet they said nothing about it, even when Barry and Barr were asked by Ed Dunlap the reason for the interrogation. Why?

The action taken was swift, extensive, coordinated. Both Cris Sanchez and his wife and also Nestor Kuilan and his wife were now interrogated. Cris and Nestor both worked in the Spanish Translation Department where Rene served two days a week.

Harley Miller now phoned Rene and asked him if he would come to the office, saying, "We just want to pick your brains a little on some points."

The Chairman's Committee had arranged for investigating committees to be formed to handle the interrogation of these different ones. With the exception of Dan Sydlik, all the men on these committees were staff members outside the Governing Body. The Governing Body through its Chairman's Committee directed all the actions but from this point on remained in the background. They now arranged to have the various men serving on these investigative committees listen to portions of the two-hour tape that had been played to the Body so as to equip them for their committee action. That is why these committees used my name and Ed's name repeatedly in their questionings of Sanchez, Kuilan and Vazquez. Yet the Chairman's Committee had still not seen fit to inform us that the tape even existed. Why?

The objective of the investigating committees was evident from the direction their questionings took. The committee interrogating Nestor

Kuilan asked him to describe his personal conversations with Ed Dunlap and myself. He replied that he did not think his personal conversations were something others had a right to inquire into. He made clear that if he felt that anything wrong or "sinful" had been said he would not hesitate to inform them, but that this was certainly not the case. His questioners told him he should 'cooperate or he would be subject to possible disfellowshiping.' His response was, "Disfellowshiping? For what?" The reply was, "For covering over apostasy." Kuilan said, "Apostasy? Where is the apostasy? Who are the apostates?" They answered that this was still being determined, but that they were quite sure that such existed.

This is somewhat like a man's being threatened with imprisonment unless he cooperates by giving information about certain persons, and when he asks why, he is told that the imprisonment would be for complicity in a bank robbery. When he asks, "What bank was robbed and who are the robbers?" he is told, "Well, we don't know yet what bank was robbed or who did it, but we're quite sure there was a bank robbery somewhere and unless you answer our questions we will find you guilty of complicity and you will be subject to imprisonment."

Nestor explained that he had studied in Gilead School under Ed Dunlap as one of his instructors and so knew him since then, and that he had known me from the time I served as a missionary and Branch Overseer in Puerto Rico. He acknowledged that he had conversed with each of us on occasion but that those conversations involved nothing sinful or bad and were his personal affair.

By April 22, when Albert Schroeder responded to my request and phoned me, the judicial machinery of the organization was in full operation and moving rapidly. As Chairman of the Governing Body he, better than anyone else, knew all these facts, for all the investigating committees involved were under the direction of the Chairman's Committee.

He knew that his Committee had had the earlier-mentioned two-hour tape played to the Governing Body one week before his phone call.

He knew that the various investigating committees had all been "briefed," hearing portions of the tape and that, at the very time he spoke to me, they were using my name, along with that of Ed Dunlap, in their interrrogations.

He knew that the extremely grave charge of "apostasy" was included in the committee hearings. He had to know the very serious effect this could have on us two men he had known for decades, men he called his "brothers."

What, then, was said to me in his phone conversation? Consider:

After a brief exchange of greetings, I said, "Tell me, Bert, what's going on in the Writing Department?"

His reply was:

> "Well—the Governing Body thought it well that some of us make an investigation of the Department to see what could be done to improve the coordination, cooperation and efficiency of the Department—and—to see if any of the brothers had reservations on some points."

This final expression, as to persons having reservations, was stated in a rather offhand way as if of secondary importance. He had had a clear opportunity to tell me the facts as to what was taking place. He chose not to do so.

I then asked what reason there could be for such a full-scale investigation? He now had a second opportunity to give me an honest explanation of the situation. His answer was:

> "Well, the Department isn't operating as efficiently as it should. The book for this summer's convention is going to be late getting to the factory."

A second time he chose to give an evasive answer rather than a straightforward reply to my question. As to his statement, I replied that this was nothing new, but that the previous year both the *Commentary on the Letter of James* (written by Ed Dunlap), and the book *Choosing the Best Way of Life* (written by Reinhard Lengtat) had reached the factory by the first part of January, in good time. (I knew this since it was my assigned responsibility to see that these books were developed on time. The book for 1980, titled *Happiness, How to Find It*, was being written by Gene Smalley, who had never written a book before, and the project was not under my supervision.) I added that I didn't see why this should be cause for such an investigation.

Schroeder continued:

> "And then some of the brothers aren't very happy about the way their articles are being reworked. Ray Richardson said he had turned an article in [here he gave the subject of the article] and he was very unhappy with the way it was worked over."

I said, "Bert, if you know anything at all about writers you know that no writer likes to have his material undergo 'surgery.' But that is nothing new either, as long as there's been a Writing Department it's been that way. What does Lyman [Swingle, the Coordinator of the Writing Department] think about this?"

He replied, "Oh, Lyman isn't here now."

"I know he isn't there," I answered, "he's on a zone trip. Have you written to him?"

"No," he said.

I then stated, "Bert, I find this very strange. If, for example, Milton Henschel [the Coordinator of the Publishing Committee which supervises all factory operations] were away and another member of the Publishing Committee were away, let's say Grant Suiter, and reports came to the Governing Body that the factory there was not functioning as efficiently as it should—do you think that the Governing Body would begin a full-scale investigation of the factory and its operations in the absence of those two brothers?" (I knew such an action would not even be contemplated.)

He hesitated somewhat and said, "Well, the Governing Body asked us to do this and we're simply making a report to them. We're going to make our report tomorrow."

My response was, "Well, I'd appreciate it if you would express my feelings on the matter. I think it's an insult to Lyman Swingle, to the man, to his years of service and to his position to take an action like this without consulting him or even letting him know."

Schroeder said he would convey this expression. I added that if there was anything of genuinely great importance that required discussion, I could always go up there. He said, "You could?" I replied, "Of course I could. It would simply be a matter of taking a plane and going up there." He asked if I could come the following Wednesday. I replied, "What would be the purpose if Lyman Swingle won't be there then?" The conversation ended there.

The Chairman of the Governing Body of Jehovah's Witnesses had had multiple opportunities to respond openly and honestly to my requests for information by saying, "Ray, what we feel is a very serious matter has come up and there are even charges of apostasy being made. We think you should know that your name has been involved and before we do anything we thought the only Christian thing to do was to talk to you first."

Instead he said nothing, not one word, to indicate that this was the case. Of course, he could not very well have made the latter part of that statement since he and the other members of the Chairman's Committee had already put into motion a large-scale operation of tapings, investigating committees and interrogations. The picture given me by the Governing Body representative was, plainly put, deceptive, fictitious. But I had no way of knowing then just how deceptive and fictitious it was. I soon began to learn, but primarily from sources outside the Governing Body.

If the conduct of the Governing Body and its Chairman's Committee in this regard is difficult to understand, I consider it even more inexplicable—and unjustifiable—that they were not open and above board with Ed Dunlap who was right there at the headquarters. When he asked Barry and Barr what the purpose of their interrogation was, simple fairness should have moved them to tell him why the Governing Body assigned them to question him, what grave charges were being made. Certainly Scriptural principles, including the statement of the Lord Jesus Christ that we should do to others as we would have them do to us, would have *demanded* that someone say to his face what accusations of "apostasy" were being made behind his back. The ones who knew this chose not to do so at that time. They chose not to do so for *nearly a month thereafter*. Yet his name, like mine, was passed on to the members of investigating committees and then of judicial committees—to at least a dozen or more men—and *still* no one from the Governing Body approached him to tell him what grave charges were being linked to his name. *Yet many of them saw him on a daily basis.*

I do not understand how that course of action can be considered worthy of the name Christian.

On Friday, April 25, just three days after Schroeder's phone call in response to my request, judicial committees, operating under the sanction and direction of the Chairman's Committee of the Governing Body, disfellowshiped Cris Sanchez and his wife and Nestor Kuilan. Rene and Elsie Vazquez were also disfellowshiped by another committee as was an elder of a congregation adjoining that in which Rene served. The names of all except the congregation elder were read out to the entire headquarters staff, stating that they had been disfellowshiped. The Governing Body thus informed well over a thousand five hundred persons. They did not see fit to inform me. I eventually heard it, of course, but from phone calls from those so treated, not from any of my fellow members on the Governing Body.

Diane Beers, who had been serving as a member of the headquarters staff for ten years and who was well acquainted with the San-

chezes and Kuilans, described her impression of the events of the
week of April 21 to 26 in this way:

"I think the thing that was impressed on my mind the most during that week
was the cruel way these friends were being treated. They never knew when
they would be required to go to a committee meeting. Suddenly the phone
would ring and there would go Cris. Then he would come back, the phone
would ring and there would go Nestor. On and on it went. They were kept
constantly up in the air during that week. One day when I was talking to
Norma, she told me that the committee wanted her to talk to them without Cris
there and she didn't know what to do. I suggested that Cris should be there at
all times because otherwise she would never have a witness to what they said
to her and how she replied. They could say anything, and she would have no
way of proving that it was different. It was becoming apparent that they were
trying to pit Norma against Cris.

"Finally on Friday afternoon [April 25] at 4:45 p.m., the Committee came
marching on to the 8th floor where we all worked and headed for the conference room that was directly behind my desk. Shortly, everyone began to leave
work and go home, but I stayed around to see what the outcome would be.
They called Cris and Norma and Nestor and Toni in and as they each came
out, I went to see what the 'verdict' was. I remember that when I went into
Nestor's office to talk to Toni and him, they told me I had better leave before
I too got into trouble for being seen with them. I walked home by myself
fighting all the way not to break down in tears. I was just devastated. I couldn't
believe what was happening. It's a feelng I will never forget. This place had
been my home for many years and I had enjoyed my time there—now it was
like I was in a place totally foreign to me. I thought about Christ saying that
by their fruits you will know them and I just couldn't reconcile what I had
seen and heard about during that week as being Christian. It was so harsh and
unloving. These were people who had given years and years of service to the
Society, had good reputations and were much loved by everyone. And yet no
mercy could be shown to them. It was incomprehensible to me.

"I had a meeting that evening, but I refused to go as I was just too upset.
Later on that evening when Leslie [Diane's roommate] had come home from
the meeting, we were talking and we heard a knock at the door. This was
around 11:00 p.m. It was Toni Kuilan. She didn't even get in the door before
she broke down and just sobbed. She didn't want Nestor to know how upset
she was. We all sat there and cried together and talked. We let her know that
she and Nestor were our friends now the same as always and tried to encourage
her as best we could. I couldn't sleep very good that night and got up once
around 2:00 or 3:00 in the morning. I just sat in the bathroom thinking about
what had happened and felt like it was a nightmare—it didn't seem real to me.

"Saturday morning I went to see Nestor and Toni and Cris and Norma and
when I got to Kuilan's room, they had just had a visit from John Booth [a

member of the Governing Body]. He was sent to tell them that their appeal had been rejected by the Governing Body. The committee had told them Friday evening that they had to have the appeal in by that next morning at 8:00 a.m. This in itself was ridiculous, but they complied and had an appeal in by 8:00 a.m. Booth was sent to tell them No. Nestor asked him why and he told him that he [Booth] was just a 'messenger boy'—he made it obvious that he did not want to discuss anything with any of them."

Here were people who had been associated for decades, had given many years of their life wholesouled and full time to what they believed was God's service, and yet in the space of six days, from Monday, April 21 to April 26, all that was set aside and they were disfellowshiped. During that week, when Scriptures were employed by their interrogators, it was in an accusatory, condemnatory way, not in the way that the apostle Paul describes at Second Timothy, chapter two, verses 24 and 25, when he instructs:

"And the Lord's servant must not quarrel; instead he must be kind to everyone, able to teach, not resentful. Those who oppose him he must gently instruct, in the hope that God will give them a change of heart leading them to a knowledge of the truth."—*New International Version.*

I believe it speaks poorly for any religion if it is unwilling to take time to reason with persons by means of God's Word—not for a few hours or even a few days, but for weeks or months—when those persons question the Scripturalness of that religion's teachings. When those being interrogated at the headquarters brought up Scriptural points, they were told in so many words, "We are not here to discuss your Bible questions." Harley Miller told Rene Vazquez, "I don't claim to be a Bible scholar. I try to keep up with the Society's publications and that is about all I can do." In the minds of the interrogators the prime issue was, not loyalty to God and his Word, but loyalty to the organization and its teachings. In this, as has already been shown, they had ample backing from the publications of the Society.

It can be truthfully said that none of the persons disfellowshiped had had any thought of separating themselves from Jehovah's Witnesses nor had they any thought of encouraging others to separate. Their attitude is poignantly expressed in this letter written by Rene Vazquez in appealing the disfellowshiping action taken against him and his wife:

Rene Vazquez
31-06 81 Street
Jackson Heights, NY 11370

May 4, 1980

Judicial Committee
c/o Claudius Johnson
1670 E 174 Street   Apt. 6 A
Bronx, NY 10472

Dear Brothers:

I find it necessary once again by this means to appeal to your
sound reasoning and impartial judgement and see that we are not
guilty of the accusation brought against us, my wife and I. We, in
fact do not really understand or know who our accusers are.

During our hearing, time and again, we stated from the heart,
in all truthfulness before Jehovah God that the very idea of
promoting a sect or being apostate is utterly unthinkable on our
part. Is this not borne out by my dedicated service to Jehovah God
for the past 30 years, to the extent of giving minimal attention to
my own family and to my secular work? Why should my recent actions
in regard to discussing some Bible points in private conversation
with some dear brothers and friends, all of a sudden be taken as an
attack on the organization or as apostasy? Why should such extreme
action as disfellowshiping be taken, when sound reasoning, kindness,
true christian love and mercy, could mend and heal any miunderstandings
or heartache that resulted from imprudent talk or repetition of things
not in harmony with what has been published by the Society? Where
is the evil, wicked person, the hater of Jehovah, the rebellious
individual, the unrepentant doer of wicked acts that should be
stamped out? Why should a legalistic definition of apostasy be used
in such a cold and unmerciful way to condemn people who have done
nothing but serve faithfully and pour out their souls in behalf of
the brothers for so many years?

Who are the ones causing reproach on Jehovah's name and giving
a bad name or image to the organization? Are not the drastic actions
that are being taken, and the unloving methods being used, and the
slanderous rumors being spread, and the lack of mercy and christian
love, the suspicion, fear and terror of inquisitory investigations,
multiplying a thousand times any misunderstanding or unintentional
harm due to people repeating improperly some things said?

Brothers, there is nothing but love in our hearts for the entire
association of our brothers, and in no way has my wife or I ever wanted
to act with or had any evil design to cause confusion or disturbance of
their faith. How would Christ Jesus handle a situation like this?

It appears that the main objective of the committee was to eatablish
guilt by establishing that there was apostasy. In spite of our repeated
expressions from the heart, that pursuing a course of apostasy is

Judicial committee
May 4, 1980
Page 2

unthinkable, that such a thing never came into our heart, that charge
continued to be pressed. The committee appears to have been committed
to proving that we were apostates by showing that private personal
conversations we had with some of our dear friends, were in fact part
of an evil scheme to form a sect or cause a division by apostasy.
In two different occasions Brother Harold Jackson used the illustration
of a young girl who committed fornication, but the idea of doing that
was so rejected by her mind, that she in fact believed that she did not
commit fornication, but she was pregnant. The application would be that
no matter how abhorrent is to us the idea of being apostates, that no
matter if our heart and conscience tell us that it is unthinkable for
us to do such a thing, still we are apostates.

But Brothers, we know the difference between our right and left
hand. This is not the case of a young girl lacking in understanding
and experience. But for the sake of argument, even if such were the case,
that we are something that we are not, because we are not in our heart,
mind and conscience, how would Christ Jesus handle the matter? Would he
not extend his lovingkindness and mercy to that girl, so that sin may
not rule as king because he died so that we may be shown mercy?

On the other hand, would it be the wisdom from above to use the
example of that girl as a principle to judge another case where the girl
is sure that she did not commit fornication but her belly is big? What
if proper examination shows that she had a cyst in her womb, so that
she was in fact telling the truth, but was so pressed by questionings
and mental anguish that she would be made to suffer, and in addition
to that, slanderous rumors would begin to circulate saying that she
was pregnant, that she was going to have twins, that she already gave
birth to triplets, and so on. Would that not be a great injustice? Who
would be the ones causing the real harm? Would not the love and mercy
of Christ Jesus avoid such a great injustice?

For this very same reason Christ Jesus told those who condemned
him for doing works of healing on the Sabath: "Stop judging from the
outward appearance, but judge with righteous judgement."--John 7:24

Brother Episcopo, as one on the judicial committee, stated, by
a number of leading questions, that an apostate could be very sincere
in what he would be teaching, but he still was an apostate. The
application would be that in spite of our continued expressions
indicating that such an apostate course of action is unthinkable on our
part, that we have never engaged in any evil design against the
organization, nor in forming a sect, that we still are to be dealt with
as apostates because of the things we discussed in our private
conversations with our friends.

However, if we were to use that definition of apostasy, then we
would have to conclude that our history as an organization as Jehovah's
witnesses is full of acts of apostasy. When we were teaching that the
invisible presence of Christ Jesus began in 1874, we were very sincere.
But Jehovah knew that what we were teaching was not in harmony with
Bible truth. Then He would have to have considered us apostates, by the
definition put forth by Brother Episcopo. Time and again, as an

Judicial Committee
May 4, 1980
Page 3

organization we have taught, with godly devotion and sincerity, what resulted not to be in harmony with the Word of God, and the faith of many was disturbed when things did not turn out to be the way we taught. Would it be in harmony with mercy and love to judge the organization as apostate on that basis? Would it be sound reasoning to put the organization in the class of Hymeneaus and Philetus, who were subverting the faith of others, saying that the resurrection had already occurred?

The basis of the action against us is our having discussed certain points from the Bible with a few brothers in private conversation with them. One of the fundamental privileges each one has as an individual is that of talking confidentially to a friend or trusted person. If this privilege is taken away, or if we are told that we have to confess such confidential talk and then be judged on the basis of such expressions, or if the individuals we took into our confidence are forced by fear of action against them, to accuse us of talking to them, what sort of subjection are we demanding as an organization? Would not that become total subjection or absolute subjection? Would'nt that be in effect violating the headship of Christ Jesus over the congregation?

We can give various examples of such kind of conversations in the past on the part of many, including some of those in our committee, of things not published or taught by the organization. If I know of such conversations, how many more know or knew about them? To how many did they speak about those things? Should we now start an inquisitory investigation to determine that, and to argue that they are apostate? The very reason that I did not mention such examples, giving names, is that I know it would be unjust to do such a thing. We did not want to give the idea that we were pointing the finger at someone else. Are the brothers now to be under an atmosphere of terror so that the very mention of reading the bible at home would be viewed as suspicions and possible apostasy, or should we say "heresy."?

In our hearing, when I expressed that we were very sorry for the disturbance that somehow was traced back to us due to a very imprudent repetition of some points to a number of brothers, and when we gave the assurance that we would in no way again talk about such things to others, but rather tell anyone who would mention such things that such talk should be stopped, Brother Harold Jackson strongly stated that I had to give them some kind of assurance about that, and then proceeded to say that we were a danger to the organization, and to imply that I was following a pattern of covering up things, and that he did not personally believe what I was saying. What is the direction given in the bible in this regard? How can that "assurance" be given? Even if there were valid reason for someone to be accused of promoting a sect, Titus 3:10 says: "As for a man that promotes a sect, reject him after a first and second admonition." The second admonition would be due to the individual's continuing with new offenses indicating that he insisted on promoting a sect. Even if we were viewed as that kind of persons, from the very first unfortunate misunderstanding, we have

Judicial Committee
May 4, 1980
Page 4

even become abnormally non-comunicative in order to avoid any further
misunderstanding. Since a mere verbal assurance would not be enough,
as implied by the counsel of Paul, the conduct of the individual,
not necessitating a second admonition, and then a re-ocurrence of the
wrong, would be the assurance needed. Even that benefit of the doubt
is not given to us.

more than one time it was stated by brother Jackson that the
things comented constituted an attack on the very heart of the
organization. but in the first place, such attack does not exist,
and I personally do not know of anyone conducting an attack. Could
it be that an expression is being used which was coined by an
undiscerning person who made a hasty judgement and made a complaint?
Should a statement, or hasty judgement like that, all of a sudden
be taken as an absolute truth and measure everybody by that? Brothers,
the extreme and strange actions taken in this situation are very
disturbing and perplexing.

We appeal on the basis of righteousness and mercy, because we
have been judged on a wrong we have not committed.

be assured of our prayers to Jehovah for this matter to be
clarified for the blessing of His name and the spiritual well-being of
his people.

Your brothers,

Rene Vazquez

Elsie Vazquez

Some thirty years earlier, Rene had left his father's home to escape
what he felt was an oppressively intolerant atmosphere, narrow-
mindedness. He sought freedom to pursue his interest in Jehovah's
Witnesses. From then on he had given himself, heart and soul, to
service among them. Now, in the space of two weeks, he saw those
thirty years set aside as of no particular weight, he was subjected to
intense interrogation, his sincerity of motive was impugned, and he
had been labeled a rebel against God and Christ. His letter voices his
painful anguish on finding himself in the same atmosphere of religious
intolerance and narrow-mindedness he thought he had escaped.

Rene was granted an appeal and again met with a committee (formed
of five other Elders). Every effort he made to be conciliatory, to show
that he was not seeking to make an issue of specific doctrinal matters,

that he had no desire to be dogmatic about such, was rejected as evasive, as evidence of guilt.

At one point, after hours of being plied with questions, he was interrupted by Sam Friend, a member of the Appeal Committee, who said, "That is a lot of hogwash. Now I'm going to read this list of questions to you and I want you to answer them yes or no." To Rene, whose native language is Spanish, the term "hogwash" was unfamiliar and, although afterward deciding it was simply some regional expression, he says that at the time it hit him with such a literal image of filth that something "gave" inside him and he responded, "No! I'm not going to answer any more of your questions. You men are trying to sift my heart and I'm not going to endure any more of it." A recess in the session was called; Rene walked out and on reaching the street broke down in tears.

The committee upheld the disfellowshiping decision.

Of all the persons Rene had known and worked with in the Brooklyn Service Department, including those who had been willing to make use of his kindness and helpfulness over many years, not one appeared to say at least something in his behalf, to express any request for a similarly kind treatment toward him.[26] On the organization's scales of justice his undeniable sincerity, his unmarred record of the past thirty years—none of this carried any weight if he did not totally agree with the organization and maintain unquestioning silence. Somewhere in all this it would seem that the words of the disciple James have application, when he writes:

> "Talk and behave like people who are going to be judged by the law of freedom, because there will be judgment without mercy for those who have not been merciful themselves; but the merciful need have no fear of judgment."[27]

Finally, on May 8, 1980, the Governing Body officially informed me that my name was involved in this. A phone call came from Chairman Albert Schroeder and he said that the Governing Body wanted me to go to Brooklyn to appear before them. This was the *first time* they gave me any indication whatsoever of my being in any way under question.

Fifteen days had passed since our previous conversation in which

26 While it is true that all these proceedings were carried on in "secret star-chamber" style, there were many in the Department who knew what was taking place, either through direct knowledge or by departmental "gossip."

27 James 2:12, 13, JB.

the Chairman repeatedly evaded telling me what was actually taking place. I still was unaware of the existence of the two-hour taped interview or that it had been played to the Governing Body in full session. Twenty-three days had passed since that was done.

In those twenty-three days they had not only played that tape to the Governing Body but had played portions of it including my name and that of Ed Dunlap to at least seventeen persons outside the Body (those forming investigative and judicial committees), they had disfellowshiped three members of the headquarters staff and three person outside, one of them a friend of mine for thirty years, they had taped another interview with a man named Bonelli (a tape that will be discussed later), and in general had not only invited but had actively sought any evidence of an incriminating nature that could be obtained from members of the Bethel family or others, the threat of disfellowshiping even being used to extract information from some.

Only after all this did the Governing Body through its Chairman's Committee think it advisable to let me know that they viewed me as in any way implicated in what was taking place. Why?

What I knew I had learned entirely from other sources, not from the Governing Body of which I had been a member for nine years. The Bethel headquarters members who were grilled and put on trial had phoned me, voicing their dismay at the unkind, intolerant attitude shown. They expressed their belief that the ones directing the whole process were simply going through them in order to reach their true objective, Edward Dunlap and myself. They felt that such ones were taking what they considered to be the more strategic course of beginning with the "small people," the lesser known and less prominent ones, establishing their "guilt," making it seem as if the situation was of great and dangerous proportions, and then, having laid as strong a foundation as possible, proceeding to deal with the better known and more prominent ones. Rightly or wrongly, this was the impression they had. It would be interesting to hear from those of the Chairman's Committee, to whom all reports ultimately went and who answered all requests for direction by the investigating and judicial committees—to hear what possible reasons that Committee could have had for proceeding in the manner they did.

When Chairman Schroeder phoned me on May 8, I expressed my feelings, how difficult I found it to understand why, after living and working together, week in and week out, for nine years with the members of the Governing Body (fifteen years with some), not one of them had the brotherly considerateness to communicate with me as to what was taking place. (In all fairness to the members as a whole, it must be granted that they may not have known in detail how the Chairman's Committee was handling matters. They may not have known the content of Albert Schroeder's phone conversation with me on April 23 and the misleading responses my questions received—though it seems possible, even probable, that the conversation was taped, as later developments would indicate. Either way, it must be acknowledged that some or many of the members may have expected and believed that the Chairman's Committee was conducting matters on a high level, in accord with Christian principles, doing to others as they would have done to themselves.)

I then asked Albert Schroeder what his feelings would have been if, at the time he was in Europe conveying his thoughts of a different application of the critical phrase "this generation," some in Brooklyn, on hearing of this, had brought accusations of "apostate leanings" on his part, and then had begun gathering together any other expressions he might have made anywhere at any time to anyone as evidence to substantiate that grave charge—and had done all this without even communicating with him to advise him of what was taking place. How would he feel?

He gave no reply. I told him I would go to Brooklyn as requested and the conversation came to a close.

By the time I arrived in Brooklyn on May 19, the continual toll on my nerves had brought me to a state of near shock. There seemed to be something so irrational about what was happening, the methods used. Some called it a "nightmare." Others felt a stronger term was needed, namely, "paranoia." Innocent Christians were being treated as if they were dangerous enemies.

Recently I ran across an item I had read and clipped some years ago from the *New York Times*. Headed "Mistrust Found in Nixon's Staff," among other things it said:

"A psychiatrist on the White House staff from 1971 to 1973 says the inner group around Richard M. Nixon deeply mistrusted the motives of other people, viewed concern for people's feelings as a character flaw, and could not respect loyal opposition or dissent.

"Dissent and disloyalty were concepts that were never sufficiently differentiated in their minds,' Dr. Jerome H. Jaffe said. 'That really was the tragic part. To dissent was to be disloyal. That is the theme that recurred again and again.' . . .

"'The Administration admired people who could be cold and dispassionate in making personnel decisions,' he said. 'To make concessions to people's feelings, to recognize that a particular objective was not worth destroying people in the process of its attainment, was not something that elicited any admiration. Such a concern was viewed as a fatal flaw.'

"'They deeply distrusted the motives of other people and were unable to believe that people could rise above selfish motives,' he said."[28]

I find a frighteningly close parallel between this and the attitudes shown in Brooklyn in the spring of 1980. "To dissent was to be disloyal. That is the theme that recurred again and again." The kindness of Jesus Christ seemed so seriously missing. Any warmth of friendship, and the compassionate understanding that gives friendship its warmth, seemed replaced by a cold organizational approach that assumed the worst, gave no benefit of doubt, and viewed forbearance and patience as a weakness, inimical to the interests of the organization, to its goals of uniformity and conformity. It was as if some massive legal machine had been put in motion and was grinding along in an unfeeling, unrelenting way toward its ultimate objective. I found it hard to believe it was actually happening.

At the headquarters, among other things on my desk I found an item prepared by the Chairman's Committee back on April 28, 1980. (See next page.) Some of the points were surprising to me, since I had never even considered them, much less discussed them with others. I was repelled by the dogmatic terms in which all the points were stated. And I thought the "Notes" at the bottom really presented the true issue. For those notes focused repeated emphasis on the *"basic Biblical 'framework' of the Society's Christian beliefs,"* the *"'pattern of healthful words' that have come to be Biblically accepted by Jehovah's people over the years."*

This had a familiar ring, for it was an argument so frequently used in Governing Body sessions, the argument that long-standing traditional teachings of the Society must be adhered to, as if the years they had been believed necessarily gave proof of their rightness. Those traditional teachings, and not the Word of God itself, lay at the crux of the issue.

On May 20 I met with the Chairman's Committee and they played me a tape of the report they gave to the Governing Body on the interviews with members of the Writing Staff, and about the Chairman's

---

28 *New York Times*, January 12, 1976, p. 12.

(To Governing Body)   RECENT EVIDENCES OF WRONG TEACHINGS BEING SPREAD ABOUT

Following are some of the wrong teachings being spread as eminating from Bethel. These have been brought to the attention of the Governing Body from the field from April 14 onward.

1.   That Jehovah does not have an organization on earth today and its Governing Body is not being directed by Jehovah.

2.   Everyone baptized from Christ's time (C.E. 33) forward to the end should have the heavenly hope. All these should be partaking of the emblems at Memorial time and not just those who claim to be of the anointed remnant.

3.   There is no proper arrangement as a "faithful and discreet slave" class made up of the anointed ones and their Governing Body to direct affairs of Jehovah's people. At Matt. 24:45 Jesus used this expression only as an illustration of faithfulness of individuals. Rules are not needed only follow the Bible.

4.   There are not two classes today, the heavenly class and those of the earthly class also called "other sheep" at John 10:16.

5.   That the number 144,000 mentioned at Rev. 7:4 and 14:1 is symbolic and not to be taken as literal. Those of the "great crowd" mentioned at Rev. 7:9 also serve in heaven as indicated in vs. 15 where it is claimed that such crowd serves "day and night in his temple (naoŝ" or K. Int says: "in the divine habitation of him."

6.   That we are not now living in a special period of "last days" but that the "last days" started 1900 years ago C.E. 33 as indicated by Peter at Acts 2:1? when he quoted from the Prophet Joel.

7.   That 1914 is not an established date. Christ Jesus was not enthroned then but has been ruling in his kingdom since C.E. 33. That Christ's presence (parousia) is not yet but when the "sign of the Son oi man will appear in heaven" (Matt. 24:30) in the future.

8.   That Abraham, David and other faithful men of old will also have heavenly life basing such view on Heb. 11:16.

Notes: The above Biblical viewpoints have become accepted by some and now being passed on to others as "new understandings." Such views are contrary to the basic Biblical "framework" of the Society's Christian beliefs. (Rom. 2:20; 3:2) They also are contrary to the "pattern of healthful words" that have come to be Biblically accepted by Jehovah's people over the years. (2 Tim. 1:13) Such "changes" are condemned at Prov. 24:21,22. Hence the above are 'deviations from the truth that are subverting the faith of some.' (2 Tim. 2:18) All considered is this not APOSTASY and actionable for congregational discipline. See ks 77 page 58.

                              Chairman's Committee   4/28/80

Committee's subsequent steps in getting investigative and judicial processes in motion. They then gave me two tapes to take and listen to, one being the two-hour interview with the Cuban couple (the Godinezes) and the other a shorter taped interview with a Witness named Bonelli. I learned for the *first time* of the existence of the two-hour tape and that they had played it to the Governing Body over a month before. I find it almost ludicrous that after all the havoc that had been wreaked on people's lives since the time of playing that tape, they were just now getting around to letting me hear it, the day before my hearing in a plenary session of the Governing Body.

I took the tapes to my office and played them. It made me feel ill. Everything was given such an ugly cast. I had no doubt that the Godinezes were seeking to repeat things as they had heard them, for I knew them and had always found them to be decent persons. But, as Harley Miller led them through the interview, I kept asking, "Were the things said to them actually presented in the extreme way that they here sound?" I was effectively cut off from determining this since the Chairman's Committee had already directed the formation of the judicial committees that had produced the disfellowshiping of those involved.

At the end of the tape, I heard the three members of the Chairman's Committee individually express themselves as though satisfied that they now had a clear picture of matters and, first, commending the couple interviewed for their loyalty, while, thereafter, condemning those implicated. This increased my feeling of illness. How could they do this without even having talked with Cris Sanchez? Why was he not there? Why was Rene Vazquez in effect "set up" by Harley Miller's suggestion (expressed on this very tape) that Godinez phone Rene and "tactfully" see if he would commit himself? What was the interest that these men had, what were they seeking to accomplish? Was it sincerely to help people, to understand their viewpoint and work toward a peaceful solution, to seek to clear matters up with a minimum of difficulty and hurt, through kind counsel, through exhortation to moderation and prudence if these were lacking—or was it to build up a case against persons? I found nothing in the entire tape to indicate anything but the latter goal.

If the contents of that first tape were bad, the second was far worse. The Godinezes had expressed their recollections of a conversation in their home and the way the things said had struck them and, as stated, I believe they did so sincerely. The second tape was filled largely with rumor. But the most disheartening aspect of the whole recording were the expressions made by the headquarters interviewers.

Bonelli was a member of a Spanish-speaking congregation adjoining that of Rene's. The tape began with Albert Schroeder introducing Bonelli as a man who had been a "ministerial servant" (or "deacon") in two previous congregations but who was not presently such. He quoted Bonelli as having said that he was not appointed as a ministerial servant in his present congregation because of an adverse attitude of one of the elders there, named Angulo.

Bonelli then gave testimony against this same elder that he said had contributed toward his not being appointed as a ministerial servant. (Angulo was one of those who was disfellowshiped.) He also said that after the Memorial service (the Lord's Evening Meal) on March 31, he had gone to Rene Vazquez' home where he saw Rene's wife and mother partake of the emblems of bread and wine.[29] Bonelli said he also partook of the emblems.

This last statement produced surprised comments from his interviewers, Albert Schroeder and, from the Service Department, Dave Olson and Harold Jackson. Bonelli went on to say in explanation—and I here quote his exact words as they are recorded on the tape: "I'm sneaky." He said he had gone to Rene's home to get information about them.[30]

He went on to say that he understood from another Witness that the elder named Angulo had already obtained a building in which he and Rene would hold meetings, that they had already baptized persons in their new belief.

There was, in reality, *not a single word of truth* in those rumors. The interrogators did not ask where the supposed location of meetings was, or what the names of the persons supposedly baptized were. None could have been supplied if they had asked, for they did not exist.

Farther along in the tape, Bonelli had difficulty expressing one point in English and Harold Jackson, who speaks Spanish, had him state it in Spanish and then Jackson put it into English. Bonelli chuckled and

---

29 Previous to my departing on my leave of absence, Rene told me that he and his wife and mother all felt conscientiously that they should partake of the emblems. He said he was certain that if all three did so at the Kingdom Hall it would cause a lot of talk (it is rare for any of the Spanish-speaking congregations to have one professing to be of the "anointed" among them). He said he felt the course that would cause the least problem would be for his wife and mother to wait until after the congregation meeting and partake quietly at home. He said that Bonelli was not in their congregation and was not asked to accompany them home but asked to do so himself. (Rene's mother had at one time conducted a Bible study with Bonelli and knew him well.)

30 I personally doubt that that was his motivation at the time.

said: "My English is not so good, but the information I am giving is."
Dave Olson's voice then came in quickly saying, "Yes, Brother, you're
giving us just what we need. Go on."

When I heard those words it was as if a crushing weight came down
on my heart. In the whole interview, this man had not said one thing
that could possibly be viewed as helpful if the aim was to try to aid
persons who had a wrong understanding of Scripture. Only if the aim
was to build up a case, to obtain incriminating, damning evidence,
then only could he be said to be 'giving just what was needed.' But
even the evidence supplied was half rumor, unfounded, utterly false,
and the other half could be viewed as significant only if one upheld
the view that a religious organization has the right to prohibit private
conversations about the Bible among personal friends if these do not
adhere totally to that organization's teachings, as also the right to judge
the conscientious actions of persons even when done in the privacy of
their own home.

At the close of Bonelli's taped testimony, Dave Olson asked him if
he could supply names of other "Brothers" who might give similar
information. Bonelli had claimed that a large number of persons were
spoken to about the "apostate" beliefs. He replied to Olson's request
by saying that he thought he knew a "Brother" in New Jersey who
might be able to give some information. Olson asked his name. Bonelli answered that he didn't remember but thought he could find out.
Olson said, "But there must be many others who could supply information." Bonelli then said he thought he knew some "Sisters" who
might be able to do that. What were their names? That, too, he would
have to find out.

Albert Schroeder then expressed gratitude to Bonelli for his cooperation in testifying and counseled him to 'keep himself spiritually
strong by attending the meetings regularly,' and added that if Bonelli
heard any other information to come to them with it.

In my opinion, nothing expresses more clearly and forcefully the
direction taken in the entire process of investigation, interrogation and
ultimate condemnation than does this particular tape. I can think of
nothing that would be more helpful to all of Jehovah's Witnesses
everywhere to enable them to have a balanced, not a one-sided, view
of what took place, the "climate" that prevailed, how the men connected with God's "channel" at headquarters conducted themselves,
than for them to hear this tape and compare it with what has thus far
been told them by the organization or what they have heard through
gossip. But they should also have the right to ask questions as to what

was done to verify the testimony of this man, to separate fact from rumor, and also the right to ask why this kind of testimony was viewed by the headquarters men as of such value, "*just what we need.*"

The likelihood of the organization's doing that, allowing this tape to be heard (with no portions erased) and for questions to be asked is, I believe, virtually nonexistent. I personally think they would destroy it rather than allow that to happen. I still do not understand why the Chairman's Committee did not feel ashamed to let me hear it as they did.

The Governing Body knew that within days after the disfellowshiping of the headquarters staff members, rumors of the same kind contained in this tape began circulating within the Bethel family. The "apostates" were forming their own religion, had been holding separatist meetings, baptizing people, their new belief went under the name of "Sons of Freedom"—these and similar expressions were common talk. They were also totally false. Governing Body members presiding at the morning Bible discussions made many comments about the "apostates" but did not see fit to expose the falsity of the rumors circulating. Those rumors went unchecked and eventually spread all over the globe. Yet every Witness who passed these on was speaking, even if unwittingly, false testimony against his neighbor. The only ones in position to expose the falsity of those rumors and thus help stop the false testimony were those of the Governing Body. Why they did not choose to do so only they know. I do not doubt that among them there were some who honestly believed that the things they were hearing were factual. But I believe that in their position and with their weight of responsibility they had an obligation to investigate and to help others to realize that it was not factual, it was fiction, and not only fiction but hurtful, even vicious, fiction.

I would not argue that errors of judgment were all on one side. I do not doubt in the least that among those of us "brought to trial" there were cases of injudicious statements. The evidence indicates that some of the most extreme statements were made by a man who, on being approached, quickly offered to become a 'witness for the prosecution,' testifying against a fellow elder. I do not personally know that man, have never met him, nor do I know the other elder. They are total strangers to me.[31]

I do not think it was wrong for the headquarters to make at least some inquiry into the matter as a result of the information that was brought to their attention. It would be entirely natural for them to do

---

31 These elders were in the congregation adjoining the congregation Rene attended.

so. If they believe that what they teach is truth from God it would be wrong for them not to do so.

What I find very difficult to understand and to harmonize with Scripture is the *manner* in which this was done, the precipitous reaction and hastiness, the methods employed—covering over and withholding information from persons whose life interests were intimately involved, whose good name was at stake, the devious approaches employed to obtain damaging information, of coercion through threat of disfellowshiping to obtain "cooperation" in getting such incriminating evidence—and, above all, the spirit shown, the crushing despotism, the unfeeling legalistic approach, and the harshness of the actions taken. Whatever injudicious statements may have been made by a few of those 'put to trial,' I think the facts show them to have been far surpassed by the means used to deal with the matter.

As in the Inquisition, all rights were held by the inquisitors, the accused had none. The investigators felt they had the right to ask any question and at the same time refuse to answer questions put to them. They insisted on maintaining their judicial proceedings secret, entirely away from observation from anyone else, yet claimed the right to pry into the private conversations and activities of those they interrogated. Their judicial secrecy was proper, the exercise of "confidentiality," their evasiveness was simply being "practical," strategic, but the efforts of the accused to maintain the privacy of their personal conversations was labeled as being devious, as evidence of a hidden conspiracy. They expected their own actions to be taken as evidence of zeal for God, for "revealed truth," while at the same time they suspected the worst in all that the accused had done, made no allowance for their sincerity in wanting to put God first, for their love of truth even when that truth was contradicted by traditional teachings.

When Rene Vazquez, for example, on being interrogated, endeavored to express himself moderately, undogmatically, to show that he had no desire to make flaming issues of minor doctrinal matters, and to make clear that he was not being insistent that anyone else see things as he did or adopt his views, he found that this was very unsatisfactory to the judicial committee members. They sought to pin him down on his inner feelings, his personal beliefs. As he put it, when a question from one direction did not accomplish this, then a question from another direction attempted to force him into some categorical reply. In his hearing before the first judicial committee, another elder, named Benjamin Angulo, was also "on trial." Angulo was very positive, even adamant in many of his expressions. When Rene spoke in moderate terms, one of the Committee members, Harold Jackson, told Rene, "you are not even a good apostate." Saying that Rene did not clearly defend his beliefs, Jackson continued:

> "Look at Angulo, he defends them. You talked to Angulo about these things and look how he now talks about them. He may be disfellowshiped, and yet you are not definite about these points."

In the second hearing with the appeal committee, as has been shown, Rene's efforts at being moderate brought forth the expression "hogwash." Mildness, moderateness, a willingness to yield where the issues permit yielding, these qualities do not make good evidence for disfellowshiping persons as rebellious "apostates." Yet they are qualities that are part of Rene Vazquez' nature, and those who know him know that this is true.

Two years after his disfellowshiping I talked to Rene about the whole affair and asked him how he now felt about having spoken to others on what he saw in the Scriptures. What would he say to someone who advanced the argument that, as in the case of someone working for a business organization, as long as he is part of that organization he should uphold all its policies and if he could not he should first leave before saying anything. His reply was:

> "But that is a business organization and I did not think of matters in those terms. I viewed the matter as involving a higher relationship, one with God. I know what my feelings were then and what was in my heart, and no one can tell me otherwise. If I were in some scheme, why should I now deny it? When the hearings came, I prayed that I would not be disfellowshiped. Others did the same. Yet it happened.
>
> "If I had wanted to stay in the organization just to proselytize, I would now be a militant. Where is the 'sect' that I was working for? Where is the afterfact to prove that is what I was working for? To this day, even when people have approached me to talk with me, afterward I prefer to let them call me rather than take the initiative.
>
> "If I had it all to do over again I would be facing the same dilemma. I feel that so much good came from what I learned from the Scriptures, that it proved such a blessing to have things cleared up and brought me closer to God.
>
> "If I had had some 'scheme,' I could have programmed the way I would do things. But what I did was simply human and I was acting according to human reaction. That human element took precedence over fear of an organization. It was never my idea to disassociate myself from the Witnesses. I was just rejoicing in what I was reading in the Bible. The conclusions I came to were as a result of my personal reading of the Bible. I was in no way trying to be dogmatic.

"The question I ask is, after all these thirty years as a Witness, the feelings I had of mercy and compassion—why were these not felt by *them*? Why the conniving way of framing questions? The hearings were held as if to gather information proving guilt, not to aid an 'erring' brother."

One rumor that circulated widely, in fact internationally, was that these three men (Vazquez, Sanchez and Kuilan), all of whom worked in the Spanish Translation Department, were deliberately making changes in material when translating and that I knew of this and had condoned it. (In French-speaking countries the rumor was adjusted to apply to French translation work.) Rene's comments on this were:

"That is ridiculous. It would have been impossible to do. There were no changes made and that never came into our minds. No one ever accused us of that. Everything translated had to go through about five different persons for checking, Fabio Silva being the last one to read it. In translating it was always necessary to strive to be faithful to the original idea."[32]

Probably the most vicious rumor, passed on as "truth" by elders and others in various parts of this country, was that there was homosexuality being practiced among the "apostates." Where such a blatant lie originated is difficult to imagine. The only explanation I can think of is that, about a year before the inquisition tactics began, an organizational member in a position of considerable responsibility had been accused of homosexual tendencies. The Governing Body handled the case and endeavored to keep the matter quiet. Nonetheless, it seems that some talk did circulate. In the rumor mills this man's actions were now transferred over to the "apostates." This was easy to do since spreaders of rumors are seldom concerned about facts. I can think of no other possible explanation.

Why would people priding themselves on their high Christian principles pass on such vicious rumors when they had absolutely nothing but gossip on which to base them? I believe that in many cases it was simply because many felt a need somehow to justify in their own minds and hearts what had happened. They had to have reasons other than the true ones to explain why such summary and harsh actions were taken against people with unblemished records, people whom

32 Not only was everything checked by a number of different persons in Brooklyn, but a large percentage of Branch Office personnel in Spanish-speaking countries know English and read the publications in both languages. Had such charge of deliberate alteration been true, it would have been quickly reported. To think otherwise simply betrays an ignorance of the facts or a lack of concern for facts on the part of those originating and spreading the rumors.

even their closest associates knew to be peaceful, unaggressive persons. To see the ugly label of "apostate" suddenly placed on these people required *something more* than the facts of the matter provided. Without such, those who knew these people, and others who heard of them, would have been obliged to face up to the possibility that the organization they viewed as God's sole channel of communication and guidance on earth was perhaps not what they thought it to be. For many this was to think the unthinkable. It would severely disturb their feeling of security, a security that rests largely (far more so than most would acknowledge) on their unquestioning trust in a human organization.

SANHEDRIN EXPERIENCE

"Now it is required that those who have been given a trust must prove faithful. I care very little if I am judged by you or by any human court; indeed, I do not even judge myself. My conscience is clear, but that does not make me innocent. It is the Lord who judges me." —1 Corinthians 4:2–4, *New International Version.*

When I arrived in Brooklyn, all the information that had been withheld from me was given in one large dose. The next morning I was due to appear before the Governing Body in full session.

Afterward, I could review it and see just what had been done, the program of action followed, the methods employed. But at the time it only created a sense of shock. There was no opportunity to ask those involved about the accuracy of what was now given to me—they were already disfellowshiped, their testimony now unacceptable to the Body.

I still found it hard to believe that people, the people within whom I had my lifelong religious heritage, would ever do what I saw being done. My feelings on going to the Brooklyn headquarters were strangely comparable to my feelings when making trips to the Dominican Republic during the regime of the dictator Trujillo. In Puerto Rico, my point of departure, everything was so free and open, people on the street or in public conveyances talked with no sense of restraint. But as soon as my plane landed at the airport of what was then Ciudad Trujillo (now Santo Domingo), the change was almost palpable. People were so guarded in their speech, in public conveyances conversation was minimal, people were concerned lest any remark be taken as unfavorable to the dictator and be reported by the spy system that proliferated during that regime. Conversation and interchange of ideas that were viewed as completely normal in Puerto Rico were dangerous in the Dominican Republic, liable to bring upon one the label of an enemy of the state. In the one country, a man could express an opinion that differed from that of the majority and feel no sense of concern if he later learned that he had been quoted. In the other, a man expressing any thought that did not conform to the existing ideology afterward found himself engaging in self-recrimination, feeling as if he had committed some wrong, something over which to feel guilt, and the thought of being quoted was a foreboding one. In this latter case, the issue was not whether what one had said was true; it was not whether his saying it was honestly motivated and morally proper. The question was, how would it be taken by those in power?

Any feeling of this latter kind that I had had at the headquarters before the spring of 1980 had been only fleeting, momentary. Now it surrounded me, seemed overwhelming. The view those exercising governing authority had already taken was obvious from the "briefing" given me by the Chairman's Commmittee, and by the remarks they and the Service Department men expressed on the tapes. In the highly emotional atmosphere and the climate of suspicion that had developed, it was difficult to keep in mind that what I or others had said could be viewed in any other light than the harsh way these men had expressed it. To keep in mind that what might be condemned from an organizational standpoint as heretical, could, from the standpoint of God's Word, be right, proper and good, was hard to do, particularly after a life of intense service in the organization. I knew that I had not sought out people to whom to speak on these matters; they had approached me and I felt an obligation to point them to God's Word for answers, even if the answers found there differed from those of men in authority.

I felt sure that by far the majority of the men before whom I would appear would see the matter from the organizational viewpoint only. If, from the start, there had been any other point of view taken, I was satisfied that the whole affair could have been quietly, peacefully and simply worked out, through friendly, brotherly conversation, encouraging moderation if any immoderate speech had been made, urging considerate restraint if inconsiderate restraint had been shown. By avoiding condemnatory confrontations, refusing to resort to high-handed methods and legalistic approaches, it would not have been necessary for private conversations and incidents that involved a small handful of persons to have blown up to such proportions that they became a *cause célèbre*, a full-scale affair with violent impact on the lives of many persons, one that produced reverberations and gossip on an earthwide scale.

On going before the Governing Body, I felt no desire to add fuel to the fire already raging. It had already consumed some much-loved friends. I was willing to acknowledge that something I personally deplored—statements of an extreme or dogmatic nature—might have been made by a few of those involved, though I had no way of determining at this time to what extent this was true, for it related primarily to persons with whom I had had no Scriptural discussion, some of whom I did not even know.

On Wednesday, May 21, the Governing Body session opened with Albert Schroeder as Chairman. He first stated that the Chairman's Committee had asked me if I was willing to have the Governing Body's discussion with me taped and that I had agreed, with the provision that a copy of the taping be provided to me.

The Governing Body conference room contained one, long oval table capable of seating about twenty persons around it. The full Body of seventeen members was present. Aside from Lyman Swingle, who sat to my left, no member had conversed with me; the day before, no one (not even the member related to me) had visited me, either in my office or in my room. If there was any warmth or brotherly compassion in the Governing Body conference room, I failed to discern it. I felt only the feelings I had experienced when appearing in secular court trials of the past, with the exception that in those cases I felt freer to speak and knew that other persons were present who could witness what was said, the attitudes expressed. This instead was a closed secret session; the attitude displayed seemed only to confirm what Rene Vazquez had told me of the attitude manifested toward him.

The Chairman said that the Body first wanted me to express myself on each of the eight points the Chairman's Committee had drawn up as evidences of apostasy (in their memo of April 28). I did, in each case endeavoring to be moderate, undogmatic, as yielding and conciliatory as I could be without going against my conscience by being either dishonest or hypocritical. The absolutist form in which these were presented by the Chairman's Committee in their memo—as if one either accepted fully the organization's teaching on these points or else viewed them in the dogmatic way expressed in the memo— simply did not fit my case. None of their eight points expressed what I felt were the true issues. The issue was not whether God had an "organization" on earth but *what kind* of organization—a centralized, highly structured, authoritarian organization, or simply that of a congregation of brothers where the only authority is authority to help, to guide, to serve, never to dominate? Thus my response was that I believed that God had an organization on earth in the sense that He had a congregation on earth, the Christian congregation, a brotherhood.

The issue was not whether God had guided (or would guide) those forming this Governing Body, but to what extent, under what conditions? I did not doubt or question that God would give his guidance to these men if that was sincerely sought (I felt that some of the decisions made, particularly in earlier years, had been good decisions, compassionate decisions), but I certainly did not think this was automatic; it was always conditional, contingent on certain factors. So my response included the statement that I believed such guidance always was governed by the extent to which God's Word was adhered to; that to that extent God grants his guidance or withdraws it. (I think that that is true for any individual or any collective group of people, whoever they are.)

My responses to all the questions were made in this manner. If any of those accused had spoken about these matters in the dogmatic, absolutist way that the Chairman's Committee presented them, then I felt a desire to do whatever I could to restore a measure of reasonableness and moderation, to conciliate rather than exacerbate, and I bent as far as I could bend.

Other questions asked me were relatively few. Lyman Swingle asked about my view of Bible commentaries, from which I gathered that this had been a subject of discussion in the Body. I replied that I had begun to use them more extensively as a result of my uncle's encouragement (during the *Aid* project) and that if the view was that they should not be used then there were entire sections of the Bethel library that would need to be emptied, since there were dozens, scores of sets of commentaries there.

Martin Poetzinger, who had spent several years in concentration camps during the Nazi regime, expressed dissatisfaction with my responses to the set of eight doctrinal points. How could it be, he asked, that I felt as expressed if these other people were making such strong statements? (As was true of the others, he had never talked personally to any of them.)[33] I answered that I could not be responsible for the

---

33 Lloyd Barry also expressed similar dissatisfaction, saying that I had "equivocated" on every one of the 8 points the Chairman's Committee had drawn up as proof of "apostasy."

way others might express things, and I directed his attention to Romans, chapter three, verse 8 and Second Peter, chapter three, verses 15 and 16, as examples of how even the apostle Paul's expressions were wrongly expressed or wrongly understood by some. Though I did not say so, I frankly felt my circumstance was like that described at Luke, chapter eleven, verse 53, as among men who were trying to 'draw me out on a great many subjects, waiting to pounce on some incriminating remark.'[34] The conduct of the Body during the preceding weeks gave basis for no other feeling.

Poetzinger went on to make known his view of the disfellowshiped "apostates," saying, with strong feeling, that they had shown their real attitude by "throwing their Watch Tower literature into the garbage before leaving!" (This was one of the rumors that circulated most widely in the Bethel family, in fact, it was reported to the entire Bethel family by a Governing Body member one morning.) I told Martin Poetzinger that I would never want to arrive at a conclusion when I had not talked with those involved to learn the facts. I said that in the fifteen years I had been at the headquarters it was a rare thing to go into one of the closets containing "dirt hoppers" without seeing quantities of Society literature—older magazines and books—discarded by members of the family; that, from what I knew, some of the disfellowshiped ones of the Bethel staff were departing by plane for Puerto Rico and that the heaviest items, and the most easily replaceable, would be such books. I repeated that I did not think it right to make a judgment on the basis of hearsay and that I thought it was especially unfitting for one sitting as a judge to do so. He stared at me but said nothing further.

Another question was asked with regard to the Memorial service (the Lord's Evening Meal) I had conducted the month before (April) at Homestead, Florida.[35] Was it true that I had not discussed the "other sheep" (those with earthly hopes) in my talk there? I said that was true, and related to them my experience the first year I had come to Brooklyn from the Dominican Republic. My wife and I had attended a Memorial service at a congregation that held this meeting quite early in the evening. Thus we returned to the Bethel headquarters in time to hear my uncle, then the vice president, give his entire talk. After the talk we were invited, along with my uncle, to the room of staff member Malcolm Allen. My wife immediately said to my uncle, "I noticed

---

34 *Philips Modern English* translation.
35 Jehovah's Witnesses hold this service as an annual celebration only, approximately at the time of Passover.

that you didn't mention the 'other sheep' anywhere in your talk. Why was that?" He replied that he considered the evening one that was special for the "anointed" and said, "So, I just concentrate on them." I informed the Body that I still had my notes from that talk by the vice president and had used them many times in conducting Memorial services. They were welcome to look at them if they wished. (Fred Franz was, of course, present if they cared to question him about his talk.) The subject was dropped.[36]

My regret at what had happened, based on the premise that some persons had apparently been extreme in their statements, was sincere. I told the Body that if I had been informed I would have done all in my power to bring such to a halt. I did not deny that injudiciousness had been shown, nor did I exclude myself in saying this, but I stated that I felt it was wrong to equate what is injudicious with what is malicious. I expressed my respect for and my confidence in the Christian qualities of those I personally knew who had been so viewed and treated. I told them of what I knew of the thirty years of service of Rene Vazquez, his sincere devotion, his unblemished record in Puerto Rico, Spain and the United States. I also expressed dismay that, after having lived and worked with them as fellow Body members for so many years, not one of them had seen fit to communicate with me and convey the honest facts as to what was taking place.

Chairman Schroeder was the only one to respond. He quickly said, "But Ray, you didn't level completely with us either. You didn't say [in the phone conversation] how you knew about the investigation of the Writing Department." I replied, "Did you ask me?" "No," was his answer. I said, "If you had I would have told you without hesitation. Ed Dunlap phoned me and mentioned it." Shortly afterward, Karl Klein, another member of the Chairman's Committee, smilingly acknowledged that "We didn't level fully with Ray," and added that "if Rene Vazquez had responded to the questions the way Ray did he would not have been disfellowshiped." Since neither Karl nor any other member of the entire Governing Body had made any effort to talk with Rene, to attend the first "investigative" interview held with him, or the first judicial hearing with him, or the appeal hearing with him, they could

---

36 Typical of the rumors circulated (and I had questions written to me about this from as far away as New Zealand) was that I had given a talk encouraging everyone to partake of the emblems and that an entire congregation had done so (which would be a truly spectacular event for Jehovah's Witnesses). The fact is, however, that at the talk I gave in Florida in April 1980, there were exactly two partakers, myself and a woman attending who was not a Witness but a member of a local church.

only judge his responses by the reports passed on to them by those who had carried out such activity for them. How they felt they could judge or compare on such second-hand basis I did not know. The Chairman's Committee, which included Karl Klein, had been willing to take the time to meet with accusers, to hear accusations brought, including the adverse testimony given by the Godinez couple and Bonelli, but they had *not found the time to talk to a single one of those accused.* I hardly find this an exemplary expression of brotherly love, of fellow feeling or compassion.

The majority of those on the Body simply sat and listened, asking no questions, making no comments. After two or three hours (I was too affected emotionally to be aware of the time) I was informed that I could leave the conference room and that they would get in touch with me. I went to my office and waited. Noontime came and looking from the window I saw Governing Body members walking through the garden en route to the dining rooms. I had no appetite for food and remained waiting. By the time three o'clock came I felt too drained to remain there and went to my room. The preceding weeks, the phone conversation with the Chairman and the shock that came on finding out how misleading it had been, the distress expressed in a flow of phone calls from those who were being subjected to intense interrogation and pressure, the rapidity and relentlessness of the disfellowshipings that followed, and, most of all, the continued silence on the part of the Governing Body as to informing me of a single one of the developments in all this, had now been culminated by my experience that morning, the coldness of the attitude shown, and the hours of waiting that followed. By evening I had become physically ill.

That same evening a phone call came to our room from Chairman Schroeder asking me to meet with the Body for an evening session of further questioning. My wife had answered the phone for me and I told her to inform him that I was simply too sick to go and that I had said what I had to say. They could make their decision on what they had heard.

Later that evening, Lyman Swingle, who lived in rooms two floors above ours, came by to see how I was feeling. I appreciated this and told him what a strain the period of many weeks had been. I stated to him that what concerned me most deeply was not what action the Body might decide to take toward me, but that beautiful truths of God's Word had been made to appear ugly. I meant that then and still feel that the most serious aspect of all that took place was the way an array of organizational teachings were used as a standard against which to evaluate plain statements in the Bible, and that those plain statements (because they did not conform to the organizational "pattern" of interpretation) were depicted as distorted teachings giving evidence of "apostasy."

I had in mind such plain yet beautiful statements of God's Word as:

"One is your teacher, whereas all you are brothers."

"You are not under law but under undeserved kindness."

"All who are led by God's spirit, these are God's sons."

"One body there is, and one spirit, even as you were called in the one hope to which you were called; one Lord, one faith, one baptism; one God and Father of all persons, who is over all and through all and in all."

"For as often as you eat this loaf and drink this cup, you keep proclaiming the death of the Lord, until he arrives."

"For there is one God and one mediator between God and men, a man, Christ Jesus."

"It does not belong to you to get knowledge of the times and seasons which the Father has placed in his own jurisdiction."[37]

By contrast, the eight points used by the Chairman's Committee as a sort of "Confession of Faith" by which to judge people had *not one single point* where the Society teaching involved could be supported by simple, clear-cut statements in Scripture. What plain statement in Scripture could anyone, Governing Body member or anyone else, point to and say, "Here, the Bible clearly says":

1. That God has an "organization" on earth—one of the kind here at issue—and uses a Governing Body to direct it? *Where does the Bible make such statements?*

2. That the heavenly hope is not open to anyone and everyone who will embrace it, that it has been replaced by an earthly hope (since 1935) and that Christ's words in connection with the emblematic bread and wine, "Do this in remembrance of me," do not apply to all persons putting faith in his ransom sacrifice? *What scriptures make such statements?*

3. That the "faithful and discreet slave" is a "class" composed of only certain Christians, that it cannot apply to individuals, and that it operates through a Governing Body? *Again, where does the Bible make such statements?*

4. That Christians are separated into two classes, with a different relationship to God and Christ, on the basis of an earthly or a heavenly destiny? *Where is this said?*

5. That the 144,000 in Revelation *must* be taken as a literal number and that

---

37 Matthew 23:8; Romans 6:14; 8:14; Ephesians 4:4–6; 1 Corinthians 11:26; 1 Timothy 2:5; Acts 1:7.

the "great crowd" does not and *cannot* refer to persons serving in God's heavenly courts? *Where does the Bible say this?*

6. That the "last days" began in 1914, and that when the apostle Peter (at Acts 2:17) spoke of the last days as applying from Pentecost on, he did not mean the same "last days" that Paul did (at 2 Timothy 3:1)? *Where?*

7. That the calendar year of 1914 was when Christ was first officially enthroned as King toward all the earth and that that calendar date marks the start of his *parousia? Where?*

8. That when the Bible at Hebrews 11:16 says that men such as Abraham, Isaac and Jacob were "reaching out for a better place, that is, one belonging to heaven," this could not *possibly* mean that they would have heavenly life? *Where?*

Not a single Society teaching there dealt with could be supported by any plain direct statement of Scripture. Every single one would require intricate explanations, complex combinations of texts and, in some cases, what amounts to mental gymnastics, in an attempt to support them. Yet these were used to judge people's Christianity, set forth as the basis for deciding whether persons who had poured out their lives in service to God were apostates!

The morning after my hearing before the Governing Body, Chairman Schroeder came to my room with a tape recorder to tape my response to some additional testimony from a staff member, Fabio Silva, who recounted things said to him by Rene Vazquez when Rene was providing him transportation from the airport one day. I said I had nothing to comment with regard to such hearsay evidence.

The morning hours passed. I felt a need to get out from the place and the oppressive atmosphere it contained. When I knew the lunch period was ended, I left my room and walked upstairs and was able to speak to Lyman Swingle as he was walking from the elevator to his rooms. I asked how much longer I had to wait. He told me a decision had been reached and that I would be notified that afternoon. His remarks gave me reason to believe that some members had pushed strongly for disfellowshiping and, while speaking with me, his face suddenly became very drawn and he said, "I can't understand how some men think. I fought, oh how I fought—" and then his lips compressed, his shoulders began to heave, and he began to sob openly. I suddenly found myself trying to comfort him, assuring him that it really did not matter that much to me what their decision was, that I simply wanted the matter to come to an end. Since his tears kept coming, I walked away so that he could go on to his rooms.

I know that there is no person on the Governing Body more devoted to the organization of Jehovah's Witnesses than Lyman Swingle. I had felt admiration and affection for him because of his honesty and courage. I have no idea what his attitude toward me would be today. It might be totally opposite. I only know that, if for no other reason, I will always love the man for the sincere feeling he expressed that day in the hallway. In his sadness I found strength.[38]

That afternoon Chairman Schroeder brought the Governing Body's decision to me. Evidently those seeking disfellowshiping had not attained a two-thirds majority, for he simply informed me that I was being asked to resign from the Body and also as a member of the headquarters staff. The Body offered to place me (and my wife) on what is known as the "Infirm Special Pioneer" list (an arrangement often offered to Circuit and District Overseers who have to leave traveling work due to old age or poor health). Those on this list report each month to the Society and receive monthly financial help, but are not required to reach any particular "quota" of hours in preaching work.[39] I informed him that neither of us felt we wanted to be under any arrangement that carried any obligation, even an implied one. He then made a few remarks about "what a marvelous piece of work" the *Aid to Bible Understanding* book had been. Then he left.

I wrote out my resignation, set out on the following page. I have not failed to do what I there said up to the present time.

My wife and I went away for a couple of days to get our emotions under control and then returned to move out what belongings we would take with us. I left the bulk of my files behind, bringing primarily the files on matters in which I had been most personally involved. I felt the need to be able to document my position on such issues should that position be misrepresented in the future, as in several cases it was.

On our return, I saw Ed Dunlap standing outside one of the headquarters buildings. He was to meet that day with a judicial committee.

Ed was now sixty-nine years old. The year before, in 1979, he had talked seriously about leaving the headquarters. He knew he had been the object of personal attack both within the Governing Body and

---

38 In the months that followed, Lyman Swingle, though continuing as a Governing Body member, was removed from his position as the Coordinator of the Writing Committee and of the Writing Department, being replaced by Lloyd Barry.

39 At that time I believe the monthly allowance was about $175 per person.

May 22, 1980

Governing Body

Dear Brothers:

By means of this letter I submit my resignation as a member of the Governing Body.

I will also be terminating my Bethel service.

My prayers will continue to be offered on your behalf as well as for Jehovah God's servants earthwide.

Your brother,

R V Franz

outside thereof. At one point he had asked the Writing Committee to give him relief from harassment. The Writing Committee assigned three of its members, Lyman Swingle, Lloyd Barry and Ewart Chitty, to speak to Governing Body member Karl Klein (not then a member of the Writing Committee, though he became such after Chitty's resignation). They urged him to refrain from going into Ed's office and speaking critically to him as well as to refrain from talking to others about Ed in such manner. This seemed to have effect for a time as to expressions outside the Body, though not within the Body and its sessions.

When, in late 1979, I informed Ed of our thoughts about leaving, he said that he had weighed the idea but had come to the conclusion that it was not feasible for him. At his advanced age and in his economic situation he did not see how he could reasonably hope to support himself and his wife. By remaining, at least they would have a place to live, food, and medical care when needed. So, he said, he had decided to stay and added, "If they give me too much hassle in the Writing Department I'll just ask for a transfer to the carpenter shop or some other kind of work."

Less than a year later he found himself cited for a judicial committee hearing. The day I saw him he said, "I'm going to be very frank with them. It's against my nature to hedge." He said he had little doubt as to what the committee would do.

It was now near the end of May. Over nine weeks had elapsed since the Chairman's Committee had played the Godinez tape to the Governing Body in which Ed's name was used several times. Nearly that length of time had passed since Barry and Barr had interviewed him, assuring him that they were 'just seeking information.' During all those nine weeks—although Ed Dunlap was right in their midst, even up to the very last working on a Governing Body assignment to prepare a book on the life of Jesus Christ—*not a single one* of the Chairman's Committee approached him to discuss these matters with him, to inform him of the grave charges being made. These men were exercising full direction of the whole affair, they all knew Ed intimately, yet to the end they said not one word to him on the subject.[40]

After Barry and Barr's initial interview with him, for nine weeks *no one in the entire Governing Body* went to Edward Dunlap to talk about the matter, to reason with or discuss God's Word with this man who had been associated for nearly half a century, had spent some forty years in full-time service, professed the heavenly hope, and was now nearly seventy years of age. They themselves are witnesses that this is true. How unlike the shepherd who would leave the ninety-nine to search out and help a "strayed" sheep, for such he was in their eyes.

Again, it may well be that some injudicious words had been spoken by a few individuals among those disfellowshiped. The above actions by those in authority, to my mind, spoke far, far louder than did any such words.[41]

A committee of five headquarters staff men was assigned to do the work of judging Ed Dunlap. The Governing Body remained in the

---

40 Albert Schroeder had been a fellow Instructor with Ed at Gilead School for many years; Karl Klein worked in the same Writing Department with him, his office being right next door to Ed's; Grant Suiter, a year or so before these events, had come to Ed with an assignment he (Suiter) had received to prepare (an outline for one of the Branch seminar class discussions) and asked Ed to prepare it for him, saying that he was very busy and was sure Ed would "do a better job anyway."

41 1 John 3:14–16, 18.

background. All of the five men assigned were younger than Ed, none professed to be of the "anointed." After just one day's deliberations they arrived at their decision.

Fairly typical of the attitude shown were these expressions:

When asked about his views on the organization's teachings about two classes of Christians, Ed called their attention to Romans, chapter eight, verse 14, that "ALL who are led by God's spirit" are God's sons. He asked, "How else can you understand it?" Fred Rusk, who had served as a Gilead School Instructor for several years while Ed was Registrar, said, "Oh, Ed, that's just your interpretation of it." Ed asked, "Then how else would you explain it?" Fred Rusk's reply was, "Look, Ed, you're the one that's on trial, not me."

When questioned about the organization's forming of rules, he stressed that the Christian is not under law but under undeserved kindness (or grace). He said that faith and love were greater forces for righteousness than rules could ever be. Robert Wallen said, "But Ed, I *like* to have someone tell me what to do." Having in mind the apostle's words at Hebrews, chapter five, verses 13 and 14, that Christians should not be like babes but like mature persons "who through use have their perceptive powers trained to distinguish both right and wrong," Ed answered, "Then you need to read your Bible more." Robert Wallen smiled and said, "Me and two million others." Ed replied, "The fact that they don't do it doesn't excuse you from doing it." He stressed that this was the major problem, the brothers simply did not study the Bible; they relied on the publications; their consciences were not genuinely *Bible* trained.

Evidently the major factor that developed in all the session was that on two occasions Ed had had Bible discussions with some of those who had now been disfellowshiped. The judicial committee had no evidence that this had been the case but Ed voluntarily offered the information, having said from the start that he intended to be perfectly open with them on all points. These persons had approached him and on two occasions had had a meal with him after which they discussed portions of the book of Romans.[42] The judicial committee wanted to know if he would talk to anyone else on these points. He replied that he had no intention of "campaigning" among the brothers. But he said that if persons came to him privately seeking help and he could direct them to the Scriptures for the answers to their question, he would do

---

42 Ed was assigned by the Governing Body's Teaching Committee to conduct a regular class on Romans for the Branch Committee members in their seminars.

so, would feel an obligation to help them. In all likelihood, this was the determinative factor. Such freedom of private Scriptural discussion and expression was not acceptable, was viewed as heretical, as dangerously disruptive.

One statement made seemed particularly paradoxical. Ed had told them plainly that he had no desire to be disfellowshiped, that he enjoyed the brothers and had no desire or thought of cutting himself off from them. The committee urged him to "wait on the organization," saying, "Who knows? Perhaps five years from now many or all of these things you are saying will be published and taught."

They knew the fluctuating nature of the organization's teachings and doubtless on that basis felt they could say this. But how much conviction as to the rightness, the solid Scriptural basis for these teachings at issue, did this show on their part? If they were willing to accept the possibility that the organization's teaching on these points might be no more solid and enduring than that, how could they possibly use them as the basis for deciding whether this man was a loyal servant of God or an apostate?

If they considered that these teachings (to which the Chairman's Committee had attached such major importance) were so subject to change that it would be worth while to wait and see what five years would bring, why was it not also worth while to postpone any judicial action against this man who had given, not five years, but half a century of service to the organization?

The logic of such an approach can be understood only if one accepts and embraces the premise that an individual's interests—including his good name, his hard-earned reputation, his years of life spent in service—are all expendable if they interfere with an organization's objectives.

I feel sure that every man on that judicial committee recognized that Edward Dunlap had a deep love for God, for Christ and for the Bible—yet they felt they had to take action against him. Why? They knew the temperament prevailing within the Governing Body, expressed through its Chairman's Committee. Organizational loyalty required such action by them, for this man did not, could not, accept all the claims and interpretations of that organization.

So they disfellowshiped Ed Dunlap, and he was asked to leave what had been his home at the Bethel headquarters. He returned to Oklahoma City where he had grown up and where, now 72 years of age, he supports himself and his wife by hanging wallpaper, a trade he had practiced before he began his forty years of service as a full-time representative of the Watch Tower Bible and Tract Society.

How those responsible—genuinely and primarily responsible—for all this can approach God in prayer at night and say, 'Show us mercy as we have shown mercy to others,' is difficult for me to understand.

11

AFTERMATH

*"I know that after my going away oppressive
wolves will enter in among you and will not
treat the flock with tenderness."*
—Acts 20:29.

THERE is an old expression, "An iron hand in a velvet glove."
I do not believe that the events of the spring of 1980 produced
the hardhandedness manifested by the authority structure. I believe
the hardness was already there, that history shows it was. What took
place in the spring of 1980 merely caused the velvet glove to be removed, exposing the unyielding hardness underneath. What followed
supports that conclusion.

When the judicial committee of five Bethel elders that, by any standard of rightness, did for the Governing Body what the Governing
Body should have done for itself, finally met with Ed Dunlap and
informed him of their decision to disfellowship him, Ed said to them:

> "All right, if that is your decision. But *don't you say that it's for 'apostasy'.*
> You know that apostasy means rebellion against God and Christ Jesus, and *you*
> *know that that is not true of me."*

In the August, 1980, edition of the monthly paper called *Our Kingdom Service*, sent to all congregations, the front page contained the
statement that a number of persons in the Bethel family had been
disfellowshiped and then spoke of "apostasy against the organization."
This phrasing, though still false (for there had been no rebellion even
against the organization) was at least closer to the truth than statements made elsewhere.

On May 28, 1980, my letter of resignation was read to the family.
On May 29, a meeting of all Bethel elders was called. Jon Mitchell

was among these. He was serving as a secretary in both the Service Department and the Governing Body offices. My only contact with him had been when he obtained visas for me for my trip to Africa. He had never conversed with any of those who were disfellowshiped. He had, however, seen some of the correspondence from judicial committees passing through the offices and had heard the departmental gossip about the "heresy" trials. Relating his impressions of the Elders meeting, and the talks given by Governing Body members Schroeder and Barry, he says:

"Schroeder's talk focused on the subject of organization. He spoke about our 'finely tuned organization' and how certain ones who seemed to feel that they couldn't go along with its rules and regulations 'ought to be leaving and not be involved in the further progressive work here.' (The publication *Branch Organization* was held up to illustrate how 'finely tuned' the organization was, and he said that this publication contained over 1,000 rules and regulations regarding the operations of the Branches and the Brooklyn headquarters.) He stressed that this was not a 'witch hunt,' but there appeared to be a 'pruning' going on.

"Of those who had left, he said, "It's not that they don't believe the Bible, you'd have to be an atheist to think that way,' but 'they understand it differently,'

"He concluded his part by opening it up to questions from the Bethel elders. Harold Jackson raised his hand and suggested that there be a 'forum' or open discussion of what the issues were. Schroeder replied that they had no plans to do this. If we had a question we could send in a letter. Another elder, Warren Weil, asked if the possibility of having the brothers take 'loyalty oaths' had been considered. Brother Schroeder replied that that avenue was not being pursued at that time.

"Lloyd Barry's talk seemed to be an effort to refute some of the beliefs apparently held by those viewed as apostates and to sound a call for loyalty to the organization. He read Proverbs 24:21,22, and warned that we should beware of 'those who are for a change.' He spoke disparagingly of certain ones who were getting together to study the Bible in an independent fashion, claiming that some were even doing this instead of going to the *Watchtower* study on Monday evening.

"He likewise spoke in unfavorable terms of those inclined to use commentaries by writers of Christendom. (Barnes' *Notes on the New Testament* were possessed by men in the Service Department and kept in open display; this remark prompted them to remove these and put them in drawers.) Barry spoke about our 'rich heritage' as Jehovah's Witnesses and was visibly upset by the possibility that some did not hold it in as high esteem as he did and seemed inclined toward thinking which could be detrimental to the organization's growth and prosperity."

Though he had never discussed any Scriptural points or any of the issues involved with any of us who were the target of these talks, Jon writes:

"This meeting and the events that followed had the effect of augmenting the sickening feeling developing in me since I first heard of the startling news of the disfellowshipings and Brother Franz's dismissal.

"The August 1, 1980, *Watchtower* was to contain an article which listed what were considered to be various 'signs of apostasy.' But I already had some very clear-cut ideas of what the *actual* signs were. I was deeply distressed by the realization that the organization more and more seemed to be displaying these signs itself, as follows:

"1) The suppression of free Bible reading. Though I knew it was not likely there would be Bible burnings, nonetheless, it was apparent that complete freedom to read the Scriptures and enjoy open Bible discussions was being curtailed. Why wouldn't the Governing Body permit an open discussion of the issues as suggested, especially since it involved individuals who had contributed much to the organization and who were greatly respected as good Bible scholars? What were they trying to hide? Couldn't the 'truth' stand up to such examination?

"2) The apparent shift in emphasis from the Bible to our 'rich heritage' or organizational traditions. I knew quite well that this had been the failing of many religious sects, including the Pharisees. Matthew 15 and Mark 7 contain the words of Jesus wherein he denounced them for giving greater weight to tradition than to God's word. The suggestion that a 'loyalty oath' be required to ensure loyalty to an organization and its traditions was absolutely apalling to me. Yet it had been made in all seriousness.

"3) Inquisition tactics. It seemed clear that the Governing Body, which I had considered to be there more for the purpose of serving the brothers, was wielding a very powerful authoritarian hand and was determined to act quickly and decisively in its handling of the matter. Would it not have been far wiser and judicious for them to act carefully and deliberately, thoroughly weighing and considering matters and then *slowly and cautiously* reaching a decision?

"I remember thinking to myself at the Elders' meeting, 'Stop! Slow down! Can't you see what you're doing?' I felt this way, not because of being disloyal to the organization, but because I loved it and wanted more than anything else for it to be solidly based on a firm foundation of truth."

Like him, I initially retained hope that after the nightmare had passed, perhaps more rational thinking would begin to prevail, that the emotional, almost hysterical, 'siege mentality' which treated a small number of conscientious individuals as if they constituted a mammoth threat to the worldwide organization, would be replaced by calmer, more judicious thought and action. The opposite took place.

Perhaps nothing illustrates so clearly the incredible demands now made for total conformity as does the following letter, sent out to all traveling representatives, Circuit and District Overseers, by the Service Department of the international headquarters, dated September 1, 1980. Here presented is material from the first two pages of the letter, the section under the heading "Protecting the Flock" being of special interest in this discussion (particularly relevant points are underlined).

WATCHTOWER
BIBLE AND TRACT SOCIETY OF NEW YORK, INC.

CABLE WATCHTOWER

117 ADAMS STREET, BROOKLYN, NEW YORK 11201, U.S.A.   PHONE (212) 625-1240

SCG:SSF   September 1, 1980

TO ALL CIRCUIT AND DISTRICT OVERSEERS

Dear Brothers:

We know that you and your wives benefitted greatly from the "Divine Love" District Conventions. They impressively brought to our attention why love is the most beneficial quality that we can develop. (1 Cor. 13:13) Love enables us to remain united in spite of the limitations and shortcomings we manifest. --Col. 3:12-14.

You can be sure that by your loving example, the brothers you serve will be uplifted and strengthened in the faith. We have received a number of letters informing us of the love you brothers and your wives have displayed. One body of elders wrote concerning their circuit overseer: "(He) is truly devoted to do Jehovah's will . . . being of spiritual assistance to all . . . approachable in discussing any matter. (He) has a listening ear, showing empathy for the brothers. Such brothers we can rely upon when future problems we know will come, set in."

You can be confident that the brothers treasure your friendship, association and love when you 'genuinely care for the things pertaining to them.' (Phil. 2:19-23, 29) Therefore, continue exerting yourselves to deal lovingly with them. Never pressure them or scold them. Lead them, work hard with them, exhort them in accord with their needs. Be patient if their progress appears slow. Such loving, patient treatment will refresh the brothers.--Matt. 11:28-30.

PROTECTING THE FLOCK

A major responsibility of an overseer as he 'shepherds the flock of God in his care' is to protect it from dangers. (Acts 20:28) Acts 20:29, 30 indicates that one of those dangers can be men who apostatize. There is a fine study of this subject in the August 1, 1980, Watchtower. All of you want to get thoroughly familiar with the contents of the study articles. Encourage all of the elders and ministerial servants, especially, to do likewise. Include key points in your "Continue in the Things You Have Learned" program.

Help the elders discern between one who is a trouble-making apostate and a Christian who becomes weak in faith and has doubts. (2 Peter 2; Jude 22, 23) The former one should be dealt with decisively after extended efforts have been put forth to readjust him. (2 John 7-10) On the other hand, one weak in faith should be patiently and lovingly assisted to get the accurate knowledge that will solidify his faith.

Page 2

> Keep in mind that to be disfellowshiped, an apostate does not have to be a
> promoter of apostate views. As mentioned in paragraph two, page 17 of the
> August 1, 1980, Watchtower, "The word 'apostasy' comes from a Greek term that
> means 'a standing away from,' 'a falling away, defection,' 'rebellion, abandonment.'
> Therefore, if a baptized Christian abandons the teachings of Jehovah, as presented
> by the faithful and discreet slave, and persists in believing other doctrine
> despite Scriptural reproof, then he is apostatizing. Extended, kindly efforts
> should be put forth to readjust his thinking. However, if, after such extended
> efforts have been put forth to readjust his thinking, he continues to believe
> the apostate ideas and rejects what he has been provided through the 'slave class,'
> then appropriate judicial action should be taken.
>
> This is not to say that you or the elders should go on 'witch hunts,' as it
> were, inquiring into the personal beliefs of your brothers. Rather, if something
> reasonably substantial comes to the attention of the elders along this line, it
> would be appropriate to make a kindly, discreet inquiry so as to protect the flock.
> We cannot overemphasize the need to be cautious, discreet and kindly as such
> situations are dealt with.--James 1:19, 20.

COOPERATION BETWEEN BODIES OF ELDERS

In some of our larger cities it has been noticed that, at times, when
wrongdoing is uncovered, several congregations may be involved. There is a need
for full cooperation between the bodies of elders of these congregations. The
elders should be alert to the need to quickly pass on to the bodies of elders of
other congregations any information about publishers in their congregations that
may necessitate an investigation. Any who have indiscreetly gotten themselves
involved in wrong conduct need to be assisted right away. Any who have allowed
themselves to become hardened in sin need to be severely reproved and if unresponsive
to this, expelled from the congregation. It would be good for you to alert the
bodies of elders in your circuit to the material that was presented to you in
your seminar in the fall of 1979 in outline #13 under the heading "Elders Still
Need Assistance in Handling Intercongregational Problems." Whatever information
is needed and available should be passed on quickly to the elders of the congregation involved.

You want to help elders feel keenly the obligation before God to prevent
wrongdoing from infiltrating and spreading within the congregation. (1 Cor. 5:6-8)
The judicial committee should make great effort to see if the individual is
genuinely repentant before extending forgiveness to him for the bad name that he
has given to the congregation. Usually a person who is truly repentant can point
to some "fruit that befits repentance." (Matt 3:8) We want to have in mind that
no matter how good the counsel or reproof, if the person's heart is unresponsive,
given the same circumstances he will repeat the sin. To protect the flock the
elders must be willing to take decisive action in such cases.

The letter presents an official policy. It actually says that a person's believing—not promoting, but simply *believing*—something that differs from the teachings of the organization is grounds for taking judicial action against him as an "apostate"!

The letter makes no qualifying statements limiting such differences of belief to fundamental teachings of God's Word, such as the coming of God's Son as a man, the ransom, faith in Christ's shed blood as the basis for salvation, the resurrection, or similar basic Bible doctrines. It does not even say that the person necessarily disagrees with the Bible, the Word of God. Rather, he disagrees with "the teachings of Jehovah, *as presented by the faithful and discreet slave*." Which is something like saying that a man's accepting and obeying a King's written message is no guarantee that he is loyal; it is his accepting and obeying what a slave messenger claims the ruler meant that decides this!

The symbol at the top of the September 1, 1980 letter identifies the composer of it as Leon Weaver. But it should not be thought that this "thought-control" policy was the thinking of one individual, nor was it some momentary off-the-cuff expression of extremism which a person might make and afterward feel ashamed of as a rash, harsh and utterly unchristian position to take. The composer was a member of the Service Department Committee whose members, such as Harley Miller, David Olson, Joel Adams, Charles Woody and Leon Weaver, are all long-time representatives of the organization, with decades of experience behind them. They are agents of the Governing Body in supervising the activity of the more than 7,500 congregations and of all the Elders, Circuit and District Overseers in the United States, where one-fourth of all Jehovah's Witnesses live. They are in regular contact with the Service Committee of the Governing Body and are supposed to be thoroughly familiar with the Governing Body policies, attuned to its thinking and viewpoint and spirit.

But this only adds to the appalling aspect of the position the letter took. As I know from years on the Service Committee, any letter of this importance *must* be submitted to the Governing Body Service Committee for approval before being sent out.[1] Objection by even one member of that Committee would have resulted in the letter's going before the entire Governing Body for discussion.

Whatever the case, the letter and its policy—which evokes memories of the position of religious authorities in the Inquisition—had to have been approved by a number of headquarters representatives, including several Governing Body members. Since people's friendships, family relationships, personal honor and other life interests were all at stake, it should be presumed that these men gave long, careful thought to that statement of September 1, 1980, before approving it as an official expression from the "faithful and discreet slave" of Jesus Christ. What they there said was no light matter to be explained away later by saying, "Well, we really didn't mean it exactly the way it sounded." As the facts show, people, many persons, were actually disfellowshiped and continue to be disfellowshiped solely on the basis of this very thought-control policy sent out. The denigrating label of

---

1   The members at that time were Ted Jaracz (Coordinator), Milton Henschel, Albert Schroeder, William Jackson and Martin Poetzinger.

"apostate" is placed on their name simply because in their own hearts, they cannot accept all of the Society's interpretations.

Possibly this policy resulted from or was influenced by something that developed earlier that year in one of the New York congregations. Jon Mitchell, mentioned previously as working part time in the Service Department, relates:

> "Somewhere around this time period [referring to the early summer of 1980] a memo came down from F. W. Franz, apparently in response to a question that had been sent in by Harold Jackson [part of the Service Department staff].

> "It seems there was a pioneer (full-time preaching) sister in a Spanish congregation who felt she could not conscientiously teach that the 144,000 of Revelation 7 and 14 was a literal number. She said she would not proselytize or seek to publicize an opposing view, but she did not want to teach that the 144,000 was a literal number to those with whom she studied the Bible.

> "Brother Jackson's question apparently was to the effect of wanting to know whether or not such a person could be classified as an 'apostate.' The memo confirmed that such a person could indeed be viewed as an apostate and should be disfellowshiped if she did not agree to teach what the Society instructed her to teach. I recall someone in the Service Department referring to the outcome of this case and stating that the girl had 'recanted.' I was amazed that such terminology could be used without any sense of shame."

One might think that the extreme position taken in the September 1, 1980, letter, earlier quoted, conveyed to all elders by the traveling representatives, would produce, if not a storm of protest, at least some measurable expression of dismay from elders and others. They were too well trained for that to be the case. Some few individuals did express themselves, but cautiously, lest they also receive the label of "apostate." Certainly the lack of protest was not because they had 'proved to themselves that this was the good and acceptable and perfect will of God,' as the apostle urges.[2] Rereading the paragraph on page two, one finds not a single scripture advanced as proof that such thought-control policy has any Scriptural support. The Christian's thoughts are to be 'brought into captivity to the Christ,' not to men or an organization.[3] Why then this willingness to surrender one's conscience to such total control?

It is the concept of "the organization" that produces this. That concept creates the belief that, to all intents and purposes, whatever the organization speaks, it is as if God himself were speaking. Perhaps

2 Romans 12:2.
3 2 Corinthians 10:5.

epitomizing the spirit that the Society's pronouncements, including this letter, produced is an incident occurring at a Circuit Assembly meeting for elders of a section of Alabama. The District Overseer, Bart Thompson, held up a Society publication that had a green cover. He then said to the assembly of elders, "If the Society told me that this book is black instead of green, I would say, 'Y'know I could have sworn that it was green, but if the Society says it's black, then it's black!' Others have used similar illustrations.

True, there are many thinking Witnesses who are repelled by such blatant expressions of blind faith. Yet most are still willing to conform, even to take "judicial action" against any who express doubts about the Society's interpretations. Why?

I try in my own mind and heart to understand the feelings of all these persons, including those on the Governing Body. Based on my own experience among them I believe that they are, in effect, the captives of a concept. The concept or mental image they have of "the organization" seems almost to take on a personality of its own, so that the concept itself controls them, moves them or restrains them, by molding their thinking, their attitudes, their judgments. I do not believe that many of them would take the position they now take if they thought only in terms of God, Christ, the Bible, and the interests— not of an organization—but of their Christian brothers, fellow humans. The insertion of the existing concept of "the organization," however, radically alters their thinking and viewpoint, becomes, in fact, the dominant, controlling force.

I believe that when the men on the Governing Body think about and refer to "the organization" they likewise think of the *concept* rather than the reality. They think of "the organization" as something far bigger and grander than themselves, thinking of it in its numerical aspect, in the extent of its scope of control, as something international, worldwide. They do not realize—apparently—that this aspect relates more to the organization's *domain* than to what it itself actually is. When however, they urge "loyalty to the organization" they must know, they certainly *should* know, that they are not talking about that domain—about the thousands of congregations and their members that the organization directs. They are talking about loyalty to the *source* of the direction, the *source* of the teachings, the *source* of the authority. Whether the Governing Body members acknowledge it or whether they prefer not to think about it, the fact remains that in these crucial respects they, and they alone, are "the organization." Whatever other authority exists—that of the Branch Committees, that of the District or Circuit Overseers, that of Congregational Elder Bodies—that authority is totally dependent on them, subject to adjustment, change or removal at their decision, unilaterally, with no questions asked. The apostle at Romans, chapter thirteen, says that earthly governments "stand placed in their relative positions by God." His words could be compared to the above situation, for all the existing authorities within the organization "stand placed in their relative positions by the Governing Body," subject entirely to its control.

As stated, I doubt that most of these men think about these facts. So for them "the organization" remains something rather undefined, abstract, a concept rather than a concrete entity. Perhaps because of such an illusory view of "the organization" a man can be a Member of such a Body that has virtually unrestricted power and authority, and yet not feel a keen sense of personal responsibility for what the Body does, for whatever hurt or whatever misleading information and consequent misdirection results. "It was *the organization* that did it, not us," seems to be the thinking. And, believing that "the organization" is God's chosen instrument, the responsibility is passed on to God. It was His will—even if later the particular decision or the particular authoritative teaching is found wrong and changed. People may have been disfellowshiped or otherwise hurt by the wrong decisions. But the individual Member of the Governing Body feels absolved of personal responsibility. Any mess that has been made, God will do the cleaning up of it for "the organization."

I express the above points, not as a means of condemnation but as a means of explanation, an attempt to understand why certain men that I consider to be honest, basically kind individuals could be party to what I feel that they in their own hearts, would normally have rejected. I think the concept earlier described is tragically wrong, as pernicious as it is tragic. I believe the drastic actions taken toward those persons accused of "apostasy" were, in almost all cases, not only unjustified but repugnant, unworthy not only of Christianity but of any free society of men. Yet this effort at comprehension enables me to be free from brooding or harboring bitterness toward the persons involved, either individually or collectively. Bitterness is both self-defeating and destructive. I do not know any person among those men that I would not be willing to express hospitality to in my home, with no questions asked, no issue of apology raised. Neither I nor any of my personal friends had any thought of cutting them, or any other persons, off from association because of a difference in understanding. The cutting off was not our thought, not our action.

When I met with the Governing Body the meeting was taped and I had been promised a copy of the tape. What happened to this? I believe what occurred is illustrative of points that have just been made.

About three weeks after returning to Alabama, I had occasion to write the Governing Body and took the opportunity to ask about my copy of the tape. I received a reply dated June 26, 1980.

WATCH TOWER

BIBLE AND TRACT SOCIETY OF PENNSYLVANIA

PHONE (212) 625-1240   CABLE WATCHTOWER

124 COLUMBIA HEIGHTS, BROOKLYN, NEW YORK 11201, U.S.A.

June 26, 1980

R. V. Franz
c/o P. V. Gregerson
Route 4, Box 444
Gadsden, AL 35904

Dear Brother Franz:

    Your letter of June 14 has been received.

    We checked with the shipping department and they inform us that your furniture has been crated and it was shipped out from Brooklyn on Tuesday, June 24. So you should be receiving it soon.

    As for the tape about which you write this matter is being given attention and it will be sent to you just as quickly as a copy can be made and shipped on to you.

    We will look forward to receiving the two procedure books that you will be sending to us. Your letter also enclosed the convention talk material you mentioned returning to us.

    May Jehovah's blessing be with you and we send Christian love.

                        Your brothers,

                        Watch Tower ... . Society
                        OF PENNSYLVANIA
                        For the Chairman's Committee

Two weeks passed and then this letter came:

PHONE (212) 625-1240

WATCH TOWER
BIBLE AND TRACT SOCIETY OF PENNSYLVANIA

CABLE WATCHTOWER

124 COLUMBIA HEIGHTS, BROOKLYN, NEW YORK 11201, U.S.A.

July 10, 1980

Mr.Raymond V. Franz
c/o P. V. Gregerson
Route 4, Box 444
Gadsden, AL 35904

Dear Brother Franz:

Further with regard to our letter of June 26:

We thank you for the return of the Branch Organization and
Governing Body Procedure books, which arrived the other day.
Also, the shipping department has notified us that your furni-
ture items were sent and that they have been received by you.

While the Chairman's Committee had mentioned that the
matter of sending you the tape of May 20 (although it may be
the tape of May 21st that you have in mind of the Governing Body
meeting) was "being given attention," the Governing Body has now
thought it well not to make up and give out any copies of the
tapes for either of such dates. Also, in view of a confidential
item which had been sent to the Governing Body members in April
somehow coming into the hands of one of the members of the Bethel
family who was disfellowshiped, and which was further circulated,
the Governing Body has determined that it would not be advisable
to open the records of its sessions (be it by tapes or minutes
in writing) to anyone off the Society's premises. Furthermore,
a change of status as to yourself has occurred. If in the future
you would wish to obtain information from the tape we would not
object to making such available to you to hear at Bethel.

While we did verbally mention, and also write, that a copy
of the tape would be available to you, now the situation has
seriously changed. As you no doubt can appreciate the Governing
Body feels that this would be a more discreet course. We trust
that you will find this arrangement a reasonable one.

It is hoped all is well with you and we send our Christian love
and greetings.

Your brothers,

Watch Tower B.&T. Society
OF PENNSYLVANIA

For the Chairman's Committee

A NONPROFIT CORPORATION

The letter unavoidably brought back memories of the way matters
had been handled from the start, from the time the Chairman's Com-

mittee had first put in motion the judicial machinery and actions that produced the various disfellowshipings. I had hoped all that was passed. I had no way of knowing what they were referring to in writing of "a confidential item which had been sent to the Governing Body in April." While in Brooklyn I had not seen any of the disfellowshiped persons, nor did I see them between then and my return to Alabama. So I replied as follows:

July 19, 1980

Watchtower Society
Attention: Chairman's Committee

Dear Brothers:

    This will acknowledge receipt of your letter of July 10.
Yes, the furniture items were received by us in good condition
and we appreciate the work of the brothers in shipping in caring
for this.

    I note what you say about the decision not to send the
tape of May 21 (incorrectly stated by me as May 20). As you
must realize, the agreement was, and it was stated by the
Chairman of the body before the session, that such would be
provided to me. There were no qualifications stated, such as
my status, my being at Bethel or outside of Bethel. It was
a simple acknowledgement of the one provision that I required
before agreeing to having the session taped, and you accepted
that stipulation and agreed to it. Since you have acknowledged
in writing that this is the case then it seems you should hold
true to your agreement. What others have done cannot be used
as a basis for breaking your agreement with me. If you do not
intend to hold true to that agreement then it is plain that the
only fair thing for you to do is to destroy that tape and any
transcripts or copies thereof. For if I am not entitled to a
copy of it then neither should you be, for I only agreed to it
on the provision that I would receive a copy of it.

    I have not completed my review of my papers but believe that
I have some further material that should be returned to you and
I will do this as soon as possible.

    I will look forward to hearing from you at an early date
on the matter of the tape. I will expect to receive either the
tape or your letter to the effect that the tape and any copies or
transcripts thereof have been destroyed.

    Thank you for your attention to the above and may God aid
you in loyally upholding the high principles of his Word and
the good news about his Kingdom.

                     Yours in Jehovah's service,

                     R. V. Franz

This is the answer the Governing Body sent me three weeks later:

PHONE (212) 625-1240

WATCH TOWER

BIBLE AND TRACT SOCIETY OF PENNSYLVANIA

CABLE WATCHTOWER

124 COLUMBIA HEIGHTS, BROOKLYN, NEW YORK 11201, U.S.A.

August 8, 1980

Raymond Franz
c/o P.V. Gregerson
Route 4, Box 444
Gadsden, AL 35904

Dear Brother Franz:

Your letter of July 19 with reference to the Chairman's Committee letter to you of July 10, has been received.

The Governing Body decided for the time being not to send you the tapes of the May 21 meeting as mentioned in our letter to you of the 10th of July. As described in our letter if you desire to hear the information on these tapes they are available to you for listening at Bethel.

We send our greetings.

Your fellow servants of Jehovah,

Watch Tower B.&.J. Society

OF PENNSYLVANIA

For the Chairman's Committee

They answered not a single point I had raised. The sense of unreality I had experienced before now came back. It seemed difficult to believe that men in responsible positions could act so irresponsibly. The letter's tone conveyed the attitude that all rights belonged to them (to "the organization") and that the rights of individuals could simply be ignored, if that appeared desirable and advantageous, summarily set aside as of no particular consequence. I wrote once more, as follows:

August 23, 1930

Chairman's Committee
Brooklyn, New York

Dear Brothers:

I have received your letter of August 8 which is in
response to mine of July 19 with regard to the tape you
agreed to send me.

Your letter is a response but not a reply. It simply
repeats in abbreviated form your letter of July 10 and makes
no reply to the points presented in my letter of July 19.

The fact is that you have in your possession tapes of
the May 21 meeting only as a result of an unkept agreement.
To set up new conditions after an agreement has been made,
doing so unilaterally and arbitrarily, is certainly not fair
by any standards. In your letter of June 26 you acknowledged
in writing that you had made an agreement to provide me a
copy of the tape of the meeting and stated your intention of
preparing such copy and sending it to me. My status had already
changed at that time, yet this was subsequently used as one
basis for not keeping your agreement. The reasons given for
not carrying out your agreement, as stated in your letter of
July 10, are in no way a justification for a breach of contract.

May I urge you to meditate upon the consequences of such
a course, keeping in mind the principle set forth at Leviticus
19:15; Romans 1:31. In view of your evident concern about
releasing a copy of the tape, I have offered you the only
honorable alternative, that of eliminating the tape and any
copy or transcripts thereof. If you wish to keep the tape then
the only just thing to do is to keep the agreement by which you
obtained it. I have no doubt that if the circumstances were
reversed, with the tape being in my possession and you being the
petitioners for an agreed-upon copy, you would take the same
position that I have taken.--Matthew 7:12.

Please accept the above as an expression of concern for
your own spiritual interests as well as for that of brothers
everywhere. Though my status may be viewed as a lowly and not
a high one, I will appreciate your manifesting consideration for
the points made in this letter and my letter of July 19.

Your brother,

R. V. Franz

Nearly one month later, another letter came, shown on the facing
page.

As the correspondence already presented shows, my "wishes" actually were for the copy of the tape to be sent as promised. Since they
clearly were unwilling to part with it (recalling somewhat the "Water-
gate" attitude), I had offered them an option, which they finally exercised. At any rate, I was glad to have the matter settled and hoped that
was the end of any further dealings with the Body. It was not.

Some weeks after my return to Alabama, the Society had sent me a
check for $10,000, as a gift 'to aid in reestablishing in the South.' I
had made no request for money and the action taken was both unex-

PHONE (212) 625-1240

WATCH TOWER
BIBLE AND TRACT SOCIETY OF PENNSYLVANIA

CABLE WATCHTOWER

124 COLUMBIA HEIGHTS, BROOKLYN, NEW YORK 11201, U.S.A.

GT/A   September 24,1980

Raymond V. Franz
Route 4, Box 440F
Gadsden, AL 35904

Dear Brother Franz:

Your letter of August 28, 1980 has been received and has been given consideration.

This is to inform you that the tapes of the May 21, 1980, meeting to which you have made reference have now been destroyed. There are three witnesses of the Governing Body who were present when such tapes were destroyed. There were no written transcripts made of the material that was taped, nor were any taped copies made of the recordings. The tapes have been totally destroyed.

This is in accordance with your wishes as set out in your correspondence to us.

Your brothers,

Watch Tower B.& T. Society
OF PENNSYLVANIA

For the Chairman's Committee

pected and appreciated. It took a loan of another $5,000 to obtain a mobile home, and Peter Gregerson allowed us to park this on his property. I was grateful to be able (as well as economically obliged) to do strenuous physical labor for Peter in yard work. Each day was spent mowing lawns, cutting weeds, trimming hedges, being stung by wasps and yellow jackets, bitten innumerable times by fire ants, sweating through one period when for thirty consecutive days the temperature passed 100° Fahrenheit. I cannot recall any other time in my life when I experienced the constant physical pain that I did during those months. Yet I was glad for it, as it served to offset the emotional hurt I felt.

The greatest help, for both my wife and myself, was, however, our daily reading of the Scriptures. Each morning we read four of the Psalms, doing this consecutively until completing them. Though read many times before, they seemed almost new to us now. We could relate to them so much more. For if any one part of the Bible makes clear the very *personal* relationship that can and should exist between God's servants and himself, the Psalms seem to do this, outstandingly so. The emotional upset, the sighing, the feeling of helplessness and despair that the writers so often expressed, their ultimate acknowledgement in each case that their full and final hope was and must be, not in men, but in Jehovah God as their Rock and high place of protection, struck a very responsive chord in both of us.

My determination on leaving the international headquarters had been not to precipitate problems. I did not go looking for trouble. The trouble came looking for me.

For a number of months we enjoyed a pleasant relationship with the members of the East Gadsden Congregation of Jehovah's Witnesses, sharing in their meetings and in the "field activity." A few months after my arrival the local body of elders wrote to Brooklyn recommending my appointment as an elder in the congregation. The brief reply that came back said succinctly that the Society did not think it advisable for the elders to recommend me as such (or as a ministerial servant). The only reason given was that the notice of my resignation (published in the same *Our Kingdom Service* as the information about the disfellowshiping of several staff members) was still recent. The presiding overseer of the congregation seemed upset by the spirit of the letter but I recommended he simply forget about it.

With this letter, plus the information given out to elders as a result of the September 1, 1980, Society letter (stating that mere belief that differed from the published teachings of the Society was grounds for disfellowshiping), the atmosphere gradually began to change. The *Watchtower* magazine began publishing articles clearly designed, not to calm matters, but to focus discussion on the supposed "apostasy" taking place. From then till now, by word and by printed page, a concerted campaign has apparently been under way to justify the extreme treatment meted out to those brothers in Brooklyn who were so swiftly expelled. Rather than a lessening of dogmatism the claims of divine authority and the accompanying calls for unquestioning loyalty became more strident. Issue after issue of the *Watchtower* magazine focused on points that had been questioned, insisted on their rightness, and in general produced a definite entrenchment of position rather than a moderating thereof. The argumentation used to achieve this seemed to reach new lows in misrepresentation of any contrary views.

An atmosphere of both suspicion and fear developed. Elders who were by nature moderate men felt hesitant about calling for moderation lest this be viewed as evidence of disloyalty. Those who were inclined toward tough action found favorable opportunities to express their hard-line attitude. It recalled the McCarthy period in the United States, when anyone who spoke on behalf of civil rights and freedom and expressed disapproval of ruthless methods of crushing unpopular ideologies was in real danger of being classed as a "Communist sympathizer," a "fellow traveler" of radical elements.

Under these circumstances, meeting attendance for me became more and more depressing, as it meant hearing God's Word misused, made to say things it did not say, as well as hearing the constant self-authentification and self-commendation of the organization. It made one wish that there was at least the freedom of expression found in the first-century synagogues that granted persons, such as the apostles, opportunity to speak out in favor of truth (though even there this inevitably led to a hardening of attitude that eventually would close the doors of the synagogue to them). But, as I remarked to Peter Gregerson, I considered myself simply a guest at the Kingdom Hall; it was their Hall, their meetings, their programs, and I had no desire to put a "damper" on their carrying them out. So, I limited my comments to the reading of relevant scriptures, simply emphasizing whatever portion was applicable. It was a rare meeting that someone, often an older member, did not come up afterward and make some expression of appreciation.

The "crusade" atmosphere developing, however, gave me reason to believe it was just a matter of time until some further action would be taken toward me. And so it happened.

THE CRIME AND THE SENTENCE

"Both the Pharisees and the scribes kept muttering, saying: 'This man welcomes sinners and even eats with them.'" —Luke 15:2

One meal was all the evidence needed. It happened this way:

Within about six months of my return to northern Alabama, the Society sent a new Circuit Overseer into the area. The previous man had been a moderate, inclined to play down problems rather than make issues of them. The man who replaced him had a reputation for greater aggressiveness. This was about the time the Society's letter to District and Circuit Overseers had come out saying that "apostasy" included persons who even *believed* something different from the organization's teachings.

On his second visit to the East Gadsden Congregation (March 1981) the new Circuit Overseer, Wesley Benner, arranged to meet with Peter Gregerson, going to his home along with a local elder, Jim Pitchford. The reason? Benner told Peter that there was a "lot of talk" about him in the city and in the Circuit. Peter said he was very sorry to hear that. Where was the "talk" coming from? Benner was reluctant to say, but Peter pointed out that he needed to know to remedy the situation. Benner then said the source was an in-law of Peter's family.

Peter made clear that he had put forth every effort to be circumspect in his expressions and that any conversations on Scriptural matters he had had with anyone in the area were strictly with his own relatives. He was deeply concerned that persons outside his family relationship were now engaging in "a lot of talk," as the Circuit Overseer had said. "How could that be?" he asked. Wesley Benner offered no explanation.

What, then, were they talking *about*? Benner brought up a point in a certain *Watchtower* article that Peter had reportedly objected to. Under no circumstances could the point be called a "major teaching" of Scripture; it actually involved a technicality.[4] Nonetheless, since Peter had not agreed with the organization it became important. After long discussion, the Circuit Overseer was finally obliged to acknowledge that the point might indeed be in error. (In actual fact, it was subsequently dropped from the *Watchtower* magazine in all foreign-language translations, although readers in English were never informed.)

Peter said afterward, "I was determined not to let a 'confrontation' situation develop and I did everything I could to keep the conversation calm and reasonable." When the Circuit Overseer and the local elder left, Peter felt the matter had ended on a friendly basis and was glad that was the case. It was not.

The following week, the Circuit Overseer sent word that he wanted a second meeting to pursue the matter further.

Peter told me he felt that the time had come to make a decision. The spirit that had been generated by the Governing Body, its Service Department and its letter of September 1, 1980, and a succession of

---

4   The article, in the August 15, 1980, issue of the *Watchtower*, endeavored to show that the Greek term *naos* (temple or sanctuary), used in Revelation 7:15 with regard to the "great crowd," could apply to the temple courtyards. In doing so it said that Jesus chased the moneychangers out of the *naos*. (See page 15, box at the bottom of the page.) Since the Bible account itself, at John 2:14–16, clearly uses another term (*hieron*), the claim was obviously false, as one elder expressed it, "either an example of intellectual dishonesty or intellectual ignorance."

Watchtower articles, had built up to the point where a "witch hunt" atmosphere prevailed. He felt it would be naïve on his part if he failed to recognize the strong likelihood that efforts were under way to bring about his disfellowshipment. His befriending me, he felt, was at least a contributing factor. As he saw it, he had two choices: Either voluntarily disassociate himself from the congregation or let the efforts under way continue to their goal of disfellowshiping him. He found neither choice desirable but of the two he believed he should take the first, voluntarily disassociate himself.

When I expressed doubt as to whether things had reached that stage yet, he said he had weighed the matter, prayed about it, and felt it was the wiser course. The factor that most concerned him, he said, was his family. Of his seven children, three were married, some had children, and he had three brothers and two sisters living in the area and many nephews and nieces. All of them were Jehovah's Witnesses.[5] If he allowed the organization's representatives to push matters to the point of disfellowshiping, it would make for a very difficult situation for all these family members. It would put them in a serious dilemma as to whether to associate with him as their father or grandfather or brother or uncle, or, instead, to be obedient to the organization and shun him. Additionally, there were about thirty-five Witnesses in the employ of his grocery company. Voluntary disassociation seemed better since, as he understood it, it simply meant that he was no longer a member of the congregation. But it did not call for the rigid cutting off of relations that organizational policy required in cases of disfellowshiping.[6]

Peter submitted his letter of resignation on March 18, 1981. It was read to the congregation. Although normal comment followed, inasmuch as Peter had been a Witness from childhood and had taken the

5 His wife's family also included many Witnesses.

6 I knew personally that the Governing Body had till then equated disassociation and disfellowshipment *only* in the case of persons entering politics or the military, *not* for a simple resignation from the congregation. I had, in fact, been assigned to undertake a revision of the *Aid to Answering Branch Office Correspondence* manual which spelled out all such policies and I knew that no such extreme position had been reached on disassociation. Persons who resigned were not treated the same as those disfellowshiped, with the sole exception that if they desired to re-enter the congregation they had to submit a request to that effect. After hearing that the Service Department had sent out some letters making such equation, I talked with a member of the Service Department Committee and pointed out that the matter had never been presented to the Governing Body and that any such action had to be of the Service Department's own doing (an example of the Department's occasional unauthorized "policy-making" actions). He acknowledged that nothing on this had come through from the Governing Body.

lead for many years in local congregation activity, the letter seemed to clear the air since it calmly presented his reasons and expressed no animosity. With rare exception, Jehovah's Witnesses in Gadsden, on meeting up with Peter, treated him in a manner that was at least cordial. I think they would have kept on doing so had they been governed by their own sense of right and wrong. It seemed that a crisis situation had been averted.

Within six months the *Watchtower* magazine published articles changing the whole picture. Some commented to me, "They did everything but put your name and Peter Gregerson's in the magazine." I do not believe the situation in Gadsden was solely responsible for the articles. I do believe, however, that it did have some effect on the ones motivated to prepare these. What was the change made in these articles?

Back in 1974 the Governing Body assigned me to write articles on the treatment of disfellowshiped persons. (The Body had just made a decision that made this advisable.)[7] Those articles, duly approved by the Body, greatly moderated the attitude that had prevailed up to that time, encouraged Witnesses to manifest a more merciful attitude in many areas of their contacts with disfellowshiped persons, reduced the rigidity of policies governing dealings with a disfellowshiped family member.

The September 15, 1981, *Watchtower* not only reversed this, on some points it carried the matter backward to an even more rigid position than had existed previous to 1974. (An example of "tacking" backwards, this time to a point *behind* the starting place.)[8]

A major change made was with regard to any voluntarily disassociating themselves (as Peter Gregerson had done a few months previous). For the first time the policy was officially published that anyone doing this was to be treated in the same way as if he had been expelled from the congregation.[9]

---

7 Two cases had come before the Body of disfellowshiped persons who wanted to attend meetings but needed assistance. One was a young girl living in a rural area in New England, the other a woman in a drug rehabilitation center in the Midwest. Neither could get to meetings without assistance as to transportation. The Governing Body's decision was that it would be acceptable to provide transportation in such cases.

8 The *Watchtower* of December 1, 1981, carried an article attempting to justify all the shifting back and forth on various doctrinal points on the Society's part. It used the analogy of a boat tacking against the wind. The problem is that the shifting of teaching often brings them back virtually to the point where they began.

9 This was directed primarily toward those who resigned. While those entering politics or the military were classed as "disassociated," this was not some voluntary action on their

When I read the material, viewing it against my background of experience on the Governing Body (and particularly in the light of my recent experiences with the Chairman's Committee) I had little doubt as to where this would lead. I did not have long to wait.

What is now related is given in detail not because my own case is involved or because it is so unusual, but instead because it is so typical of what others experienced, the methods and actions of elders of Jehovah's Witnesses in case after case of this kind. It is illustrative of the thinking and spirit inculcated in them, a thinking and spirit derived from a central source.

Though published with a September 15 date, the *Watchtower* magazine in question arrived over two weeks before that date. Within a few days, came a visit from a local elder of the East Gadsden Congregation of Jehovah's Witnesses, Dan Gregerson, Peter's youngest brother. He asked if he and a couple of other elders could come out and speak to me. I said that would be all right; what did they want to talk about? After some hesitation, he said first that it was to discuss my having made remarks of an adverse nature about the organization. When I inquired who was the source of such a claim, he said the person preferred to remain anonymous. (This 'shooting of spears out of the fog' is quite common and the one accused is supposed to take this all as quite normal and proper.)

I asked him, however, if he did not think that Jesus' counsel at Matthew, chapter eighteen, verses 15 to 17, should apply (the counsel there being that one with a complaint against a brother should first go himself and talk with his brother about the problem)? Dan agreed it did apply. I suggested that as an elder he see the individual and recommend that he come and talk to me about the matter and thus apply Jesus' counsel. He replied that the person did not feel "qualified." I pointed out that that really was not at issue, that I had no interest in arguing with anyone, but that if I had disturbed someone I would appreciate that person's telling me personally so that I could apologize and set matters straight.[10] Dan's reply was that I had to realize that the elders also had "a responsibility to protect the flock and watch out for the interests of the sheep." I agreed fully and said I was sure he realized that doing this certainly meant that elders should encourage

---

part, not on their request. It was an automatic action taken by the elders in accord with Society policy. So the new position dealt with those *voluntarily* withdrawing.

10 I still do not know of whom he was speaking.

everyone in the flock to hold carefully to God's Word and apply it in their lives. In this case, they could help the party involved to see the need to apply Jesus' counsel and come and speak with me, then I could know what had offended the person and make whatever apology was needed.

He said he would drop that point and went on to say that they wanted to discuss my "associations" with me. They would be welcome to do that, I said, and it was agreed that he and another elder would come two days later. Dan and an elder named Theotis French came. The conversation started with Dan's reading Second Corinthians, chapter thirteen, verses 7 to 9, and informing me that they were there to "readjust" my thinking in connection with the September 15, 1981, *Watchtower*, particularly as regards my association with his brother, Peter Gregerson, now disassociated. Dan had been in a restaurant in August when Peter and I and our wives had a meal there.

I asked them if they realized they were right then on Peter's property, that in that sense he was my landlord. That I was also in his employ. They knew that.

I explained that, as in all matters, I was governed by conscience as regards my associations and I discussed Paul's counsel about the importance of conscience in his letter to the Romans, chapter fourteen. Whatever the Scriptures instructed, I would be happy to do, but I saw no evidence to support the view now adopted as to disassociated persons. What Scriptural support was there?

The conversation now followed an easily predictable course: Dan referred to First Corinthians, chapter five, in support of the position. I pointed out that the apostle there spoke of not associating with persons called brothers who were fornicators, idolaters, revilers, drunkards and extortioners. I had no such persons among my associates and would not want them in my home. But surely they did not consider Peter Gregerson as included among that kind of people? Neither responded.

Dan then referred to the apostle John's words at First John, chapter two, verse 19: "They went out from us, but they were not of our sort; for if they had been of our sort, they would have remained with us." When asked what the context showed as to the kind of persons John spoke of, they acknowledged that he was speaking of "antichrists." I pointed out that the same was true in John's Second Letter, verses 7 to 11, which deals with association with such ones. I assured them that I would never fellowship with an antichrist, one who had rebelled against God and Christ, but that again I had none such among my acquaintances. Surely they were not saying that Peter Gregerson was an antichrist? Again no response.[11]

This was, *actually*, the extent of the Scriptural "readjustment" that I received from these two shepherds of the flock. From that point on their only references were to the *Watchtower* magazine. Did I accept what it said on this subject, did I submit to the organization's direction? I stated that in the end the real question was what God's Word says on any matter, that some teachings are clearly solid, founded immovably on God's Word; other teachings can be subject to change.

In illustration, I asked Dan if he thought it possible that the organization could, at some future time, change its view as to the application of Jesus' expression about "this generation" in Matthew, chapter twenty-four? (I did not tell them that Governing Body members Schroeder, Klein and Suiter had in fact suggested a change that would have moved the start of that "generation" from 1914 up to 1957.) Dan's reply was, "If the organization sees fit to change it at some future time, then I will accept it." While not a direct answer, that indicated he recognized the possibility of a change. I then asked him if he thought the organization could possibly change as regards the teaching that Jesus Christ gave his life as a ransom for mankind? He just looked at me. I said I was sure that he did not think that could take place, for that teaching was solidly based on Scripture. The other teaching was a "current understanding," subject to change, certainly not on the same level with the teaching of the ransom sacrifice. I viewed the material in the September 15, 1981, *Watchtower* and its prohibitions regarding association with disassociated persons in the same light.

Dan now began speaking of the "need to be humble" in accepting God's direction. I could wholeheartedly agree to that and said I was sure they would also agree that those who preach humility should be the first in exemplifying it.

Again to illustrate, the example was given them of a group of people in a room, conversing. One person expresses his views very emphatically on a variety of matters. When he finishes, another person in the room comments, saying he agrees wholeheartedly with the initial speaker on several points; however, he feels differently on a couple of them, giving his reasons. At this the first individual becomes incensed and calls on the group to expel this person from the room as unfit

11 Dan acknowledged that he had never spoken to his brother, Peter, about Peter's differences of viewpoint, although Dan was fully aware of them.

company—because he did not agree with him on *every* point. Who, I asked, is the one needing to learn humility? Again, no response. The conversation ended not long thereafter and they left.

Peter visited me that evening to find out the results. He was very sorry about the position taken toward me and knew to what it could lead. He said he wanted me to know that if I thought it advisable not to have any further association with him that he would understand.

I reminded him of an incident that took place a year and a half earlier one evening shortly before I went to Brooklyn in May, 1980, for my final session with the Governing Body. He and I were alone in his car and I told him that Cynthia and I had talked things over and decided it would be better not to return to Alabama after the session, but instead go to the home of members of Cynthia's family. I said that I did not know what might come of the meeting, perhaps "the worst," and I did not want to create problems for him and his family.[12] We felt there was less likelihood of problems being made for my wife's family if we went there. He replied that they very much wanted us to return, were counting on it. I told him we appreciated that greatly, but that he had a large family—wife, sons and daughters, brothers and sisters, grandchildren and in-laws, all Witnesses—and that if disfellow-shiped, my returning could result in considerable difficulty and un-pleasantness for them on the part of the organization.

His response was, "I realize that, and don't think I haven't thought a lot about it. But we've talked it over among ourselves and we've crossed that bridge. We want you to come back no matter what."

It would be difficult to say how much those words had meant to me at that particular time. I told him that I did not see how I could do any less now that the situation was the other way around. I could not be party to something that labeled a man wicked who had simply acted according to conscience, out of concern for truth and for the interests of others.

After the "readjustment" meeting with the two elders of the East Gadsen Congregation, nothing further was said to me until the arrival of Circuit Overseer Wesley Benner, some weeks later. He arranged to come to my home with Dan Gregerson. Tom Gregerson, also a brother of Peter and the second of the four sons of the Gregerson family, was also present at his own request.

The discussion followed the same predictable pattern, except that

---

12 Peter at that time had not yet disassociated himself. His disassociation came nearly a year later.

the Circuit Overseer was inclined to interrupt my statements to the point that I finally had to ask him, as a guest in my home, that he at least wait until I had finished an expression before breaking in.[13] The "readjustment" was once more based on the *Watchtower*, not on Scripture. Again, when asked if they really considered Peter Gregerson to be a "wicked" man of the kind described at First Corinthians, chapter 5, or an "antichrist" as described by the apostle John, neither had any comment.

I drew their attention to Romans, chapter fourteen, where the apostle stressed the need to be true to conscience, that anyone who does something while doubting that it is approved of God thereby sins, since "everything that is not out of faith is sin." Since the Scripture states that, "Anyone pronouncing the wicked one righteous and anyone pronouncing the righteous one wicked—even both of them are detestable to Jehovah," I could not conscientiously violate that principle by viewing or treating Peter Gregerson as a wicked person, when all I knew about him told me otherwise.[14]

Benner's response was that, if I had to be guided by my conscience, so did the elders have to be guided by theirs. That if this was my position then "they would have to take action accordingly." (Evidently the conscience of the elders did not allow for respecting the conscience of another man, showing tolerance.) What kind of "action" was meant was made quite clear by his further expression. He said he simply viewed himself as one who conveyed the things provided by the organization. Using his own words, he said, "I parrot what the Governing Body says." This was stated with evident pride, for what reasons I could not understand. I have never viewed being a parrot as an achievement of any great merit.

Not long after this the conversation ended and they left. Tom Gregerson shook his head in disbelief, saying the experience had been revealing but depressing; that he would not have believed that men would say things such as he had heard.

By the first of November the same judicial machinery that had functioned in Brooklyn, began functioning in Gadsden. Phone calls asking one thing after another came from the elders. I was advised that a judicial committee would meet with me.

I had been planning to write to the Governing Body to submit my

---

13   During the conversation a clear "beeping" sound came a couple of times from the direction of the Circuit Overseer. I have since wondered if he was taping the conversation, inasmuch as this seemed to have become a favored practice with the Governing Body.

14   Proverbs 17:15.

resignation to membership in the Society's corporations. (I had been a voting member of both the Pennsylvania and the New York corporations for several years.)[15] Along with informing the Body that I was resigning from such membership, on November 5, I wrote:

> Locally, certain elders have taken the information in the September 15, 1981, Watchtower as authorization to demand a change in my relationship with the man on whose property I live and for whom I work, Peter Gregerson. They state that, since he has disassociated himself, I should view him as among those with whom one should not eat--wicked persons and antichrists--and that failure to conform to this position requires disfellowshiping. Approaching 60, having no financial resources, I am in no position to move or to change my employment. So I would very much appreciate knowing if the intent of your statements in that issue of the magazine is truly as they present it, namely that my accepting an invitation from my landlord and employer to eat with him is grounds for disfellowshiping. If, instead, they have exceeded the intent of what was published, some counsel of moderation would grant me relief from a situation that is potentially oppressive. I will appreciate whatever clarification you can give, whether directly or through one of your departments.

That same day a phone call came from the elders. Their calls had been so numerous and the approach so unbrotherly that my wife and I both began to feel emotionally upset every time we heard the phone ring. I instructed my wife that if the elders phoned and I was not there that she should inform them that anything they had to say to put it in writing. So, she now passed this information on. The next day the appointed judicial committee wrote, the letter arriving November 10, 1981.

Many of Jehovah's Witnesses find it incredible that I was actually disfellowshiped because of eating a meal with a man, Peter Gregerson. Some insist that this could not be the case. I believe the correspondence that now developed makes the matter plain. The first letter, sent by the judicial committee, was dated November 6, 1981.

This letter makes clear that one charge, and one charge only, formed the basis for their "judicial action," namely, my 'association with a disassociated person.'

In my written response, I pointed out to the Gadsden elders that, I had written to the Governing Body for clarification of the meaning of

---

15 That membership continued after I left the headquarters. Both in 1980 and 1981 I received the usual "Proxies" for voting at the annual meeting. The first year I mailed the proxy in, but in 1981 I could not find it in myself to do so, particularly in view of the material being published in the Society's magazines.

2822 Fields Avenue
East Gadsden, AL 35903
November 6, 1981

Raymond V.Franz
Route 4, Box 440F
Gadsden, AL 35904

Dear Brother Franz:

As per your instructions given us by Sister Franz on Thursday,
November 5, this is to ask you to meet with a judicial committee
on Saturday, November 14, at 2:00 p.m. at the East Gadsden Kingdom
Hall. The purpose of the meeting is to discuss with you your
continued association with a person disassociated from the congregation.

If you are unable to meet with us on the above date, please contact
one of us to arrange another meeting.

Your brothers,

Theotis French
Theotis French

Edger Bryant
Edger Bryant

Dan Gregerson
Dan Gregerson

---

the material published in the September 15, 1981, *Watchtower*, and
wondered why they had given no consideration to this, evidently being
unwilling to allow time for me to receive a reply. I also pointed out
the unreasonableness of having Dan Gregerson serve on the judicial
committee when he had already presented himself as my accuser. I
expressed the hope that the judicial committee might be enlarged to
make more likely a fair and impartial discussion of this new policy
and its application.[16]

---

16 For the reader's information this letter is presented in full in the Appendix.

I sent this letter and a week later, on Friday, November 20, when I arrived home from work, my wife told me that Elder Theotis French had phoned. They would be meeting as a judicial committee the very next day, Saturday afternoon, he said. They had sent me a letter to that effect.

In that afternoon's mail there was a notice of a certified letter. I hurriedly drove to the Post Office and was able to obtain the letter before closing time. The letter was dated November 19, 1981.

2022 Fields Avenue
East Gadsden, AL   35903
November 19, 1981

Raymond V. Franz
Route 4, Box 440-F
Gadsden, AL   35904

Dear Brother Franz:

As a body of elders, we have reviewed your letter and would like to respond. First, we would like to let you know that the body of elders had been made aware that you had mailed a letter to the Watchtower Society and we had determined that we should proceed with the judicial committee hearing. Second, in view of Dan Gregerson's being an accuser the body of elders has decided to replace him on the judicial committee with Larry Johnson.

Third, there are persons other than Dan who could serve as witnesses regarding the matter in question, but we feel that it is not necessary to disclose their names in view of your acknowledging that you have been fellowshipping with persons who are dissassociated from the congregation.

Fourth, the body of elders has determined that three elders will serve on the committee. We would like to assure you that the brothers designated have not prejudged you and that they will approach the meeting objectively.

Finally, Brother Franz, the appointed judicial committee would like to schedule a meeting with you on Saturday, November 21, at 4:00 p.m. at the Kingdom Hall. If you are unable to attend we request that you notify one of the brothers shown below to arrange a more convenient meeting.

Your brothers,

Larry Johnson

Edgar Bryant

Theotis French

The letter was not merely formal. It might as well have come from some civil court, for, although signed "Your brothers," it conveyed none of the warmth of a Christian brotherhood. Cold legalism dominated its tone. Yet, unless I had already been prejudged (which they affirmed was not the case), there surely should have been a brotherly spirit expressed, a sense of compassionate concern for the life interests of the man to whom they wrote. Setting aside my entire adult life's service among Jehovah's Witnesses or my having served on their Governing Body or my age and existing circumstances—setting all that aside, they still should have manifested some measure of loving interest, even if they viewed me as '*one of the least* of Christ's brothers.' (See Matthew chapter twenty-five, verse 40.) I do not believe the unfeeling spirit expressed originated with these men. It had another source. The letter was typical.

My wife had already informed Elder French in the phone conversation that we had guests arriving from out of state on Saturday and that there was no way to communicate with them or change our plans.

The following Monday, November 23, I again wrote to express my dismay at the hurried and inconsiderate manner in which the judicial committee was proceeding.

That very afternoon a phone call came from Elder French stating that the judicial committee would meet two days later, on Wednesday evening (November 25) and make their decision whether I was present or not. I decided that it was useless to mail the letter I had written to them.[17] They seemed to be in an enormous hurry, a "rush to judgment." I do not personally think that this was of their own initiative. As the chairman of the committee later acknowledged, they were in communication with the Society's representative, Circuit Overseer Wesley Benner. Many of their expressions and attitudes reflected remarkably those made by him in my home. He, in turn, was almost certainly in touch with the Service Department of the Brooklyn headquarters, and that department was—beyond any doubt—in communication with the Governing Body. This is not unusual; it is the usual way in which things work. The methods employed were not surprising to me; they were simply depressing.

When Wednesday (November 25) came, I decided that, rather than

---

17 See the Appendix for the letter's contents.

be tried *in absentia*, I would go to their meeting which Elder French said would be held "Wednesday evening". That afternoon I called the home of one of the committee members to ascertain the exact time. The man's wife said that he was already at the Kindgom Hall. I phoned the Hall and found that they were going to have the meeting in the afternoon—to them the "evening" apparently meant any time after 3 p.m. I told them that I had not understood that, that no specific time had been given me and asked it they could postpone their meeting till after 6 p.m. They agreed.

Tom Gregerson had said that he wanted to accompany me and I now phoned him. On arriving at the Kingdom Hall we went into the conference room where the judicial committee, Elders French (Chairman), Bryant and Johnson were. They informed Tom that he could not be present except to give testimony. He said he wanted to be present since about thirty-five Jehovah's Witnesses worked for the company (Warehouse Groceries) of which he was an officer. He wanted to know just what position was being taken on this issue. Their answer was still, No.

After his departure, the committee opened the hearing and called in the witnesses. There were two: Dan Gregerson and Mrs. Robert Daley.

Dan spoke first. He said he had seen me in the Western Steak House along with Peter Gregerson (and our wives). This was the essence of his testimony. When he finished, I asked him when this was and he acknowledged that it was in the summer and hence before the September 15, 1981, *Watchtower*, with its new ruling that called for treating anyone voluntarily disassociating himself the same as though he were disfellowshiped. I told the committee that unless they believed in *ex post facto* laws, Dan's testimony was irrelevant.

The other witness was then asked to present her testimony. She testified to essentially the same thing as Dan, except that the occasion in the restaurant was after the publishing of the September 15, 1981, *Watchtower*.

I readily acknowledged that I had indeed had a meal with Peter at the time she referred to. I also asked her if it was not the case that she and her husband (an elder in the East Gadsden congregation) had also eaten a meal with Peter? (Peter had gone to Morrison's Cafeteria one day and found himself in line right behind Elder Daley and his wife. Since, previous to his present marriage, Daley had been Peter's stepfather, having married Peter's mother after his father's death, Peter now nudged Daley and Daley turned, began talking with Peter and asked Peter to sit with them and the three conversed throughout the meal. This, too, was after the September 15, 1981, *Watchtower's* appearance.)

The witness became quite excited at this and said that while that was true, afterward she had told some of the "Sisters" that she knew it was not right and would never do it again. (Later, after the hearing, I mentioned this to Peter and he said, "But they ate with me twice! Another day I went into Morrison's and they were already seated and when they saw me they waved to me to come and sit with them." The witness said nothing of this second occasion, which was unknown to me at the time of the hearing.)

That was the absolute sum and substance of the "evidence" against me. The two witnesses left.

The judicial committee then began asking me about my position toward the September 15, 1981, *Watchtower*. I inquired why they had not been willing to wait for the Governing Body's response to my inquiry on this, written on November 5? The chairman, Theotis French, brought his hand down on the September 15 *Watchtower* open before him and said, "This is all the authority we need."

I asked if they would not feel more confident if they had confirmation of their viewpoint from the Governing Body? He repeated that 'they had to go by what was published,' and that, anyway 'they had called Brooklyn on the matter.' This was the first I had heard anything about such a call. Evidently that was why, when I spoke to the committee chairman, Elder French, on the phone two days earlier he had said that the body of elders "did not feel it was necessary" to wait for the Governing Body to answer my letter! They followed the same secretive course followed earlier by the Chairman's Committee and apparently did not feel any need whatsoever to let me know that they had already communicated by telephone with the Brooklyn headquarters.

I asked if they spoke with someone on the Governing Body. The answer was, No, that they talked with a member of the Service Department. What had they been told? French said they were told, "Nothing has changed and you can go ahead."

French said that his understanding was that "the Society has taken a hard look at the previous position [in the 1974 *Watchtower*] and they are now going back to the way it was before." (This is basically the way Circuit Overseer Benner expressed himself in my home.) Theotis went on to say that "the *Watchtower* helps us to see where to draw a fine line" in these matters. Elder Edgar Bryant added, "We are all trying to put ourselves in line with what the *Watchtower* requires."

Up to this point none of the three men had made any reference to the Bible. I stressed that this was my guide. On what *Scriptural* basis should I consider Peter Gregerson as a person unfit to eat with?

Elder Johnson turned to First Corinthians, chapter five, began reading a couple of verses, hesitated and stopped, making no application of the information. I asked each member of the committee individually, if he himself could say he honestly believed Peter Gregerson was the kind of person described in such texts, including John's writings about "antichrists"? Theotis French reacted with some agitation, saying 'it wasn't up to him to make a judgment of the man,' that 'he didn't know everything about Peter so as to make such a judgment.' I asked him how, then, they could possibly ask me to make such a judgment and be governed by it, when they themselves were not willing to do so?

His response was, "We didn't come here to have you teach us, Brother Franz." I assured him that I was not there to "teach" them, but that my whole course of life as a Christian was being put in question, was at issue, and I felt I had a right to express myself. Neither Edgar Bryant nor Larry Johnson would make any clear statement as to how they viewed Peter Gregerson, eating a meal with whom was now being treated as a "criminal" act.

The chairman then said he saw no purpose in further discussion. Tom Gregerson was called in to see if he had any testimony to give. When he asked what effect this *Watchtower* position would have on Witness employees in his company who periodically might travel with, or attend a meal in company with, a disassociated person, Larry Johnson said they were not there to answer that question, Tom could bring the question up at another time.[18] Tom replied that he had been asking the question for some time, had asked the Circuit Overseer, and still had no answer. There was no response, the meeting concluded and we left. The judicial committee remained behind to discuss the "evidence."

About a week later, the phone rang and Larry Johnson informed me that the committee's decision was for disfellowshiping. I had seven days from the date of his phone call in which to appeal their decision.

I wrote them a lengthy letter, my "appeal" letter. I felt that whatever

18   Tom Gregerson was at that time the president of Warehouse Groceries.

I had to say it would be best to put it in writing. What is spoken can be easily changed, twisted or simply forgotten; what is written remains and is not so easily ignored. My experience at the previous hearing made it obvious that a very unhealthy climate prevailed and that even in an appeal hearing the likelihood of any calm, reasoned Scriptural discussion of matters was quite remote.

In the letter I called their attention to the Society's published counsel that elders on a judicial committee should "weigh matters carefully," that they should not look for "rigid rules for guidance," but "think in terms of principles," they should "be sure the counsel is based solidly on God's Word," should "take sufficient time and endeavor to reach the heart of the person," should "discuss the application of the scriptures that apply and be sure that he [the one accused] understands." That was what was said; it was not what was being done (yet what was being done was known to the ones responsible for the publishing of that same counsel). The essence of my position is perhaps summed up in these two paragraphs:

Perhaps it may be said that I have not expressed repentance for having eaten with Peter Gregerson. To express repentance I need first to be satisfied that doing so is a sin before God. The only means for providing such conviction must rightly come from God's Word, which alone is inspired and unfailingly reliable. (2 Timothy 3:16, 17) My understanding from the Scriptures is that loyalty to God and to his Word is of supreme importance and supercedes any other loyalty or whatever kind. (Acts 4:19, 20; 5:29) My understanding also is that it is not for me or any other human or group of humans to add to that Word, under pain of being "proved a liar" or even receiving divine plagues. (Proverbs 30:5, 6; Revelation 22:18, 19) I cannot take such scriptural warnings lightly. In view of all the scriptural admonition against judging others, I have a healthy fear of setting myself (or any human or group of humans) up as legislator and feel compelled to let God's Word alone do such judging. To do that I need to be certain that I am not simply following some humanly devised standard that poses as a divine standard but which is in fact uninspired, unsupported by God's Word. I do not wish to be guilty of presumption and impertinence in judging someone whom God by his own expressed Word has not so judged.--Romans 14:4, 10-12; James 3:11, 12; see also Commentary on the Letter of James pages 161 to 168.

I assure you that if you will help me to see from the Scriptures that the act of eating with Peter Gregerson is a sin I will humbly repent of such sin before God. Those who have talked with me thus far have not done this but have cited the above-mentioned magazine as their "authority" (the term used by the chairman of the judicial committee). My understanding is that all authority within the Christian congregation must derive from and be solidly based on the Word of God. Proverbs 17:15 states that "Anyone pronouncing the wicked one righteous and anyone pronouncing the righteous one wicked--even both of them are something detestable to Jehovah." I have no desire to be detestable to God and hence am very concerned about this matter.

I closed making yet another appeal that they honor my request to wait for a reply from the Governing Body to my letter of November 5.[19]

By now, however, I had little doubt but that the Governing Body had no intention of answering my letter. One month had already passed and they were well aware of my circumstances and how critically some statement from them was needed. From my years of experience on the Body I knew that, though preferring to remain in the background, they were very definitely kept informed of every development in my case. The Service Department would be expected to pass on all information, and it in turn would be supplied with reports from the Circuit Overseer. Both the actions and the expressions made by the local elders indicated that procedures were orchestrated from the center of authority, through the Circuit Overseer. The center of authority, the Governing Body, was willing to communicate with those who were judging me, doing so through their Service Department, but they were not willing to respond to my petition written to them, not even to acknowledge receipt of the letter.

So, on December 11, seven weeks after my initial letter, I again wrote the Governing Body, sending them a copy of my "appeal letter" and reminding them of my letter to them dated November 5.[20]

Exactly seven days after submitting my appeal letter, Elder French phoned to tell me an appeal committee had been formed, naming the members selected. Three days passed and another phone call came; he was informing me that the appeal committee would meet with me on Sunday. I told him I had written him asking for the specific names of the committee members (he had only given me family names of a couple of them) and said I would be asking for a change in the committee membership. When I inquired why these particular men had been selected, his reply was that Wesley Benner, the Society's representative, had selected them.

Those he had chosen as appeal committee members were Willie Anderson, Earl Parnell and Rob Dibble. In view of the fact that the principal charge against me was my association with Peter Gregerson I found this selection incredible.

19 See the Appendix for the letter in its entirety.
20 See the Appendix.

Every one of these men was very unlikely to show objectivity where Peter was concerned.

As I pointed out in a letter to the Gadsden elders (although they themselves already knew it), Willie Anderson had been at the head of a committee that created a considerable stir in Gadsden in its handling of a large number of young people in the local congregations. Peter Gregerson had appealed to the Brooklyn headquarters to send in a review committee and when this was done the committee headed by Willie Anderson was found to have been excessive in a number of its actions. This had a noticeable effect on the relationship between Elder Anderson and Peter Gregerson thereafter.

Circuit Overseer Benner's selection of Earl Parnell was even harder to fathom. One of Peter Gregerson's daughters had been married to a son of Elder Parnell but had recently obtained a divorce from him. The strained relations between the two sets of parents was obvious; Circuit Overseer Benner knew of the divorce action and, one would think, would also have been sensitive enough to have realized how inappropriate it would be to assign Elder Parnell to a case in which Peter Gregerson was a central figure.

Similarly with Rob Dibble. He was Elder Parnell's son-in-law, his wife being the sister of the Parnell son recently divorced by Peter Gregerson's daughter.

As I wrote to the Gadsden elders, I found it difficult to think of a committee of three men that would have less to recommend it for an unbiased, objective hearing. (The only way I could see any logic to the selection would be if an adverse decision was somehow being deliberately sought.) In my letter I requested that a totally different appeal committee be selected.[21]

The same day I wrote these letters (December 20), yet another phone call came from Elder French. The appeal committee wanted to inform me that they would meet on the next day, Monday, and 'would hold the hearing whether I was present or not.' I told Elder French I had written requesting a change in the committee and had written to the Brooklyn headquarters as well. I delivered copies of these letters directly to his home the next day, Monday.

Two days later, Wednesday, December 23, the following note came by registered mail:

21 See the Appendix.

RAY FRANZ,
THE MEETING THAT WAS SET FOR THURSDAY
DEC. 24 AT 7:00 PM AT THE EAST GADSDEN
CONGERATION HAS BEEN CHANGED, TO DEC. 28
1981 AT 7:00 PM AT THE EAST GADSDEN CONG.
Would VERY MUCH LIKE To SEE You. THERE.

Theotis French

No one had said anything to me about a proposed meeting on Thursday. But the above note was my official notice of a December 28 meeting, Monday.

During the two days after delivering the letters to Elder French's home, I learned that he was trying to obtain information to support a new and totally different charge. Mark Gregerson, another brother of Peter's, informed Peter that Theotis French had called long distance to Mark's home in Florida. Elder French spoke to Mark's wife and asked if she could recall ever hearing me make any remarks against the organization. She told him she never had heard me make remarks against anybody, including the organization. Why did he want to know? He replied that he was 'just seeking information.' He did not ask to speak with her husband.

This, too, brought memories of the nightmarish situation I had experienced a year and a half before, and of the conduct of the Chairman's Committee of the Governing Body then.

Approximately seven weeks had passed since I first wrote the Governing Body asking for an expression on the material in September 15, 1981, *Watchtower*, telling them why it was of serious importance to me. I had now written them two more times, petitioning them to make some expression. They did not see fit to answer or even to acknowledge any of this correspondence. Is it unbelievable that the leadership of a worldwide organization with over two million members, one that claims to be the outstanding example of adherence to Christian principles, could conduct itself in such manner? No, not if one is familiar with the attitude prevalent among its leadership. I have personally been witness to similar ignoring of letters when the Governing

Body felt it was not to their advantage to provide an answer. They clearly felt so in my case.

From the beginning I had had no doubt as to the ultimate goal of all that was being done. I was thoroughly sickened by the whole conduct of the affair, what I can only describe as a narrow-minded approach, an obvious determination to find something, no matter how trivial or petty, that could serve as a basis for bringing adverse action against me. So I wrote my last letter, dated December 23, 1981, sending copies to the Governing Body and to the East Gadsden Congregation Body of Elders.

                                          December 23, 1981

East Gadsden Congregation Body of Elders
Gadsden AL

Dear Brothers:

     By means of this letter I am withdrawing my appeal of the
decision to disfellowship me. My reason for doing so is as
follows:

     On the basis of testimony that I had eaten a meal on one
occasion with Peter Gregerson since the publication of the
September 15, 1981, Watchtower, the initial judicial committee
decided to disfellowship me. That forty years of full-time
service could be discounted on such a petty basis indicates
to me that there is no real concern to take into account my
conscientious feelings, expressed in detail in my letter of
December 8, 1981, nor concern to show me from Scripture wherein
I have erred.

     Additionally, the selection of the membership of the appeal
committee, as made by the circuit overseer, gives no real basis
for expecting a fair consideration in my case. The selection
made, as pointed out in my letter of December 20, 1981, was of
three persons who are obviously among those least likely to be
able to handle my case in an objective way, free from the
influence of personal feeling. I can think of no justification
for the selection made, and believe it makes a travesty of justice.

     There seems to be no evidence to indicate that the Governing
Body is desirous of providing any aid or relief for me, since my
letter of November 5, 1981, has now gone approximately seven weeks
with no response to me. While the chairman of the initial
judicial committee has stated that he called the Service Department
on more than one occasion, the conversations give no indication
of relief since, according to the chairman, they said that 'nothing
has changed and to go ahead.'

     Finally, I now know that effort is being made, by phone, even
by long distance, to try to find something to use against me in
an effort to incriminate me. This has been done in the last few
days, since my turning in my letter of December 20, 1981, request-
ing a different appeal committee. Even though the person contacted
has never made any complaint about me, the request is made to
see if they can remember anything I said that might be viewed as
improper. Surely if I were responsible for making a disturbance
in the congregation, one of a genuinely perverse or malicious
kind, it would never be necessary to resort to such methods to
substantiate such a charge.

East Gadsden Congregation Body of Elders
December 23, 1981, Page II

The continuation of such method can only result in further damaging of my good name and character. It is an open invitation to suspicion and gossip.

My feelings are as those of the apostle at Galatians 6:16: "Henceforth let no one be making trouble for me, for I am **carrying** on my body the brand marks of a slave of Jesus." For the past eight weeks my wife and I have been subjected to much mental anguish, not merely by the repeated visits and more than a dozen phone calls (to the point where the ring of the phone became an unpleasant sound), but more especially by the attitude manifested. Now there is added to all this the knowledge that a surreptitious inquiry is being carried on that is clearly adverse to my rightful interests. I experienced similar treatment last year in New York, where similar efforts were made for one month--and not one word was said to me during that time to indicate to me that my conduct was in any way under accusation, this despite the fact that a clear opportunity was given by me for those conducting the inquiry to express such. I have no desire to undergo similar mistreatment again, particularly since there is nothing to indicate that the truth of the matter can be made known in such a way as to remove the unwarranted stain produced. That must rest in God's hands. --Matthew 10:26.

My withdrawal of my appeal should in no way be construed as an acknowledgment of guilt or an acceptance of the disfellowshiping decision as being in any sense proper, just or Scriptural. Again with the apostle I can say: "Now to me it is a very trivial matter that I should be examined by you or by a human tribunal. Even I do not examine myself. For I am not conscious of anything against myself. Yet by this I am not proved righteous, but he that examines me is Jehovah." (1 Corinthians 4:3, 4) My confidence in his righteous judgment is implicit and my confidence in the rightness and truthfulness of his Word is only strengthened by what I have experienced. And as long as I have life I will endeavor to make the truth of that Word known to others for their blessing and God's praise.

As for my brothers among Jehovah's Witnesses, I can say that the good will of my heart and my supplication to God are on their behalf. I have labored conscientiously since 1938 in their spiritual interests and I assure you that if I saw any hope that my subjecting myself to further trial would result in benefit to them I would gladly endure such.--Compare Romans 9:1-3.

Respectfully,

Rt 4, Box 440-F
Cadsden AL   35904

There was little question in my mind but that those directing the whole affair had begun to feel that the "evidence" used to disfellowship me—one meal with Peter Gregerson—might appear rather weak. Rather than seek to provide the evidence from God's Word (demonstrating that my act was truly sinful) which I had requested in my appeal letter, they tried to build a stronger "case" by soliciting adverse testimony. I saw no good in further submission to this.

Eight days later, a phone call came from Larry Johnson informing me that they had received my letter and that in view of my withdrawal of my appeal, the disfellowshiping action taken by the first committee was counted as remaining in force.

That the call came on the day it did, seemed rather appropriate. I had been baptized on January 1, 1939, and exactly forty-three years later, on December 31, 1981, I experienced excommunication—the only charge serving as the basis for this being testimony that I had eaten a meal with a disassociated person.

Do I personally believe that this was the true reason for their taking the action they did? No. I believe it was simply a technicality used to achieve an objective. The end justified the means in their minds. That an organization would make use of a technicality of such pettiness, to my mind betrays a remarkably low standard for conduct and a great insecurity.

Based upon my past experience on the Governing Body of Jehovah's Witnesses, upon the conduct of its Chairman's Committee during the spring of 1980, and also upon the material published from that time until the present, my personal belief is that it was considered "advantageous" that I be disfellowshiped so as to eliminate what they considered a "threat." If so, then this too, I think, reveals a very great sense of insecurity—particularly so for a worldwide organization that claims to be God's chosen instrument, backed up by the Sovereign power of the universe, the reigning King's appointee as supervisor of all his earthly interests. This would surely *not* be the action of an organization fully at ease with its own teachings, calmly confident that what it presents is truth, solidly supported by God's Word. Nor is it the action of an organization having genuine confidence in its body of adherents, confidence that the instruction and training given have produced mature Christian men and women who do not need some maternal *magisterium* to prescribe what they shall read, discuss or think about, but who are instead capable of discerning for themselves between truth and error, through their knowledge of the Word of God.

The action *is* typical, however, of many religious organizations of the past, all the way back to the first century, organizations that felt a compelling need to eliminate anything that, *in their view*, threatened to diminish their authority over others.

In his book, *A History of Christianity*, Paul Johnson writes of methods employed during the dark period of religious intolerance which produced the Inquisition, and says:

> "Convictions of thought-crimes being difficult to secure, the Inquisition used procedures banned in other courts, and so contravened town charters, written and customary laws, and virtually every aspect of established jurisprudence."[22]

The methods employed regularly by judicial committees formed of Witness elders would be considered unworthy of the court systems of any enlightened country. The same withholding of critically important information (such as the names of hostile witnesses) also the use of anonymous informers, and similar tactics, described by historian Johnson as practiced in the Inquisition, have been employed with great frequency by these men in dealing with those not totally in agreement with the "channel," "the organization." What was true back then, is true in the vast majority of cases now, as Johnson puts it:

> "The object, quite simply, was to produce convictions at any cost; only thus, it was thought, could heresy be quenched."[23]

SHEPHERDING THE FLOCK

"Diotrephes . . . lays baseless and spiteful charges against us; not satisfied with that, he refuses to receive our friends, and he interferes with those who would do so, and tries to expel them from the congregation." —3 John 9, 10, *New English Bible*.

When questioned by outsiders, including newspaper and newsmagazine reporters, about treatment accorded to any who cannot conscientiously embrace every teaching of the Watch Tower Society, organization representatives present a picture of almost benign tolerance.

An article in the *Chicago Tribune* of June 25, 1983, quotes a Watch Tower representative, Samuel Herd, as saying:

22   Paul Johnson, *A History of Christianity* (New York: Atheneum, 1979), p. 253.
23   Ibid., pp. 253, 254.

". . . the unrest has been generated by a relatively few 'disgruntled' former members who, in most cases, 'have turned their back on Scripture.'

"'We're not spiritual policeman,' Herd said, 'We don't try to stifle anyone in his opinion.'"

The public relations director for the Canadian Branch of the Watch Tower, Walter Graham, is quoted in a Toronto newspaper as unable to understand why dissenters "feared reprisals" from the church. The article states:

"'If someone doesn't want to live by our principles, he's free to leave. There's no badgering here, no physical or emotional harassment,' he said.

"Mr. Graham added that grievances are handled at the congregational level by committees of elders. 'We don't dictate from headquarters. We have a very open organization that allows for a great deal of individuality,' he maintained."

At the international headquarters in Brooklyn, public relations representative Robert Balzer responded in similar fashion.

Those "public relations" words, however, in no way fit the facts.

Though scores of examples could be cited, one that is perhaps as illustrative as any has its source in the country of Ireland.

Two men in Dublin, friends and fellow Witnesses, read the article in *Time* magazine describing my disfellowshipment. They phoned the reporters who wrote the article, questioning them in disbelief. Then they phoned Peter Gregerson and finally me. Both were elders, one was a full-time "Pioneer," and they were among the most active Witnesses in their country. They arranged to fly to the United States in March of 1982. They spent five days with us. Each in his own way seemed prototypically Irish—Martin Merriman was rosy-cheeked with dark, curly hair and quick of wit, John May was lean and blond with a rather poetic nature and speech. They were both completely uninhibited in the questions they put to us.

After five days, they told us that their real interest in coming to the United States was to express to the Governing Body personally the concern they and others in Ireland felt as to the harsh trend evident in the organization. They asked what possibility I saw of their being heard by the Body? I told them I thought it remote in the extreme, a virtually futile effort, that at best they might hope to have one or two Members meet with them in a private room. They seemed inclined to doubt that this was really so. To them it was the most natural thing in the world that the members of the Governing Body, being their Christian brothers, would be willing to give them at least a brief audience in the interest of the Irish field in which they were so active. As Martin Merriman later expressed it:

> "We had complete confidence that our Governing Body would meet with us and straighten the whole matter out—no question about it."

Following their departure from Gadsden, they telephoned Governing Body member Jack Barr. Barr's wife had been a missionary in Ireland and knew John May's family well. They told Jack that they had been in Gadsden, had talked with Peter and me and had questions they wanted resolved. Startled, he asked, "Do you think that was wise?"

John May replied, "It may not be wise organizationally, but we're lovers of truth and the truth is what is important."

Jack told them that the members of the Governing Body were "very busy" and that he doubted that a meeting with them would be possible. They had traveled thousands of miles at great expense, they said, and wanted to speak with someone who could give them a definite answer.

The following morning they phoned Lyman Swingle, the current chairman of the Body that year. When John May introduced himself, the chairman replied, "I know who you are. You're the man who spent five days with disfellowshiped and disassociated persons. So, now you're the knight in shining armor riding a white horse across the Atlantic to set matters s†raight?" Martin says that from the look on John's face, and knowing his poetic nature, he could almost hear John say to himself, "I never thought of meself that way, but that sounds very beautiful." John, however, simply replied that he and Martin would very much like to convey to the Governing Body what they knew of matters, things that might be helpful to the Body to aid them to understand the feelings of many in Ireland. He invited Swingle to phone the Branch Office in Ireland to find out what sort of men they were, that they had not come to create trouble but simply wanted answers to honest questions in order to help the brothers back home.

He was told, "Put it in writing." He continued to urge that they be heard, but each time the reply was, "Put it in writing."

Martin then spoke, saying:

> "I can't believe that you're saying this, that you won't meet with us. If I go home and tell my brothers and sisters back in Ireland that you won't meet with us, the Governing Body won't meet with us, they'll call me a liar. In Ireland we go to the doors and brag to people that 'they can't get in to see their bishop, but that we can meet with our Governing Body.'"

He was told, "It's unprecedented." Martin responded, "Well, Brother Swingle, may I respectfully bring to your attention what it says in Acts, chapter fifteen, that Paul and Barnabas went up to Jerusalem to meet with the Governing Body." The reply was, "So, now you're Paul and Barnabas?" Martin expressed himself as hurt by the attitude taken. Again the reply, "Put it in writing."

After about twenty minutes Martin then told the Governing Body chairman:

> "Fourteen years ago I was a Roman Catholic. Jehovah's Witnesses came to see me, they raised questions in my life that I couldn't answer. So I went along to the priest, the parish priest. He said, 'Well, come in and sit down,' and he gave me tea and biscuits. Now, he couldn't answer any of me questions, Brother Swingle, but at least he paid me the courtesy of sitting down and talking to me.
>
> "Brother Swingle, I'm not asking you to meet with me. I'm not telling you to meet with me. I am *begging* you to meet with me. Because I am now at the crossroads again that I was at fourteen years ago. I am confused, I am disturbed, and I simply want my shepherds to help me."

The response to this plea? "Put it in writing." Martin says he was extremely hurt, felt like saying many things. But he says that, instead, "I wished him Jehovah's blessing, said I would certainly pray for him for I felt that he did need prayer with an attitude like that, being an elder and having that attitude."[24]

They left their phone number with the chairman and waited. Three days passed and no call came. So, they took their flight back to Shannon, Ireland, feeling, as they put it, stunned and with a feeling of disbelief at what they had heard; their whole world seemed so gloomy, for they had not wanted to hear what they heard, nor to believe that things were as they had actually found them to be.

Recall the Canadian public relations representative's statement that "we don't dictate from headquarters. We have a very open organization that allows for a great deal of individuality." Compare that with what resulted to these two Irish Witnesses.

One week after their return, a visit to the Branch Office in Ireland was scheduled and Lloyd Barry of the Governing Body arrived to carry out the assignment. Martin and John thought he might arrange to talk with them, to discuss their questions with them. He did not.

---

24 I think that the attitude expressed by the chairman was likely the attitude adopted by the Governing Body in general and which attitude he felt obliged to reflect.

But he did do something. He put in motion the judicial operations in Ireland.

The following week, John and Martin were contacted by the Branch Office, requesting that they meet with the Branch Committee. Their trip to America was the subject of considerable questioning. The upshot of the meeting was that the Branch Committee asked them not to discuss with others what they had heard in the United States.

I found personally interesting the comparison of the handling of their case and that of my own, the inequality of application of the Society's own policies. Testimony that I had eaten one meal with a disassociated man was counted as sufficient grounds for taking disfellowshiping action against me. Here, by contrast, were men who had spent five days and nights in the home of this same man, had eaten with him and me numerous times, discussed issues with us for hours on end. The Governing Body was informed of their 5-day visit. Yet no action was taken toward them.

I think the reason is evident. The Branch Office was well aware of the attitude of the Irish Witnesses, their disinclination to be dominated and dictated to; they knew the respect with which both these men were held by Witnesses throughout all the north of Ireland. They doubtless felt that they had a situation on their hands that made it "politically" advantageous not to take any strong measures.

However, *similar* to my own case, about six months later a Circuit Overseer (E. G. Watt) was sent in to the Dublin area. Not long afterward a judicial committee was formed to investigate John May and Martin Merriman. When John told Circuit Overseer Watt that their sole concern was to know the truth of matters, he was told, "What is true or false, right or wrong, is not the point. It's, 'is it in harmony with the Society's policy, and are you talking about it.'"

This statement brought John May to a point of decision. He thereafter submitted his resignation from the organization. He felt he could no longer support a system that operated according to such standards.

Martin now became the focus of attention. The Circuit Overseer visited many of the Witnesses in the Dublin area, inquiring as to any statements that Martin might have made. A number of these phoned Martin after the visit to tell him of the questioning going on. This was the action of a Society that the Canadian representative described as "a very open organization that allows for a great deal of individuality."

Martin was cited for a hearing. He notified those in charge that he wanted in writing three things: Who would form the committee; what the accusation was; who the accusers were. Returning home one day, he found Circuit Overseer Watt there. Watt told him that he did not need the information in writing (a remarkably opposite approach to matters than that which had been presented to Martin in Brooklyn where he repeatedly was told, "Put it in writing"). Martin spent about three hours in finally convincing the man that he had a right to such information in writing, eventually taking a piece of paper from one of his children's notebooks for the information to be put down. Watt gave the names of the committee members and then said there were no accusations and no accusers. Martin did not accept that and finally Watt wrote that the hearing was to 'discuss the situation that is disturbing the congregation.' (Martin felt that Watt's visits and interrogations were the factor that had produced the greatest disturbance among the Witnesses.) He asked Watt to sign the paper. It took another half an hour to persuade him to do so.

On a Saturday afternoon in the Dun Laoghaire Kingdom Hall of Jehovah's Witnesses the hearing was held. More than forty Witnesses expressed to Martin their desire to accompany him to the hearing. He accepted the request of only twenty of these. The judicial committee, composed of the Branch Coordinator, the Circuit Overseer and a local elder, were startled to see these people at the Hall. To their credit, they listened to the testimony of these people that Martin had in no way endeavored to stir up matters, had, to the contrary, tried to avoid creating any disturbance.[25]

For Martin the most surprising incident in the hearing came when he began to recount to the committee the phone conversation he and John May had had with the chairman of the Governing Body of Jehovah's Witnesses. The Branch Coordinator interrupted Martin to tell him that they had already heard the tape. Momentarily stunned, Martin said, "Tape? What tape?" The Branch Coordinator appeared somewhat flustered and then said that the Governing Body had sent the Branch Office a tape of the telephone conversation.

Thus, if any have doubt as to the content of that conversation, related earlier in this chapter, that content is confirmable at Brooklyn. This is why I have earlier expressed the thought that my telephone conversation with Chairman Albert Schroeder in the spring of 1980 is similarly confirmable. The strange concern to have on tape what others said was now plainly and undeniably compounded by the Govern-

25 The wife of the local elder on the committee sent a letter expressing these same points, having asked her husband's permission beforehand.

ing Body's admitted secret taping of the phone conversation between Lyman Swingle and the two Witnesses from Ireland, John May and Martin Merriman.

No action was taken against Martin Merriman by the judicial committee. The Branch Coordinator, Arthur Matthews, openly stated that the motives of Martin and John were never in question. This was a commendable expression. Yet the official Governing Body policy was that John May, as a disassociated person, was not to be spoken to by other Witnesses.

Subsequently, a special visit to Ireland by Governing Body member Jack Barr, accompanied by a man from the Brooklyn Writing Staff, Robert Pevy (who had once served in Ireland as a missionary), was arranged by the Governing Body. They addressed the Witnesses in the Dublin area, their talks emphasizing the importance of "loyalty to the organization."

After the talks, Martin Merriman approached Jack Barr on the platform, introducing himself by saying, "Brother Barr, I'm the face behind the telephone." When Barr looked puzzled, Martin gave him his name. Barr replied, "Oh, Brother Merriman—it's good to see your face." Martin replied, "Well, that's very nice of you to say that, Brother Barr. The only thing is I'd rather have heard it six months ago when I was in New York." He asked if Barr would take the time to meet with him to discuss his questions. He pointed out that there was widespread concern in Ireland about the Governing Body's policy regarding persons who disassociated themselves, the implication that even to say "hello" to such was improper. He referred to John May as a "good, decent man," and, turning to Branch Coordinator Matthews who was standing alongside, he said, "Isn't that right, Arthur?" Arthur replied, "John is a righteous man." Martin informed Governing Body Member Jack Barr that he had made it clear to the Branch and was now making clear to Barr that 'he would not treat John May as a wicked person, that he would eat with him at any time.' Again, the Governing Body member did not find it convenient to meet with Martin to discuss his questions.

Following this visit of the representatives from Brooklyn, word reached Martin that Witnesses were again being interrogated, questioned as to any conversations with him. Having heard that a "harder line" had been decided upon, on October 27, 1982, after fourteen years of intensely active association, Martin submitted his resignation from the congregation.

Why did he and John May (and their wives) reach this decision? It was not what these men heard in conversation with Peter Gregerson and myself that brought them to that decision. They left Gadsden with the expressed intent to continue as members of Jehovah's Witnesses, contributing in whatever way they could for the good of the organization. They left with the strong hope that improvement was possible, that the Governing Body would recognize their sincerity and honest intent.

The real credit (if it may be called that) for their decision to disassociate themselves rests outside Gadsden, Alabama. It rests in Brooklyn—where their conversations with members of the Governing Body took place, where one of those conversations was secretly taped, and from where the directives went out to the Branch Committee in Ireland to put in motion the program of investigation and interrogation of two sincere Christian men who wanted only good for Jehovah's Witnesses. I am satisfied that if it had not been for what they saw of the organization's actions and spirit *after* they left Alabama, they would still be associated with Jehovah's Witnesses. The organization had no time to discuss their questions and concerns with them when they were at its doorstep. But it was willing to send emissaries across the ocean, at great expense, and to have long hours spent in investigation and in interrogation of others, to protect "the interests of the organization." The Governing Body may not want to accept the responsibility for the decision these men arrived at, they may deny that responsibility, but it remains theirs nonetheless. It was, more than anything else, their speech, their attitude, their course of action that were the decisive— and disillusioning—factors.

The experience of these two men has essentially been that of hundreds of others. The closer they got to their "shepherds," the more the outward velvety softness gave way to unyielding, iron-cold hardness.

May I say once more, a final time: I do not think the coldness or the hardness, the aloof, superior, even smug attitude experienced, is owing to the normal personality of most of the men involved. I believe it owes very definitely to the false teaching that allows an organization to make claims of exclusive authority and unapproachable superiority that are both immodest and unfounded. That concept deserves not only to be questioned, it deserves to be exposed for the hurtful, God-dishonoring doctrine that it is.

12

PERSPECTIVE

"Therefore we do not lose heart. Though out-
wardly we are wasting away, yet inwardly we
are being renewed day by day. For our light
and momentary troubles are achieving for us
an eternal glory that far outweighs them all.
So we fix our eyes not on what is seen, but on
what is unseen. For what is seen is temporary,
but what is unseen is eternal."
—2 Corinthians 4:16–18, *New International*
Version.

THIS, then, is my account. These are the fundamental issues that
produced in me a crisis of conscience. The effect they had, my
feelings, reactions, conclusions reached, are set forth. The reader can
assess them for whatever they are worth. Simply put, my question is:
How would your own conscience have been affected?

What with some four thousand million people on earth and only
God knows how many generations in the past, the life of any one
person is but a minute fraction of the whole. We are very tiny drops
in a very big stream. Yet Christianity teaches us that, small and inconsequential as we are, we can each contribute good to others that is out
of proportion to our own smallness.[1] Faith makes that possible, and,
as the apostle expresses it, "the love the Christ has compels us."[2]

We do not need the bulk of a big organization to back us up, nor its
headship, control, proddings and pressure, to accomplish this. Heart
appreciation for God's undeserved kindness in making life a "free gift,"

---

1 1 Corinthians 3:6, 7; 2 Corinthians 4:7, 15; 6:10.
2 2 Corinthians 5:14.

not dependent on works but on faith, is sufficient, more than enough, to motivate us. "Since God so loved us, we also ought to love one another."[3] If we respect and cherish our Christian freedom, we will respond to no other compulsion. Neither will we submit to any other yoke than the one offered in these words:

> "Come to me, all you who are weary and burdened, and I will give you rest. Take my yoke upon you and learn from me, for I am gentle and humble in heart, and you will find rest for your souls. For my yoke is easy and my burden is light."[4]

I feel certain that when life comes to its close the only thing that will, in retrospect, bring any true sense of satisfaction is the extent to which life was used to contribute to the welfare of others, primarily spiritually, and, secondarily, emotionally, physically and materially.

I cannot believe that "ignorance is bliss," or that there is any kindness in encouraging people to live in illusions. Sooner or later, illusion must meet up with reality. The longer it takes for this to happen, the more traumatic the transition—brought on by disillusionment—can be. I am only glad it did not take any longer than it did in my own case.

That is why I have written what I have written. I have sincerely sought to be accurate throughout the account. Based on what has happened already and what has been published and circulated through rumors and gossip, I have no doubt but that effort will be made to disparage the significance of the information. If anything that could be called error—even if it be the difference of one day in a date, the difference of 1 in a figure, a misplaced comma in a quotation, misspelled name, or any other such mistakes—can be found, I think it entirely likely that there are those who would use such things or comparable ones, to say, "The book is full of errors." Whatever may be said, I can only say that I am willing to stand by what I have presented. If there are errors, I will be grateful to anyone who will point such out to me and will do whatever I can to make correction.

What does the future hold for the organization of Jehovah's Witnesses and its central Governing Body? Though often asked this, I have no way of knowing. Time alone will tell.

There are some things that I feel a measure of certainty about, but only a few. I do not personally think there will be any mass movement

---

3 1 John 4:11, NIV.
4 Matthew 11:28–30, NIV.

out of the organization. It presently is reporting fair growth in a number of countries. The vast majority of Jehovah's Witnesses are simply unaware of the realities of the authority structure. From lifelong experience among them, in many countries, I know that for a large percentage the organization has a certain "aura," as though a luminous radiation surrounds it, giving its pronouncements an importance above and beyond that normally accorded the words of imperfect men. The teachings take on an esoteric quality, "esoteric" referring to "that which is designed for and understood only by the specially initiated," generally those of a private, exclusive group. Most assume that Governing Body sessions are on a high level, manifesting more than ordinary Scriptural knowledge and spiritual wisdom. As Witnesses, all are, in fact, admonished thus:

> "After being nourished to our present spiritual strength and maturity, do we suddenly become smarter than our former provider and forsake the enlightening guidance of the organization that mothered us?"[5]

There are constant admonitions to be humble, which translates into accepting whatever the organization provides as coming from a source of superior wisdom. The fact that the average Witness has only a misty idea of the way that the leadership arrives at its conclusions adds to the aura of esoteric wisdom. It is, they are told, "the only organization on earth that understands the 'deep things of God'."[6]

Few of them have ever confronted the issues dealt with in this book, the challenge to conscience they raise. I incline to believe that many, perhaps most, would prefer not to face them. Some have personally expressed their feeling to me that they enjoy their friendships within the organization and would not want to see these disturbed. I also enjoyed mine and had no desire to see them disturbed; I felt, and still feel, affection for the people with whom I spent most of my life. But I also felt that there were issues of truth and honesty, of fairness and justice, of love and mercy, that were bigger than those friendships and my enjoyment of them.

By this I am not saying that I think anyone should precipitate difficulty, seek or force a confrontation that is unnecessary. I can sympathize wholeheartedly with those who are of families composed of Jehovah's Witnesses and who know full well the wrenching effect it could have on family relationships if the members were called upon

---

5 The *Watchtower*, February 1, 1952, p. 80.
6 The *Watchtower*, July 1, 1973, p. 402.

to treat a son or daughter, brother or sister, father or mother, as an "apostate," a God-rejected, spiritually unclean person. I have never encouraged anyone to precipitate such a situation; I tried to avoid precipitating it in my own case.

But given the present climate in the organization, it is becoming increasingly difficult to avoid this without compromising conscience, without 'acting a part,' pretending to believe what one may not believe, what one may actually believe to be a perversion of the Word of God, producing unchristian fruitage, hurtful results.

I know a number of persons who have tried to withdraw quietly and some who are, in a sense, "in hiding," persons who have actually gone to the extent of moving to another area and who have sought to keep their whereabouts unknown (organizationally) so as to avoid harassment. I could cite case after case where, despite all efforts at avoiding confrontation, elders have sought the persons out, their only concern apparently being to extract from them some statement of their position—not toward God, Christ or the Bible—but toward "the organization." If the persons fail in this "loyalty test," presented as a clear ultimatum, they are almost always disfellowshiped, cut off from friends and family if these are members of the organization.

Typical is the recent experience of one young woman, a wife and mother, in southern Michigan. She had been interrogated by the elders because of her doubts about certain teachings and had been so emotionally affected by the experience that she had withdrawn from attending meetings. After some months, a phone call came from the elders requesting that she meet with them again. She said she did not want to undergo that experience again. They urged her to do it, saying that they wanted to help her with her doubts and that this would be the last time they would ask her to meet with them. Her husband, not a Witness, recommended that she go and "have it over with." She went.

As she said, "Within the first ten minutes I could see the direction they were taking." Half an hour from the start of their questioning they had disfellowshiped her. She says the time factor alone stunned her. As she put it, "I couldn't believe they were doing this. I sat there the whole time sobbing and within thirty minutes they had 'kicked me out of the Kingdom.' I would have thought they would have got down on the floor with tears in their eyes, pleading with me for hours, to prevent that from happening." One of the five elders, a man who dozed off during the discussion, later said in her hearing, "The nerve of that woman to say that she wasn't sure if this was God's organization or not."

If efforts to avoid the unwanted confrontation fail, I think there is consolation in knowing that the reason for any family distress and heartache rests on one side only. It is fully and entirely the fruitage of an organizational policy, one that is backed by the threat of expulsion for anyone who does not comply with the policy, anyone who fails to treat disassociated or disfellowshiped persons, no matter how sincere and devoted one may know them to be, as though they were rejected by God. The religious intolerance that acts as the divisive force, destructive of family oneness and affection, is not mutual therefore. As in Jesus' day, it comes from one side, one source, a source that equates conscientious disagreement with disloyalty.[7] There is where the real responsibility for the emotional hurt and distress ultimately rests.

Many Witnesses, though deeply concerned over what they see, find it difficult to adjust to the thought of serving God without being connected to some powerful organization, having the benefit of its largeness, its strength of numbers. True, Jehovah's Witnesses are a small organization compared to many, but they are widespread. Their visible structures are not as impressive as those of the Vatican or of other major religions; nonetheless, the expanding international headquarters, which now owns a sizeable chunk of Brooklyn, the many Branch facilities, some with large printing establishments, all built or bought at the cost of millions of dollars and staffed by hundreds of workers (in Brooklyn, by about two thousand), the large Assembly Halls and the many thousands of Kingdom Halls (not a few costing more than a quarter million dollars to build), are sufficient to impress the average person. Every new acquisition or expansion of material properties is hailed as indicative of divine blessing and evidence of the organization's spiritual prosperity and success. Above all, the teaching that they are, exclusively, the one people on earth with whom God has dealings, and that the direction they receive from the Governing Body is from a divine "channel," helps produce a sense of cohesion, of specialness. The view of all other persons as "worldings" contributes to this feeling of a close-knit relationship.

Because of this, I think it is equally as difficult for the average Witness to contemplate serving God without these things as it was for Jewish persons in the first century to contemplate such service apart from the religious arrangements they were accustomed to. The impressive temple buildings and courtyards at Jerusalem, with temple service carried out by a large staff of hundreds and thousands of ded-

---

7 Matthew 10:17, 21; Mark 13:9–12; Luke 21:16.

icated workers, Levites and priests, their claim to be exclusively the chosen people of God, with all others viewed as unclean, stood in tremendous contrast to the Christians of that time, who had no large buildings, who met in simple homes, who had no separate priestly or Levite class, and who humbly acknowledged that 'in every nation the man that fears God and works righteousness is acceptable to him.'[8]

Quite a number, particularly among elders of Jehovah's Witnesses, express the sincere hope that some kind of "reform" will take place to correct the wrongs they are conscious of, both doctrinally and organizationally. Some suggest that this may come about by a change of personnel in the leadership. Even before I went on my leave of absence from the headquarters in early 1980, a member of a Branch Committee of a major country, a discerning person who realized the distress I felt over the existing attitudes and situation, said to me, "Ray, don't give up! These are old men, they will not live forever." This expression was not reflective of a hard, unfeeling, cynical personality, for the person who spoke it is just the opposite of that; he is a very kind, warmhearted man. Such expressions are often born of a belief that some change *must* come, that the trend toward an ever harder line and an increasingly dogmatic stance *must* give way to a more Christian approach, a more humble presentation of beliefs.

Personally, I do not believe that any fundamental change will come simply through men in authority dying. I say *fundamental* change, for there have been changes in varying degrees throughout the history of the movement, some as a result of the deaths of Russell and Rutherford. Whatever these changes, the basic foundation has remained the same. The change in the authority structure in 1975–76 was as major an adjustment as has taken place in the whole history of the organization. Authority was spread out to a body of men, with many new faces coming to the fore. Yet the power of traditional beliefs and traditional policies has overcome any effort to bring about a change from speculative interpretations, dogmatism, Talmudic legalism, control by an elite group, repressive measures, in favor of a simple brotherhood, united in essentials, tolerant and yielding in non-essentials, both in belief and practice.

As was true of previous Society presidents, the present president, Fred Franz, has been a leader figure and, although the presidency itself was stripped of virtually all its intrinsic power in the decentral-

8 Acts 10:35.

izing action of 1975–76, he personally remains very influential. He is now in his nineties. There is no question but that his passing would affect and alter the picture, for there is no one of a charismatic personality like his (or like that of his predecessors, Russell, Rutherford and Knorr) among the remaining members of the Governing Body. Since the doctrinal superstructure that developed from the death of Judge Rutherford in 1942 onward is essentially the product of the writings of Fred Franz, and much of the basic policy regarding "disfellowshiping" issues likewise his, the possibility of doctrinal changes or "adjustments" clearly becomes greater in his absence.

I am, however, personally inclined to feel that whatever changes come will be minor and will not alter the basic doctrinal position and attitude of the organization to any major extent. Of the Governing Body members who would remain, there is no one with the ability to couch new interpretations in the impressive language and intricate argumentation found in his writings. Most of the members do very little writing, some none at all. Lloyd Barry is the only one who has written books and these have been simply restatements of existing views with nothing new advanced.[9] The organization's other principal writers are not members of the Body nor do they profess to be of the "anointed" class.

If the ultimate effect of the restructuring of 1975–76 was like moving the inner walls of a house around, then any future changing of personnel within the administration might be compared to a rearranging of the furniture or adding new pieces—in both cases the house itself remains the same. Aside from the president, of the fourteen remaining members of the Governing Body, those exercising the most powerful influence currently are Milton Henschel, Ted Jaracz and Lloyd Barry.[10] It would be unusual if anything these members combined in favoring were not unquestioningly supported by members Carey Barber, Martin Poetzinger, Jack Barr and George Gangas. Though somewhat more individualistic than these last four mentioned, Albert Schroeder and Karl Klein would probably follow suit in most cases. The votes of this number would be determinative.

If the past is any indication, the direction taken by those leading members will follow a conservative line, resisting any course or rec-

9 Books written by Lloyd Barry include *Good News to Make You Happy* (published in 1976) and *"Let Your Kingdom Come"* (published in 1981).
10 Grant Suiter would have been included with these three, largely from his having long been an officer of the Society. However, in 1983 he suffered a tragic accident which left him completely paralyzed. He died a few months later.

ommendation that does not uphold and promote the traditional teachings, methods and policies now in force. What has been published and done in the past few years gives no basis whatsoever for expecting the kind of "reform" some feel must come. It is true that many of the Governing Body members are in their seventies and eighties. Any new replacements, however, will have to meet the approval of the remaining members and particularly of those with dominant influence. There is no question but that it is becoming more and more difficult to find "suitable" candidates for membership on the Body in view of the dwindling number of "anointed" men. This may some day oblige the Governing Body to back away from its fundamental requirement that its membership is open only to those of such class. That would be difficult to harmonize with their doctrine about the privileged status of the "faithful and discreet slave class," and may be avoided as long as possible. They may be helped by the fact that periodically younger members of the organization decide that they are "of the anointed" and thus become possible candidates for membership in the Body.

A major mistake in looking for reform from the direction of personnel changes is, I believe, in thinking that the situation owes to the men in charge. Only in a secondary sense is that the case. Primarily, it is not the men. It is the *concept* that controls, the *premise* on which the whole movement is founded.

It can never be overlooked that what most markedly distinguishes the beliefs of Jehovah's Witnesses is not their disbelief of eternal torment or of the inherent immortality of the soul or of the trinity, nor their use of the name Jehovah, or their belief in a paradise earth. Every one of these features can be found in other religious organizations.[11]

What especially distinguishes their teachings from any other denomination is the keystone doctrine centered on 1914 as the date when Christ's active rulership began, his commencing judgment then and, above all, his selecting the Watch Tower organization as his official channel, his assigning full control of all his earthly interests to a "faithful and discreet slave class" and, factually, giving ultimate authority to its ruling body. Any abandoning of that keystone teaching would affect

11 Not only the various "Bible Student" associations, several of which are international, but also some Church of God affiliations hold nearly identical beliefs in these same areas; the Seventh Day Adventist churches believe in soul sleep, do not believe in eternal torment, do believe in a paradise earth ruled by Christ's kingdom.

the whole doctrinal structure and is extremely unlikely, would be very difficult to explain. The past few years have seen just the opposite, a determined effort through the columns of the *Watchtower* and other publications to shore up their defense of the interpretations surrounding that date or resulting from it, to sustain faith in the claims based on it. Most important among those claims is that related to organizational authority, and here again there is presently a very intensive campaign to solidify support of, and loyalty to, that authority structure.

True, each year that passes places more of a strain on that teaching and those claims. 1984 marks seventy years since 1914. Eventually the teaching about the "generation" living in 1914 may become just too difficult to sustain with any credibility. But there are various "adjustments" that might be advanced, some of these having been considered in Chapter 9, and the claims could still be retained in an altered form.

Organizationally, moves are being made to go back to more centralized authority (additional "tacking"). In the spring of 1983, a new organization manual restored the position of a more or less permanent presiding overseer as chairman in the bodies of elders, as well as other centralizing features designed to give greater control on down the line of organizational supervision. Whether this will lead to a re-centralization of authority on the Governing Body itself, with a permanent chairman or overall coordinator, remains to be seen. It seems rather unlikely that the present president of the Society would be so selected, since he has no particular propensity toward administrative work. His logical successor would be Milton Henschel, and such a restructuring within the Body with him filling the new position would seem considerably more likely.

Whatever the changes that come, they will most certainly be heralded as the product of divine direction, and the past doctrines or arrangements that may be discarded will be depicted as 'God's will for that time,' perhaps some kind of "maneuvering' by the heavenly Captain, Christ Jesus, in working toward an end that was ultimately beneficial. As in the past one hundred years of the organization's history, there is little reason to believe that the changes will be acknowledged for what they are—generally the result of failing to hold to the Scriptures in the first place, and, in most cases, changes made under the pressure of circumstances, designed to ward off foreseen dilemmas because of a position that has become untenable. This is not at all the same as corrections that are made by persons who search the Scriptures and, as a result of what they discover there, freely admit that they have been in error and wish to rectify their mistakes.

In all of this the basic premise will be persistently upheld, the concept that dominates the thinking, the writing and the action. It is that premise—that God *must* deal with humans through an organization and that his king Jesus Christ has chosen the Watch Tower organization for this role—that hinders many discerning persons from seeing where the true problem lies. As the saying is, they 'cannot see the forest for the trees.' They can see the individual inconsistencies and injustices, the falsity of many teachings, the devious nature of many of the arguments, the unchristian spirit of many of the approaches. But they cannot see what this all adds up to, what the sum total is. They see the parts but not the whole. Some of these persons are in positions of major responsibility. They cling to the hope—even as I clung to the hope—that the future will see great improvements, because their thinking is molded to the organizational premise. They feel that God *must* do something to straighten matters out because that premise or concept must be proved true; God must uphold and vindicate it. Yet that premise lies at the root of the very wrongs they personally lament. It is a concept that did not originate with God. There is no reason to believe that He will feel compelled to support it.

I think here of a saying that was passed on to me by a friend. It says:

> "The mind which renounces, once and forever, a futile hope, has its compensation in ever growing calm."

I have found that saying true in my own case. I know that it has proved true in the case of many others.

Whatever the initial distress—a distress that sometimes follows the demeaning experience of being interrogated by men who, in effect, strip one of human dignity, make the weight of their authority felt, and presume to judge adversely one's standing with God—however torn one may feel inside, afterward there does come a distinct feeling of relief, of peace. It is not just knowing that one is finally outside the reach of such men, no longer subject to their ecclesiastical scrutiny and pressure. Truth, and the refusal to compromise truth, brings freedom in other fine and wonderful ways. The more responsibly one makes use of that freedom the finer the benefits.

The greatest freedom enjoyed is that of being able to serve God and his Son—as well as serve for the good of all persons—untrammeled by the dictates of imperfect men, the freedom to serve according to the dictates of one's own conscience. The sense of having a great burden lifted off, the lightening of a heavy load, comes with that freedom. If genuinely appreciated, this gives one the desire to do, not less, but more in service to the Ones giving that freedom.[12]

Traumatic as the initial transition may be, it can lead to the development of a truly *personal* relationship with these two greatest Friends. The organization has so persistently pushed its own self to the fore, has occupied such a large place on the spiritual scene, focusing so much attention on its own importance, that it has kept many from the closeness of fellowship with the heavenly Father that should have been theirs. The figure of the organization has loomed so large that it has overshadowed the greatness of God's own Son, has clouded the vision of many from appreciating the warm relationship he invites persons to share with him, has distorted their perception of his compassionate personality.[13] It is not surprising, then, that many persons, if expelled from the organization, feel a sense of aloneness, of being adrift, floundering, due to no longer being tied to some visible authority structure, no longer having their lives channeled into its rigid routine of programmed activity, no longer feeling the restrictive pressures of its policies and rulings.

In a sense, it seems that often one must undergo a measure of such painful adjustment to come to appreciate fully what complete dependence on God and his Son really means. I do not know personally of anyone who, in such circumstances, has recognized the need to draw closer to God, to give serious attention to the reading of his Word, to show interest in others by trying to be of spiritual uplift and encouragement, who has not been able to weather the experience well, to come through it feeling greatly strengthened, more strongly fixed on the only solid foundation, faith in God's provision of his Son.[14] They have realized more than ever before the intimate relationship they have with their Master and Owner as *his* disciples, whom he treats as personal friends, not like sheep that men have penned off in a mass enclosure, but sheep to whom the Shepherd gives individual, personal attention and care. Whatever their age, whatever the length of time it took them to come to this realization, the feeling they have fits the

12 Galatians 5:1, 13, 14; 1 Corinthians 9:1, 19; Colossians 3:17, 23–25.
13 Matthew 11:28–30; Mark 9:36, 37; 10:13–16; Luke 15:1–7; John 15:11–15.
14 Psalm 31:11–16; 55:2–6, 12–14, 22; 60:11, 12; 94:17–22; Romans 5:1–11; 8:31–39.

well-known saying, "Today is the first day of the rest of my life." Their outlook is both happy and positive, for their hopes and aspirations are dependent, not on men, but on God.

To feel this way does not imply any failure to recognize that there is indeed a flock of God, a congregation headed by Christ Jesus. God's Son gave the assurance that he would have true followers, not just in the first century or in this twentieth century, but in all the centuries in between, for he said, "I am with you *always, to the close of the age.*"[15] Intermixed though they were among all the "weeds" that were bound to come, he would know who these genuine disciples were, *not* because they belonged to some organization but because of what they *were*, as *persons*. Wherever they were, however indistinguishable from the human standpoint their being part of his congregation may have been, down through the centuries he has known them and led them as their Head, their Master. His apostle tells us, "But God's firm foundation stands, bearing this seal: 'The Lord knows those who are his.'"[16] Why should we doubt that this continues to be the case right up to the present time? God's Word shows that it is not up to men—not even possible for men—to separate people out so as to say that they have now gathered all the "wheat" into one neat enclosure. The Scriptures make clear that only when God's Son makes known his judgments will that identification become manifest.[17]

It is a pleasure now to be free to meet people and not feel obliged to look for some "label" in order to know how to view them. One feels no need to classify them automatically as either a Witness or a "worldling," as either "in the Truth" or "part of the Devil's organization," as either someone who, by virtue of having the Witness "label", is automatically one's "Brother" or "Sister" or, because of lacking such, is a person only to be "witnessed to" but unworthy to associate with on a friendly basis. In place of this, there is a healthful feeling of being able to do what is fair and just by assessing each person in an unbiased way for what he or she is—as a person. It is reassuring to be able to do this because of knowing that "God is not partial, but in every nation the man that fears him and works righteousness is acceptable to him."[18]

---

15 Matthew 28:20, RSV.
16 2 Timothy 2:19, RSV.
17 Compare Matthew 13:37–43 with Romans 2:5–10, 16; 14:10–12; 1 Corinthians 4:3–5; 2 Corinthians 5:10; 10:12, 18; 2 Timothy 4:1.
18 Acts 10:35.

Certainly one of the most painful experiences for many who have tried to be true to conscience is to realize how quickly long-term friendships can end, how abruptly an atmosphere of apparent love can change to one of cold distrust. A Witness in a southern state, one of the most active in her congregation, began to see how far the organization had strayed from Scriptural teaching. She told an acquaintance that, despite this, she had no thought of withdrawing. As she expressed herself, "There are so many people in our congregation that I personally studied the Bible with and helped to bring into association with the congregation. I feel a deep love for them and for others and for that reason I feel I should stay. I can't walk away from these people I love." Not long after this, the elders, becoming aware that she had reservations about some teachings, began questioning her "loyalty." Almost overnight, attitudes toward her underwent change. She found herself being convicted by congregational innuendo and gossip. As she said, "I discovered that the deep love I thought existed was actually a one-way thing. Without even talking to me to find out how I really felt, persons I had dearly loved suddenly turned cold to me."

When your very reverence, devotion and integrity toward God have been defamed—the greatest calumny possible—it is a chilling experience to hear someone that you considered a solid friend say, "I don't know what happened and I prefer not to know." Or to learn that such a one has said, "I don't know the facts but whatever the organization did there must have been a good reason."

All too often the vaunted love claimed as part of the "spiritual paradise" shows itself to be quite superficial. In a phone conversation, a Witness in a nearby state, still actively associated, told me that her husband, a prominent elder in their city, had for some time been under considerable pressure from other local elders. "If they could get anything at all against him, they'd hang him from the highest tree," she said. My comment was that this reminded me of the saying, "With friends like these, who needs enemies?" "You don't know how many times we've repeated that," she replied.

My feelings are like those contained in a letter from a person who had experienced cold rejection and who wrote:

> "Even the hurt I felt when many former friends of many years chose to believe these stories rather than come to me and find out the truth, was dimmed by my joy . . . and also the knowledge that the reason they were acting this way was because of the fear in them. I can really forgive them from my heart because I truly know how they felt—at best that I had abandoned Jehovah (by leaving his organization) and at worst that I was deceived and led astray by

Satan. Either way put me in an unapproachable position. I am really sorry for any hurt that I have caused them or anyone in the organization. I really love them and would do anything in my power to reach them and try to explain the truth of what is happening to me."

My feelings coincide because I believe that the turning off one's affection with the apparent ease of turning off a light switch is also a product of organizational indoctrination, not something normal to most persons' natural feelings.

Whatever the case, the Witness who follows his or her conscience may indeed find terminated virtually every friendship that he or she has had. In such circumstance, one surely needs to embrace the attitude voiced by the psalmist:

"In case my own father and my own mother did leave me, even Jehovah himself would take me up."[19]

Only an increased awareness of God's friendship and that of his Son can compensate, can put all other relationships in proper perspective as to their relative worth. Though it may take time, there is good reason to trust that other friendships will become available, if one is willing to make the needed effort. And there is a likelihood that they will prove more enduring, the affection being predicated, not on organizational membership, a sort of "club spirit," but on what one really is as a person, on the Christian qualities demonstrated, the realities of one's heart. I did not personally lose all my friends by any means. But for every one that I did lose I have found another. They are persons who have made clear that they are determined not to let differences of opinion or viewpoint have a disruptive effect on that friendship. This follows the counsel given:

"Accept life with humility and patience, generously making allowances for each other because you love each other. Make it your aim to be at one in the Spirit, and you will be bound together in peace."[20]

It may be difficult, because of being so long accustomed to the extreme emphasis placed on numbers and the pretension that numerical growth is proof of divine direction and blessing, to take a humbler, more modest outlook, to scale down one's viewpoint in such areas. For the first time, one may come to appreciate and cherish Jesus' assurance that 'where two or three are gathered together in his name

19   Psalm 27:10; compare Psalm 31:10; 38:11, 50:20; 69:8, 9, 20; 73:25, 28.
20   Ephesians 4:2, 3, *Phillips Modern English* translation.

he is present with them.' In my own experience, I can say that sharing with only one or two others in reading and discussing the Scriptures has proved fully satisfying and rewarding. True, when at times a larger number of persons have shared with us in these Bible discussions, there has been a greater degree of interest and variety of comment. Yet the fundamental strengthening power and richness of God's Word have not been diminished on those occasions when we have been just "two or three." I can honestly say, in each case, that it has resulted in my carrying away with me things worth remembering to a greater extent than on so many occasions in the past when I met with hundreds, thousands, tens of thousands of persons in organizationally pro- grammed functions.

It takes faith to trust that this will prove true. But this is related to another of the benefits of the freedom that upholding God's truth brings, namely, that in place of feeding on a strictly regimented "diet" pre- pared by a human authority structure, one can rediscover God's Word for what it really is, for what it actually says. It is surprising how refreshing it can be to read the Scriptures and simply let them speak for themselves, without being "overprinted" by the traditional teach- ings of men. One person, in a southern state, who said that in her association as a Witness she had never failed to report activity every month for forty-seven years, with equally regular attendance at all meetings, expressed how thrilling she now found her reading of the Scriptures, saying, "I never felt moved to stay up until 2 a.m. reading the *Watchtower* but now I find myself doing just that with the Bible."

After being accustomed to intricate interpretations, complex argu- ments, and imaginative allegorizing of the Scriptures, it may also be difficult to recognize and accept the remarkable simplicity of the Bible's actual message. It may be hard to realize that Jesus meant exactly what he said when, after stating the principle that "whatever you wish that men would do to you, do so to them," he went on to say, "for this *is* the law and the prophets."[21] That shows that the whole intent, the whole thrust of all the inspired Scriptures then in existence was to teach men and women to love. This harmonizes with Jesus' declara- tion that on the two commandments of loving God and loving one's neighbor "depend all the law and the prophets."[22] Note, not only the law but also "the prophets."

21   Matthew 7:12, RSV.
22   Matthew 22:40, RSV.

Prophecy then has as its aim not the development of some speculative interpretation and highly imaginative application to certain dates and events in modern times (which application often changes as the passing of time makes it unsuitable), nor to supply the means for boasting of an organization's supposed superior relationship to God. All prophecy is designed to lead us to the "son of God's love," that we might learn love through him, and live in love as he lived in love. Thus, we read that, "The bearing witness to Jesus is what inspires prophesying."[23]

Whenever Scripture is employed in any other way, whenever dogmatism and sectarian argumentation becloud and complicate this simple design of the Scriptures, it demonstrates that those so arguing have missed the whole purpose of the Bible.

Those who think that the imaginative interpretations just described actually constitute the "deep things of God," betray a lack of understanding of what that phrase Scripturally applies to. When the apostle Paul used the phrase (in his First Letter to the Corinthians), he had shortly before stated:

> "When I came to you, brothers, I did not come with eloquence or superior wisdom as I proclaimed to you the testimony about God. For I resolved to know nothing while I was with you except Jesus Christ and him crucified. I came to you in weakness and fear, and with much trembling. My message and my preaching were not with wise and persuasive words, but with a demonstration of the Spirit's power, so that your faith might not rest on men's wisdom, but on God's power."[24]

What he describes is exactly contrary to the type of teaching that makes people feel dependent on a human organization which produces intricate and often perplexing interpretations of prophecy that few can explain without a particular publication in their hands.

This, too, is a blessing, to be able to recognize that the truly "deep things" of Scripture relate to learning the "depth of the riches, the wisdom and the knowledge of God" expressed particularly in his mercy through Jesus Christ, that "out of his glorious riches he may strengthen you with power through his Spirit in your inner being, so that Christ may dwell in your hearts through faith. . . . that you, being rooted and established in love, may have power . . . to grasp how wide and long and high and deep is the love of Christ, and to know this love

---

23 Revelation 19:10.
24 1 Corinthians 2:1–5, 10, NIV.

that surpasses knowledge—that you may be filled to the measure of all the fullness of God."[25]

That the "good news" centers on this very expression of mercy by God through Christ and his ransom can be demonstrated by anyone who will take the time to look up each occurrence of that phrase by means of a concordance. Of the more than one hundred occurences of the expression "good news" in the Bible, there are eight references to the good news "of the kingdom," but there are scores of references to the good news "about the Christ." This is because God's kingdom, the expression of his royal sovereignty, is all centered in his Son and the things that He has done through him and will yet do through him. It is on Christ Jesus, and not on some human organization, that our attention and interest should focus, for "carefully concealed in him are all the treasures of wisdom and knowledge."[26] When compared with study, meditation and prayer that concentrate on a greater understanding of the depth of God's mercy and love and goodness, the writings found in some explanations of prophecy, however intriguing or mystifying or exotic, prove superficial indeed.

It is pleasant, then, to be able to read God's Word without feeling compelled to fix with absolute precision the meaning of every portion, or to explain every prophetic statement in an authoritative application. For what the apostle Paul wrote still holds true:

> "For our knowledge and our prophecy alike are partial, and the partial vanishes when wholeness comes. . . . Now we see only puzzling reflections in a mirror, but then we shall see face to face. My knowledge now is partial; then it will be whole, like God's knowledge of me. In a word there are three things that last for ever: faith, hope, and love; but the greatest of them is love."[27]

If our love for God, his Son and fellow humans is enhanced and upbuilt by our reading of the Scriptures, then that reading has undeniably served its major purpose. There are many points in the Scriptures that are so stated that they simply cannot be pinned down to one explanation as the only possible, right explanation. If there are alternative explanations, both of which allow for harmony with the rest of the Scriptures, both of which contribute to faith, hope and love, why fall into the sectarian trap of adamantly insisting on just one of these?

I appreciated an expression made along this line by a person in one of the Pacific Islands, who wrote:

25 Romans 11:33; Ephesians 3:16–19, NIV.
26 Colossians 2:3.
27 1 Corinthians 13:9, 10, 12, 13.

"I will not believe or support any teaching I feel is false, and I will stand on what I believe to be true, but I can no longer judge others who love God and feel I am better than they, because I may know some things they don't. God deals with us all from the point of where we are. We're all wrong in some areas, and judging, comparing, competing and separating ourselves from others who love God and who are also seeking him, is not God's way. His way is love, which unites and heals and covers over a multitude of sin and error. In time we will all come to know the whole truth, but in the meantime we must share what we have, and help and encourage others, not draw battlelines."

After all the arguing and debating is done over certain points or doctrinal issues that so often involve things not clearly spelled out in Scripture, what genuine good has been accomplished? The real question remains, what are we as persons? How well do we reflect the qualities of our heavenly Father and his Son? Does our life, our manner of dealing with others truly exemplify their teachings? Any teaching, organizational or individual, that does not genuinely contribute toward one's being compassionate, considerate and helpful in one's treatment of others, could never be from God, for "this commandment we have from him, that the one who loves God should be loving his brother also."[28]

The question is asked, Where then do I go? What do I become?

I feel no need to "go" anywhere. For I know the One who has the "sayings of everlasting life."[29] I appreciate the strengthening companionship of those I have with whom to associate (either personally or by correspondence) and hope that the future will add to my acquaintance with yet other sincere persons whose concern is for truth, not simply in doctrine, in words, but as a way of life.[30]

I am simply trying, then, to be a Christian, a disciple of God's Son. I cannot see why anyone would want to be anything else. I cannot understand how anyone could hope to be anything more.

The past is now past. I have much to be grateful for, comparatively few things to regret. By this I am not minimizing the seriousness of error. When the sands of time begin to run low in one's life, the damaging effects of having allowed any measurable degree of error to affect one's earlier decisions and life course can become rather painfully apparent. I have no regrets as regards hardships endured in the

---

28 1 John 4:21.
29 John 6:68.
30 1 John 3:18.

past. I feel I have learned valuable lessons from them. The trusting confidence I placed in a human organization, however, has proved to have been misplaced. Having spent the greater part of my life endeavoring to direct people to God and his Son, I find that that organization views such ones as if their flock, answerable to them, subject to their will. Nonetheless I am happy in the knowledge that I personally sought to encourage such ones to build their faith on God's Word as the sure foundation. My trust is that that labor will prove to have been not in vain.

At an age where other men contemplate retirement, I find myself just trying to make a start in providing for future needs of myself and my wife. Yet, along with the Bible writer, I can "say with confidence, 'The Lord is my helper; I will not be afraid. What can man do to me?' "[31] I do not regret in any way having held to conscience; the good that has resulted far outweighs any unpleasantness experienced.

Some early decisions, based on false presentations of God's will, produced effects that seem well nigh irreversible. I still get a hollow feeling inside whenever I think of leaving behind a wife with no son or daughter to supply emotional support and comfort, or to provide, perhaps, for her economic needs more adquately than I may be able to do in the years that yet remain. But there is a future beyond the immediate future and it is hope in that future, and the divine promises related to it, that calm the heart.

Though I find some of their actions incomprehensible, I feel no more authorized, or inclined, to pass judgment on those individuals who have rejected me than I feel they had the right to pass judgment on me. My sincere wish would be that the future might bring them better days, for I feel that there is so much that they could do that would broaden their outlook and lives and cause their days to become far richer in more meaningful ways.

I hope I have learned from mistakes of the past and, although I will certainly make more, I trust that at least there will be improvement, for the good of others as well as my own. I do regret that I cannot personally apologize to some whom I have wronged in one way or another, but my prayers are that no lasting hurt will come and I trust in God's providence in those areas that are beyond my ability to do anything about. Hopefully, the remaining years of my life may see a measure of peace for my wife and me and God's blessing on our united efforts to serve him all our days.

31 Hebrews 13:6, NIV.

After his summary expulsion from the international headquarters, Edward Dunlap passed through Alabama on his way to Oklahoma City and his beginning life anew there at sixty-nine years of age. In talking with him, he said, "It seems to me that all one can do is try to lead a Christian life and help people within whatever sphere of influence he normally has. All the rest is in God's hands."

I am grateful to have been able to make available information that I feel others have a right to hear. There is much more that could be said, perhaps that needs to be said to give a complete picture. But whether time, life and circumstances allow for saying it or not, I am content to let the results of what has now been said rest in God's hands.

Appendix

For Chapter 3

WILL AND TESTAMENT OF CHARLES TAZE RUSSELL

Having at various times during past years donated to the WATCH TOWER BIBLE AND TRACT SOCIETY all of my personal possessions except a small personal bank account of approximately two hundred dollars, in the Exchange National Bank of Pittsburgh, which will properly be paid over to my wife if she survives me, I have merely love and Christian good wishes to leave to all of the dear members of the Bible House Family—and all other dear colaborers in the harvest work—yea, for all of the household of faith in every place who call upon the name of the Lord Jesus as their Redeemer.

However, in view of the fact that in donating the journal, ZION'S WATCH TOWER, the OLD THEOLOGY QUARTERLY and the copyrights of the MILLENNIAL DAWN SCRIPTURE STUDIES Books and various other booklets, hymn-books, etc., to the WATCH TOWER BIBLE AND TRACT SOCIETY, I did so with the explicit understanding that I should have full control of all the interests of these publications during my life time, and that after my decease they should be conducted according to my wishes. I now herewith set forth the said wishes—my will respecting the same—as follows:

AN EDITORIAL COMMITTEE OF FIVE

I direct that the entire editorial charge of ZION'S WATCH TOWER shall be in the hands of a committee of five brethren, whom I exhort to great carefulness and fidelity to the truth. All articles appearing in the columns of ZION'S WATCH TOWER shall have the unqualified approval of at least three of the committee of five, and I urge that if any matter approved by three be known or supposed to be contrary to the views of one or both of the other members of the committee, such articles shall be held over for thought, prayer and discussion for three months before being published—that so far as possible the unity of the faith and the bonds of peace may be maintained in the editorial management of the journal.

The names of the Editorial Committee (with such changes as may from time to time occur) shall all be published in each number of the journal—but it shall not in any manner be indicated by whom the various articles appearing in the journal are written. It will be sufficient that the fact be recognized that the articles are approved by the majority of the committee.

As the Society is already pledged to me that it will publish no other periodicals, it shall also be required that the Editorial Committee shall write for or be connected with no other publications in any manner or degree. My object in these requirements is to safeguard the committee and the journal from any spirit of ambition or pride or headship, and that the truth may be recognized and appreciated for its own worth, and that the Lord may more particularly be recognized as the Head of the church and the Fountain of truth.

Copies of my Sunday discourses published in the daily newspapers covering a period of several years have been preserved and may be used as editorial matter for The WATCH TOWER or not, as the committee may think best, but my name shall not be attached nor any indication whatever given respecting the authorship.

Those named below as members of the Editorial Committee (subject to their acceptance) are supposed to me to be thoroughly loyal to the doctrines of the Scriptures—especially so to the doctrine of the ransom—that there is no acceptance with God and no salvation to eternal life except through faith in Christ and obedience to his Word and its spirit. If any of the designated ones shall at any time find themselves out of harmony with this provision they will be violating their consciences and hence committing sin if they continue to remain members of this Editorial Committtee—knowing that so to do would be contrary to the spirit and intention of this provision.

The Editorial Committee is self-perpetuating, in that should one of these members die or resign, it will be the duty of the remainder to elect his successor, that the journal may never have an issue without a full Editorial Committee of five. I enjoin upon the committee named great caution in respect to the election of others to their number—that purity of life, clearness in the truth, zeal for God, love for the brethren and faithfulness to the Redeemer shall be prominent characteristics of the one elected. In addition to the five named for the committee I have named five others from whom I prefer that selection should be made for any vacancies in the Editorial Committee, before going outside for a general selection—unless in the interim, between the making of this Will and the time of my death, something should occur which would seem to indicate these as less desirable or others as more desirable for filling the vacancies mentioned. The names of the Editorial Committee are as follows:

> WILLIAM E. PAGE,
> WILLIAM E. VAN AMBURGH,
> HENRY CLAY ROCKWELL,
> E. W. BRENNEISON,
> F. H. ROBISON.

The names of the five whom I suggest as possibly amongst the most suitable from which to fill vacancies in the Editorial Committee are as follows: A. E. Burgess, Robert Hirsh, Isaac Hoskins. Geo. H. Fisher (Scranton), J. F. Rutherford, Dr. John Edgar.

The following announcement shall appear in each issue of THE WATCH TOWER, followed by the names of the Editorial Committee:

ZION'S WATCH TOWER EDITORIAL COMMITTEE

This journal is published under the supervision of an Editorial Committee, at least three of whom must have read and have approved as TRUTH each and every article appearing in these columns. The names of the Committee now serving are: (names to follow.)

As for compensation, I think it wise to maintain the Society's course of the past in respect to salaries—that none be paid; that merely reasonable expenses be allowed to those who serve the Society or its work in any manner. In harmony with the course of the Society, I suggest that the provision for the Editorial Committee, or the three that shall be actively engaged, shall consist of not more than a provision for their food and shelter and ten dollars per month, with such a moderate allowance for wife or children or others dependent upon them for support as the Society's Board of Directors shall consider proper, just, reasonable—that no provision be made for the laying up of money.

I desire that the OLD THEOLOGY QUARTERLY continue to appear as at present, so far as the opportunities for distribution and the laws of the land will permit, and that its issues shall consist of reprints from the old issues of THE WATCH TOWER or extracts from my discourses, but that no name shall appear in connection with the matter unless the same is required by law.

It is my wish that the same rules apply to the German, the French, the Italian, the Danish and the Swedish or any other foreign publications controlled or supported by the WATCH TOWER BIBLE AND TRACT SOCIETY.

I will that a copy of this paper be sent to each one whose name has appeared above as of the Editorial committee or the list from whom others of that committee may be chosen to fill vacancies and also to each member of the Board of Directors of the WATCH TOWER BIBLE AND TRACT SOCIETY. This shall be done immediately on my death being reported, so that within a week, if possible, the persons named as of the Editorial Committee may be heard from, their communications being addressed to the Vice-President of the WATCH TOWER BIBLE AND TRACT SOCIETY—whoever may be holding that office at that time. The answers of those appointed shall be to the point, indicating their acceptance or rejection of the provisions and terms specified. A reasonable time shall be allowed for any one mentioned who may be absent from the city or from the country. Meantime the remainder of the committee of at least three shall proceed to act in their capacity as editors. It shall be the duty of the officers of the Society to provide the necessary arrangements for these members of the Editorial Committee and to assist them in their duties in every possible manner, in compliance with the engagements made with me bearing on this matter.

I have already donated to the WATCH TOWER BIBLE AND TRACT SOCIETY all my voting shares therein, putting the same in the hands of five Trustees, as follows: Sr. E. Louise Hamilton, Sr. Almeta M. Nation Robison, Sr. J. G. Herr, Sr. C. Tomlins, Sr. Alice G. James.

These Trustees shall serve for life. In event of deaths or resignations successors shall be chosen by the WATCH TOWER SOCIETY Directors and Editorial Committee and the remaining Trustees after prayer for divine guidance.

I now provide for the impeachment and dismissal from the Editorial Committee of any member thereof found to be unworthy the position by reason of either doctrinal or moral laches, as follows:

At least three of the Board must unite in bringing the impeachment charges, and the Board of Judgment in the matter shall consist of the WATCH TOWER BIBLE AND TRACT SOCIETY'S trustees and the five trustees controlling my voting shares and the Editorial Committee, excepting the accused. Of these sixteen members at least thirteen must favor the impeachment and dismissal in order to effect the same.

DIRECTIONS FOR FUNERAL

I desire to be buried in the plot of ground owned by our Society, in the Rosemont United Cemetery, and all the details of arrangements respecting the funeral service I leave in the care of my sister, Mrs. M. M. Land. and her daughters, Alice and May, or such of them as may survive me, with the assistance and advice and cooperation of the brethren, as they may request the same. Instead of an ordinary funeral discourse, I request that they arrange to have a number of the brethren, accustomed to public speaking. make a few remarks each, that the service be very simple and inexpensive and that it be conducted in the Bible House Chapel or any other place that may be considered equally appropriate or more so.

MY LEGACY OF LOVE

To the dear "Bethel" family collectively and individually I leave my best wishes, in hoping for them of the Lord his blessing, which maketh rich and addeth no sorrow. The same I extend in a still broader sweep to all the family of the Lord in every place—especially to those rejoicing in the harvest truth. I entreat you all that you continue to progress and to grow in grace, in knowledge, and above all in love, the great fruit of the spirit in its various diversified forms. I exhort to meekness, not only with the world, but with one another; to patience with one another and with all men, to gentleness with all, to brotherly kindness, to godliness, to purity. I remind you that all these things are necessary for us, necessary that we may attain the promised kingdom, and that the Apostle has assured us that if we do these things we shall never fail, but that "so an entrance shall be ministered unto us abundantly into the everlasting kingdom of our Lord and Savior Jesus Christ."

It is my wish that this my last Will and Testament be published in the issue of THE WATCH TOWER following my death.

My hope for myself, as for all the dear Israel of God, is that soon we shall meet to part no more, in the first resurrection, in the Master's presence, where there is fulness of joy forevermore. We shall be satisfied when we awake in his likeness—

"Changed from glory unto glory."

(Signed) CHARLES TAZE RUSSELL.

PUBLISHED AND DECLARED IN THE PRESENCE OF THE WITNESSES WHOSE NAMES ARE ATTACHED:

MAE F. LAND,
M. ALMETA NATION,
LAURA M. WHITEHOUSE.

DONE AT ALLEGHENY, PA., JUNE TWENTY-NINE, NINETEEN HUNDRED AND SEVEN.

The preceding document is the will prepared by Charles Taze Russell, founder of the Watch Tower Society and its magazine, as published in the *Watch Tower* of December 1, 1916.

For Chapter 10

The issue regarding the use of the term "ordained minister" first arose in 1974. I have a complete file on the matter, one that has been puzzling to many Witnesses since virtually none are aware of the background.

In 1974 Grant Suiter had suggested a convention talk on the subject "Ordained Ministers of God." It followed the current practice of applying the title of "Ordained Minister" to every man, woman and child who had undergone baptism as a Witness. President Knorr assigned me to develop a talk outline on the subject. (His letter dated February 15, 1974.) It seemed to me that the title was simply something adopted from the clergy and I could see no Scriptural basis for the application given to it, equating baptism with an ordination ceremony. More importantly, when working on the *Aid* project, I had been impressed with the fact that the original language terms for "minister" (both in Hebrew and in Greek) meant simply a "servant," the humble quality inferred being in contrast with the elevated prestige often attached to the title "Ordained Minister."

Due to my concern for holding closely to the Scriptures, I first spoke with my uncle, Fred Franz, about the matter. He stated quite definitely that baptism could not rightly be called an "ordination." I doubt seriously that I would then have had the courage to write to President Knorr about the matter had it not been for this expression from the vice president. The letter I wrote resulted in a Governing

Body discussion and Knorr personally spoke very strongly against any change in the current practice of using the term. (In actuality, it was not used congregationally; it was only used when speaking or dealing with persons of the public, including officials.) I expressed my reasons for my questioning the practice, stressing the Scriptural meaning of the term "minister." It would, however, be contrary to all fact to say that my voice carried any particular weight in the discussion. For one thing, I was the youngest person on the Body, then consisting of eleven members, I held no position of any particular responsibility, and, during the discussion of the "Organization" book, had been the object of some fairly caustic remarks by the president. Without equivocation I can say that one factor and one factor only resulted in a change of position on the use of the term "Ordained Minister" as applying to every man, woman or child baptized. That was the voice of Fred Franz. He very firmly stated, repeatedly, that baptism and ordination do not refer to the same thing. Those surviving members of that group of eleven members know that this was the case.

After rather sharp discussion, there eventually was a *unanimous* vote that three members of the Body, Fred Franz, Raymond Franz and Lyman Swingle, be assigned to develop written material giving the reasons for a change in position. Fred Franz was elected to do the writing and prepared a 46-page argument for publication in the *Watchtower* (a copy of which argument I still have). When it was presented to the Body, however, they found it obscure, so written that it was difficult to know just what was being said. I was then assigned to do a "rewrite."

The material I wrote laid primary emphasis on the humility surrounding the original language terms for "minister" in the Bible. This was my main concern. I also knew that the very expression "minister" was a term restricted to only a handful of languages (English, French, Italian, Spanish and Portuguese) and that in our own publications, when translated into other languages, such as German, it often was rendered by the corresponding word for "clergyman." A large number of modern Bible translations rendered the original language terms by the word "servant." The material I wrote clearly stated that *in that sense* every Christian is a "minister." (See the *Watchtower* of December 1, 1975, page 732, paragraph 18.)

I could not limit my writing to these points however. In a 3-page letter, dated September 11, 1974, President Knorr went into great detail as to points he felt should be covered, particularly as to specific application of the term to the various categories of Witnesses, such as Elders, Ministerial Servants, Pioneers, Bethel Family members, and so forth. He stressed that anything written would have to deal with this. Milton Henschel wrote on some similar points (his letter dated September 18, 1974). These letters resulted in the material found in the last several paragraphs of the final article I wrote, in which suggestions were offered as to how one might answer if asked by government officials whether one was an "Ordained Minister."

The material I submitted was thoroughly discussed and argued by the Governing Body. Again the respect for, and the influence of, the vice president resulted in final approval of the material for publication. The vote was unanimous, as it had to be at that time when the two-thirds majority arrangement had not yet gone into effect.

All this information is presented because the facts about this matter have, since the spring of 1980, been grossly misrepresented, both by Governing Body members and others. As stated, I have a complete file, containing signed letters, in confirmation of the accuracy of what is said above.

I feel that Grant Suiter took the matter quite personally, though my questioning of the point was as to an organizational policy, not a criticism of anything originated by him. He brought the matter up in Governing Body sessions on three occasions during the years following, each time expressing his disagreement with the position published by the Society. The last time was at the February 6, 1980, Governing Body session when letters from three Witness lawyers were considered. These letters had resulted from an invitation to write on the subject extended at a meeting of doctors and lawyers. In the Governing Body session Grant Suiter referred to the changed policy as having constituted "an attack on the organization." Yet many of the members present knew that it was the voice and influence of Fred Franz, then vice president, that had brought the Body around to accept the change, even overcoming the objections of the president, Nathan Knorr. And, in every one of the three occasions when the matter was brought up for review by Governing Body member Suiter, it was the firmness of position expressed by Fred Franz, now the president, that baptism is not an "ordination" that was the deciding factor. In each case the decision of the Body was not to return to the previous application of the title "Ordained Minister" as applying to every baptized Witness. Every member of the Governing Body present at the three separate sessions involved knows that this was the case.

One year after my resignation from the Governing Body, President Fred Franz gave a speech at a Gilead School graduation in which he reinstituted the earlier policy of calling every baptized man, woman and child among the Witnesses, not simply a "minister" or "servant" of God, but an "Ordained Minister." He now argued that they had as much claim to such designation as do the clergy of Christendom.

And, one might very properly say, they have the same right to use the term "bishop" in place of "overseer," since that term is simply an anglicized form of the Greek word for "overseer" (*episkopos*), and "deacon" which is simply an anglicized form of the Greek word (*diakonos*) for "servant" or "minister."

The simple fact is that in none of the sessions did those who argued in favor of calling every baptized man, woman and child among the Witnesses an "ordained minister" ever express concern about the Scriptures as *requiring* such—in all cases their arguments were based on the *advantages* this brought. Those advantages were the advantages and privileges granted to the clergy—exemption from military service, exemption from certain taxation. This, and not Scriptural teaching, was the overriding concern.

For Chapter 11

This is my letter in response to the citation to a judicial hearing by the East Gadsden Congregation of Jehovah's Witnesses:

November 12, 1981

Body of Elders
East Congregation of Jahovah's Witnesses
2822 Fields Avenue
East Gadsden, AL   35903

Dear Brothers:

Your letter of November 6 arrived Tuesday afternoon, November 10. This letter I am writing may or may not reach you before Saturday, so I will contact Theotis by phone in order that the brothers will not make an unnecessary trip to the Hall then.

I asked Dan to let you know that I was writing a letter to the Governing Body requesting information and would appreciate your waiting until an answer was received before following through on your judicial proceedings. Your letter does not make mention of this. Perhaps you can write me as to your decision on that request, if it was indeed given consideration. As you perhaps know, forty years of my life were spent in full-time service, as pioneer, special pioneer, circuit overseer, district overseer, missionary, Branch overseer, Bethel family member, Governing Body member. I do not know if you consider those forty years as allowing for a measure of forbearance on your part in the sense of patiently waiting whatever period of time it takes for Brooklyn to respond. I would hope that such would be the case and that your interest in their response would equal mine.--James 2:12, 13.

Do the three signatures at the end of the letter represent those forming the judicial committee? If so, then may I respectfully petition the body of elders to reconsider their selection? From what was stated at the meeting with Wesley Benner and Dan Gregerson, Dan presented himself as the accuser in the matter, stating at the beginning of the conversation that 'he had seen me eat with Peter Gregerson' (the occasion being some months ago, previous to the publication of the September 15, 1981, <u>Watchtower</u>). Till now I know of no other accusation of a supposed offense. Are there such? (I would need to know what such are—and by whom raised—if I am to be in position to have witnesses on my behalf.) Whatever the case in that respect, by any standard of justice it would hardly seem proper for the accuser to form part of the judging body. There are additional reasons for viewing Dan as not qualifying to serve in that capacity but I see no need to add them to that which is stated.

In your consideration of the above point, it would be much appreciated by me if you would weigh the advisability of enlarging

Body of Elders
East Gadsden Congregation
November 12, Page Two

the judicial committee. The charge involves a new position taken by the Governing Body (the placing of disassociated persons in the same class with disfellowshiped persons has heretofore been limited in publications only to those entering military service or political activity). Besides this, I have heard comments regarding condemnatory remarks about me made by some elders on the body. Since they have not spoken personally to me, I cannot know to what extent this testimony is accurate. But since it does raise the question of prejudgment it would be viewed as a kindness if additional elders in the congregation were included so as to contribute toward a fair and impartial discussion.

This letter is somewhat lengthy but perhaps you will pardon this considering that my devotion to God, his Son and his inspired Word are all being called in question. Accept my thanks for considering the points raised and may Jehovah God and our Lord Jesus Christ be with the spirit you show.—2 Timothy 4:22; Philemon 25.

Your brother,

RV Franz

Rt. 4, Box 440-F
Gadsden, AL 35904

The following letter, dated November 23, 1981, was never sent due to the rapidity of the action of the judicial committee and their unwillingness to allow needed time for correspondence on matters. The letter, nonetheless, is helpful in that it gives some idea of the handling of the case by the judicial committee:

November 23, 1981

Body of Elders
East Gadsden Congregation

Dear Brothers:

I am writing this letter to the body of elders since I would like to know if all of you actually approve of the handling of my case as it has been conducted till now.

As you know, I wrote a letter to the Governing Body (under date of November 5) requesting information on the application of the material in the September 15, 1981 <u>Watchtower</u> as it relates to my personal situation.   Part of my letter dealt with other points; I am enclosing a copy of the part that deals with the local circumstances and the elders here.

When cited for a hearing to be held on Saturday November 14 I called to your attention that the judicial committee made no mention whatsoever of my request to allow the Governing Body time to respond to the letter.

On November 19, Thursday, the judicial committee wrote a letter to me that was mailed on Thursday afternoon and in that letter cited me for a hearing on <u>Saturday</u>. They could not possibly have expected the letter to reach me before Friday and if I had not returned home early on Friday afternoon and gone to the post office the letter would not have reached me until Monday, <u>two days after</u> the time indicated for the hearing. Brother French called by phone about <u>twenty-four hours</u> before the time for the hearing, otherwise I would have known nothing of the letter. My wife explained that we were due to receive company on Saturday (the visit having been arranged as the result of a long-distance phone call from a person out of the state). When I returned home I learned for the first time of the letter and went to the post office to obtain it. The obvious hastiness manifest I find saddening indeed.

Perhaps you brothers view this as a proper way of handling matters. I would hope that that is not the case.

Adding to this, this afternoon I received a phone call from Brother French informing me that the judicial committee will meet this Wednesday evening to hear my case whether I am present or not. This means that they view their handling of matters as normal and proper and that my response justifies their classing me as one who 'repeatedly refuses or fails' to be present for a judicial hearing.

Against the background of the facts, do you really believe

East Gadsden Body of Elders
November 23, 1981, Page II

this is so? In none of my communications have I expressed a refusal
to meet with a judicial committee but instead I have expressed what
I believe to be a valid and sensible reason why the date set was
not agreeable.

      At the time Brother French called this afternoon I was pre-
paring a letter in response to that of the judicial committee.
In that letter the statement was made that "the body of elders
had been made aware that you had mailed a letter to the Watchtower
Society and we had determined that we should proceed with the
judicial committee hearing." The letter contains no explanation
or reason for not allowing the Governing Body time to respond to
the letter. When I asked Brother French this afternoon what
possible reason there could be for not allowing them to respond
first, his reply was that the body 'did not feel it was necessary.'

      I accept the fact that my having devoted fully two-thirds
of a life of nearly sixty years to God's service is discounted now
as a reason for showing any consideration for my request. But do
you brothers really feel that saying 'we did not feel it was
necessary' is a fitting response to such a request, by whomever
made?

      Do you believe the oft-repeated counsel that it is better to
err on the side of patience, forebearance and mercy rather than on
the side of hastiness, harshness or rigidity? Does mere 'necessity'
or rather the lack of it justify not heeding that counsel? Whatever
personal attitude some of you may have toward me, I sincerely
believe that my request deserves a better reply than it has thus
far received. Principles such as those at Proverbs 14:29; 25:8-10
would seem to give basis for your wanting a far better reason than
what has been advanced as justification for the course now pursued.

      May your decision be one that you can sincerely believe has
God's blessing and is in accord with the example and teachings of
his Son while on earth.--Matthew 5:5; 12:7.

                          Respectfully,

                          [signature]

      Following is the complete letter sent as an appeal from the decision
of the judicial committee to disfellowship me:

December 8, 1981

East Gadsden Congregation Body of Elders

Dear Brothers:

By means of this letter I would like to appeal the decision to disfellowship me that was made by the judicial committee you appointed.

Speaking of judicial matters, one of the Society's publications says that "elders serving as a judicial committee must weigh matters carefully, knowing that certain factors may distinguish one situation from another. Instead of looking for rigid rules for guidance, you will need to think in terms of principles and judge each case on its own merits." As to giving counsel, the same publication says, "Be sure the counsel is based solidly on God's Word. Take sufficient time, and endeavor to reach the heart of the person. Take time to listen. Be sure you have all the facts. Discuss the application of the scriptures that apply and be sure that he understands. Take time for research, if that is needed, before you give counsel or answer his questions. If you cannot take the necessary time, it would be well to let another elder handle the matter." (Xerox copies enclosed.)

I do not feel that these things have thus far been done in my case. I find it saddening that an attitude of unusual haste has been shown and an apparent reluctance or inability to 'discuss the application of the scriptures that apply for full understanding.' I feel that a brotherly approach would call for patience rather than haste; compassion and understanding rather than a rigid application of rules.

My circumstances should not be unknown to you. After forty years of full-time service, in which I endured privation, poverty, hunger, thirst, cold, heat, fever, dysentery, jailings, dangers of mob violence, of gunshots and war, the risk of life and liberty in dictatorial lands, along with constant toil, I found myself at the age of 58 facing the problem of finding a home and employment to provide for myself and my wife. Since I began pioneering upon graduation from high school in 1940, I had no experience in secular employment and no financial resources to sustain me. The funds given me by the Society (evidently viewed as some type of compensation for my forty years of service) were less than most persons earn in one year of secular employment and covered no more than a portion of our initial expenses.

Peter Gregerson provided me with employment and a place to park the mobile home I obtained and am still in debt for. He thus became both my landlord and employer. About six months ago, under pressure, he resigned from the local congregation. As you know, the sole basis for the judicial hearing with me was the accusation that I had eaten at a local restaurant with Peter Gregerson.

East Gadsden Congregation Body of Elders
December 8, 1981, Page II

Some elders in the area feel that their employment with
Warehouse Groceries allows for their remaining free from accusation when eating with Peter Gregerson, who is Chairman of the
Board. Yet my relationship is closer, more involved than theirs,
since I not only work for Warehouse Groceries but also work for
him personally, doing work on his property and home in a way that
calls for regular conversation and discussion, often in his home,
at mealtimes and on other occasions. I am unable to understand
why a brotherly approach would not call for a compassionate,
understanding attitude, weighing my circumstances and recognizing
the "factors that distinguish one situation from another."

At the judicial hearing, only one of the two witnesses gave
testimony that relates to anything subsequent to the publication
of the September 15, 1981, Watchtower, which places disassociated
persons in a category with disfellowshiped persons. One witness
stated that he had seen me at the restaurant with Peter and Janet
Gregerson but acknowledged that the occasion was in the summer,
hence previous to the publication of that magazine. Unless one
believes in ex post facto laws, his testimony would hardly seem
relevant.

The other witness testified to a more recent occasion, having
seen me enter a restaurant in company with my wife and Janet Gregerson (who is not disassociated) and then subsequently seeing Peter
enter. This same witness, along with an elder of the East Gadsden
congregation, ate at a restaurant with Peter Gregerson on two
occasions subsequent to the publication of the September 15, 1981,
Watchtower. In neither case did Peter ask to sit with them but
in both cases he was invited to sit at their table and to engage
in free conversation with them. Apparently this was not viewed
as meriting a judicial hearing, but the one occasion in my case
was viewed as meriting such. I mention this only because your
letter of November 19 assured me that the elders handling my case
were free from prejudgment and would be objective in their approach.
The inconsistency apparent makes it difficult for me to feel satisfied that such was the case. It raises serious questions as to the
motivation for the judicial action itself and the decision rendered.

I find it equally hard to understand the accusation directed
at me when viewing it against the background of what is happening
in the Gadsden area. To list the occasions when elders and others
have eaten or otherwise had social contact with disassociated and
disfellowshiped persons would be difficult since they are numerous.
Yet for some reason I have been singled out for accusation. If the
view be taken that it is simply a matter of starting with someone,
why should the testimony of only one witness to one occasion since
the appearance of the September 15, 1981, Watchtower, result in my
being selected as the one to begin with? This too raises questions
as to objectivity and impartial motivation.

Perhaps it may be said that I have not expressed repentance

East Gadsden Congregation Body of Elders
December 8, 1981, Page III

for having eaten with Peter Gregerson. To express repentance I
need first to be satisfied that doing so is a sin before God. The
only means for providing such conviction must rightly come from
God's Word, which alone is inspired and unfailingly reliable.
(2 Timothy 3:16, 17) My understanding from the Scriptures is that
loyalty to God and to his Word is of supreme importance and supercedes any other loyalty or whatever kind. (Acts 4:19, 20; 5:29)
My understanding also is that it is not for me or any other human
or group or humans to add to that Word, under pain of being "proved
a liar" or even receiving divine plagues. (Proverbs 30:5, 6; Revelation 22:18, 19) I cannot take such scriptural warnings lightly.
In view of all the scriptural admonition against judging others,
I have a healthy fear of setting myself (or any human or group of
humans) up as legislator and feel compelled to let God's Word alone
do such judging. To do that I need to be certain that I am not
simply following some humanly devised standard that poses as a
divine standard but which is in fact uninspired, unsupported by
God's Word. I do not wish to be guilty of presumption and impertinence in judging someone whom God by his own expressed Word has
not so judged.--Romans 14:4, 10-12; James 3:11, 12; see also
Commentary on the Letter of James pages 161 to 168.

I assure you that if you will help me to see from the Scriptures that the act of eating with Peter Gregerson is a sin I will
humbly repent of such sin before God. Those who have talked with
me thus far have not done this but have cited the above-mentioned
magazine as their "authority" (the term used by the chairman of
the judicial committee). My understanding is that all authority
within the Christian congregation must derive from and be solidly
based on the Word of God. Proverbs 17:15 states that "Anyone
pronouncing the wicked one righteous and anyone pronouncing the
righteous one wicked--even both of them are something detestable
to Jehovah." I have no desire to be detestable to God and hence
am very concerned about this matter.

I fully accept the scriptural teachings at 1 Corinthians 5:11-13
and 2 John 7-11 and have assured those with whom I spoke that I
have no desire to associate with or eat with or have in my home
persons of the kind there described, wicked persons and antichrists.
My problem is seeing how these scriptures apply to the person who is
at the crux of the case directed against me, Peter Gregerson.
Under pressure he resigned from the congregation of Jehovah's
Witnesses, but, as you know, he stated the following in his letter:

"It was brought to my attention yesterday that I have caused
many brothers throughout Gadsden and our circuit to be disturbed.
I had tried very hard to prevent that.

It is true that I have been experiencing serious doubts
regarding certain teachings of the Watchtower Society. However,
I would like to make clear two points of importance. First, I
have not been actively discussing these matters within the congregation. I have not even discussed them with the Body of Elders for
fear of accidentally causing conversation within the congregation.
I have had "confidential talks" with very few people, almost all in

East Gadsden Congregation Body of Elders
December 8, 1981, Page IV
 my own family.

      Secondly, my views have not changed regarding Jehovah God Jesus
Christ and the plain teachings of the Bible such as resurrection.

      As Jehovah God is my judge, I am conscious of no conduct unbe-
coming a Christian. For almost 50 years, since the winter of 1931-
1932, when my dad started taking me to meetings, I have been a
regular and hard working Jehovah's Witness. My good name and reputation is of great value to me, both among you and in the community
at large.

      So that my "good name" can be preserved, and so that there will
be no further trouble and disturbance within and among you, I hereby
resign from association with the organization.

      This does not change my respect for the good done by the Watch-
tower Society. It does not change my friendship and love for you
as individuals. Of course, I will accept whatever attitude you
choose to show me.

                           Respectfully,

                           Peter V. Gregerson

[End of the copy of Peter Gregerson's letter. What follows is the continuation of my appeal letter.]

      He states that he is "conscious of no conduct unbecoming a
Christian" which would mean that he is not the kind of person
described at 1 Corinthians 5:11-13. He expresses his faith in
Jehovah God, his Son and the plain teachings of the Bible which
would rule against his being among the kind of persons described
at 2 John 7-11. To my knowledge no one has disputed those claims
or refuted them. For me to treat him as a wicked man or an antichrist without clear scriptural basis for doing so would, I believe,
make me liable for divine disapproval.

      I have asked each of the elders who has spoken with me, inclu-
ding the three members of the judicial committee, if they themselves
view Peter Gregerson as the kind of person described at 1 Corinthians
5:11-13 and 2 John 7-11, namely a wicked person or an antichrist.
They themselves were obviously hesitant to say that these scriptures
apply to him, yet these are the only scriptures that set out the
injunction identifying persons with whom a Christian should not eat.
Is it truly fair to ask of me that I apply these scriptures to him and
thereby judge him as an unfit person with whom to eat when those
sitting in judgment upon me are themselves either unwilling or
unable to do so? As of now I do not see that these scriptures apply
to Peter Gregerson. In order to see that they do I would need your
assistance.

East Gadsden Congregation Body of Elders
December 8, 1981, Page V

I can understand why the elders would be reluctant to say
that they themselves would place Peter Gregerson among the kind
of persons described by the inspired apostle at 1 Corinthians 5:11-13,
fornicators, greedy persons, idolaters, revilers, drunkards and
extortioners. I seriously doubt that any one of you on the body
of elders would admit that as even a remote possibility. Please
correct me if I am wrong.

That leaves those described at 2 John 7-11, antichrists. Can
you understand why in my heart I feel the need for genuine conviction before I could apply these verses to anyone? The apostle John,
who is tne sole user of the term, describes such a one in these
words: "Who is tne liar if it is not the one that denies that **Jesus**
is the Christ? This is the antichrist, the one that denies the
Father and the Son." (1 John 2:22) "But every inspired expression
that does not confess Jesus does not originate with God. Furthermore, this is the antichrist's inspired expression . . . ." (1 John
4:3) "For many deceivers have gone forth into the world, persons
not confessing Jesus as coming in tne flesh. This is the deceiver
and the antichrist." (2 John 7) On this basis, some commentaries
(used on a number of occasions in Society publications) make these
points:

   Barnes' Notes on the New Testament says: "From this it is
   clear, that John understood by the word all those who
   denied that Jesus is the Messiah, or that the Messiah had
   come in the flesh. . . . They arrayed themselves against
   him, and held doctrines which were in fact in entire
   opposition to the Son of God."

   From Lange's Commentary: "$\dot{\alpha}\nu\tau\iota$ [anti] may mean both
   hostility and substitution. In the former case it denotes
   the antagonist of Christ, the antichrist, in the latter the
   pretender-Christ or pseudo-Christ . . . . The antichrists
   deny that Jesus is the Christ; that He did not come in tne
   flesh, that He is not the Son of God, that He is not of God.
   The doctrine is the denial of the truth, the lie, they
   themselves are LIARS, and according to John viii.44, the
   children of the devil, of the father of the lie ([1 John]
   iii.3-10) . . . . The antichrist and the antichrists are
   to be taken 'as expressly connected with Satan,' and the
   two words here denote not substitution but hostility to
   Christ . . . ; the antichrist is pre-eminently the instrument and tool of Satan."

Do any of you on the body of elders seriously believe that
Peter Gregerson is to be classed among such kind of persons?

Jesus Christ said that "whoever addresses his brother with
an unspeakable word of contempt will be accountable to the
Supreme Court; whereas whoever says, 'You despicable fool!' will
be liable to tne fiery Gehenna." (Matthew 5:22) For myself, I

East Gadsden Congregation Bouy of Elders
December 8, 1981, Page VI

had far rather be called a "despicable fool" than to be labeled an
"antichrist." Surely there is no uglier term to be found in the
Bible. Since even the unjust application of the expression "despicable fool" can make one liable for Gehenna, how much more so the
application of "antichrist" if unjustly used? I am very concerned
not to run such grave risk and I trust that you as individuals
will weigh that risk with equal concern. At Matthew 12:36, Jesus
says: "I tell you that every unprofitable [careless, RSV;
unfounded, Jerusalem Bible] saying that men speak, they will
render an account concerning it on Judgment Day." How could any
of us take such warnings lightly? Or how could we feel that we
can let the responsibility for our action rest with others if we
erroneously, without genuine foundation, declare someone a person
unfit to eat with as a person 'hostile to Christ'? Emphasizing
our personal relationship and responsibility to himself, as to his
Father, God's Son says: "Know that I am he who searches the inmost
thoughts and hearts, and I will give to you individually according
to your deeds."--Revelation 2:23.

Loyalty to God obliges me to be guided by my conscience which
is molded by these scriptures. Does such a conscientious course
make me subject to condemnation? It is true that the circuit
overseer said in my home that 'the Governing Body can overrule
our conscience.' While he stated--to use his own words--that he
"parrots what the Governing Body says," it would seem that in
this case he spoke of his own originality, for I know of no publication of the Society that makes a statement like his. More importantly, I know of no scripture that supports such view. The inspired
apostle tells us that, even where an action is right in itself, if
a person does it having doubts "he is already condemned," since
"everything that is not out of faith is sin." (Romans 14:23) If
my conscience is to change, it must be by the power and force of
the Word of God, not by mere human reasonings, for I am determined
to "let God be found true, though every man be found a liar," and
hence determined to be among those not "adulterating the word of
God, but by making the truth manifest recommending ourselves to
every human conscience in the sight of God."--Romans 3:4; 2 Corinthians 4:2.

I have set out this information in detail to enable you to
see the problem I face in accepting unquestioningly and with no
qualms of conscience the view advanced, namely, that the letter
written by Peter Gregerson (copied herein)--by itself and with no
other justifying evidence in support--gives anyone the right to
say that he automatically has become a wicked person unfit for
Christians to eat with. Have I missed the sense of the scriptures
that now restrain me from making such automatic judgment? Do they
not say what I understand them to say? And does my conscientious
concern to be true to God's Word now make me subject to condemnation
as also a wicked person, unfit to eat with? Three men among you
have rendered such judgment. I write this as much for their benefit,
and out of concern for them, as for the rest of you. If I am wrong
and God's Word says something different than what I see there, then

East Gadsden Congregation Body of Elders
December 8, 1981, Page VII

your reproving me by setting forth the proof from that inspired
Word of God will not only be accepted but welcomed.

    I am supplying a copy of this letter for each member of the
body of elders since the judicial committee that rendered its
decision against me received its appointment from you. I am
also sending copies to the Governing Body and its Service Department
since your appointment as elders comes from them. As you know,
I wrote the Governing Body on November 5, 1981, requesting information as follows:

    "Locally, certain elders have taken the information in the
September 15, 1981, Watchtower as authorization to demand a change
in my relationship with the man on whose property I live and for
whom I work, Peter Gregerson. They state that, since he has disassociated himself, I should view him as among those with whom one
should not eat--wicked persons and antichrists--and that failure to
conform to this position requires disfellowshiping. Approaching 60,
having no financial resources, I am in no position to move or to
change my employment. So I would very much appreciate knowing if the
intent of your statements in that issue of the magazine is truly
as they present it, namely that my accepting an invitation from my
landlord and employer to eat with him is grounds for disfellowshiping.
If, instead, they have exceeded the intent of what was published,
some counsel of moderation would grant me relief from a situation
that is potentially oppressive. I will appreciate whatever clarification you can give, whether directly or through one of your departments."

    I have repeatedly petitioned you to allow them time to answer
this request for information. Thus far you have not seen fit to
honor that plea. I hope that you will now do so.

             Sincerely,

             R. V. Franz

A copy of this letter was sent to the Governing Body along with the
following letter:

                       December 11, 1981

Governing Body of Jehovah's Witnesses
Brooklyn, New York

Dear Brothers:

    On November 5, 1981, I wrote to you seeking some clarification
as to the position taken in the September 15 Watchtower and its
placing of disassociated persons in the same category with disfellowshiped persons and detailing the manner in which all of
Jehovah's Witnesses should view and treat such persons. In that
letter I expressed concern over the probable consequences of the
material.

    Since then local elders in the congregation where I have
been associated have taken that material as "authority" to take
disfellowshiping action toward me, the charge being that I had
eaten a meal with a disassociated person at a restaurant, the
person being my landlord and employer.

I am enclosing a copy of the appeal letter I have turned in to the local body of elders. If the judicial committee's action meets with your approval and is in accord with the intent of the material you have published, then the appeal letter may be of no interest to you. If, however, that is not the case and you do feel concern over this action (not solely as relates to me but as it is indicative of the probable reaction generally to that published material) then you may wish to do something to moderate the effect of that material. The company I work for, Warehouse Groceries, employs from thirty-five to forty Witnesses in its offices and ten stores. The Chairman of the Board is disassociated as is the head of the Non-Foods section; other personnel, including the manager of one of their larger stores, are disfellowshiped persons. So the clarification requested in my letter could be of benefit to a number of persons in this area.

It seems clear that the position taken in your published material will have a progressively cumulative effect, with more and more persons being affected. If applied consistently, rather than in a selective, arbitrary manner, in the way it has been applied to me, it could easily lead to the disfellowshiping of dozens of persons in just this area whose names come readily to mind. Do you genuinely feel that such action is justified scripturally?

Since the responsibility for the results of the earlier mentioned material rests ultimately with you brothers, it seems of benefit to pass this information on to you and to your Service Department.

Sincerely,

RW Franz

Rt. 4, Box 440-F
Gadsden, AL 35904

Following is my letter of December 20, requesting a change in the appeal committee selected by Circuit Overseer Wesley Benner:

December 20,1981

East Gadsden Congregation Body of Elders
Gadsden AL

Dear Brothers:

By means of this letter I am requesting that a different appeal committee be appointed. I am sending a copy of this letter to the Service Department of the Governing Body and of the Watchtower Society since I am requesting that a committee be formed of brothers outside of this area and outside of this circuit. My reasons are as follows:

On December 15 I received a phone call from Theotis French saying that an appeal committee had been selected, composed of Willie Anderson, either Earl or Felix Parnell (he wasn't sure which) and Brother Dibble (whether the father or the son was not said to my knowledge). I told him that I would write a letter and that I would have something to say about the composition of the committee. I asked why elders from the East Gadsden congregation were not used and he said that that was not the way it was done anymore and that he had called on the circuit overseer to make the selection.

On December 18, Friday, I wrote to Theotis asking him to
supply me in writing the names of those definitely selected to
serve on the committee. I mailed the letter that morning. That
evening Theotis called saying that the appeal committee would
meet on Sunday. I informed him that I had written a letter which
he should receive in a day or so. Saturday evening he called
again, saying he had received the letter and that the committee
wanted to meet with me on Monday, evidently December 21. He did
not state either time or place, as he had not done when informing
me of the planned Sunday meeting. He gave me the names of the
proposed committee members: Willie Anderson, Earl Parnell and
Rob Dibble. I again requested he send the information in writing.
This morning he phoned yet again, stating that the appeal committee
was going to meet on Monday (again failing to state either time or
place). I told him that the proposed committee ought to write me
direct rather than have him phone me and told him that I objected
to the composition of the committee as selected and would be writing
this letter requesting a new committee. He said that the proposed
committee would meet anyway on Monday. I stated that in my forty
years of experience I had never seen such an obvious rushing of
matters, to which he replied that the last school provided by the
Society had brought changes (what these were he did not say).
Despite my objections to such inconsiderate haste he said that the
committee would meet anyway and that anything I had to say should
be said then. I again stated that I was requesting a different
committee.

East Gadsden Congregation Body of Elders
December 20, 1981, Page II

I believe my reasons for such request are substantial. I
will detail them for your benefit and that of the Service Department as well as as a matter of record.

I was serving on the Service Committee of the Governing Body
at the time that Gadsden experienced a very disturbing period for
many families, one involving a large number of the young people
in the area. By way of the Service Department I was made aware
of serious mishandling of matters by the local committee, requiring
the sending in of a special committee to straighten matters out.
The matter is fresh enough in my mind to assure you that I could
not feel confident of a competent hearing if the appeal committee
included one who played as prominent a role as Brother Anderson did
in the committee responsible for such serious errors. Additionally
I know, both through information from the Service Department at
that time and from personal knowledge since, that Peter Gregerson
was active in seeking the review of the local committee's action
and thus contributed substantially to the bringing in of the outside
committee assigned by the Society. When the whole picture is put
together, the selection of Brother Anderson to serve on my case,
in which my relationship with Peter Gregerson is the central issue,
is a selection not conveying great likelihood either of judicious-
ness, impartiality or objectiveness. While it might be hoped that
Brother Anderson profited from the correction given by the review
committee, the present conduct of the proposed appeal committee,
their haste to 'rush to judgment,' the irregularity of their
methods, only strengthen the memory of the past mishandling of
matters. I think you can understand why I would rightly object to
such a selection and find it completely unacceptable.

As to the selection of Earl Parnell, the reasoning that led
to such choice is indeed hard to fathom. May I say once more,
that my relationship with Peter Gregerson is the point on which
this whole cases revolves, about which the whole testimony of
the adverse witnesses was based, and because of which relationship
the first committee decided that I should be disfellowshiped.
How then could there be any rational justification for the selection
of Earl Parnell to serve on my appeal committee? He is, as you
well know, and as the circuit overseer knows, the father of Dana
Parnell who was recently divorced by Vicki Gregerson, Peter Gregerson's daughter. Without going into matters in detail, it should be
sufficient to say that for some time now very strained feelings
have developed between the two families and more particularly
between the two fathers. The circuit overseer was certainly aware
of the very strong feeling that exists in this regard, since Dana
was brought up in his conversation with Peter during his previous
visit to Gadsden. It would seem clear to anyone of even average
comprehension that the selection of Dana's father to serve in a
matter where Peter Gregerson is involved, would be flying in the
face of all that good judgment, fairness and just plain common
sense would lead one to expect. What possible reasoning or
proper motivation could lead to such a choice?

East Gadsden Congregation Body of Elders
December 20, 1981, Page III

The circumstances involving Brother Parnell unavoidably
affect the third member of the proposed committee, Rob Dibble.
He is Earl Parnell's son-in-law, being the husband of Dana's
sister Dawn. If necessary, I believe that testimony is available
showing that Rob's wife has been very much affected by Peter
Gregerson's daughter's divorcing of her brother and has been
fairly vocal about the matter. It seems most unlikely that what
she has expressed to others has not also been expressed to her
own husband. To expect that he could enter a case in which one's
association with Peter Gregerson is a central issue and do so
with the necessary freedom from personal feelings and the needed
objectiveness is, I believe, asking more than good judgment would
indicate.

In view of all this, I am respectfully requesting that a
different committee be formed, made up of brothers outside this
area and outside the circuit. With perhaps one exception I
cannot conceive of a comittee of three individuals that would
have less to recommend itself for an objective, unbiased hearing
of my appeal than the one that has been selected. Perhaps the
circuit overseer's selection was the product of a hurried decision
without due consideration of the factors here stated. While
attempts could be made to argue or explain away those factors,
a love of fairness and justice would certainly rule out such a
course. It will, I hope, move you to acknowledge that the appeal
committee should be one that does not require such attempted
justification but, rather, be one that can stand on its own, free from
serious question.--1 Timothy 5:21, 22.

You may also wish to write to the Society about these points
and I would welcome your doing so.

For your information, I am expecting today the arrival of
some guests who are traveling over 500 miles to visit us and who
have only a few days to spend with us. Monday afternoon I have
an appointment in Birmingham (made some days ago) that will likely
result in my getting home late that evening. Later that week we
are scheduled to go on a trip out of the state, one planned some
time ago, with arrangements made by those with whom we will be staying.
During the days before and after New Year's day, a family of friends
will be visiting us, flying in from out of state to do so. However,
after January 5 I should have time to meet with the new committee
selected and this should also give time for the Society to arrange
for such.

May I also request that your communication with me be in writing
so that the frequent omissions and difficulties already experienced
may not continue to multiply. Thank you for your consideration of this.

                                        Sincerely,

Rt 4, Box 440-F
Gadsden AL 35904

Copies of this letter were went to the Governing Body and to the
Service Department along with the following letter:

                                        December 20, 1981

Watchtower Bible and Tract Society
Brooklyn N Y

          Attention: Service Department

Dear Brothers:

By means of this letter I am appealing to you to arrange
for an appeal committee to hear my appeal, a committee formed
of brothers outside the Gadsden area and the circuit in which
it lies. My reasons for making such appeal are set out in
the enclosed letter directed to the East Gadsden Congregation
Body of Elders, under this same date.

The chairman of the original judicial committee has informed
me of conversations with you so you are not unaware of the case.

I am requesting that the committee be formed of brothers
outside the circuit, in part because of the large amount of rumor
and gossip that has circulated, much of which has filtered back
to me. But I also believe that the selection made by your
appointed representative, the circuit overseer, when compared with
the information presented in the enclosed letter, shows that
his judgment is, put simply, quite deficient.